Post-Ireland?

POST-IRELAND?

ESSAYS ON CONTEMPORARY IRISH POETRY

*Edited by Jefferson Holdridge
and Brian Ó Conchubhair*

Wake Forest University Press

Wake Forest University Press
Post Office Box 7333
Winston Salem, NC 27109
wfupress.wfu.edu

ISBN: 978-1-930630-76-5
Library of Congress Control Number 2016932677

Designed and typeset by Nathan W. Moehlmann,
Goosepen Studio & Press.

Cover Image: "Burren After Rain" by Manus Walsh, used with permission from the artist and Kenny's Bookshop, Ireland.

Publication of this book was made possible in part by generous support from the Boyle Family Fund and the Institute for Scholarship in the Liberal Arts, College of Arts and Letters, University of Notre Dame.

Contents

Post-Ireland?

Introduction

With certain members of the younger generation of Irish poets, there is what may be termed a post-national, trans-historical urge, which often but not always has an inward and/or metropolitan focus. Justin Quinn titles the last chapter of his 2008 *The Cambridge Introduction to Modern Irish Poetry, 1800–2000*, "The Disappearance of Ireland." He ends with these words on such a disappearance: "Poets such as Heaney and Hartnett, even though they have invested much of their imaginative life in matters of 'Ireland,' clearly also relish the prospect of getting rid of it. These more recent poets do not move in concert with a larger nationalist objective, as the poets of a century before did. Rather they bear witness to the multitudes the island contains, and have extended its borders to include a fair piece of the known world."[1] Clearly these words are meant as a statement of his own poetic as much as anyone else's. In a likeminded vein, Conor O'Callaghan explains how such a sensibility works in his introduction to the third volume of *The Wake Forest Series of Irish Poetry* (2013), when after detailing the social forces of the 1990s in Ireland, he writes: "It is equally difficult to find direct correlations between such social forces and the poems included here, and foolish even to attempt that. Poetry continues to happen, as it should, in silence and solitude. That remains as true of the work of the poets of this post-Troubles, Celtic Tiger generation as it ever was." Yet he adds this important rider: "However, those events and changes are often visible and audible as background."[2]

The title of this collection of essays, *Post-Ireland?*, acknowledges the question of the disappearance of a certain version of Ireland, that the old definitions may no longer apply, and implies with the question mark that perhaps Ireland can never be left behind because, as a colonial entity, the formulation of its identity has always been linked to its possible dissolution or absorption. Once, the larger threat was England, the United Kingdom, then America, now it is the European Union or globalization. Unlike Quinn's declaration of the disappearance of Ireland, but very similar to the phrase "after Ireland," *Post-Ireland?* is balanced on the tension between opposites. The phrase "after Ireland" has been used at least twice as a byword for the end of Ireland as it is known: Declan Kiberd uses it interrogatively in a 2009 article for *The Irish Times* that surveys the ruins of the economy and its influence on Irish culture.[3] It was also used by Harry Clifton as a title of a poem included in his selected works, *The Holding Centre* (2014).[4] Both writers play on the notion of an Ireland that is lost and an Ireland that survives to be sought. Both writers seem to think that the Irish landscape provides a sustaining sense of place. Kiberd, however, laments the loss of a strong sense of nation, believing, unlike Justin Quinn who sees the disappearance as liberating, that the loss is corrosive and leaves only commerce in its wake. Kiberd writes: "That is the background to the tragedy of many contemporary artists and intellectuals. They have declared their embarrassment in the face of simple-minded notions of nation, faith and fatherland; and have helped to erode these forces. But in the collapse of all other 'isms,' the market itself becomes the sole remaining ideology — and its idea of a Croatian or an Irish identity is Disneyesque in its naivety."[5] As a returning ex-patriot and cosmopolitan writer, Clifton is often considered to be a bridge between younger and older Irish poets, between Ireland and post-Ireland. He is prized as a deracinated émigré by some of the next generation and is sometimes critiqued by others for this same trait.[6] Yet his position is more nuanced than a mere lack of a sense of place can explain. As recent poems have shown, his sense of place is always being redefined by his migrations, and in this respect he is an important exemplar by neither rejecting nor embracing essential identities. Rather he writes with a mysterious migratory sense of crossing the borders between the local and the universal, of recognizing the cultural desecration of the deforested place left behind and yet dreaming of its forested, primeval origins:

> [...] Sloe-berries
> In autumn, whiskey
> In winter, deer returning
>
> To dark re-forested hills.
> Selfconsciousness
> Without God. A solitude,
>
> A self-sufficiency
> Feeding, not on roots,
> But the dream of roots.[7]

For though the definitions of "Ireland" and the "Irish" no longer apply as they once did, for some writers and artists they remain relevant, even for those who would turn or have turned away. The relative stability or instability of identity has long been debated in Ireland as in other postcolonial societies.

Such concerns go back to Yeats himself who thought that though the parlance of English journalism had corrupted nineteenth-century English poetry, it hadn't tarnished the peasant speech of Ireland of his day and wouldn't the poetry. This belief buttressed his hope for a new national literary movement. Similarly no careful reader can dispute the premise that twentieth-century Irish poetry attained distinctiveness through its struggle to confront the debilitating elements of Catholicism or Protestantism, as well as to explore the religious insights of these traditions, much as it did through its concomitant struggle with the traumatic after-effects of British colonialism and the assertion of an independent identity. Nor may we demure from the conclusion, however much we might want to, that as Ireland becomes as thoroughly post-Catholic as it is postcolonial, its poetry will have lost another one of the few remaining cultural influences and inflections differentiating it from its anglophone counterparts across the globe. In this regard, Irish Catholicism mirrors the Irish language. Without religion's persistent influences on secular society and the rise of vernacular, often Americanized English in Ireland, will Irish literature and culture maintain a distinctive character? Again, many of the younger generation seek to question the necessity of such themes in identifying Irish poetry, in poetry in English as well as the Irish language. In his preface to the forthcoming fourth volume of *The Wake Forest Series of Irish Poetry*, David Wheatley writes, "Even as I disavow any common front among my writers [chosen for his selection], however, another part of my intention is to suggest an alternative perspective on the business of Irish canon-formation, and the ways in which non-dominant strands such as experimental writing have been unfairly overlooked; how the Irish language is treated; and how (or whether) younger poets can ever escape what Beckett termed the 'accredited themes' of the past — the shibboleths of belonging, identity, and nation that still form the horizon of expectation for so much Irish poetry."[8]

For some very fine poets of the post-Heaney generation these questions and the above critical issues of identity maintain relevance, even if some entertain them at a distance. When one examines what has been written about contemporary poetry in general, but of the younger generation in particular, certain concepts do appear consistent: How to negotiate the history of Ireland, its sectarianism, its provincialism (or parochialism as the case might be), the experience as a colonial subject of the British empire and/or its role as an agent of said empire, its cultural inheritance from folklore and myth or the rejection of that inheritance, its religious inheritance or the contemporary insignificance of that legacy. Then there is the linguistic inheritance, the importance of acquired language and the grammatical influences of the suppressed one, that is, the Irish language. Does contemporary Ireland and the current generation of poets look toward Europe? America? Boston or Belgium? New York or London? These dichotomies of influence have long bedeviled the Irish and Irish poets. In Barry Sheils's book *W. B. Yeats and World Literature: The Subject of Poetry*, Yeats himself notes how Irish subjectivity was caught "between the influence of America and the influence of England." Yeats concludes that it was "hard to say" which of "the two is denationalising us most rapidly."[9]

As Irish society has changed since independence and through its role in the European Union, so also has Irish poetry entered a time of transition. With "the Troubles" in Northern Ireland now fading from younger memories, the next generation of Irish poets may not draw inspiration from the experience of living in a violently divided country. The country will still be divided, however, whatever attitude is taken toward this division. Whatever one can say of future Irish poetry, one can say with confidence that it will be different. In fact, it already is different, as this collection illustrates; poets, especially younger writers, have recently added many new strings to their repertoire, such as reflecting in new ways on global culture and poetic form, and expressing ecological concerns.

The essays that follow suggest various avenues into understanding the trends that Irish poetry has taken from the 1960s until now. *Post-Ireland?* includes essays covering the work of Colette Bryce, Michael Davitt, Michael Donaghy, Vona Groarke, Seamus Heaney, Aifric Mac Aodha, Pádraig Mac Fhearghusa, Tomás Mac Síomóin, Derek Mahon, Campbell McGrath, Maureen McLane, Dorothy Molloy, Sinéad Morrissey, Paul Muldoon, Eiléan Ní Chuilleanáin, Caitríona Ní Chléirchin, Nuala Ní Dhomhnaill, Ailbhe Ní Ghearbhuigh, Áine Ní Ghlinn, Doireann Ní Ghríofa, Bríd Ní Mhóráin, Conor O'Callaghan, Simon Ó Faoláin, Liam Ó Muirthile, Caitríona O'Reilly, Cathal Ó Searcaigh, Séamus Barra Ó Súilleabháin, Derry O'Sullivan, Gabriel Rosenstock, and Eithne Strong. The collection closes in an essay on Irish interminglings with global poets of diverse backgrounds, such as Christopher Okigbo, Derek Walcott, E. A. Markham, Sujata Bhatt, and Daljit Nagra. Though coverage is short of complete, the editors hope that there is a wide enough range of poets to help the reader toward his or her own conception of what post-Ireland might mean, that is, how much and to what extent are "Irish" poets searching for their own national and/or poetic identity and how much are they leaving certain identity politics and paradigms behind. Wake Forest University Press also hopes that these essays will converge with the various anthologies it has published in order to broaden the audience of a greater number of contemporary Irish poets.

Matthew Campbell's essay ("The Irish Longing for Rhyme") seeks to explain why Irish poets have a formal feeling, and why they haven't been so subject to the turf wars over formal vs. free or rhyming vs. blank verse, which American poets have fought. The difference between David Caplan's ideas, which Campbell quotes, and this article is precisely this: Campbell believes that there is nothing controversial in the belief that rhyme matters, that it helps to shape a poem, that rhyme, as Brodsky said, is "smarter than the poet." Caplan has to make a case for it. Campbell is less pressed to do so. But knowing some of the wider concerns, he delves deep to explain why rhyme is important to Irish poetry, and in so doing formulates a convincing apologia for it. Rhyme can be quite "revelatory," as Muldoon is quoted as saying. Campbell concludes: "Weighing up rhyme from foot to foot and rhyming it with the future: this by no means amounts to an Irish theory of rhyme or a theory of Irish rhyme. But it does fit with a certain preoccupation with time, loss, and longing, of finding and binding." Rhyme, whether half or full, assonantal or consonantal, as he shows, gives a space and method for such emotions to resonate.

As the title suggests, ERIC FALCI's essay ("Contemporary Irish Poetry and the Problem of the Subject") is concerned with the position of the lyric "I" in Irish poetry. Falci begins by acknowledging that Irish poets are often seen as standard bearers for traditional forms of poetic subjectivity (which we can see in especially pronounced ways in the poetry of Seamus Heaney and Eavan Boland). He proceeds, though, to point out how, from the version of Irish modernism developed by Thomas Kinsella up through later poets including Medbh McGuckian, Ciaran Carson, and Paul Muldoon, there has been a competing strain of poetry that has tested the stability of the lyric "I" and the presumption of representational discourse. We can track this competing strain questioning lyric subjectivity even further back to the poets of the 1930s and 1940s (such as Samuel Beckett, Thomas McGreevy, and Denis Devlin) and later to a school of poetry connected to such contemporary poets as Trevor Joyce and Maurice Scully. Modernist de-centering has a tradition in Irish poetry that is often overlooked. By outlining two competing views of lyric subjectivity, Falci aims to show how the traditional lyric "I" and the decentered subject are in constant conversation in Irish poetry. Often, this conversation occurs in the work of a single author. For instance, as Falci states, "the recessive subject of Eiléan Ní Chuilleanáin's poetry, its frequent presentation of a speaker who seems partially unavailable within the diegesis of the poem or whose perspective seems collaged rather than cohesive, allows both for a renewal of lyric subjectivity beyond its poststructural fracturing and for a continuation of performative elusiveness that quietly critiques models of representative subjectivity that are ideologically doubtful." This essay takes as its primary focus the poetry of Sinéad Morrissey and Caitríona O'Reilly, two of the most important voices in their generation who both, albeit in different ways, continue an ongoing conversation over lyric subjectivity. Morrissey and O'Reilly undertake substantive and complex investigations into the delineation of subjectivity within poetic texts: for Falci, the sophistication of their poetry "allows us to articulate a much more capacious notion of what lyric subjectivity might involve."

KELLY SULLIVAN's essay ("Derek Mahon: Letters to Iceland") considers Auden and MacNeice's *Letters from Iceland* (1937), written on the eve of World War II as an entry into a discussion of the ecological poetry of Derek Mahon. She sees the anti-pastoralism of the first, with its insistence on the human element in the landscape as a reaction to the coming war. Sullivan proceeds to discuss how Mahon deploys this example and merges it with a more contemporary consciousness of the importance of landscape and human relations to it. As Sullivan concludes: "Ultimately, Mahon's letters to Iceland acknowledge the same problem with looking at a landscape as an aesthetic object that Auden and MacNeice's *Letters from Iceland* do: in both cases, removing the human element abdicates responsibility. The difference is that Mahon implies our ultimate, human responsibility is precisely to that landscape, that ecosystem to which we belong, 'not as discrete / observing presences but as born / participants in the action.'" The European ecological tradition has always emphasized the house in the etymology of ecology. Partly this tradition is due to the lack of wilderness in Europe, partly the importance of how landscape mirrors history in ways that are not immediately, or so deeply available, in the new world. Either way, the essay is an eloquent reflection of how the human and non-human must be interlinked for the sake of both entities. This ecological responsibility is central to how Ireland faces its future while respecting its past, as we have seen in the controversies concerning Tara some years ago and the landscape of Seamus Heaney more recently. Such ecological responsibility in the

Anthropocene is also a transnational as well as Irish preoccupation, which further connects the search for Ireland in its landscape with the migratory place of the human in the larger landscape of Earth.

An emerging poet in her own right who resides outside Ireland, AILBHE DARCY grounds her essay ("Dorothy Molloy: Dual Citizenship in the Kingdom of the Sick") on the move from a national framework to a post-national one, often inflected with a sense of liberation and even progress, in contemporary Irish criticism. She opens with a memory of a reading she gave with another poet, when someone in the audience asked them how they could claim Irishness as their identity if they were not living in Ireland. Those questions of internationalism and nationalism, as well as disease and gender underlie her discussion of the deceased poet, Dorothy Molloy. For Darcy, national and transnational poetries are less a matter of poetic form or figure, and more a matter of poetic topic. She contends that the privileged speaking position enjoyed by the current generation of Irish writers, in tandem with a colonized past, "is precisely what now makes our poetry 'Irish.'" She asserts that to read a poet born in Ireland but living elsewhere, or writing about not very Irish things, as merely a post-national English-language poet would be to miss the opportunity to fully tease out the different forces that meet, collide and negotiate in that poet's language. While this essay argues that the Irishness of Molloy's poetry is rarely obvious, it nevertheless acknowledges that we must attend to its context within Irish literary traditions to fully appreciate its accomplishments. In so doing, we discover Molloy's engagement with a literary tradition that values formal control and intellectual rigor by showing precisely what can be achieved when poetry questions the values of control and intellectual rigor.

DECLAN KIBERD's essay ("Seamus Heaney: The Death of Ritual and the Ritual of Death") establishes ritual and art as ways of understanding personal, historical, and cultural experiences. The inwardness of the poem finds it objective correlative in the ritual enactment of culture. This complex of individual and community is ritual's central focus. Kiberd, of course, is subtly using the etymology of religion itself, which is concerned with linking, in order to make a case for how the poet perilously performs this sacerdotal role. Poetry or aestheticization seems to risk betraying the rituals of faith and community. For Heaney, as Kiberd demonstrates, the pressures on the poet in a time of political upheaval, which has family implications for everyone concerned, takes its toll. Heaney uses anthropology and ritual to offset the risk of poeticizing the suffering. Kiberd states of the anthropological bent to the controversial volume *North* (1975): "The poet suggested that to understand the strange clash, the 1600s were scarcely more helpful than the morning newspapers: better to re-read Tacitus. The mythical was reasserting itself in a world stripped of useful ritual. Such an analysis shocked left-wing Nationalists, able to quote hard-and-fast statistics of discrimination on housing and jobs." He goes on to note how Heaney, by mourning the death of ritual through references to ancient myth and ritual practice, is endeavoring to do no less than bring the dead to life. This process is of an oracular quality in which the dead speak through him as well as to him. The etymology of "person" reminds us that it is both a mask and a sounding through of something larger than we are. This can be an intricate process. During a time of death and violence, of history being overturned, Heaney was trying to remember the history that was being dismembered around him and to ensure "that there will be a life before death."

In his essay ("Writing by Night: Nuala Ní Dhomhnaill's Dream Notebooks"), JOHN DILLON examines Nuala Ní Dhomhnaill's Turkish Irish-language diaries to trace and uncover correlations between them and her published poems. On leaving Ireland for Turkey in the 1970s after her marriage to Dogan Leflef, Ní Dhomhnaill kept a series of diaries in which she chronicled her dreams. This essay investigates how an Irish poet living in Turkey recorded and reordered her dreams, in Berryman fashion, to craft an aesthetic that embraced her emigrant experience and folkloric heritage and in doing so raised questions about the nature and origin of influence, inspiration, and the impact of location and place on the poetic process. Dillon's essay illustrates how these diaries can unfold the conscious rendering of subconscious currents in the displaced poet.

In her essay ("Reconfigurations in Colette Bryce's Poetry"), AILBHE McDAID contends that Bryce reinvents and reimagines the spatial configuration and codes of behavior dictated through inherited structures to question the very boundaries that limit identity and restrict performance. Here migration is considered a version of disappearance that challenges societal expectations in public spaces, while memory works as a form of reappearance in the way it revisits and reconstructs the past, the self, and identity. Bryce engages poetic strategies of escape, erasure, and invisibility as she explores the motif of borders and boundaries to probe questions of enclosure and exclusion, transitions, and emigration. For Bryce, McDaid argues, disappearing through migration means having to continually reappear on return; furthermore, such a strategy requires a renegotiation of the terms of public space.

BRIAN Ó CONCHUBHAIR's essay ("Contemporary Irish-Language Poetry: After *Innti*") considers the contemporary state of Irish-language poetry: the nature and type of poetry published by those millennial poets, many of whom have now published several volumes. He considers whether the Innti poets, who revolutionized and popularized Irish poetry in the 1970s and 1980s, ever formed a coherent group. Did they share a common vision or aesthetic, or were they more a collection of individuals? He proceeds by questioning if the attention they deservedly attracted may have unintentionally skewed readers' and critics' perceptions of the variety and diversity of poetry available in Irish, thereby blinding critics to other less colorful poets. What role did Seán Ó Tuama play in shaping the canon of Irish-language poetry, and did the dominance of the Innti style of poetry restrict alternative poetic forms and distinct voices emerging in the 1990s? The essay concludes by briefly considering some millennial poets now coming to the fore in contemporary Irish-language poetry.

Issues of language and tradition are central to DANIELA THEINOVÁ's innovative essay on Aifric Mac Aodha ("Original in Translation: The Poetry of Aifric Mac Aodha"). In a multilingual poetic tradition such as Irish, language issues are impossible to disregard and notions of a linguistic community are complex. Writing in Irish, contends Theinová, is simultaneously a statement of affiliation and a way to accommodate differences. Mac Aodha not only seeks to secure the continuance of tradition but simultaneously insists that such is unattainable where the fractured tradition and ruptured continuity bequeath unanticipated freedoms. The liberating detachment from writing in a language which is not one's own, which has lost continuity with its historical development and a community that would be exclusively defined by it provides a template, Theinová argues, for encompassing and thematizing the questions of identity and ultimately allows her to declare herself undeniably an Irish poet. As Colette Bryce's poetry enacts an imagistic desire for disappearance, Mac Aodha mines a language whose identity is often forced to the margins and whose speakers are perceived as vanishing.

Like Campbell's, NATHANIEL MYERS's essay ("End Rhymes and End-Rhymes: Paul Muldoon's Echoic Elegies") is deeply concerned with form. This focus, as we see in many poets, may provide a definition of Irish poetry and/or a complication of the dilemmas of Irish identity. Either way, form is essential to an understanding of contemporary poetry. Myers's thorough discussion of elegy and end rhymes reflects on both Muldoon's prowess as an elegist and the virtuosity of his rhymes. He begins his essay with a declaration that Muldoon's elegies are his "most acclaimed poems" and a question that tests his assertion: "How would Muldoon, whose poetry is generally characterized as ludic, erudite, and often opaque, find critical favor for his work in a genre that often demands a certain gravitas and emotional transparency from its poet?" His essay seeks to show that Muldoon's poetry is often profoundly self-interrogating, especially his elegies. Myers understands that it is this poetic self-critical metanarrative that has made Muldoon's formidable elegies some of his most famous work. Aestheticizing grief is a questionable act. Mourning must dismantle the aesthetic itself. He concludes: "Muldoon's elegies are cries that echo themselves, that through rhyme give the poet (and reader) the very means by which grief can be sounded and experienced, and ultimately puzzled over by poet and reader alike."

FLORENCE IMPENS ("Writing Ireland: Seamus Heaney, Classics, and Twentieth-Century Irish Literature") focuses on Seamus Heaney and considers how he negotiates the challenges of place through his classical representations of his locality and of Ireland to transcend the particularism of local experience and define his position within the modern Irish literary tradition. She explores the complex intertextual nature that the Classics perform in Heaney's poetry as a means to subsume his double cultural heritage as an Irish writer in the English language. The young Heaney reworked classical representations modeled by other Irish writers, but on migrating south to the Republic in 1972, his relationship with his home evolved. It was then that he began to re-write classical poems celebrating the Irish countryside and his locale in the years of the peace process. Those changes affected not only his choice of classical narrative, but also the ways in which he alluded to the Irish poetic tradition. He moved from a framework influenced by the revival and parochialism to one encompassing modernism, thereby putting the transnational dimension of his poetry to the fore. If relocation proved fruitful for Heaney, it was no less productive for other poets like Conor O'Callaghan, Paul Muldoon, Derek Mahon, or Nuala Ní Dhomhnaill.

JEFFERSON HOLDRIDGE's essay ("The Autonomous Tear: Caitríona O'Reilly's *Geis* and Conor O'Callaghan's *The Sun King*") discusses how the epithet "Irish" poet sits uneasily for twenty-first-century poets, especially those coming after Heaney, Mahon, Boland, and Muldoon. For poets writing in the twenty-first century, poetry instead remains a bridge between such poles as the abstract and concrete, history and myth, inwardness and identity, religion and philosophy, science and art. In doing so, their writing emphasizes the remarkable flexibility of "Ireland," "Irishness," and subjectivity. Holdridge focuses on the ways in which O'Reilly investigates our sense-experiences of the natural world and her belief that the human finds its image reflected perhaps most startlingly in the encounter with the non-human. O'Callaghan's poetry is concerned with how memory, especially when dislocated and disconnected, relies on sensual images and their slippery, often opaque capacity to "mean" as well as to "be." The fundamental premise beneath this consideration of both poets is that poetry has its own ways of producing theoretical vision and philosophical knowledge.

THEO DORGAN's essay ("Southern Wind") argues against theory-driven criticism if not against criticism per se. It is also a defense of poetry in the Irish language that makes no excuses but only points out the hegemony at work in the preference of critical circles for poetry in English. It aims toward a restoration of the ancient severe conversation between poet and scholar, each working to be flexible and adaptable. It proposes that theory, always operating inside a circumscribed horizon, can adapt to the unexpected. In tandem poetry, always making itself new, is predicated on the unexpected as much as, if not more than, it depends on tradition — on what is already known. None of this, Dorgan asserts, means we can afford to dispense with "rigorous criticism," but this essay asks for a different *kind* of criticism. Putting forth such questions on the nature and future of criticism, Dorgan investigates the foundation for the collection as a whole, each essay of which queries tradition, engages in rigorous criticism, and often submits what is most unexpected in the poetry which is surveyed.

JAMES CHANDLER ("Three Contemporary Irish-American Poets: Donaghy, McGrath, and McLane") begins his essay with the question central to this collection: "How do we identify an Irish poet 'post-Ireland'?" His answer is "to consider three American poets of Irish descent, each with a discernible relationship to Ireland and its poetic traditions." The three poets, Michael Donaghy, Campbell McGrath, and Maureen McLane, are all former students of the University of Chicago. After discussing their relationships to the academy and to the poetic tradition both here and in Ireland, Chandler wonders if it might be best or most appropriate to call them Irish-American poets. Circumventing any final conclusion to this question, Chandler concludes that it might be better not to ask whether they are poets who write in light of Ireland (i.e., post-Ireland) or in search of Ireland, but rather to concentrate on the transnational poetic inheritances in the English language, in America, in Ireland, and in England. In this Chandler approaches Dorgan, in that poetry matters most as it renews itself, and is its own theory. Chandler also echoes Matthew Campbell (especially regarding McLane) in his assertion that form, like rhyme, can be a technique shared across the Atlantic as well as across the Irish Sea.

As this collection attests, there is no disputing the ways in which Ireland is *in* and *of* the world. In the field of postcolonial studies and world literature more broadly, there have been extensive studies of the significance of canonical Irish writers upon postcolonial authors of narrative fiction including Jean Rhys, Chinua Achebe, J. M. Coetzee, Salman Rushdie, Jamaica Kincaid, Arundhati Roy, and Junot Díaz (to name some of the most recognized). In poetry studies, scholars have mapped the significance of US, Eastern European, Greek, French, and Japanese literary and cultural influences upon contemporary Irish poetry as well as the literary circuits and institutional networks connecting Ireland with Caribbean, African, and South Asian spaces of poetic production in the post–World War II era. But what are "Ireland's afterlives" in global anglophone poetry? In what ways have postcolonial, English-language poets engaged with "Ireland" — here understood as a "relay," a densely layered, multifaceted site, comprising its historical, political, cultural, aesthetic, linguistic, and imaginative dimensions — as a way to mediate a wide range of crises due to the sweeping disjunctures of modernity, from struggles over independence and decolonization, experiences of ethnic migration and diaspora, through globalization and cosmopolitanism? OMAAR HENA's concluding essay ("Ireland's Afterlives in Global Anglophone Poetry") conducts a comparative study of an Irish-inflected global poetics, beginning with Yeats's late great poem "Lapis Lazuli" through poems by Christopher Okigbo (Nigeria), Derek Walcott (St. Lucia), E. A. Markham (Montserrat/UK/France), Sujata Bhatt (India/US/Germany), and Daljit Nagra (UK). Ireland's afterlives feature as a testament to Irish literature's institutional standing in the world republic of letters. Hena maintains that we can account for postcolonial poets' engagement with Ireland through the sheer sophistication of its literature, especially through its recurring preoccupation with aesthetics and politics and shared experiences of dislocation, estrangement, and cultural in-betweenness. Figuring this collection's title as a question, Hena posits that "Post-Ireland?" functions less as a descriptive reality (political borders have decidedly *not* gone away, no matter how transnational our critical lens) than as an open-ended debate, a horizon of possibility, even an ongoing problem for understanding how literature negotiates past and present, local and global, familiar and strange, self and other. Ultimately, this chapter demonstrates how English-language poets from around the world have contributed to a vibrant conversation over the many ways in which Irish cultural resources both survive (*sur-vivre*, "live on") and flourish as they become uprooted, appropriated, recycled, and renewed in the global era.

NOTES

1. Justin Quinn, "The Disappearance of Ireland," in *The Cambridge Introduction to Modern Irish Poetry, 1800–2000* (Cambridge: Cambridge UP, 2008), 210.

2. Conor O'Callaghan, preface to *The Wake Forest Series of Irish Poetry*, Vol. 3 (Winston-Salem: Wake Forest UP, 2013), xiv.

3. Declan Kiberd, "After Ireland?" *The Irish Times*, Aug. 29, 2009, http://www.irishtimes.com/news/after-ireland-1.728344. *After Ireland* will be the title of a forthcoming book by Kiberd, published by Head of Zeus and Harvard University Press.

4. Harry Clifton, "After Ireland," *The Holding Centre: Selected Poems 1974–2004* (Winston-Salem, NC: Wake Forest UP, 2014), 144–45.

5. Kiberd, "After Ireland?"

6. Richard Tillinghast, "The Future of Irish Poetry?" in *Finding Ireland* (Notre Dame: Notre Dame UP, 2008), 193–217.

7. Clifton, *The Holding Centre*, 145.

8. David Wheatley, preface to *The Wake Forest Series of Irish Poetry*, Vol. 4 (Winston-Salem, NC: Wake Forest UP, forthcoming 2017).

9. Barry Sheils, *W. B. Yeats and World Literature: The Subject of Poetry* (New York: Ashgate, 2015), 15.

1

The Irish Longing
for Rhyme

Matthew Campbell

The novelist Jonathan Safran Foer gives a wry account from his student days of an attempt to procure money for photocopying from his enigmatic Director of Creative Writing, Paul Muldoon. He offers a little allegorical fantasy of a conversation he never had in the Professor's office, concerning a man searching for something he had lost deliberately:

> I asked: "What are you doing?"
> He said: "I'm looking for something important."
> I asked: "What are you looking for?"
> "Well," he said, "ostensibly I'm looking for a nickel. But I hid it from myself, and it's only a nickel, so pretty clearly that isn't the important thing."
> I said: "You hid it from yourself?"
> He said: "So I could go looking for the important thing."
> I asked: "What's the important thing?"
> He said: "Exactly."[1]

This conversation is lifted straight from the pages of *Alice in Wonderland* — who plans the serendipitous? But the novelist suggests that the poet taught him a writing lesson, of the necessity of serendipity, or serendipity as necessity — and when serendipity doesn't come along of itself, the need to go and find it.

Elsewhere in this memoir Foer alludes to one of the poems in the Gallery Press interim collection *The Prince of the Quotidian* (1994), in which Muldoon records his attempt at writing a poem a day through the month of January 1992, responding to TV news, personal letters, newspapers, and reviews. In the case of this sonnet, the poet offers the versification of a local bar and the shrub outside his back door. It is a poem about unimportant things, about randomness, criticism and triviality:

> Not for nothing would I versify
> 'The Alchemist and the Barrister', rhyme (pace Longley) 'cat'
> with 'dog', expand on the forsythia
> that graces our back door: 'humdrum', 'inadequate',
>
> 'inconsequential journalese', 'a klieg light
> masquerading as the moon'; none will
> I trust, look for a pattern in this crazy quilt
> where all is random, 'all so trivial',
>
> unless it be Erasmus, unless
> Erasmus again steel
> himself as his viscera are cranked out by a windlass
>
> yard upon 'xanthous' yard;
> again to steel himself, then somehow to exhort
> the windlass-men to even greater zeal.[2]

Foer says:

> The poet Joseph Brodsky — to whom Muldoon dedicated a wonderful poem — was fond of saying, "The rhyme is smarter than the poet." I take

that to mean there are reasons greater than the prettiness of rhyming
to write within forms. When you are forced to end a line with a word
that rhymes with "tree" — or, in the case of a Muldoon poem, with
"forsythia" — you are taken to a place you wouldn't have chosen, had
you been unconstrained. The constraints allow you to exceed yourself.
The handcuffs are also the keys to the handcuffs.[3]

Actually, in Muldoon's sonnet, "forsythia" suggests itself for an equally
difficult rhyme ending, "versify." But if "[t]he rhyme is smarter than the
poet," the rhyme allows games of form in which there is at least a knowing
fiction that the rules are unknown. "Rhyme" appears to orchestrate the
proceedings of a poet who elsewhere assumes an imaginary self as an erotic
adventurer, "the Prince of Serendip," a poet who blasphemes on Wilfred
Owen, "the poetry is in the serendipity."[4]

Foer's handcuffs analogy echoes a phrase of Muldoon's that has been
elevated to platitude in many reviews of his work — "Form is a straitjacket
in the way that a straitjacket was a straitjacket for Houdini."[5] But for all
intents and purposes, when Muldoon says "form" he means the handcuffs or
straitjacket of rhyme, the widely-shared convention of describing the formal
arrangement of a poem with reference to its "rhyme scheme," as here, in
the fourteen lines of an irregular Petrarchan sonnet. But a "scheme" is not
a "key," and this poet still tends to remain enigmatic on the whereabouts of
that relieving implement.[6] The meter as such in "Not for nothing" remains
remarkably "free," and if there is some anchoring in sonnet-logical structure (a volta or turn in the ninth line at the word "unless"), there is also
often extravagant end-line rhyming: "versify/forsythia," "light/quilt," "yard/
exhort," not cat with dog, but "cat" with "inadequate." Of course there is one
example of a formal organization we might also call extravagant: this poem
recites the alphabet in sequence at the opening letter of twenty-five words,
beginning with "Alchemist and Barrister" and "cat" and ending with "xan-
thous," "yard," and "zeal."[7] There is one exception, although it hides inside
and is consequently exposed by the word "none," a negative containing
the o where o should be, where o becomes a zero. The sonnet is in its way
about "nothing," beginning with the twistedly idiomatic, "Not for nothing":
the sense of the double negative is that it must be for something, but that

something might be the negative itself. Muldoon's other abecedarius in *The Prince of the Quotidian*, the much-loved and anthologized, "The Birth," piles up an alphabetical list to celebrate the wonders of word and world at the moment of the birth of his daughter, and in it, "the windlass-women" are midwives to the miracle. Such secular versions of the numinous are absent in "Not for nothing," from the double negative onwards. In the zero in the word "none," we get as close to the contentlessness of a mere "formalism." In Muldoon's case, the suspicion is that the form is the content, and that only within listening-distance of its rhymes can we grasp what might, or more probably what might not, be going on.

Rhyme is something that Muldoon has been unable to shake off, or to escape from, as it has been for at least the last three generations of Irish poets. It doesn't look like the important thing, but looking for it, certain rhyming Irish poets may very well have found that it was there in rhyme all along. It takes poet-critic Peter McDonald four pages of interpretation of this poem, working from the etymology of the word "trivial," to show that from unimportant beginnings extraordinary things can come.[8] If such a willful tuning down of the import seems small matter in the face of Irish history and politics, say, which has been no trivial thing in the lives of the last three generations of poets and their fellow citizens, why retain rhyme? One answer is offered by a critic and rhymer of a different hue, Simon Jarvis, who sees a cognitive purpose in the triviality of rhyming in the apologia at the beginning of Alexander Pope's *The Rape of the Lock*, "What mighty contests rise from trivial things": "the irony rebounds [...] on whoever would imagine that he himself could never be so foolish as to get upset about something so insignificant."[9] Rhyme is one insignificant thing, yet it persists across the centuries and between two rhymers in English, Pope and Muldoon. In one sort of English and American poetry the persistence of rhyme is more noted by its rarity — and thus Jarvis's apology is an exception in the criticism. But why is it, no matter how difficult they make it for themselves, no matter how long British and American poets follow free verse and experiment with it after Whitman and Williams and Pound and Olson and Prynne, why in this day and age when all the formal accoutrements of so many art forms have gone through the mill of modernism and its various postisms, why do so many Irish poets still long for rhyme?

If rhymed poems appear to be "formal," tending to "closure," there is nevertheless a switching within them as the present tense of rhyme longs in two temporalities, for the future and for the past, both as originating sound seeking a mate and as echo seeking its progenitor. The hunch of a critic such as Jarvis is that rhyme is a form of cognition and, like music, can be thinking itself, what he calls "musical thinking."[10] It may require a metaphysical as much as epistemological jump to think that texts can long, or that they have agency, cognition, or emotions, an interiority in which rhymes can think. If rhyme had its own agency and powers of expression, it would express both desire and memory, and frequently the memory of desire — or even the desire for memory. But if we participate in the fiction that mere rhyme can be cognitive or active, we could say that as it is used by (or uses) poets, and is then read by (or reads) readers, the present tense of rhyme can be articulated between present and past. It both expresses and represents subjectivity and history, the past of the self and the past of the formations and traditions of poetry and society, as well as the future of rhymes not made, artistic, ethical, and political selves in a state of becoming. The form of the poem is one small modeling in textual time of the chances for the future as thrown up by the coinciding of the sound of words — chances that begin in but are not constrained by the matter of sonic coincidence.

Muldoon's poem proceeds by rhyme, in the first place a coupling of sounds, but one that involves other rhyme sounds in further sonic proliferation. In other Irish poems written in English, rhyme may play only a local part in such large psychic, formal, and historical patterning of sound. But rhyme is everywhere apparent, prolific even, in its refusal to become a memory in the history of Irish poetry in the English language. Regardless of trends like the "new formalism" of American and British poetry and criticism, Irish rhyme has been successively revived during the century of innovation enjoyed by other, perhaps more metropolitan, poetic traditions. Irish poet Conor O'Callaghan says that rhymed verse returned strongly in the 1980s, replacing the "expressive, quasi-mystical, affirmative free verse"[11] then being written. In O'Callaghan's account, rhyme (unlike quasi-mystical affirmation), sounds like a serious matter, and from the long history and practice of Irish rhyme both in English and Irish-language poetry, memory (the past-obsession of Irish history and culture) and desire (the seeking for the futurity of a sovereignty grounded in the imagined completeness of culture and self in the past) continue to circle around each other in ways that are not that easily given up. In one story of Irish poetry, these are poetic inheritances from the dispossession suffered by the Gaelic tradition, its linguistic rupture, and associated cultural compensations in the English language (through translation, writing for song) in contemporary Irish culture. For all that Prague-based poet Justin Quinn could, in 2001, talk of "the first genuinely post-national generation" of Irish poets, this still comes from an Irish poetic scene in many ways operating outside Anglo-American experimental/conservative, neo-modernist/formalist turf wars. As critic Fran Brearton has recently said, "a formal feeling never went away."[12]

Such formalism is partly a matter of an inheritance from the various artistic ways in which English has been fashioned for Irish poetic traditions, the new authenticity of something poet Patrick Kavanagh called "the synthetic Irish thing."[13] To add in the English influence of church and street (as in the hymnal and the ballad) might seem one way of accounting for an Irish longing for rhyme from various political and aesthetic persuasions. But English-language verbal culture after Percy's *Reliques* and The Beatles, not to mention American culture since The Sugarhill Gang,[14] bear just as much evidence of this persistence of the rhyming linguistic and musical structures which still revert to the oral performances through which experiences of field and street find expression and form. For many contemporary Irish poets, rhyme has been all of these things, performing a longing both for form and for the creativity that comes from not needing to look for it.

So, for a number of contemporary Irish poets, training in rhyme involves an embrace both of the determination of meaning by narrowing lexical choice as well as the labor involved in submitting to the laborious trivialities of mere technique. In the words of English modernist poet Charles Tomlinson, writing in 1969, the poet remains in thrall to "the *chances* of rhyme," and they are "like the chances of meeting — / In the finding fortuitous, but once found, binding."[15] The unsophisticated — childish even — pleasures and attractions of rhyme come fraught with immense difficulty for the poet who chances the semantically unforeseen when narrowing the limits of the foreseeable when choosing to rhyme — or being chosen by rhyme (the finding is binding, as Tomlinson would have it). If it is indeed a matter of choice or even of art, the memories of an organicism of form and naturalness of expression still persist through any talk which touches on authenticity. And the Irish might be said to major in authenticity, technique masked by *sprezzatura*. Roy Foster quotes J. J. Sheehan's revivalist *Guide to Irish Dancing* from 1902 on how to be Irish in dancing, and the terms might well apply to poetry-writing: "In short, be natural, unaffected, easy — be Irish and you'll be alright."[16] Or, as Yeats would put it, "Labour is blossoming or dancing where / The body is not bruised to pleasure soul."[17]

The example of rhyme is strong in other ways for the contemporary Irish poet from Irish poems which would not have come into being without it, and in particular the influence of Muldoon himself spreads over British and American poetry as well — how could it not from the poetry editor of *The New Yorker*? But to look at his precursors, at either end of Irish poetry's great renaissance since the end of the nineteenth century, William Butler Yeats and Seamus Heaney have exerted great influence on the development of successive generations of poets and their clinging on to the difficulties of rhymed verse. The first example here, by Yeats, hinges on the word "difficult" itself. As the many critics who have studied his compositional practices have shown us, Yeats started many poems in prose and worked them up into strict rhyming and stanzaic verse, a habit he never lost even given the experiments in free verse going on around him as the twentieth century progressed. In a diary entry, we gain an insight into one task that the poet set himself:

> September [1909]. Subject: To complain of the fascination of what's difficult. It spoils spontaneity and pleasure and it wastes time. Repeat the line ending 'difficult' three times, and rhyme on bolt, exult, colt, jolt. One could use the thought of the wild-winged and unbroken colt must drag a cart of stones out of pride because it's difficult, and end by denouncing drama, accounts, public contests — all that's merely difficult.[18]

The serendipitous follows from the initial decision to end the first line with the word "difficult," and then the need to structure the poem according to the available rhyme words. So, the longing for a rhyme sound comes first, and once rhymes are found, image, thought, and theme follow. The theme ("It spoils spontaneity and pleasure and it wastes time") is fully conversant with the terms of the writing task the poet has set himself.

The result was one of Yeats's finest lyric achievements of his middle period: a poem about the forms of poetry and the determinations of public life, as well as about the limits of an aesthetic of serendipity and a practical decision-making which merely guesses at the uncontrollable in art and politics.

> The fascination of what's difficult
> Has dried the sap out of my veins, and rent
> Spontaneous joy and natural content
> Out of my heart. There's something ails our colt
> That must, as if it had not holy blood
> Nor on Olympus leaped from cloud to cloud,
> Shiver under the lash, strain, sweat and jolt
> As though it dragged road metal. My curse on plays
> That have to be set up in fifty ways,
> On the day's war with every knave and dolt,
> Theatre business, management of men.
> I swear before the dawn comes round again
> I'll find the stable and pull out the bolt.[19]

No matter that in the finished poem he couldn't find a place for three repetitions of "difficult," nor even for the one projected full rhyme ("exult"). There is a happy accident in the seeking for sense to justify the rhyme endings. The introduction of the sound "colt" and then the meaning of the word "colt" (an "unbroken" young horse) allow serendipity to enact an untamed violence on meter and rhyme in ways that deliberately court dissonance, both in meaning and in prosody. The imagery and sound of the lines packs in extreme complications: the "holy blood" of the pedigree, the punishment of the breaking-in conveyed in packed stresses that sonically "lash, strain, sweat and jolt" across the lines, the teeth-on-edge sound-image of "dragged road metal." The whole must resolve itself in an uncoupling of the colt, a freeing of the constraint, in the freeing of final closing rhyme itself: "pull out the bolt." The poem is an exemplification of — and complaint against — the compulsions of closed as opposed to open form, its truculent refusal of sonnet form notwithstanding. (It should have happened in line 8, "My curse on plays," the moving on of argument at the volta.) Yeats has thrown in the "jolt" rhyme to upset such stabilities, untaming the expectations of form just as he has triumphantly asserted the difficult in his control of the colt. "Bolt" is both fastener of rhyme and, in the threat to pull it, liberator of this structure. Yeats also offers an instance of the paronomasia of rhyme — its invitation to wordplay — in the pull of contraries for and against closure in the final rhyme: the colt will bolt without the bolt.

"The Fascination of What's Difficult" is a drama of chance and control, setting a random (though not trivial) strain of word-sounds and their meanings in motion, grappling for control of them and demonstrating success even when they most threaten to escape. The poem advertises its availability to the windlass-men — literary critics with an MBA — in its complaint against "the important thing": "Theatre business, management of men." It is a dangerously prosey line, which requires a sardonic drawl in order to fill out the pentameter: "Theatre bus-i-ness, management of men," or even "The-atre business." The poem also stages a struggle with sound as evidenced by rhyme. In the returns of rhyme it doubles back on poetry itself — and through that it returns to the self itself.

By that I mean something that has a long pedigree in thinking about rhyme in European poetry, comparatively short-lived as it is in the Western European tradition — maybe just over a thousand years old. The origins appear to have been in Irish-language poetry, carried across by Irish clerics into their translations of Latin verse which were then imported into medieval European poetic traditions through the lyric verse written for sacred song.[20] Contemporary writers in rhyme, or about rhyme, merely address a crisis already evident in Dantean arguments for an extension of vernacular verse. Giorgio Agamben thinking about Dante in "The End of the Poem" essay, Paul Muldoon in his End of the Poem lectures written serendipitously with Agamben in mind, and Simon Jarvis thinking about Hegel's account of rhyme in the Aesthetics, all advert to the disparity between sound and meaning in verse. Dante, according to Agamben, opposes "cantio as unit of sense (sententia) to *stantia* as purely metrical units," and quoting directly (Agamben's emphasis), the *stanza* provides "a capacious storehouse or receptacle for the art in its entirety" while "*just as the* canzone *is the lap of its subject-matter, so the stanza enlaps its whole technique.*"[21] Rhyme is one structuring element of the stanza, but structure and content may not be one and the same: in fact structure may mean the end of content and the end of the poem means the end of its music along with the end of its thinking. "Closure" is thus one satisfaction — or risk — as in Yeats's explanation to his friend Dorothy Wellesley of the completion of a process which is singular to poetic composition: "The correction of prose, because it has no fixed laws, is endless, a poem comes right with a click like a closing box."[22] Geoffrey Hill adds to the memorability of this formulation by calling it an, "atonement of aesthetics with rectitude of judgement."[23]

As many readers, Hill among them, have noted, Yeats's poetic practices as opposed to his official pronouncements can tell us other stories, and as at the ending of "The Fascination of What's Difficult," what appears to have been enclosed — the colt, rhyme, meaning — is far less secure than a cursory reading might suggest. The ensuing ambiguity allows Yeats to ask difficult questions about competing sonic and semantic urges. Content or meaning as well as the semantic unit of the poem — what Foer might call "the important thing" — are not really at issue here. From Dante onwards, Agamben phrases the "crisis of poetry" as "the point in which sound is about to be ruined in the abyss of sense."[24] This is the closing box at the end of the poem, when the rhyming has to stop. In "The Chances of Rhyme," Tomlinson's concluding couplet calls for "energies to combat confusion. / Let rhyme be my conclusion," putting rhyme in relation with syntax and, more precisely, with what his teacher and contemporary Donald Davie called "articulate energy." This is a conception which finds its apogee in an English tradition culminating in the poetry of Hill. What Davie says about Yeats's syntax works from an insight of Richard Ellmann, that "in his art [Yeats] remained stubbornly loyal to the conscious mind's intelligible structure."[25] We might also say that about Yeats's loyalty to rhyme:

> Systems of syntax are part of the heritable property of past civilisa-
> tion, and to hold firm to them is to be traditional in the best and

most important sense […] it is hard not to disagree with Yeats that the abandonment of syntax testifies to a failure of the poet's nerve, a loss of confidence in the intelligible structure of the conscious mind, and the validity of its activity.[26]

Despite the reference to "heritable property," the influence of Davie's thinking is more than just neo-Burkeanism, though Davie and Yeats before him might have found the idea politically congenial. Rhyme is further evidence of the verbal activity of syntax, linking the stranded images of a semantically impoverished symbolism in poetic form organized for sound. It is an element which connects semantic materials and also exercises the active aesthetic energies which can combat confusion. Energy is directed toward conclusion but is also the resistance against it. As the poem is going on, lines passing from couplet to couplet or stanza to stanza, rhyme can exceed or forestall syntax, since in enjambment, "the rhyme ends without the meaning of the sentence having been completed."[27]

Rhyme, according to Hegel, may suggest some consolation for this phenomenon of closure and continuance. Rhyme has "the sole function of bringing us back to ourselves through the return of the same sounds. In this way the versification approaches what is as such musical, i.e. the sound of interiority, and it is freed from the materiality, so to say, of language […]."[28] A latter-day Hegelian like Jarvis then reads rhyme as the return of subjectivity, stating one of its psychic functions thus:

> Rhyme marks off the time of innerness against the world's time. Rhyme, through the return of similar sounds, does not merely lead us back to those sounds. It leads us back to ourselves. […] The musical thinking of the 'unhappy consciousness' […] chimes with the approximation of verse to the musical as such. And at this point we are given a strik- ing definition of what the musical as such might be: the sound of interiority.[29]

Jarvis is aware that one danger of this interiority is that what was "the soul" for Hegel may be (to shift from sonic to visual metaphors) an illusion, or worse, "nothing at all," an emptiness of self, "something which has no content … Insofar as it must express abstract subjectivity, there is nothing at all to express." Jarvis answers by saying that "the illusion of pure interiority is a real illusion, a shape of feeling which is really present."[30]

Hegel and Jarvis are talking about the sound of words, swiveling between the "nothing" of "abstract subjectivity" and the real presence of "a shape of feeling." In both accounts, the sound of rhyme is both a fiction and immaterial. It has become "pure interiority," cognition or emotion without conceptual content. Tracking rhyme back into this version of cognition as interiority, do we simply discover that there is no object of thought, no thinking, mere hollow sound? To bring back Yeats's "Theatre business, management of men" might be one way around this, reversing Foer's parable of the poet's hunt for the nickel, looking for the important thing in the expectation that the unimportant thing will be found along the way:

> none will
> I trust, look for a pattern in this crazy quilt
> where all is random, 'all so trivial' […]

From the random and trivial coupling of sound, hovering over the content-less self as it might be, the seeming hollowness of the echo of rhyme is one way in which poetry tells us about the *past* of the sounding of the self into the present of a written verse. For all that it may be trivial, longing after the sound of thought itself, a thought which has no object, Irish rhyme hangs between such positions. As Muldoon knows (and McDonald has pointed out), the modern sense of the word "trivial" comes from the *trivium*, which is the basis of a classical education (Grammar, Logic, Rhetoric). Pope's mighty contest arising from trivial things is also playing in the background. But triviality is not arbitrary, though the procedure of the poem may be "random." Creative procedures of serendipity are not necessarily mystical but an object may be found, whether it be interiority or soul or indeed something which sounds into the unforeseen, the future.

Rhyme is a musical aid in the discovery of the self, caught in the doubleness of sound and sense, of word and image as an auditory bouncing back, a reflection of rhyme word and its partner as echo. To take my second example of Irish rhyme, Seamus Heaney's early poem "Personal Helicon" is about the past of a forming self, about the poet's youth ("As a child, they could not keep me from wells") and being drawn by a sensation which is barely verbal, "the smells / Of waterweed, fungus and dank moss." There is more than one well: one is "Fructified like any aquarium," another offers "echoes [...] With a clean new music in it"; and another was "scaresome, for there, out of ferns and tall / Foxgloves, a rat slapped across my reflection." The poem ends in the present tense adult "now," exchanging the sensations of touch and smell and self-reflection and self-echo:

> Now, to pry into roots, to finger slime,
> To stare, big-eyed Narcissus, into some spring
> Is beneath all adult dignity. I rhyme
> To see myself, to set the darkness echoing.[31]

In its way the poem is as childish as its subject-matter, written in a simple four-line stanza, alternately rhyming, near the common measure of English-language ballad. The childhood memory is openly Wordsworthian, recalling the deliberate cacophony provoked by the boy of Winander, who hooted at silent owls. The owls answered back, "Redoubled and redoubled; concourse wild / Of jocund din." Wordsworth's poem was in blank verse, so it is as if the animals rhyme back with the human, only not in words: it is never clear whether it is boy or owls who "shout [...] quivering peals, / And long halloos, and screams, and echoes loud."[32] At least the owls are animate — Heaney's younger self is depicted calling into inanimate echoing and reflecting places which prolong the delight which is "beneath all adult dignity." There is a typical Heaney note of self-deprecation which nevertheless refuses to apologize for the childishness of rhyme, or even the childishness of poetry itself; rhyming is the metonym for poetry which is the true childish thing. Similar small-scale apologies lurk in Muldoon's stacking up of the sins of his own triviality and in Yeats's rejection of the proper worldly stuff of "Theatre business, management of men."

The Wordsworthian echoes of the theme and form of the childish are one thing. The title is another and leads to other matters that the poem can explore as sight and sound and allow to cross over one into another. The well of inspiration at the Greek Mount Helicon is transplanted into Derry farmyards and ditches. The words "fructified" and "aquarium" sound their Latinate elegance across this rural Irish place and against an English that is resolutely inelegant: "fungus and dank moss … crash … ditch … soft mulch … rat slapped … finger slime." The Middle English verb "to fructify" (from French and Latin) has gone the way of echo: the OED records no entries since 1878 (and has yet to catch up with its appearance in this poem). Once such far-off linguistic histories are heard, so are longer histories of language and metaphor. Mention of echo usually means that Narcissus is moping around somewhere, and Heaney drafts in a set of Ovidian allusions that are far from childish, though keyed into a modern psychic vocabulary for linguistic and child development. The synesthesia of sight and sound and touch in these watery contexts means that Narcissus and Echo can be worked into one another, where sensation merges into the undifferentiated, the collapse of subject and object along with eye and ear and feel. This goes from "slime" to its rhyme word "rhyme": "I rhyme / To see myself," where the making of sound is the making of sight sounding back to the touch. It is also the making of the sound of the rhyme of the self, or self in rhyme: "I rhyme." And then the darkness visible, reflection echoing as sound: the final dactyl in "to set the darkness echoing" echoes on in half- or even feminine-rhyme with "spring." Because it is half-rhyme in a falling rhythm, it neither shuts the bolt nor locks the handcuffs.

This effect was learnt from his master by Paul Muldoon in his parable-sonnet from 1980, "Why Brownlee Left," where rhyme words act as adjectival modifiers back up into the octave (famous/farmhouse, black/bullocks) and conclude with a couplet which is no conclusion at all. All we are given is the falling foot of the word "future," itself rhymed with the word foot, where the shifting foot belongs both to the animal (Muldoon's ubiquitous horses) and to prosody (in the final couplet, that rare thing in post-Attridgean prosody, a poetry which measures by "foot," in this case quantitative, trochaic meter):

> By noon Brownlee was famous;
> They had found all abandoned, with
> The last rig unbroken, his pair of black
> Horses, like man and wife,

Shifting their weight from foot to
Foot, and gazing into the future.[33]

The scansion of the last two lines falls thus, dwelling on long and short: "*Shift*ing their *weight* from *foot* to," and then, "*Foot*, and *gazing into* the *fut*ure." Given the Armagh parable in the poem, "foot" can be pronounced "fut," accented as in Percy French's song "Shlathery's Mounted Fut," where "fut" rhymes with "uncut."[34] "Foot to" and "future" may then be vernacular sight rhyme or even skewed half-rhyme: "fyut-your" in the Armagh accent, with a pronounced yet still falling *r* at the end. Either way, even if full, the rhymes offer futurity as a dying fall.

If the sound of Heaney's poem about the past and not the future of sound is the sound of the self, then is its content its own thinking? Does the poem lack thought, perhaps willfully so? It does offer an *ars poetica* emerging from the swamp: of slime and echo and self-reflection, and a sort of passivity before the echo chamber of the well from which it comes to self-realization, both of the external world and its chosen medium, a historicized English language and its classical past. As such it also provides an account of psychic becoming and an aesthetic which is shaping itself on the page, handling a not-so-simple stanza and rhyme, a setting of sound in motion as a sort of mastery — or at least a virtuosity. In a way those half-rhymes in the final line of Heaney's and Muldoon's poems don't actually end them, but allow a life beyond the ending, as the echoing continues into the future. Yeats's last line had suggested its opposite in the pulling of the bolt, no matter that colt, dolt, bolt are fully stressed end-rhyme. The Muldoon sonnet, too, has a third answering poem in the *Prince of the Quotidian* sequence, in which a talking horse takes the persona of one his more politically-engaged tormentors and becomes the poet's own anti-self or *anima*, telling him,

you know it's dross;
you know that 'Erasmus' stuff is an inept attempt
to cover your arse [...][35]

Why Irish? Why *Irish* rhyme? Well, for one reason, the influence of the practice and teaching of Yeats and Heaney remain immense. Heaney wrote in 1974,

> Technique involves not only a poet's way with words, his management of metre, rhythm and verbal texture; it involves also a definition of his stance towards life, a definition of his own reality. It involves the discovery of ways to go out of his normal cognitive bounds and raid the inarticulate; a dynamic alertness that mediates between the origins of feeling in memory and experience and the formal ploys that express these in a work of art.[36]

He developed this in a 1993 lecture, this time engaging with Yeats's rhyming in an extraordinary poem about the terror in his belief in immortality, "The Cold Heaven":

> When such things occur [rhymes], the art of the poem is functioning as a corroboration of the positive emotion and intellectual commitments of the poet. To put it in yet another and perhaps provocatively simple way, 'The Cold Heaven' is a poem which suggests that there is an overall purpose to life; and it does so by the intrinsically poetic action of its rhymes, its rhythms, and its exultant intonation. These create an energy and an order which promote the idea that there exists a much greater, circumambient energy and order within which we have our being [...] when a poem rhymes, when a form generates itself, when a metre provokes consciousness into new postures, it is already on the side of life. When a rhyme surprises and extends the fixed relations between words, that in itself protests against necessity.[37]

The invocation of energy, articulate energy even, in relation to rhyming is familiar from English thinking about rhyme and syntax. But to this Heaney adds high ethical stakes to the aesthetic question, perhaps even an answer to the contentless soul from which Hegel would not demur. Heaney finds a personal God missing from his and Yeats's universe. In its place, will his word "life" do? It is maybe no wonder that another strong influence in regard to Irish rhymed verse, Muldoon, tends to suffer epistemological vertigo in proximity to the high ground of Yeats and Heaney's commitment to such intent in art (the poet's "stance towards life," the rhyming poem "on the side of life") and is happier with the "formal ploys" if not quite form as a ploy. His rhymes continuously surprise, but may also be said to acquiesce in necessity.

Current practitioners of rhyme exercise a formal arrangement of language for some of the very good historical reasons I have outlined above. And certain schools of Irish poetry, in Belfast and Dublin (perhaps less so for the Cork modernists), have been wary of the way the innovations of modernism transgress into the matter of form or form as matter. It is only in the struggle with form that these divergent and then returning conceptions of rhyme can be worked out — that is when sound and sense move apart and then attempt to come back together again. I will take two recent statements of poetical positions in regard to technique, rhythm, and rhyme. First, the Dublin-born Justin Quinn, a poet and critic aware of an inheritance from Yeats, Heaney, and Muldoon yet unafraid to mix that inheritance up in ways that nowadays would be called "cosmopolitan," by contact with Wallace Stevens, Jorie Graham, Allen Ginsberg, or Richard Wilbur, as well as the Czech poets in the country in which he lives. Matters of technique and rhyme nevertheless remain paramount:

> Take a dancer, for instance: one doesn't ask a dancer if he's able to do what he does organically, spontaneously. Or a painter. Artists and writers can reach a point where they wield the hard-won techniques naturally, like a dancer. The form becomes a mode of thought, not a mould for it. A way of measuring breath and cadence. Which is a way of life, and a trajectory of emotion and sensibility.[38]

That moves with ease from an American tradition rooted in Olsen's projective verse and Ginsberg's breath unit, back to Heaney's stance towards life, "a way of life," if not quite "on the side of life." Yet the ethical and the aesthetic remain in play. Rhyme may be just one more artistic technique, perhaps no more interiority than it is the determination of content: something must happen between these two positions as Irish poets continue to work around their fraught relation with historical conditions which have over a difficult century made certain demands on the content of the writing. This sense of a historicized aesthetic which stubbornly remains in play is one reason why so many recent Irish poets have dragged themselves back to established, if not even ancient, forms.

For a number of contemporary Irish poets, part of this sustained longing for poems to rhyme stems from the initial act of reading poetry not your own: as Belfast poet (and exuberant arch-technician) Alan Gillis has put it in the context of a discussion of the legacy of Heaney, an "initiation to the heart of poetry [...] describes an engrossed kind of reading, an immersion in the auditory imagination, that seems to be ever more under threat, but without which poetry means little." Gillis states that Heaney's "language" is "almost always his subject-matter, and yet he has offered unwavering and sure solidity of selfhood throughout his work [...] anathema to the many critics informed by the 'linguistic turn' [...] of continental literary theory." Whether or not an early poem like "Personal Helicon" actually offers solidity of selfhood, Gillis's get-out is via the reanimation of sonic authenticity in his poetry and the poetry of his generation: "Let us not worry about his [Heaney's] work as a total system or coherent philosophy. Let us appreciate his insistence on the present-tense of rhythmic utterance."[39] If such poetics remain "beneath all adult dignity," hearing rhyme in a counter-turn against the theoretical positions of the poetics in which they have been trained, Gillis and Quinn and their contemporaries have reanimated the sound of selfhood, maybe not always its "sure solidity," but certainly its challenges, its reflecting and echoing and frequent dividedness. Theirs are not conservative positions, what we might detect in the neo-Burkeanism of Yeats or Davie, inflected by Eliotian notions of "tradition." Quinn and Gillis belong to a critical generation which occupies a position in which it would be considered childish to renounce histories of reading and the "immersion in the auditory imagination." Regardless of political positioning, rhyme, like syntax, is "a part of the heritable property of past civilisations."

Given the relation of the content of these poems to desire and longing, whether in the private or public sphere, looking before and after in the temporal marking is one function of rhyme (metrical beat being a smaller marker, stanza form and refrain bigger ones). Yet the commitment in the poem is to "the present-tense of rhythmic utterance." Jarvis glosses Hegel thus: "Rhyme, through the return of similar sounds, does not merely lead us back to those sounds. It leads us back to ourselves."[40] Being led in such ways is a recurrent, temporally backwards movement, in which there will always be delay, either in the speed of light split-second between looking and reflection or the slower speed of sound and its echo. It is also a delay continuously updating itself in the present, with hope for its future. That future also contains the anxiety which is apparent in all of the poems and poets discussed so far, how they come to an ending, how that ending might pull back the bolt in some way. We are hard up against Giorgio Agamben's crisis of verse as picked up by Paul Muldoon, "the last verse of a poem is not a verse,"[41] where verse comes from *versure*, the word in Latin for the point where the plough turns round and heads in the opposite direction: or, as Heaney would have it, "Vowels ploughed into other: opened ground."[42] If the end of the poem can be just that, a crisis of ending, or closure, the final rhyme can also offer "opened ground."

Whether they be about fear of the windlass-men or just "management of men," poems must countenance an interiority that is not entirely that of their "selves" — imagined or illusory or actual. By that I mean something which occupies the subject position and may be the biographical entity which is "poet," but also related literary protagonists: character, speaker, persona, and so forth. As such, poems can be about love and about community, all in their way concerned with freedom and constraint. The concern with bindings and unbindings, voluntary and involuntary, is, I contend, one significant subject of Irish poetry. If the limits on artistic liberty have been predominant in this discussion, it is largely to show how the limits which may be found in contingency are then freely held in place by these poets ("In the finding fortuitous, but once found, binding"). But equality and fraternity are also in play — equality being implicit in the fact that you need at least one other person to be equal with; and fraternity, meaning social and communitarian connection in the broadest possible sense. Let me take three more recent examples by the poets Peter McDonald, Conor O'Callaghan, and Vona Groarke: two poems about marriage and family at a point after their break-up, and the other about community facing redundancy at a point when its political loyalties seek analogies of resistance to separation. All three are poems of return of a sort, and returns into the self, albeit in a tangible and not-so-subjectivist Hegelian sense — political as well as personal. And all make a return in location as well as rhyme to see that while change has occurred or is occurring, in recognition of that change the personal and communitarian longing from present to past while facing an uncertain future comes into play. With that longing also comes the play of rhyme.

This is the ending of a poem from 2007 by Peter McDonald, "Quis Separabit," or "who shall part us?" The title is the motto of the state of Northern Ireland and various Irish-associated regiments in the British Army including the now-disbanded Ulster Defense Regiment (UDR); it is also employed by more recalcitrant organizations keen to display their loyalty to the British crown, such as the formerly-paramilitary Ulster Defence Association (UDA). The motto is not so much about longing as for stasis, things as they are, what we have we hold, no surrender. Driving home to East Belfast from the airport, the poet notices first the rain and then the flags, in particular, the Israeli flag.

> And then the Braniel's show of flags:
> as I speed past, I leave behind
> an Ulster flag, Ulster's red hand
> drenched up there it slaps and flaps,
>
> beside it — as clear as day — the Star
> of David, staunch beneath black skies,
> flown in defiance where it flies
> glaring into the backward mirror,
>
> surviving as one mote of white
> lodged like a flaw behind the eyes —
> white edged with blue. The message is
> a downright question: who will part
>
> blood from blood, and who desert us,
> daring to stand here, while we stand?

The road loops back, and has no end.
Here we remain and who shall part us?[43]

The lyric is written in Tennyson's *In Memoriam* stanza. The delayed echo of the *a* rhymes stretches them far enough apart to diminish the accord between them; the inner *b* rhymes hold the lines much faster together. As McDonald has said in his recent book on Victorian rhyme, "Parting and restoration, distance and proximity, are concepts with obvious relevance to the predicament and procedures of *In Memoriam*."[44] If, as regards the content, the execution is in creative, pleasing accord, that content is also difficult material. What is the predicament and what are the procedures of those on the Braniel estate in East Belfast? The "Quis Separabit" motto is phrased in the poem's grammar as two repeated questions (not assertions) about inseparability, "who will part // blood from blood [...] while we stand?" and "Here we remain and who shall part us?"

Of course, these are "rhetorical questions," and they do not ask for an answer. Also at play in this investigation of rhetoric is the Unionist planting of the Star of David flag as an act of analogy, one that is tested poetically as inherent separation. Analogy, like rhyme, is the putting of two things together in difference — the contested territories of the state of Northern Ireland and the state of Israel.[45] For all of their seeming parallels, these are irreconcilables: as McDonald might say about the *In Memoriam* stanza, "Parting and restoration, distance and proximity." In Yeatsian terms these may also be antinomies and at the limits of a rhetoric of similarity. As employed here, the rhyme establishes historical predicament without the corresponding longing of its Victorian precursor for a freedom in the future, the freedom of death and immortality. If the "last verse of a poem is not a verse," the last verse of *In Memoriam* points away from memory to desire and asserts a belief in futurity, seeking the eternal rhyme of the *Commedia* (which runs throughout much of the discussion in this essay):

That God, which ever lives and loves,
    One God, one law, one element,
    And one far off divine event,
To which the whole creation moves.[46]

Tennyson cannot allow a full rhyme at the end of his poem (loves/moves), so speaking out of the mortal sounds of language, the satisfactions of such oneness, the destination of immortality or eternity cannot quite be allowed. There can be no closing box at the end of the *In Memoriam* — one procedure and predicament of the poem had been at the very start, half-rhyming with this conclusion: "Believing where we cannot prove," where "prove" rhymes with "love."

The longing in McDonald's version imagines those who desire that things stay as they are, "daring to stand here, as we stand," no matter that the extravagance, the shock even, of the flag analogy, is matched by the ventriloquized Tennyson stanza. The finding of analogy is also a matter of fortuity, or serendipity even, a matter of luck. As McDonald puts it in his book on rhyme in nineteenth-century English verse:

> [...] the effect of response is made for the writer by his awareness of the reality of language's degree of resistance in the demands and limitations of form. Rhyme is, of course, the most extreme instance of both resistance and response as far as many poets are concerned, and at its crudest level might figure first as a barrier made out of language which form itself puts in the way of a writer's intentions. Not finding a rhyme, and having to say something differently, or say something different from what was first in mind, is an instance of writerly bad luck. So, in rhymed poetry, intentions need to have luck and to know about luck.[47]

The bindings of rhyme — a longing to rhyme — may of course come loose, as in these linked love poems. The poet (and the community and the self) can run out of luck. The first, "Kingdom Come," published in 2013 by Conor O'Callaghan is dedicated *for Vona.* It replays his former wife, the poet Vona Groarke's poems about houses, most notably the poem "Other People's Houses" from 1999, dedicated *for Conor.* The second poem, from 2014, is Vona Groarke's "Furrow." It rhymes visually with O'Callaghan's "Kingdom Come," replicated on separate pages in a separate book printed in the same font by the same Irish publisher, adding a single verse more to his fifteen two-lined stanzas.

The closing stanzas of O'Callaghan's "Kingdom Come" attempt to recreate chimes:

In the yard each lost wish still chimes
even though there's no wind.

There is a barometer stalled on 'Fair',
a slow air remastered on the squeezebox.

The sea, gone miles out of its way, is there
as a screensaver reflected in the screendoor.

And our heirs are there in the ping-pong
and hip-hop of the garage's murk.

And I, in some shape or form,
am there as well. And you are there.[48]

An end-of-marriage poem, "Kingdom Come" plays through extreme sonic coincidence in the past and the disjunction of the lives it represents. The tone is not quite regret, and certainly not guilt: it gets away with avoiding both, seeking a poise which is both broken in the life and conclusive in the poem. The rhyming of the poem turns around cacophonous internal echoing and repeating devices which lead the speaker back through sound to the real illusion of a former self — sundered from his present self — "I ... am there as well. And you are there." The end of the poem is the simple deictic "there," and the sound of the word is repeated four times and heard also in "Fair," "remastered," "door," and "murk" until it finally points to an absence in actuality which is an imagined presence in both memory and fantasy: "And you are there." Space and time interchange with a longing for a lost permanence and immutability; the internal rhymes allow that longing to sound through the percussive detritus of an off-rhymed family life: squeezebox, screensaver, ping-pong, hip-hop.

Groarke's poem picks this off-rhyming again, understandably less impressed with the tonal *sprezzatura* of the absent regret and guilt in the first-published poem. But the sonic organization offers a music unable to come to resolution or "conclusion":

> There is at stake an honesty
> in knowing, definitively, what is meant
>
> by waking into a moment
> and taking the measure of it,
>
> of what the first hand might have to declare
> if the second weren't so loud
>
> of how they occupy each other,
> to arrive at a single end.
>
> How little I comprehend any of this,
> the faithless slippage of things.
>
> How years, like words, silt up in themselves:
> how, when I'm taking the bus home,
>
> I'm also hitchhiking to years ago
> to fill in our names on a form
>
> or am sitting at a yellow table
> in a restaurant called *Now*.
>
> You have come on foot to visit
> And I am waiting for you.[49]

The wavering over a fantasy of temporality plays all the way through the two hands of the blind machine of the watch to that imagined date "in a restaurant called *Now*."

Meaning remains provisional throughout: this poem comes from a book called X, partly an "ex," but primarily an undefined algebraic *x*, a signifier-self which is seeking a signified-self. Such rhymes as there are sound in ironic relation or mystified semi-achievement, at line end and in cross- and assonantal-rhyme: stake/waking; meant/moment; hand/second; declare/ other; end/comprehend; home/names/form; ago/*Now*/you. The speaker is uncomprehending, suffering from "the faithless slippage of things": the internal half-rhyme there, of "faithless" and "slippage," redeems this from the theoretical vocabulary that the speaker is grasping, though unquanti- fiable sibilance slithers through "silt," "hitchhiking," "sitting," "visit." At the poem's opening, the furrow that "Furrow" inhabited was part writing scored on a page and part burial chamber. By its ending, it seems to sound a longing only for the past of the self which is hardly regret and only tan- gentially desire. For all its autobiographical frankness and the completely unhidden invitation that this poem and the O'Callaghan poem offer to readers of Irish poetry (indeed readers of Irish publisher Gallery Press), these are material contexts which are never quite "confessional." The poem halts before its expression of the "honesty / in knowing" what is "at stake," just as it does before any narrative of what happened, or what has been lost, either as longing or desire. And in a way it does this by not rhyming — or not fully rhyming. It is not quite incompletion, but neither is it freedom. Groarke's poem pushes beyond imagined former selves, seeking for form in the "furrow" of thought-lines and the field of thought, writing etched in furrows of verse across the page.

Weighing up rhyme from foot to foot and rhyming it with the future: this by no means amounts to an Irish theory of rhyme or a theory of Irish rhyme. But it does fit with a certain preoccupation with time, loss, and longing, of finding and binding. This is a practice of the unforeseen result- ing in the art object, a practice grounded in the happy accident that some English words sound like each other, just as poets and poetry insist on alternating contact with, and division from, each other, either in intimacy or the longer histories of reading. This is only sometimes "closure": Irish poets continue to be drawn to the risks involved, especially when defensiveness and separation are in the air. To end with one last critical statement of many here, an actual, not imagined, interview with Paul Muldoon from 2004 in *The Paris Review*, prodded by his interviewer James S. F. Wilson into the compositional usefulness of rhyme — and its dangers:

INTERVIEWER: You're never tempted to rush ahead? Not even to write down the next rhyming word?

MULDOON: Never. Or hardly ever. That will look after itself. That will provide itself, if it's going to happen. I'm always open to the possibility that it won't rhyme at all.

INTERVIEWER: That's not an idle threat?

MULDOON: No, it's not, as far as one would have it within one's power. I certainly have no brief for or against rhyme. There's nothing intrinsically good about it.

INTERVIEWER: But it is a terrific engine for you.

MULDOON: I find it so. I find it an engine that is most useful in the composition of the poem. In fact I find it quite revelatory. I don't mind being led by rhyme. But I'm not led like a lamb to the slaughter. I hope.[50]

NOTES

1. "Jonathan Safran Foer on Paul Muldoon," *Poetry Society of America*, accessed July 6, 2015, https://www.poetrysociety.org/psa/poetry/crossroads/tributes/jonathan_safran_foer_on_paul_mul/. Originally published in *Crossroads*, Fall 2004.

2. Paul Muldoon, *The Prince of the Quotidian* (Loughcrew, County Meath: Gallery Press, 1994), 29.

3. "Jonathan Safran Foer on Paul Muldoon."

4. Paul Muldoon, "Blissom," in *Hay* (London: Faber and Faber, 1998); "Getting Round: Notes Towards an *Ars Poetica*," *Essays in Criticism* XLVIII, no. 2 (Apr. 1998): 109.

5. Paul Muldoon quoted by Ian Kilroy, "Transatlantic Poet" (interview), *The Irish Times*, Apr. 19, 2003, B7.

6. See "The Key," introductory poem to *Madoc* (London: Faber and Faber, 1990). As soon as this prose poem (which rhymes) is on the verge of offering an introduction, it gets deliberately side-tracked: "I wanted to say something about Marina, something about an 'identity parade' in which I once took part, something about the etymology of 'tuxedo,' but I found myself savouring the play between 'booth' and 'bathy — ,' 'quits' and 'mesquite,' and began to 'misquote' myself: [...]."

7. I am grateful to Duncan Large for noticing this.

8. Peter McDonald, *Mistaken Identities: Poetry and Northern Ireland* (Oxford: Clarendon Press, 1997), 154–58.

9. Simon Jarvis, "Why rhyme pleases," *Thinking Verse* I (2011): 40.

10. Simon Jarvis, "Musical Thinking: Hegel and the Phenomenology of Prosody," *Paragraph* 75 (July 2005): 57–71.

11. Conor O'Callaghan, preface to *The Wake Forest Series of Irish Poetry*, Vol. 3 (Winston-Salem: Wake Forest UP, 2013), xv.

12. See Quinn, "The Irish Effloresence," *Poetry Review* 91, no. 3 (Autumn 2001): 46. Cited in Fran Brearton, "'The Nothing-could-be-simpler-line': Form in Contemporary Irish Poetry," in *The Oxford Handbook to Modern Irish Poetry*, eds. Fran Brearton and Alan Gillis (Oxford: Oxford UP, 2012), 644.

13. See the first chapter of my *Irish Poetry Under the Union, 1801–1924* (Cambridge: Cambridge UP, 2013), 1–20.

14. See David Caplan, *Rhyme's Challenge: Hip Hop, Poetry, and Contemporary Rhyming Culture* (New York: Oxford UP, 2014).

15. Charles Tomlinson, "The Chances of Rhyme," in *Collected Poems* (Oxford: Oxford UP, 1985), 194–95.

16. R. F. Foster, *Vivid Faces: The Making of a Revolutionary Generation* (London: Allen Lane, 2015), 122.

17. W. B. Yeats, "Among Schoolchildren," in *The Variorum Edition of the Poems of W. B. Yeats*, eds. Peter Allt and Russell K. Alspach (New York: Macmillan, 1957), 445.

18. W. B. Yeats, *Memoirs*, ed. Denis Donoghue (London: Macmillan, 1972), 185.

19. Yeats, *Variorum*, 260.

20. T. V. F Brogan, "Rhyme," in *The Princeton Encyclopedia of Poetry and Poetics*, 4th edition, eds. Roland Greene et al (Princeton: Princeton UP, 2012), 1184.

21. Giorgio Agamben, "The End of the Poem," in *The End of the Poem: Studies in Poetics* (Stanford: Stanford UP, 1999), 110. The passage from Dante is also quoted from Agamben by Paul Muldoon, *The End of the Poem: Oxford Lectures in Poetry* (London: Faber and Faber, 2006), 152.

22. Sept. 8, 1935. *Letters on Poetry from W. B. Yeats to Dorothy Wellesley* (Oxford: Oxford UP, 1964), 22.

23. Geoffrey Hill, "Poetry as Menace and Atonement," in *Collected Critical Writings*, ed. Kenneth Haynes (Oxford: Oxford UP, 2008), 12.

24. Agamben, 113; quoted Muldoon, *The End of the Poem*, 152.

25. Richard Ellmann, "Joyce and Yeats," *Kenyon Review* 12, no. 4 (Autumn 1950): 636.

26. Donald Davie, *Articulate Energy* (London: Routledge, 1955), 124 and 129. See also Geoffrey Hill, "'The Conscious Mind's Intelligible Structure': A Debate," *Agenda* 9, no. 4 – 10, no. 1 (Autumn–Winter 1971–72): 14–23.

27. Nicolò Tibino, quoted by Agamben, 110.

28. George Wilhelm Friedrich Hegel, *Aesthetics: Lectures on Fine Art*, trans. T. M. Knox, 2 vols. (Oxford: Clarendon Press, 1975), Vol. II, 1023 (2.3.3.3, "Poetry"). I follow Jarvis, "Musical Thinking," 64, by substituting Knox's word, "stuffiness," by the word "materiality." With thanks to Michael Perraudin.

29. Jarvis, "Musical Thinking," 64.

30. Ibid., 65.

31. Seamus Heaney, *Opened Ground: Poems 1966–1996* (London: Faber and Faber, 1998), 15.

32. William Wordsworth, "There was a boy" (1800), later *Prelude*, V (1850), in *Poetical Works*, ed. Ernest de Selincourt (Oxford: Oxford UP, 1904–1969), 145 and 525.

33. Paul Muldoon, "Why Brownlee Left," in *Collected Poems* (London: Faber and Faber, 2001), 84.

34. Percy French, *Prose, Poems and Parodies*, ed. De Burgh Daly (Dublin: Talbot Press, 1929), 135–37.

35. *Prince of the Quotidian*, 40. In "Yarrow," from *The Annals of Chile*, this figure becomes full blown republican anima, the character "S—."

36. Seamus Heaney, "Feeling into Words," in *Finders Keepers* (London: Faber and Faber, 2002), 19.

37. Heaney, "Joy or Night: Last Things in the Poetry of W. B. Yeats and Philip Larkin" (1993), in *Finders Keepers*, 319 and 327.

38. O'Callaghan, interview with Justin Quinn, *The Wake Forest Series of Irish Poetry*, Vol. 3, 46.

39. Alan Gillis, "Heaney's Legacy," *Irish Review* 49–50 (2015): 144–46.

40. Jarvis via Hegel, see notes 28 and 29.

41. Agamben, 112.

42. Heaney, "Glanmore Sonnets I" (1979), *Opened Ground*, 163.

43. Peter McDonald, *Collected Poems* (Manchester, UK: Carcanet Press, 2013), 151.

44. Peter McDonald, *Sound Intentions: The Workings of Rhyme in Nineteenth-Century Poetry* (Oxford: Oxford UP, 2012), 173.

45. Paul Muldoon makes the contrary analogy, of Republicans with Palestinians, in "Rita Duffy: *Watchtower II*," in *A Thousand Things Worth Knowing* (London: Faber and Faber, 2015).

46. Alfred Tennyson, epilogue to *In Memoriam*, in *Poems*, ed. Christopher Ricks, 2nd ed. (London: Longmans, 1987), 2:459.

47. McDonald, *Sound Intentions*, 30.

48. Conor O'Callaghan, *The Sun King* (Loughcrew, County Meath: The Gallery Press, 2013), 48–49.

49. Vona Groarke, X (Loughcrew, County Meath: The Gallery Press, 2014), 24–25.

50. James S. F. Wilson, "Paul Muldoon: The Art of Poetry, No. 87," *The Paris Review* 169 (Spring 2004), accessed July 6, 2015, http://www.theparisreview.org/interviews/30/the-art-of-poetry-no-87-paul-muldoon.

2

Contemporary Irish Poetry
and the Problem of
the Subject

Eric Falci

One of the unsettled subjects around twentieth- and twenty-first century poetry in Ireland is that of the subject itself. That is, the subject of poems, what we variably describe as the speaker, the self, the poetic "I," the lyric subject, the lyric "I," or the voice of a poem. This problem is, of course, not limited to contemporary poetry in Ireland, but it has taken on quite particular dimensions within Irish poetry because, from a number of angles, it can appear as though the matter of subjectivity simply hasn't been taken up *as a problem* by contemporary Irish poets. The great majority of poets emerging from the Republic of Ireland and Northern Ireland in the past forty years have presumed, to differing degrees, the stability — and utility — of a coherent "subject" of and in a poem. This is quite different from the course of poetry in England and America over the same period; these countries have had much more robust experimental and avant-garde traditions that have taken as at least part of their charge the dismantling or critique of the poetic subject.

The subject of a poem — its lyric "I," its present-via-absence speaker, its ventriloquized voice — has been seen, whether by Language poets in North America or by J. H. Prynne and Cambridge school poets in England, as deeply problematic: a silent purveyor of a patriarchal and colonialist enlightenment subject, an easy container for the ideologies of consumer capitalism, a naive stand-in for a bourgeois subject, a discursive fiction ripe for deconstruction. The major contemporary poets on either side of the Atlantic — Lyn Hejinian, John Ashbery, Denise Riley, Prynne, among, of course, many others — have all, over the course of long careers, spent significant time disturbing and fracturing the idea (and instantiation) of a poetic or lyric subject. A number of poets have attempted to do away with it altogether, placing at the generative center of a poem not a speaker or voice, but a procedure, concept, or set of rules so that the poem might produce itself, without, to return to a well-trod moment from Charles Olson's "Projective Verse," the "lyrical interference of the individual as ego."[1] Olson's essay and his poetics more broadly have been deeply influential on both sides of the Atlantic, and although the specific context of his prescriptions has long passed, it is clear that the kind of "interference" that the self or subject has caused for and within poems has not at all abated. One of the major debates about poetry since the middle of the century, perhaps the major debate, has been concerned with the status of the "individual as ego," not only about the relationship between the author of a poem and whatever sort of "I" appears within the poem (its speaker or lyric subject), but also about whether poems can — or should — continue to be spun around the notion of an organizing subject who is the source of its language and the locus of its voicing.

It is at least somewhat surprising, then, that this debate hasn't really been taken up within Irish poetry. Nearly all poetry produced throughout Ireland in the past half century (and before that) has taken the notion of an organizing "I" or speaker as, to a greater or lesser degree, a given. This has been read as a sign of the fundamental conservatism of Irish poetry as compared to other parts of the English-language canon. Even among more experimentally-minded poets in Ireland, such as Thomas Kinsella,

Catherine Walsh, or Maurice Scully, whose work cleaves away from models of the "well-made poem" and toward the processual and open field texts typical of post-Poundian modernist poetics, there tends to be a relatively stable speaker or "mind" from which a text can be thought to emerge even as other aspects of poetic discourse and form become unmoored. This isn't to say that Irish poets have unthinkingly clung to an attenuated or outdated model of the lyric subject, but, rather, that they have tended to experiment within this model rather than fully abandon or overturn it.[2]

At the same time, the major Irish poets of the past several decades have each offered powerful and distinctive versions of lyric subjectivity, even if they haven't grappled with its underpinnings. For some poets — Seamus Heaney and Eavan Boland might stand as primary instances — the lyric "I" entwines autobiography and history, refashioning the particulars of their own lives so that the resulting amalgam appears (whether intentionally or not) to be exemplary or representative. The projects at the heart of each of their poetics are inextricable from the subjects posited in their poems, whether Heaney's bid to articulate the personal, familial, confessional, political, and literary subject into a single complex figure for self- and cultural discovery; or Boland's aim to give voice to a female subject within a literary and political culture that has been deeply, damagingly patriarchal. Although his favored modes changed over the course of his career, the final lines of "Personal Helicon" pose a practice that covers the whole of Heaney's oeuvre: the poem and "myself" produce each other mutually, each setting the other echoing. In a similar way, Boland's splicing of individual and group in order to enunciate a female subject within Irish literature and culture has been at the core of nearly all of her work. A number of critics have taken issue with the stances that Heaney and Boland proffer and have suggested that other figures — Medbh McGuckian, Eiléan Ní Chuilleanáin, Paul Muldoon, Michael Longley, and Derek Mahon (to name only the most oft-cited poets) — construct more productively complex models of poetic subjectivity, models that are responsive to poststructural thinking or postmodern notions of selfhood, or that aren't wound so tightly into binaries of nation, gender, or religion.[3]

Putting aside the particulars of such arguments, which have been considered by a number of critics and don't need rehearsing here, it is worth pointing out that it isn't the case that the poetic subject becomes a less prominent feature in the work of, say, McGuckian or Muldoon. If anything, the gravitational pull of the subject or speaker becomes even stronger, if only because the myriad difficulties presented by their work require a reader to hold even tighter to the figure or figment of a lyric "I," because other structures of cohesion have been removed. In, for example, a typical McGuckian poem, the ties of syntax have been so loosened, the contextual frame so scrambled, and the logic of reference so shredded that one is thrown back even more adamantly upon the notion of a poetic subject who is generating and, so, holding together the poem's radically incompatible parts. Muldoon's poems operate quite differently, but the paratactic or associative quality of much of his work, along with its hermetic system of references and its baroque formal structures, have the effect of centering a poem's subject — its author, inventor, confectioner, speaker — even more definitively. I don't mean to suggest that every Muldoon or McGuckian poem appears in the same way, nor that every poem by Longley or Boland (or, for that matter, Heaney) unfolds a pre-made set of stances or forms. However, what is striking about Irish poetry of the past several decades is not that each major poet has developed a distinctive or signature style or set of styles (this, after all, is precisely what "major" poets often do), but rather that each has fashioned a style that orbits around a particular kind of "I," one that is catalyzed by a recognizable set of characteristics, tones, or tactics.

Or, to put it in a somewhat different way, most of the major Irish poets of the past fifty years have fashioned distinctive models of poetic subjectivity, whether they have hewed closely to the center of the English poetic tradition or have experimented at its edges, and not only in the service of a style from which might emanate a "self" and its expressions. These models have also been attuned to local conditions and histories, and so have been able to perform different kinds of discursive and political work. If the involuted subject of McGuckian's poetry and the free-wheeling subject of Muldoon's can be thought about as dialectical negations of the forthright and exemplary subjects in Boland's or Heaney's writings, then other poets have offered quite different alternatives. The anxious evasive maneuvers of the subject of Ciaran Carson's poetry of the 1980s and 1990s constitute a granular phenomenological account of daily life in Troubles-era Belfast. The concrete autobiographical subject that features in many of Paula Meehan's poems provides for an immanent feminist critique to emerge alongside Boland's historically-minded or McGuckian's deconstructive models, one that can take up directly the complicated politics of the Republic of Ireland's present. The recessive subject of Ní Chuilleanáin's poetry, its frequent presentation of a speaker who seems partially unavailable within the diegesis of the poem or whose perspective seems collaged rather than cohesive, allows both for a renewal of lyric subjectivity beyond its poststructural fracturing and for a continuation of performative elusiveness that quietly critiques models of representative subjectivity that are ideologically doubtful. Michael Longley's miniatures have the dual function of puncturing the pretensions of a certain kind of poetic subject positioning (especially within the context of Northern Ireland in the late twentieth century) and of turning the lyric lens from subject to object as they exhibit a naturalist's focus on animals and environments without recapitulating an Enlightenment-Romantic aim to "capture" such objects within the orbit of the sovereign self. Of course, such models have the effect of coalescing distinctive (and often commodifiable) individual styles, but together the various approaches to self-making among Irish poets demonstrate that while contemporary Irish poets have tended not to step outside the broad boundaries of first-person poetry, they have tested those bounds from nearly every direction.

The above encapsulations are, to a degree, overly general. Given the heterogeneous and capacious terrain of contemporary Irish poetry, I offer such broad strokes here for a few reasons. First, I want to gesture back to, and complicate, my initial point about Irish poetry's relative conservatism as compared to other bodies of contemporary anglophone poetry. There has been nothing like the Language poetry or conceptual poetry phenomena in the world of contemporary Irish poetry, and no Irish poet compares to Prynne in terms of the sheer force of his sustained pressure upon every aspect of the poetic enterprise. But neither have Irish poets simply accepted some devolved version of a Movement or mainstream lyric subject and asked no further questions. Rather, poets in Ireland have fashioned an array of investigations into the subject of the poem without fully overturning or abandoning it. Such a claim is also true (although differently true) of the most readily-identifiable experimental poets in Ireland — such as Walsh,

Scully, or Trevor Joyce — although their work isn't my subject here.[4] Second, these general comments about the canonical figures in contemporary Irish poetry help me to pivot to the writers who are my subject here, Sinéad Morrissey and Caitríona O'Reilly, who are each somewhat younger than those writers I've mentioned so far, but whose work thus far brings into focus a different set of questions about the ways that subjectivity has been constructed within Irish poetry more broadly. I will not argue that these two poets are significantly more experimental than their predecessors or peers or that they introduce something entirely new into Irish poetry. Rather, I will suggest that both Morrissey and O'Reilly undertake substantive and complex investigations into the delineation of subjectivity within poetic texts, and that their work allows us to articulate a much more capacious notion of what lyric subjectivity might involve.

If one side of the question about poetic subjectivity has to do with the way in which an "I" is construed and presented, then another side, though significantly less examined, concerns the delineation of the diegetic space within which that lyric subject is constituted. Quite often, the dismantling of one necessitates the abrogation of the other. The elusive subject of McGuckian's poetry, for instance, makes for an equally elusive diegesis. On the other end of the spectrum, the typical subject in a Heaney poem (or one by Boland, Mahon, Longley, or Meehan) operates within a clearly defined context — their work partakes of what we might call "lyric realism." Such poems appear as monologues not only because they are voiced by what seems to be a coherent "I," but also because that figure, in speaking, produces a backdrop that is self-unified and a set of perspectives that correspond: a story world. In the case of a good amount of experimental or avant-garde poetry, it isn't necessarily productive to inquire into the diegesis of a text. Diegesis, as a critical term, presumes some form of representational discourse, and much innovative poetry in the twentieth century aims precisely to refuse representation, to resist the tendency to "see through" language as though it gives onto a world by focusing on the materiality and opacity of language itself. Of course, it might be said that one of the characteristics of poetry *tout court* is defamiliarization or estrangement of such a kind, with such estrangement often occurring within the realm of figuration, and that this isn't necessarily a feature unique to modernist or avant-garde writing. But it seems important to distinguish between, say, "Kubla Khan," which is highly figurative but still allows for a diegetic space to be imagined by a reader, and *Tender Buttons*, which thoroughly defies attempts to bring it within the bounds of representational discourse.

Part of the point that I've been trying to make so far is that Irish poets in the twentieth and twenty-first centuries have generally not followed a Steinian path. Most contemporary Irish poets retain a coherent subject in part by constructing a coherent deictic and diegetic network. The various personal, temporal, and locational pronouns in a poem align, allowing a reader not only to imagine that the poem is emerging from an individualized voice, but also that that voice is sounding in a clearly imaginable space, a story world such as one expects (and imaginatively constructs) when reading a traditional novel. While retaining such a framework, however, poets in Ireland have also tinkered with and experimented on it, by unrigging one part of the network (say, the logic of personal pronouns in a poem) while maintaining others, by setting aspects of the discursive structure of a poem against one another so that their tensions might be productive, or by sequencing poems so that they trouble or undo one another. If this still signals a kind of literary conservatism, then it might be best to mark it as a conservatism of the experimental sort. Turning to poems by Morrissey and O'Reilly, two of the most accomplished poets of the generation after those two celebrated generations of Irish and Northern Irish poetry (the first one consisting of those poets born in the years just before or during the Second World War, and the second comprising those poets born in the decade after its end), displays the depth and breadth of what seems to be an island-wide project: to rethink from the inside the nature and stakes of the subject of poetry.

In a relatively short period of time, Sinéad Morrissey has become a central figure in the anglophone literary world. Already the recipient of myriad prizes, her fifth volume, *Parallax* (2013), won the T. S. Eliot Prize in 2014, and she was named Belfast's first poet laureate the same year. *Parallax*, along with a selection of her earlier poems, was published in an American edition by Farrar, Straus and Giroux in 2016. Like many of her predecessors among Irish poets, Morrissey makes a number of her poems out of the stuff of her life. The poems in Morrissey's first two volumes — *There was a Fire in Vancouver* (1996) and *Between Here and There* (2002) — emerge, most frequently, from her biography: her childhood, her family, her relationships, her travels, her time spent living abroad (primarily in Japan and New Zealand), and her return to Belfast. Some take up aspects of the political and cultural complexities of Northern Ireland, from Morrissey's particular vantage point, as the title of one early poem puts it, "among Communists." The child of ardent leftists, Morrissey has long been attuned to political themes in her work, and, perhaps more than any other poet, Morrissey has been able to track the complexities of Northern Ireland after the Troubles. Autobiographical poems continue to appear regularly in her subsequent volumes — *The State of the Prisons* (2005), *Through the Square Window* (2009), and *Parallax* — and Morrissey has been particularly interested in writing about pregnancy, the birth of her two children, and their own developing lives.

At the same time, these last three volumes also invert, or at least significantly disrupt, their own tendencies toward autobiography. In *The State of the Prisons*, Morrissey turns her practice outward, even in poems that have their basis in her life. The poems that are autobiographically minded are conspicuously so; and those that are not are very conspicuously the autobiographical poems of others presented as dramatic monologues. The title poem is a long monologue in the voice of John Howard, an eighteenth-century prison reformer, in which he provides a retrospective of his life and career, counterpointing his professional success with the guilt that he feels for abandoning his son, who contracts syphilis in his absence and is relegated to an asylum. Her previous volume, *Between Here and There*, allowed Morrissey to present her own autobiographical "I" as a displaced subject. Morrissey's life in these years was marked by frequent travel, long periods spent living abroad, and a return to Northern Ireland, and the volume's title encapsulates her time as a peripatetic.[5] *The State of the Prisons*, especially in its title poem, presents a more thoroughly displaced subject, one who is adamantly not Morrissey herself. Throughout the volume, Morrissey focuses on the relationship between subjects and objects, and more specifically on what might be called the space of the self. "The Second Lesson of the Anatomists" concretizes this set of concerns:

See how the inside belies our skin,
say the anatomists,
after showing us how freakishly we split.[6]

At issue is the integrity of the body, and the "effortlessly deceptive" quality
of skin, whose seeming coherence papers over its porosity and fragility.
Over the course of the poem, all manner of membrane and threshold
are called into question, and if the first lesson of the anatomists has to do
with the body's solidity — its skeleton, its organs — then the second lesson
inverts the first by forcing us to reckon with the hollows of which much of
the body is made: the passageways and openings that give on to others and
to the world. The poem begins to shed its spatial logic as different scales
are superimposed:

Are all skins as effortlessly deceptive as this?
The thin film over the ocean? Doors?
Or this evening, for instance,

in which darkness and a river
play both mother and father
in supporting a glass room?

Morrissey anatomizes the poem's subject, revealing its own reliance on
absence as a structuring principle. These questions are posed in response
to the anatomists' lesson, but they also perform that lesson: over the course
of the series of questions the body is fissured, diffused into environment,
architecture, and atmosphere. And then the poem undergoes a set change:
"There is a party going on." Whereas earlier Morrison described the body's
liquidity — "the heart-wonder bleeding, emptying, re-bleeding" — here the
party becomes the site of "spillage // in the centre," another unstable and
shifting diegetic space whose insides and outsides have switched or merged.
In this poem, the anatomists' second lesson produces forms of knowledge
not only about anatomy, but also about the configurations of space, the
relations among bodies and between bodies and environments, as well as

the "thin film" that at once separates and joins. In the final tercet, this new knowledge is enacted:

> For we have hallways to discover in one another like nerves.
> And childhoods, and love affairs, and drownings, and faithfulness
> by which language has occurred.

Architectural space is translated back into anatomy — "hallways ... like nerves" — and the poem's final sentence then unspools a kind of figural nerve pathway as it converts nerve into memory, memory into experience, experience into extremity (drowning), and extremity into something like an existential axiom — each of which subtend the production of language that the poem has made to occur. At issue in this poem, and, as I'll go on to suggest, in Morrissey's later work, is a series of questions about how subjects emerge within texts, as an effect of a network of relations that both allows subjects to form and binds that formation.

If the title poem and a number of other pieces in *The State of the Prisons* provide an antithesis to the autobiographical texts in her first two books, then *Through the Square Window* synthesizes all of their primary tendencies. The volume's unifying topic is the birth and early years of her son, Augustine, who is the volume's dedicatee. Ten of the book's thirty-two poems directly address or reference Augustine, and they are dispersed chronologically, with poems about, presumably, Morrissey's pregnancy and childbirth ("Returning from Arizona," "Found Architecture," and "'Love, the nightwatch ...'") appearing before poems about Augustine's early years ("Missing Winter," "Augustine Sleeping Before He Can Talk," "Through the Square Window," "Townhouse," "Grammar," "Cathedral," and "Dash"). And so, on one level, the book progresses through the story of two entwined lives and asks to be read as a double lyric memoir. By doing so, the volume establishes a story world that can carry over from poem to poem. Even though there are a number of poems that aren't directly about Morrissey's family, the ten autobiographical texts establish a diegetic spine, and the other twenty-two poems in the volume tend to gravitate toward that spine. As a whole, then, *Through the Square Window* posits an overarching lyric subject — a clear "I" who is, more or less, the author — and an encompassing diegesis within which the various poems can be said to take place.

Much of the previous paragraph might simply expand upon what may seem like the self-evident observation that I made at the beginning of the paragraph: that *Through the Square Window* is largely about the birth of Morrissey's son and his first few years of life. However, the other twenty-two poems in the volume produce a counter-narrative that both reinforces and undermines the primary one. Against the autobiographical poems in the volume, Morrissey sets a number of poems as either lyric monologues or lyric parables, most of which comment on, or redirect, the book's central arc. Some of these can be read as second-order autobiography, taking as their subject stories that the author might be reading to her child ("Mother Goose") or television shows that her child might be watching or that the author might have watched as a child (as in "The Clangers," a British kids' show broadcast in the early 1970s). Others, however, act as third-order autobiographical texts, retelling well-known narratives about the darkness of childhood ("The Innocents," which adapts Henry James's *The Turn of the Screw*) or presenting ominous parables about motherhood ("Fairground Music," which tells of a young woman's self-induced abortion) and parenthood ("Telegraph" tells the story of abuse and trauma passed down along several generations of a family in America). Against the volume's autobiographical progression Morrissey places a series of poems that act as warnings or nightmares, marking the fear and anxiety that surrounds the act of childbirth and the raising of children. Momentary references to Lewis Carroll and *Alice in Wonderland* in, respectively, the volume's first and last poems underscore the joys and perils that attend childhood and childrearing. Alongside of the autobiographical poems are a series of parabolic narratives — often in the first person — that present fictional or imagined subjects that shadow or invert the volume's two central figures: the author and her young son.

In multiple ways, *Through the Square Window* is a book of doubles. Not only is there a double subject at the heart of the volume (poet and child), but this double subject is itself doubled by the alternate monologues and parables strewn among the autobiographical poems. This doubleness, in addition to being narrativized, is spatialized. The volume frequently picks up on architectural discourse and spatial metaphors, usually as a way to figure and think through the author's own pregnancy, as in "Found Architecture," in which the internal space of the womb is externalized as a series of found structures or spatial arrangements: "whatever room I happen to be in" or whatever natural or built configuration the speaker comes upon projects her own bodily architecture.[7] The poem ends by describing four "mug-shot photographs from a machine," the sonogram images that concretize, "most disarmingly" for the speaker, the architecture of the double self.[8] What appears in the images is both the speaker and not the speaker — it is the speaker's body depicted, but also the fetal body of the son who is someone else, but not yet. This bodily ambivalence is subtly marked by the dead metaphor contained in "disarmingly." The end of the poem offers what we might describe as the "third lesson of the anatomists":

> From blood and the body's
> inconsolable hunger I have been my own kaleidoscope —
> five winter-bleached girls on a diving board, ready to jump.[9]

A final instance of "found architecture" is offered as the complex implications of the sonogram images — "I have been my own kaleidoscope" — produce a further set of subjective fissures: the kaleidoscopic self projects not only the speaker's intricate twoness, but also a splayed set of figures — "five winter-bleached girls" — whose jump prefigures the impending birth. One found architecture — the speaker's womb — will ultimately found another — the child's separate self — and at that moment lose itself.

As a whole, the volume thematizes the changeable space of the double subject at its heart and the complex dialectic between inside and outside. The book's opening poem, "Storm," figures this architecturally, detailing the phenomenological experience of being in a house during a storm:

> sanctuary was still sanctuary
> except more so, with the inside
> holding flickeringly, and the
> outside clamouring in.[10]

And fittingly, considering its overall topic, the volume's final poem figures this doubleness as it outlines the relationship between body and shadow:

> we breathe
> and are enveloped in an outline
>
> and when we pass,
> the outline stays suspended.[11]

Through the Square Window begins with a text that subordinates the subject to its surrounding space, its architecture and its weather, while the subject of the final poem makes its own weather and produces its own architecture, albeit a momentary one made only of the play of light. These paired images replicate the process from pregnancy to birth upon which the entire volume is based. Throughout her work, from the more directly autobiographical poems of her early volumes through the constellated perspectival subject at issue in *Parallax*, Morrissey sets selves and spaces against one another, offering lyric subjects whose seemingly coherent outlines are unmade or transformed by their surrounding contexts. In this regard, *Through the Square Window* is Morrissey's linchpin book (thus far): in it she striates the central lyric dyad (*I* and *you*, mother and son) with other subjects, some imagined, some novelistic, some parabolic, each of which complicate the volume's central pair by cutting against its logic. This formal striation becomes the governing figure for the book as a whole, which is concerned, above all else, with the strange wonder by which a single self becomes two.

As in Morrissey's work, Caitríona O'Reilly's first three volumes — *The Nowhere Birds* (2001), *The Sea Cabinet* (2006), and *Geis* (2015) — include a number of poems that deploy familiar discursive strategies of anecdote, reminiscence, and epiphany within the bounds of a well-made and delimited form. O'Reilly is interested, primarily though not exclusively, with delving into psychological complexities, and the poems most often read as meditations on, and investigations of, her own self and past. "I cannot feel found," she writes in the opening line of the opening poem in her debut volume.[12] The most noticeable presider in her work is Plath, who, along with Emily Dickinson and H. D., was the subject of O'Reilly's PhD research. Like Plath,

O'Reilly tracks and depicts moments of physiological and psychological extremity — dream, nightmare, migraine, anxiety, obsession — that shape the self, what she calls in "Possession," "fragments of jigsaw / in the rough art of assemblage whose end we are."[13] The title sequence of *Geis* recounts what seems to be a period of psychological breakdown and recovery, and takes place within a medical institution of some kind. Her three volumes are rife with Dickinsonian lyrics that stage scenes of emotional turmoil or psychological vexation, employing richly strange images within a highly figurative texture. Her work is attentive to the making of selves and to the construction of a subject as a kind of lyric object, one that is both rendered in and distanced by metaphor. As she writes in the penultimate poem in *Geis*, "what we have become folds over us / in days and years as involute as petals."[14] Selves, here, are rendered as both a figurative amalgam and as an amalgamation of figuration itself. Not only is the temporality of the collective subject ("days and years") compared via simile to the unfolding petals of a flower, but the process by which this figuration occurs is itself figural. The flower simile is enwrapped by a flower metaphor. Even before the introduction of the metaphorical petals, the experience of the collective subject ("what we have become") has already been figured as flower-like, capable of "folding over" itself.

What is at stake for O'Reilly, both in this local moment and more broadly, is the question of how poems can (or, must) transform subjects into objects. O'Reilly's work depends on systemic figuration: not only do her poems offer numerous discrete similes and metaphors, but also their entire texture seems wrought from figures. A reader often cannot decouple a poem's diegesis from its metaphorical space by positing a "realistic" story world on top of which are piled the metaphors and similes that enrich or enliven it. Rather, the two levels — figure and ground, tenor and vehicle — are collapsed. The subject of her poems, then, remains elusive, toggling between these compacted levels while appearing nowhere fully, or never quite appearing as an autobiographical subject. It is clear that her work is shaped by the materials and conditions of her life. But those materials and conditions are rarely directly available in the poems, even as momentary jumping-off points for metaphorical transformations. What results, then, is a body of work that is at the same time launched from autobiography and illegible as autobiography.[15]

This tendency is concretized in her early poem "Autobiography," whose title lofts a set of generic and discursive conventions that are both fulfilled and evaded. The poem is, as one might expect, autobiographical, in that it provides a first-person account in a long verse paragraph that focuses on an area of County Wicklow, where O'Reilly grew up. It contains several straightforward pieces of autobiographical information: "I live between three Victorian piers on the bay's industrial side"; "I live in the shadow / of the shadow of a castle's walls."[16] And in many ways it fits neatly into the prominent subgenre of Irish place poetry. It takes a broad perspective on a coastal area in Wicklow in sight of Bray Head (the only place name given) and details the play of its weather, the run of its land, its littoral scrim, the particularities of its built environment, and several of its historical and topographical details. It clearly positions a subject, an "I," who has broad access to and deep knowledge of both the local specifics and the characteristics of the region. An "I," it seems, who lives there. We are told, moreover, exactly where the speaker lives, if in somewhat cryptic terms: "between three Victorian piers," "in the shadow / of the shadow of a castle's walls." Other moments offer first-person experiences:

> The bay smiles, it is full of flattened shiny water
> sucking quietly at the shore and piers. All night
> I adjust my own breath to its eternally regular breaking.
>
> [...]
>
> I've watched the sky and sea
> go up in flames at dusk, though mostly they're an angry grey.
> Now any horizon of mine must be nine-tenths sky.[17]

The first passage, from the middle of the poem, and the second, the poem's final lines, present observations that are both deeply personal and oddly abstract. It isn't as though we can't align these sentences with what we can imagine to be O'Reilly's life — of course we can. Rather, it's that the lines seem to go out of their way to align with any number of lives. Each passage describes blatantly generic experiences: listening to the sea at night and timing one's own breath to its tidal motions, and watching a sunset from the shore. We can't, however, alter the poem's title by substituting the title of Stein's *Everybody's Autobiography*, because O'Reilly's poem provides enough specific detail to narrow down the range of possible subjects. It isn't just anybody's autobiography. But it also isn't O'Reilly's autobiography, even though it includes material that relates to her life. If it were titled something different, then this tension might not arise, but then it would also be a somewhat less interesting poem. The title tags the poem, and then the body of the text untags it, presenting something like an "objective" autobiography, a somewhat contradictory generic entanglement.

This inversion of generic conventions is clinched in the poem's final lines, in which the speaker whose putative autobiography this is complicates its temporality. The entirety of the poem is in the present tense with occasional forays into the past perfect tense, which gives the sense of a speaker making statements about her conditions at present ("I live," "I adjust") while also making statements about past experiences ("I've seen"). The final lines of the poem incorporate both past ("I've watched") and present ("Now"), but unlike earlier instances of this pairing, this final instance wrenches the temporal logic of the poem. The final line of the poem has the force of a concluding claim, although one that fissures the text's logic: if the present indicated by "now" is the same present indicated by the present tense verbs throughout the poem, then it isn't the case that the speaker's horizon "must be nine-tenths sky." The speaker has spent a great deal of time cataloguing the visible scene — its mountains, fields, meadows, and beaches. All of this can't possibly take up only the one-tenth of the total view that isn't sky. Such a perspective, if not impossible, is certainly unlikely. It is either the case that the "I" of the poem states something like a counterfactual desire — the kind of horizon that she "must" have "now" is precisely the kind of horizon that she didn't experience as part of her "autobiography" — or that the subject of the poem fractures. In this scenario, the final line is spoken from a second present, the present of the poem's enunciation, which would then be in the future of the present tense discourse that constitutes all of the lines that lead up to it. The temporal diegesis splits into two, each of which posits a discrete subject — the "I" who presently lives in the place described, and a distinct though related "I" who no longer does, but who recalls the past from the position of a lyric present ("now"), although, weirdly, speaks of the past in the present tense ("I live"). O'Reilly takes on the strange mechanics of self-narration and submits them to the quite different logic of lyric speaking. If part of the poem's charge is to render "autobiography" as an objective genre, then another part concerns the splitting and overturning of the subject putatively at the heart of what we would designate as "autobiography."

"The Harbour in January," the poem that follows "Autobiography" in *The Nowhere Birds*, revisits a similar landscape, but instead of anatomizing temporal diegesis and its relation to the construal of a poetic subject, O'Reilly investigates the matter of space and perspective. The poem subtly maps two incompatible perspectives atop one another: a view of the sea from some position on the shore, and a view of the shore from a position on the sea. An exercise in the manipulation of personification and the pathetic fallacy, "The Harbour in January" begins by silently positing a speaker taking in a littoral landscape, noting the "single crow" "like an arched eyebrow," the "birds in the hedge," and the "mercury-heavy rolls" of the tide.[18] Just before the midpoint of the poem — at the end of the third of six tercets — the perspective flips and is now that of the personified sea looking back on the shore: "It sees us bend from cockpit or quayside // and gives us shivering bodies." Instead of a singular speaker looking out at the collectivity of the sea, the sea is personified — "the sea's of mobile feature" — and looks back on the collectivity of the shore. Just as earlier a "single crow" approximated an "arched eyebrow," so now a "ship's legacy" (its wake of water) is personified, as "a smile that widens and complicates / and gapes to take in all the bay and me." This reimposition of a singular speaker on shore ("me") occurs as a form of diegetic estrangement. Earlier, the speaker notes that "we aren't ourselves in it," "it" referring to the sea whose perspective the poem has taken up. This phrase works triply: "we" are not "in" the sea in a literal sense (but rather on the shore shivering), "we ourselves" are not "in" the sea's perspective (a performative contradiction), and "we" aren't "ourselves" in the sea's perspective (we are, rather, the image of ourselves held in the sea's impossible field of vision). When the first line of the final tercet further characterizes the "me" that the sea's smile has gaped to take in, once again the speaker is removed from the poem's diegesis: "not of the sea, not in it, just looking on." Just as the previous poem fissures temporal logic, so does "The Harbour in January" unsettle its own spatial sense.

In so doing, O'Reilly makes the subject of the poem — by which I mean its complex of deictic, diegetic, and perspectival logic — an open investigative site, one that continues to be explored in her later work. The title poem of her second volume is perhaps her most explicit attempt to turn her poetry fully outward, focusing, as it does, exclusively on a series of exhibits in the Town Docks Museum in Hull, where O'Reilly lived for a time. "The Sea Cabinet" displays O'Reilly's powers of visual description, and each of the five poems in the sequence is intent on rendering the specific character and gravity of the objects upon which it gazes. At the same time, "The Sea Cabinet" is entirely outward facing, with no moments of self-reflexivity of the sort that we expect from poetry generally, and that we often get from O'Reilly. It is almost as though she aims to present a pure story world, an objective narration with no subjective interference at all. Of course, O'Reilly's visual descriptions often give on to anecdotes that must be imagined, and it isn't the case that the sequence appears as (or aspires to) objective description. *Geis*, which also contains a number of ekphrastic poems as well as many poems that — like the title sequence — can reasonably be thought about as deriving from individual experience, more directly mediates between what might be called texts of the objectively-rendered subject and those of the subjectively-rendered object.

In this way, we might think about O'Reilly's first three volumes as we did Morrissey's. Both approach the problem of the poetic subject at multiple levels: within individual poems, among poems in a volume, and among volumes. The primary dialectical tug in O'Reilly's poetry appears in her tendency either to foreground the intricacies of the self's interior — usually within a highly figurative texture — or to fully invest in the rendering of an object, or animal, or space outside the self. This allows O'Reilly to experiment with the frames of her texts: flipping figure and ground, rendering subjects as objects, and operating at the seam between description and figuration. Morrissey's poems less frequently juggle perspectives or present multiple diegetic spaces within a single poem. Even the poems in *Parallax*, which are overwhelmingly concerned with matters of visuality and perspective, tend to unfold as cohesive perspectival units. Morrissey's interest in the possibilities of lyric subjectivity appears at the macro level, in the ways that the internally coherent construction of subjectivity within a given poem is troubled, and rendered suspect, by the internally coherent construction of subjectivity within a nearby poem in the volume.

Of course, Morrissey and O'Reilly aren't alone in writing poems that unrig and transform their diegetic spaces or posit lyric subjects that are complex and incommensurate rather than singular and self-unified. Carson, McGuckian, Ní Chuilleanáin, and Muldoon all write poems that do similar work, and Ní Chuilleanáin's "Pygmalion's Image" is perhaps the signal such text within the modern Irish canon. Among its other wonders, it repeatedly flips and stretches its diegetic space, and the transformative animation that it forwards is catalyzed in part by a switching of scales. Such maneuvers remain, broadly, within the conventions of lyric poetry, but they submit those conventions to sustained scrutiny and press against inherited forms and stances. As part of a broader anatomization of the poetic "I" among contemporary Irish writers, one that has extended over several generations throughout the island of Ireland, Morrissey's and O'Reilly's work considers lyric subjectivity not as the making of a unified self, but rather as the ceaseless reinscription of shifting coordinates within a set of overlapping formal and diegetic frames. If such compositional practices signal something other than a whole scale suspicion of lyric poetry as a genre as well as a lingering resistance to the full freight of modernism, then they also reveal, and add to, the kinds of generative skepticism about the construction and place of the lyric subject that has typified Irish poetry since the 1960s and has spurred into existence many of its most vital poems.

NOTES

1. Charles Olson, "Projective Verse" [1950], in *The Norton Anthology of Modern and Contemporary Poetry*, ed. Jahan Ramazani, Richard Ellmann, and Robert O'Clair (New York: Norton, 2003), 2: 1060.

2. This is part of the argument that I make in *Continuity and Change in Irish Poetry, 1966–2010* (Cambridge: Cambridge UP, 2012). The present essay might be thought of as an extension, or refiguring, of some of the ideas forwarded there.

3. Key works in this regard include Guinn Batten, "'Where All the Ladders Start': Identity, Ideology, and the Ghosts of the Romantic Subject in the Poetry of Yeats and Muldoon," in *Romantic Generations: Essays in Honor of Robert F. Gleckner*, ed. Ghislaine McDayter et al. (Lewisburg, PA: Bucknell UP, 2001), 245–80, and "'He Could Barely Tell One from the Other': The Borderline Disorders of Paul Muldoon's Poetry," *South Atlantic Quarterly* 95, no. 1 (Winter 1996): 171–204; David Lloyd, *Anomalous States: Irish Writing and the Post-colonial Moment* (Durham, NC: Duke UP, 1993), 13–40; Clair Wills, *Improprieties: Politics and Sexuality in Northern Irish Poetry* (Oxford: Clarendon Press, 1993); and Edna Longley, *The Living Stream: Literature and Revisionism in Modern Ireland* (Newcastle upon Tyne: Bloodaxe Books, 1994), 196–227.

4. On the work of these poets, see, in particular, Alex Davis, *A Broken Line: Denis Devlin and Irish Poetic Modernism* (Dublin: University College Dublin Press, 2000); Eric Falci, *Continuity and Change in Irish Poetry, 1966–2010*, 186–204; and Niamh O'Mahony, ed., *Essays on the Poetry of Trevor Joyce* (Bristol: Shearsman Books, 2015).

5. The majority of scholarship on Morrissey's poetry concerns these poems of travel, especially those in part two of *Between Here and There*, which are all set in Japan. See Irene De Angelis, *The Japanese Effect in Contemporary Irish Poetry* (New York: Palgrave Macmillan, 2012), 138–58; Elmer Kennedy-Andrews, *Writing Home: Poetry and Place in Northern Ireland, 1968–2008* (Cambridge: D. S. Brewer, 2008), 249–86; and Nathan Suhr-Sytsma, "Haiku Aesthetics and Grassroots Internationalization: Japan in Irish Poetry," *Éire-Ireland* 45, nos. 3–4 (Fall-Winter 2010): 245–77.

6. Sinéad Morrissey, *The State of the Prisons* (Manchester, UK: Carcanet, 2005), 11. All subsequent quotations from this poem are taken from this page.

7. Sinéad Morrissey, *Through the Square Window* (Manchester: Carcanet, 2009), 18.

8. Ibid., 19.

9. Ibid.

10. Ibid., 9.

11. Ibid., 57.

12. Caitríona O'Reilly, *The Nowhere Birds* (Northumberland, UK: Bloodaxe Books, 2001), 11.

13. Ibid., 38.

14. Caitríona O'Reilly, *Geis* (Winston-Salem, NC: Wake Forest UP, 2015), 62.

15. This, of course, is often what poetry does. It might even be said to be exactly what Eliot had in mind when he postulates the impersonality of poetry, and, from a somewhat different angle, the "objective correlative." But, as a more specific response to self-making among contemporary Irish poets, the particular contours of O'Reilly's construal of subjects and (and as) objects bears close scrutiny.

16. O'Reilly, *The Nowhere Birds*, 26.

17. Ibid., 26, 27.

18. Ibid., 27. All quotations from this poem are taken from this page.

3

Derek Mahon:
Letters to Iceland

Kelly Sullivan

In 1936, two poets, one the noted social commentator W. H. Auden, the other a reticent Irishman, Louis MacNeice, take a trip to Iceland. They go at the behest of Auden's publisher, Faber, with the hopes of writing a "travel guide" to the distant democratic island. But 1936 is an inauspicious year for travel to far Northern Europe: in Spain civil war brews; in violation of the Treaty of Versailles, the German military occupies the Rhineland; in August, Berlin hosts the Olympic games, which are televised for the first time in history. Auden and MacNeice, feeling helplessly out of touch, watch Europe unravel from "this vertiginous / crow's-nest of the earth."[1]

The book the poets eventually publish, *Letters from Iceland* (1937), is saturated with a sense of escapism and self-recrimination, and especially with investment in the situation of Europe and their duty, as Auden describes it, to make themselves and their readers "more aware of … the world around us."[2] Writing a "travel guide" at a time of social and political crisis, on the eve of "total war," Auden and MacNeice felt they had to square socially-responsible tenets of poetry with their self-imposed exile in Iceland where they watched "nations germinating hell" in Europe below.[3] In order to accomplish this ethical and personal balance, they revived the Augustan form of the verse epistle. Verse letters allowed Auden and MacNeice to adopt an experimental off-handedness and a loose, conversational structure to their book, a tone and form that simultaneously made their work approachable and engaged readers in a dialogue about social and ethical responsibility. This engagement was subtle; a letter always implies a call to respond, an enforced social engagement contracted through the very act of reading. The verse epistles in *Letters from Iceland* made readers "more aware" of Europe in part precisely because they defy their audience's expectations for descriptions of scenery and tropes of travel writing. As Auden explains in a letter to an Icelandic friend, "I do not intend to expatiate upon the natural beauties of your island" because, he quips in clerihew, "Biography / Is better than Geography, / Geography's about maps, / Biography's about chaps."[4] As they observed Iceland's particular geography, Auden and MacNeice knew Europe's biography was shaping into catastrophe.

Auden and MacNeice's anti-pastoral travelogue insistently draws connections between viewing landscape as an aesthetic experience and an abdication of necessary social responsibility. Tom Paulin explains that, for these poets, "the effect of an aesthetic of landscape is to make violence and dubious political ideas acceptable. Insidiously they become part of a culture and so condition people's responses to art and politics."[5] For Auden, twentieth-century fascists are direct descendants of Byron's Romantic heroes, and the romantic inclination to praise nature with exalted language functions politically as a way of appealing "to our sensations, to our wish to be carried along and away in an excited experience of total liberation."[6] "Heroic" nature becomes essentially non-human and anti-social, and enables precisely those qualities in leaders who become inhuman dictators.[7] Auden and MacNeice ironically quote from Ebenezer Henderson, who published a guide, *Iceland*, in 1818, to show that drawing moral codes from the natural world leads to a value system devoid of fellow-feeling. Henderson's view of a geyser triggers "contemplation of the Great and Omnipotent JEHOVAH in comparison with whom these and all the wonders scattered over the whole immensity of existence dwindle into absolute insignificance."[8] Reading these

romantic lines in 1936 was a political event: if individual humans are insignificant, then so too are our democratic rights, and our individual freedoms.

Auden and MacNeice traveled on the eve of the Second World War
when the inhuman dictates of the Nazis were beginning to be clear. In
Iceland, they encountered Goering's brother and groups of Nazis studying
the culture they considered pure Germanic. The poets spoof this, too: under
the heading *"Iceland is German,"* they quote "an unknown Nazi" who claims
"Für uns Island ist das Land" (For us, Iceland is *the* Land).[9] In perhaps the
most insidiously direct critique of the connection between fascist dictates
and Nature, the poets (fabricate a?) quote from the Danish writer Svend
Fleuron under the heading *"Spread of Nazi Doctrines among the Icelandic
ponies."*[10] Fleuron was known as both a Nazi sympathizer (in 1941 he joined
the Weimar poets meeting as a voluntary collaborator) and as a writer of
nature and animal stories which he believed to epitomize a freedom of
spirit. The poets have him say, "Famous scientists, doctors, politicians,
and writers, mounted her and rode for a wonderful week's tour. Richer in
experience, strengthened and refreshed by Nature, ready for a new struggle
with the arch-fiend culture, they went home and gave lectures."[11] Nature,
with an emphasis on the capital N, stands in ready contrast to culture, and
Auden and MacNeice make it clear that to aestheticize the former without
the latter is a dangerous political game.

Derek Mahon: Ecological Ethics and Geographic Simultaneity

As MacNeice writes in the poem that closes the volume, during their travels
in Iceland, "Down in Europe Seville fell, / Nations germinating hell, / The
Olympic games were run — Spots upon the Aryan sun."[12] In MacNeice's
"Epilogue" it is the sun that is connected to the Nazi regime, an implicit
condemnation of landscape as escapist and therefore negatively political. For
Derek Mahon, writing sixty years later, the sun itself, and its place within a
wider ecological framework, becomes the primary ethical focus. Mahon takes
up the verse epistle form directly from Auden and MacNeice, but in his work it
serves a different purpose, one befitting Mahon's postmodernity and a new set
of political and environmental concerns. Mahon's *The Hudson Letter* (1995)
charts another sort of travel guide, but this one finds the speaker marooned

at the heart of social and political turmoil: 1990s Manhattan. Mahon's post-modern verse letters invert the concerns Auden and MacNeice grapple with in *Letters from Iceland.* And yet, the contemporary poet's epistolary poem with its essentially social gesture replicates the earlier poets' use of form to contend with political content.[13] Mahon's "The Hudson Letter" (the long poem sequence within the eponymous volume) initiates his environmental politics, rendering his issues-based poetry with the same deceptively "light" approach as Auden's, while simultaneously propelling readers toward inevitable catastrophe. In his more recent volume, *Life on Earth* (2008), Mahon revisits the geography of Iceland itself in order to show his readers that this landscape Auden and MacNeice found dangerously apolitical is now, at this zero hour of the day, the most politicized of all. Mahon further complicates the genre of the verse epistle in order to question the effectiveness of lyric address at times of ecological crisis, and to urge an awareness of temporal and geographical simultaneity which will, in turn, establish an ethical approach to the environment. Instead of writing to a cultured Europe from an isolated, northern space, Mahon writes letters *to* Iceland, urging a social and political connection to the land itself, emptied of human civilization.

At the heart of Mahon's environmentally-concerned poetry is a conflict about audience, and about the purpose of poetry in the face of ecological catastrophe. Auden and his generation also concerned themselves with the purpose of art at a time of historical disaster, but the brewing conflicts of the 1930s were fundamentally about civilization and society. In contrast, environmental writing often seeks to make the non-human world its focus. The recent trend toward ecocriticism as well as ecological literary writing (both in poetry and prose) sharpens the differences between the fields of ecology and of ethics, two practices central to Mahon's work. As Hubert Zapf explains, ethics is founded upon "the opposition between culture and nature, human and nonhuman life" so that "ethics appears, therefore, as an expression of precisely that logocentric and anthropocentric ideology that modern ecological thought tries to overcome."[14] Ecology, on the other hand, "posits an ecocentric instead of an anthropocentric orientation; it assumes the priority of nature over culture."[15] Ecocritical approaches have in part reshaped the study of ethics so that it is less subject-centered; literature that addresses ecological issues from a human perspective also helps challenge this binary. But there remains a fundamental tension in making an ethical demand for social responsibility toward non-human nature.

Mahon's eco-poetry insists that we pay attention to non-human elements of the environment, but his adoption of the verse epistle, and his engagement with temporal disjunction as a way of calling attention to geographical simultaneity, complicates any simple antagonistic division between *Letters from Iceland* and Mahon's letters to Iceland. Auden and MacNeice become models for Mahon, even as his politically- and socially-engaged poems try to make us think of nature as equal to culture. The difficulty of his project becomes the difficulty of ecologically-minded literature in general: if we do not direct our attention outward beyond the merely human, we will have no place to establish social and civic concerns. Mahon's poetry demands that we hold two concepts in our minds simultaneously: the world without us and our place in the world. To varying degrees of success, he uses the verse letter to call attention to this necessary simultaneity. In seeking an adequate address, Mahon's verse epistles and his later eco-poetry attempt to answer the question a critic finds central to Philippe Jaccottet's work (a Franco-Swiss poet whose work Mahon has translated): "To what extent is the project of reading humanity together with the environment still a viable option in the European literary tradition of the late twentieth and early twenty-first centuries?"[16]

Mahon's *The Hudson Letter* adopts the informal, chatty tone of *Letters from Iceland*. Yet hidden beneath the billowy organization of this eighteen-part verse letter is a structure and control that gives Mahon the tools to illustrate necessary simultaneities: temporal, geographical, and even biological. By borrowing the verse epistle from Auden and MacNeice, Mahon combines a lighter verse with almost invisible formal patterning. The run-on pentameter couplets of "The Hudson Letter" push us forward through the time of the work as a structural whole — it enacts the passage of a single day with detours to nineteenth-century New York and Key West — but the chatty, various looseness of the individual "letters" and sections within it enact and engage the passing minutes both the poet and reader experience. Through the fixed idea of a single day, and the fixed formal idea of a verse epistle, the poem reminds us that not only do moments in time co-exist (the letter we read travels from 1995 to us today) and, to a lesser degree, so

do species and various forms of consciousness co-exist (other voices pen-
etrate the poems, and birds populate the stanzas as symbols and as living
creatures), but most emphatically so do places co-exist (as a letter travels
from one location to another). For Auden and MacNeice, the epistolary
form created an ethically-guided sense of simultaneous social exchange.
For Mahon, this form predominantly emphasizes an awareness of ecological
simultaneity, with the local ecosystem or individual consciousness but a
small part of a vast complex.

Mahon uses a sense of geographical displacement to heighten simultaneity. As other critics have noted, Mahon does not write as an exile, and
yet he is nonetheless often "homeless" in an existential sense. He uses
specific place-names in poems, but unlike the poetry of Seamus Heaney,
for example, such place-naming tends to emphasize not rootedness, but
a weary cosmopolitanism.[17] As Peter Denman shows, Mahon often inter-
changes place-names in his work when it undergoes his notorious revisions.
Indeed, such endless revisions tend to destabilize our sense of a poem as a
geographical space to which we can return: from his *Selected Poems* (1991),
to his *Collected Poems* (1999), to his *New Collected Poems* (2011), Mahon
has made countless small changes — as well as some larger ones — altering
lines, titles, omitting paragraphs, and omitting poems altogether. In fact,
Mahon so persistently revises his work that even the guiding title "The
Hudson Letter" has lost both its reference to the Heraclitean river that runs
through it, and to MacNeice and Auden's travel guide: it is, in *New Collected
Poems*, "New York Time."[18] This sense of geographical destabilization with
his simultaneous emphasis on locations means that we come to see that
"places are more important than where they are."[19] In "The Hudson Letter"
in particular, the forward momentum of rhyme and rhythm, and the poet's
signature use of snatches of conversation, news, high and low registers, and
classical and contemporary allusion, enable Mahon to get at an integral
disruption in the way we view geography: what we do in this place affects
what happens in another, even if we cannot see it. His verse letters strive
to remind us our place in the world co-exists with many others in a fragile
system of equilibrium; we fail to recognize and acknowledge this at our own
peril. Our local ecology feeds into a vast, and simultaneous global ecology,
and the changes we make threaten the health of all the earth.

Pattern and Perspective in Mahon's Ecopoetics

For Auden and MacNeice, Iceland was an isolated landscape, a place out of touch with civilization; and yet, it also provided them with a panoramic view of the events of Europe through a unifying distance. In "Letter to Graham and Anne Shepard," MacNeice urges his friends not to forget him, but also alludes to the telescopic perspective he has gained:

> … please remember us
> so high up here in this vertiginous
> Crow's-nest of the earth. Perhaps you'll let us know
> if anything happens in the world below?[20]

Mahon borrows this "vertiginous" avian view in "The Hudson Letter," a sequence literally and figuratively peppered with birds, from Keats's nightingale to Respighi's via WQXR to Daisy's Cunard, from Jersey blackbirds to the Inca tern and Andean gull who escape from the Bronx zoo. These last escapees most clearly give us a view from the "crow's-nest of the earth." But importantly, their natural flight and instinct also give them lyric power: they are the catalyst that triggers a lyric flight and the ensuing sense of freedom and perspective, a signature Mahon panorama. Neil Corcoran calls this perspectival telescoping "theoptic," a term he borrows from Mahon himself in "A Globe in Carolina" where "to the mild theoptic eye, / America is its own night-sky."[21] Mahon's "theoptic" perspective — quite literally a god's-eye view — aligns with Henderson's equally theoptic contemplation of the Icelandic Geysir in Auden and MacNeice's compilation: at its most powerful, the human figure falls away. The exotic seabirds — who owe their poetic existence to a news article Mahon read in the *New York Times*[22] — provide Mahon with the perfect non-human vehicle for obtaining this view. They arrive to the lyric after a profusion of modern capitalist jabber, a lyric Times Square tickertape of stocks, ecological disasters, news headlines, and street talk. The urban cacophony comes all in capital letters, further emphasizing the Simmel-like sensory onslaught of the city:

INSIDER TRADING REPORTS ARE LINKED TO PRICE OF BONDS
NO SOLUTION AT HAND WHILE NUCLEAR WASTE PILES UP
NEW YORK TOUGHING IT OUT TO GET THROUGH THE COLD
ALT SEX MF FF NIGHT OWL SCAT PEDO SNUFF
AT&T BOEING CHRYSLER DUPONT DIGITAL DOW JONES
EXXON GENERAL MOTORS IBM NYNEX SEARS
PARANOIA WEST SIDE ROMEOS AMERICA AFTER DARK
ESCAPED BRONX SEABIRDS SPOTTED IN CENTRAL PARK …
 … On ledge and rail they sit, Inca tern and Andean gull, who
 fled their storm-wrecked cage in the Bronx Zoo
 […] they peer
 Through mutant cloud-cover and air thick with snow-dust,
 toxic aerosol dazzle and invasive car-exhaust,
 or perch forlorn on gargoyle and asbestos roof,
 fine-featured, ruffled, attentive, almost too high to hear
 the plaintive, desolate cab-horns on Madison and Fifth[.][23]

As the last two lines of all-capital text come together, the poem settles into near-regular rhyming couplets to follow the lyric flight of the birds and shift us into their perspective, abandoning the headlines and chaos by literally rising above it.

Much of the conviction in this theoptic shift comes through the poetic patterning at work, a patterning that is lyrically formal and, therefore, paradoxically rooted in human cultural conventions. MacNeice argues in *Modern Poetry* that formal arrangement "gives a sweeping movement, an impression of controlled speed and power — an impression which is enhanced when the verse is on a recognizable rhythmical pattern."[24] We are lifted aloft by meter and given a panoramic view of a massive urban area, and yet we sense that Mahon's concern with this view is not its beauty or scope, but its integration with a global geography. The heightened perspective comes obscured through "toxic aerosol dazzle and invasive car exhaust," a filter that asks us to see our own human relationship to a larger ecosystem. Mahon tells us the birds "'Won't touch garbage'; so where and what will they eat?" a question that connects to the "alien corn of Radio

City, Broadway and Times Square."[25] The sea birds are as un-homed as Ruth in Keats's "Ode to a Nightingale," but the merging of naturalistic imagery with urban wasteland burdens the poem with the apparent truths of those chaotic opening news headlines: "NO SOLUTION AT HAND WHILE NUCLEAR WASTE PILES UP."[26] The poet uncomfortably levels imagery drawn from nature with ecological degradation so that the New Yorkers "TOUGHING IT OUT TO GET THROUGH THE COLD" align with the "urban gulls, crows, and other toughs of the air," and the insistence that there is nothing to forage except garbage moves from metaphor to a geographical integration, forcing us to read the question "where on earth can they go?" as genuine.[27] The question recalls Mahon's earlier theoptic belief that our earth itself is only "a home from home" and therefore "unnervingly" irresolute.[28] Section VI's discomfort comes through the poem's shifting perspective: are the birds symbols of lyric power, of the poet's ability to organize the scattered, multifariousness of human civilization with natural beauty? Or are we meant to disengage from the merely human and take on an avian perspective, one that finds inhospitable Madison and Fifth and the "Mondrian millions" dining below? In either case, the juxtaposition of avian "nature" with lyric "culture" builds useful tension.

If Mahon borrows the verse epistle from MacNeice and Auden, he also borrows the sense of impending disaster that permeates *Letters from Iceland* as well as much of the poetry of the late 1930s. "The Hudson Letter" consistently returns to a threat of ecological catastrophe, a discomfiting theme in line with the poet's geographical disruptions and one whose inevitability he makes clear through the poem's patterned forward rhythm. The chatty "found poem" composed of snippets of bar-room conversation of section VII, "Sneakers'," crosses lyric patterning with emphatic references to environmental disaster:

'You get warm and dry, *tsunami* and tornadoes,
the trade winds move the surface water, right?'
'Peruvian currents.' 'Droughts in Indonesia.'
'You see the fuckin' dikes are crackin' up in Europe?'
'Cyclone.' 'Bermuda Triangle.' 'Black hole.'[29]

Section IV, "Waterfront," opens with MacNeice's ominous, "We shall go down like paleolithic man / Before some new Ice Age or Genghiz Khan," before it meditates on "storm-clouds in the west / that rain infection and industrial waste" and the seemingly self-renewing rivers that are actually "adrift with trash and refuse barges."[30] Like so many Mahon poems, this section offers a telescopic panorama in its conclusion, only this time the poet imagines

> [...] our millenium
> where, in the thaw-water of an oil-drum,
> the hot genes of the future seethe. The sun
> shines on the dump, not on the *côte d'azur*
> and not on the cloistered murals, to be sure.
> — QUESTION REALITY, DEATH IS BACK. MIGUEL 141.[31]

Here Mahon again uses formal patterning to bring the section's irregular pentameter couplets into an *abba* rhythm at the close, rhyming the naturalistic "sun" with the urban tag "Miguel 141" in a kind of futuristic holy book. The final line — embedded within the rhyme-scheme yet set apart from the rest of the poem with its block-capitals and punctuated short phrases — forces us into an awareness both of the forward-pressing pattern of the lyric (through the jarring interruption) and of the poem as a made thing. Here someone else's speech, interrupting in the form of graffito, alerts us that not only are we in the midst of a letter composed of the author's filtered impressions of the world, but also that others in this world have their own, separate and often impenetrable impressions. Nonetheless, coming ecological disaster in the form of lyric control implies we cannot escape a shared mortality. The tag — Miguel 141 — looks like a biblical citation, but follows the godless visionary act of reading the future in the waste and dregs of our oil-hungry culture.

Empty Landscapes: The Problem of Lyric Address

In one of the less successful sections of "The Hudson Letter," Mahon writes to his children in London. The tone of this section illustrates what John Redmond calls Mahon's "willful inconsistency," his "struggle between low-key observation and visionary splendour."[32] Mahon's sentimental, conversational letter modulates between the deeply personal and a broader appeal; he writes to his children, but also for his readers. The strain between these two registers creates an irresolvable conflict. And yet, the poem seems to take artistic address as its ultimate theme, even if it fails in its execution. Mahon pulls back to give us a view of the vastness of the natural world, even of the universe. In this, his poem reiterates Henderson's early nineteenth-century sense of the sublime in Iceland's nature: we feel that "the whole immensity of existence dwindle[s] into absolute insignificance."[33] In addressing his children in section IX, Mahon considers the "immensity of existence" alongside the compulsion to create art. Auden and MacNeice's anti-pastoral theme in *Letters from Iceland* manifests itself in the social form of the letter, which ultimately highlights the "emptiness" of landscape without human content. Yet Mahon tries to speak to that void with a human voice, somehow converging our social world with the emptiness of natural spaces. In the section's double-register, he urges his daughter to play music even if it seems "ridiculous," even as the volume simultaneously seems to chide his more art-appreciative readers for thinking themselves "post-pastoral."[34] "I saw a film recently," he recounts:

> Glenn Gould playing Bach to the Canadian wilderness,
> the great chords crashing out into empty space,
> the music of planet Earth, the music of a sphere
> no-one's remembered in any other place
> so far as we know, and thought, the glorious racket
> we use to explain ourselves in perpetuity
> to our hi-tech geological posterity
> at the frozen outer reaches of the galaxy.[35]

Mahon argues that the music of culture and civilization cannot be disentangled from "the music of planet Earth." We write and make art for an unknown future, one that we also help shape through our stewardship of the geography and ecology of the places we inhabit. Mahon urges his daughter — and all of us — to "explain ourselves" to the emptiness, thereby valuing equally the wilderness and the cultural necessity to make art.

Paulin says the ultimate effect of *Letters from Iceland* "is to make it impossible to read a volume of nature or rural poetry (especially by any poet writing after the Second World War) without being affected by a peculiar feeling of emptiness. Without human or political content nature means very little, and to describe it in isolation from that content is to abdicate the responsibility to be relevant which Auden and MacNeice impose on themselves, and us — indeed it is to recommend, however unconsciously, such an abdication."[36] But today, and even as early as 1989 when Bill McKibben's *The End of Nature* made global warming a talking point in public intellectual debate, looking at a landscape is always a political act. The benign and boring ice fields Auden refused to describe are now laden images, infused with the political and humanistic debates framing climate change. For Auden and MacNeice, to look at the emptiness of nature affected human emptiness and political irresponsibility; for Mahon, those wilderness spaces are both the necessary background for our continuation as a civilization, and our ultimate responsibility. Mahon deliberately politicizes landscape. In "A Country Road," he alludes to Yeats's "Easter 1916" to tell us, "Second by second / cloud swirls on the globe as though / political."[37] The clouds themselves cannot be politic, but our view of them certainly can be. And yet Mahon's clouds engulf the globe, not a local stream, as Yeats's did. The difficulty in addressing such ecological issues in lyric poetry lies in precisely that slippage between human-scale concerns and geographical emptiness. Do we speak for, or to, the wilderness beyond our local ken?

Derek Mahon's poetry since *The Hudson Letter* has increasingly moved in the direction of ecological responsibility and individual estrangement, with two recent volumes, *Life on Earth* (2008) and *An Autumn Wind* (2010), confronting such issues head-on. This increasing concern with ecology leads him to an increasing difficulty in knowing whom to address with poems, and how. Mahon remains a highly cultured and carefully educated poet, and, as Seán Lysaght points out, his "references to the environment and science are advertised [...] explicitly," making his eco-poetry both scientifically rooted — through references to James Lovelock's theories of ecosystems, and issues of climate change and public debate — and simultaneously devoted to his more traditional humanistic and existential themes.[38] This question of lyric address often manifests itself in a tension between the need to communicate and make known coming ecological disaster, and the equally strong desire to chase what Redmond calls his "eremeticism," an inclination to take himself out of the world and exist in isolation from others.[39] If, in *Letters from Iceland*, the presentation of a solitary landscape repudiates our responsibility to Europe, politics, and the world around us, in *The Hudson Letter* and Mahon's subsequent work, the landscape itself is that to which we are responsible. The social format of a letter calls attention to both the solitary act of writing and to the community and communication we share through language. Mahon seems to hope the empty landscape or elements within it force us to recognize our presence there even — or even especially — when we are not in view. But in choosing the form of the verse epistle in "The Hudson Letter," Mahon appeals to an epistolary "trope of thirdness" — the poet communicates to the empty landscape or an element of nature, but his work gains power through the anonymous human reader listening in to the conversation.[40]

Mahon poses the question of the importance of landscape without humans explicitly in "A Country Road" from *Life on Earth*:

Are we going to laugh
on the road as if the whole
show was set out for our grand synthesis?
Abandoned trailers sunk in leaves and turf,
slow erosion, waves on the boil …
We belong to this —

not as discrete
observing presences but as born
participants in the action […].[41]

Yet this poetics of ecology adds a further discomfort to Mahon's work, and one that is harder to solve through a verse letter or lyric poem in any form. For an appeal to reshape our actions on earth and thereby avert ecological disaster requires action at the personal, individual level; but such action must be for the benefit of a larger social group, or indeed the asocial landscape. Mahon's poetry thus confronts the tension between the ethical and ecological. In the end, his lyrics invert the concerns of Auden and MacNeice. As Auden moved from *Letters from Iceland* to the moral and religious tenets of later work, beginning with "New Year Letter," his "conversation" with an individual reader functioned at the level of individual moral choice. The conclusion of the penultimate poem in *Letters from Iceland* wishes readers the "power to act, forgive, and bless."[42] Yet Mahon's diction and his concerns want both to implicate individuals and also to minimize our physical presence — quite literally make us understand our scale in relation to galaxies. As his worries grow more terrestrial, the language of his poetry not only tries to show that we are a small part of a vast planet, but also strives to make us ethically aware of our place within that planet's ecosystem and our outsized effects in it. Mahon asks us to adjust the typically anthropocentric consciousness that guides ethics and allows an individual to make judgements based on collective good so that we instead prioritize ecocentrism. He asks us to place nature on a level with culture, but does so through lyric and epistolary address, fundamentally social, and therefore anthropocentric, modes.

Who does one address in a lyric written at a time of climate crisis, with a deliberately ecocentric agenda? Although the poems in *Life on Earth* are not explicitly verse epistles, their sustained sense of pointed address makes them cousins to Mahon's earlier verse letters, and show that, as Hugh Haughton argues, this is a form to which the poet turns at times of crisis.[43] Mahon's long sequence "Homage to Gaia" from *Life on Earth* proposes that we address the "earth" herself, and those empty spaces seemingly devoid of culture or human life. In section 1, "Its Radiant Energies," Mahon describes "how to live // in the post-petroleum age."[44] As his seemingly "light" poem navigates "cloud cover, open skies," photovoltaics and photoelectronics, it provides an updated, ecologically-motivated version of MacNeice's "suburban clatter" in "Letter to Graham and Anne Shepard."[45] MacNeice concludes, however, with a reminder that he addresses two friends back home in London: "Please remember us […] let us know / if anything happens in the world below."[46] Mahon makes the opposite address, shifting from a human recipient to speak directly to the "Great sun, dim or bright, / eye in the changing sky."[47] For Mahon, it is not "the world" that matters — that anthropocentric construction of life as civilization — but rather "the earth," a planet within a larger system. While MacNeice asks his friends to send news, Mahon asks the sun to "send us warmth and light."[48] But both poets use the epistolary nature of a lyric poem as a reminder that the writer himself exists. Mahon's concluding "Remember life on earth!" directly alludes to MacNeice's "remember us": both poets speak in a double register, addressing simultaneously the intended recipient of the letter or lyric, and reminding their readership that life on earth requires active engagement with both culture and nature. Mahon further insists on a semantic difference between "earth" and "world" in his apology to Gaia in section 2, "Homage to Gaia." "You love and hate us both," he says, "we babble about the world / while you sustain the earth."[49] Ultimately, his address acknowledges that our existence within an ecosystem depends upon our actions, and that Gaia will "prevail" whether or not human civilization does, too. His appeal to the earth goddess reads almost as a plea that she not be, ultimately, indifferent.[50]

In a section that gently alludes to MacNeice and Auden's earlier volume, Mahon revisits Iceland itself and uses the Icelandic musician Björk as a stand-in for the poet in order to question how we should navigate the border between nature and culture, and between aesthetic creation and geographical "emptiness." Playing off of what he perceives as Björk's anti-social "Fuck off" attitude,[51] Mahon updates Iceland for a time of ecological crisis:

> Here in the confused stink
>   of global warming what
> you really want, I think
> […]
> [is] mystery and mystique,
>   the hidden places where
> the wild things are and no one
>   can track you to your lair.[52]

Björk becomes more animal than human (in earlier stanzas she is "dark bird of ice, dark swan / of snow" and "not something to tame and stroke"[53]). And yet Mahon deliberately pulls away from a complete de-centering of human concerns, countering the dangerously romantic "mystery and mystique" and "hidden places" with a list of journalistic, scientific facts:

(Sea levels rising annually,
    glaciers sliding fast,
species extinct, the far north
    negotiable at last …).[54]

Like Glenn Gould sending chords of Bach out into the Canadian wilderness
from "The Hudson Letter," Mahon makes Björk's music address "the white
/ light and corrugated iron / roofs of the Arctic night."[55] Unlike MacNeice
and Auden's epistolary address to the civilization of Europe from the wilds
of Iceland, Björk speaks to the empty landscape itself:

Up there where silence falls
    and there is no more land
your scared, scary voice calls
    to the great waste beyond.[56]

These final lines address Björk, and model a cultural appeal to earth itself;
but they also describe Mahon's own "scared" voice as he searches for the
correct lyric address under the duress of climate crisis. As he calls to Gaia,
the wind, the sun, and "the great waste beyond," Mahon of course simultaneously corresponds with us, his (human) readers. His eco-poems attempt
a complicated ethical address; by allowing us to overhear the conversation,
they implicitly draw us into the correspondence between the poet and
nature, modeling a version of an ecocentric "life on earth." And yet in
their lyric construction, they remain cultural artifacts, as socially-coded
and anthropocentric as *Letters from Iceland* in their imperative that we
read, act, and respond. Ultimately, Mahon's letters to Iceland acknowledge
the same problem with looking at a landscape as an aesthetic object that
Auden and MacNeice's *Letters from Iceland* do: in both cases, removing
the human element abdicates responsibility. The difference is that Mahon
implies our ultimate, human responsibility is precisely to that landscape,
that ecosystem to which we belong, "not as discrete / observing presences
but as born/participants in the action."[57]

1. W. H. Auden and Louis MacNeice, *Letters from Iceland* (London: Faber and Faber, 1937), 35.

2. Auden discusses this kind of awareness specifically in relation to totalitarian states: "The primary function of poetry, as of all the arts, is to make us more aware of ourselves and the world around us. I do not know if such increased awareness makes us more moral or more efficient; I hope not.

    "I think it makes us more human, and I am quite certain it makes us more difficult to deceive, which is why, perhaps, all totalitarian theories of the State, from Plato's downwards, have deeply distrusted the arts. They notice and say too much, and the neighbors start talking." *The Complete Works of W. H. Auden, Prose, Vol. I: 1926–1938*, ed. Edward Mendelson (Princeton: Princeton UP, 1997), 470.

3. Auden and MacNeice, *Letters*, 259.

4. Ibid., 214. In fact, Auden misquotes a clerihew from the father of clerihews, Edmund Clerihew Bentley, who writes, in his *Biography for Beginners* (London: T. Werner Laurie, Clifford's Inn, 1905), "The Art of biography / Is different from Geography. / Geography is about Maps, / But Biography is about Chaps" (n.p. "Introductory Remarks").

5. Tom Paulin, "*Letters from Iceland*: Going North," in *The 1930s: A Challenge to Orthodoxy*, ed. John Lucas (Sussex: Harvester Press, 1978), 75–76.

6. Ibid., 61.

7. In this essay I use two different but related meanings of "inhuman," sometimes supplanting the first meaning with "non-human" to clarify use. In the first instance, nature, landscape, and the world devoid of human figures is "non-human" — that is, free of human representation. Such landscapes are not inherently negative, but they risk, especially for Auden and MacNeice and thinkers working during and just after modernism's emphasis on individual consciousness, cultivating an "inhuman" value system. This includes extreme forms of political and social thought like fascism, nazism, and eugenics. This type of "inhuman" correlates to Jean-Francois Lyotard's sense of the dehumanizing possibilities of "development" through science, economics, cybernetics, and other social systems (see Lyotard, 1–7).

    In the second instance, "inhuman" is something Lyotard believes comes from within the individual human, a pre-educational state of being that is not "human" — since humanism rests on shared, and learned, culture — but instead on something innate and pre-cultural, something he sees as erupting out through "institutional" forms: "literature, the arts, philosophy" (3). In relation to ecosystems, "inhuman" is a conception that includes states of consciousness and existence beyond the human. This second, more positive definition, pairs more closely with Mahon's ecocentric poetry: a cultural form used to address something seemingly beyond the human. This definition also relates to Bill McKibben's theory, in *The End of Nature*, that man now has such an outsized role in the ecosystem (through systems of development) that there is no "nature" as a separate state beyond human control. Nature, "as the work of some separate, uncivilizable force" no longer exists, but is "instead in part a product of our habits, our economies, our ways of life" (47). McKibben's new definition of nature now seems to anticipate the designation "Anthropocene" applied to the current epoch of human-influenced ecosystems and geology.

8.   Auden and MacNeice, *Letters*, 74.

9.   Ibid., 61 (my translation).

10. Ibid., 75.

11. Ibid.

12. Ibid., 259.

13. Several critics have noted the influence of Auden and MacNeice on Mahon's poetry in general, and on the composition of *The Hudson Letter* in particular. See Hugh Haughton, *The Poetry of Derek Mahon* (Oxford: Oxford UP, 2007), 226; John Redmond, "Willful Inconsistency: Derek Mahon's Verse Letters," *Irish University Review* 24, no. 1 (Spring-Summer 1994): 97–99; Neil Corcoran, *Poets of Modern Ireland: Text, Context, Intertext* (Carbondale: Southern Illinois UP, 1999), 148–49.

14. Hubert Zapf, "Literary Ecology and the Ethics of Texts," *New Literary History* 39, no. 4 (Autumn 2008): 847, 848.

15. Ibid., 848.

16. Joseph Acquisto, "The Place of Poetry; Nature, Nostalgia, and Modernity in Jaccottet's Poetics," *Modern Language Review* 105, no. 3 (July 2010): 679.

17. Neil Corcoran discusses this in more detail, see *Poets of Modern Ireland*, 137–55. See also Kennedy-Andrews's introduction to *The Poetry of Derek Mahon* (Buckinghamshire: Colin Smythe, 2002), 1–28; and Eamonn Hughes, " 'Weird/Haecceity': Place in Derek Mahon's Poetry," 97–110, in the same volume. See also Kennedy-Andrews, "Derek Mahon: 'An Exile and a Stranger,' " in *Writing Home: Poetry and Place in Northern Ireland, 1968–2008*, 155–79.

18. Peter Denman also remarks on the geographical uncertainty these revisions create,

noting that the "uncertainty" about where "home" is "extends as to where the very poem written about home is." See "Know the One? Insolent Ontology in Derek Mahon's Revisions," *Irish University Review* 24, no. 1 (Spring-Summer 1994): 29. For more on the connection between rhythm and revision in Mahon's poetry, see Michael Allen's "Rhythm and Revision in Mahon's Poetic Development," in *Close Readings: Essays on Irish Poetry*, ed. Fran Brearton (Sallins, Kildare: Irish Academic Press, 2015), 98–122.

19. John Kerrigan, "Ulster Ovids," in *The Chosen Ground: Essays on the Contemporary Poetry of Northern Ireland*, ed. Neil Corcoran (Chester Springs, PA: Dufour Editions, 1992), 260.

20. Auden and MacNeice, *Letters*, 35.

21. Mahon, *New Collected Poems* (Loughcrew, County Meath: The Gallery Press, 2011), 129.

22. Hugh Haughton notes that drafts for the poem include a clipping from a Feb. 6, 1995 *New York Times* article, "Exotic Birds Flee Collapse of Bronx Aviary." See *The Poetry of Derek Mahon*, 239.

23. Mahon, *The Hudson Letter*, 47. Mahon's continuous revisions make citations to his work a complex issue. In this essay, citations to "The Hudson Letter" will come from *The Hudson Letter* (1995) in order to retain the poem's original language and to analyze some sections omitted from later publications.

24. Louis MacNeice, *Modern Poetry* (Oxford: Oxford UP, 1938), 115.

25. Mahon, *The Hudson Letter*, 47.

26. Ibid.

27. Ibid., 47, 48.

28. Mahon, *New Collected*, 130; Neil Corcoran, *Poets*, 144.

29. Mahon, *The Hudson Letter*, 50. In an example of the geographical uncertainty of return in Mahon's oeuvre, this section of "The Hudson Letter" has been edited out of more recent editions of his work.

30. Ibid., 43. The MacNeice lines are from "An Eclogue for Christmas."

31. Ibid., 44.

32. Redmond, "Willful," 96.

33. Auden and MacNeice, *Letters*, 74.

34. Mahon, *The Hudson Letter*, 55, 19.

35. Ibid., 55.

36. Paulin, "Going North," 75.

37. Mahon, *Life On Earth* (Loughcrew, County Meath: The Gallery Press, 2008), 42.

38. Seán Lysaght, "What is Eco-Poetry?" *Poetry Ireland Review* 103 (Apr. 2011): 76.

39. Redmond, "Willful," 106–7.

40. Langdon Hammer, in his exploration of Elizabeth Bishop's letters, borrows this term from Jeredith Merrin. See his "Useless Concentration: Life and Work in Elizabeth Bishop's Letters and Poems," *American Literary History* 9, no. 1 (Spring 1997): 164.

41. Mahon, *Life*, 42.

42. Auden and MacNeice, *Letters*, 258.

43. Haughton, *The Poetry of Derek Mahon*, 222.

44. Mahon, *Life*, 44.

45. Auden and MacNeice, *Letters*, 35.

46. Ibid.

47. Mahon, *Life*, 45.

48. Ibid.

49. Ibid.

50. Eóin Flannery offers a reading of Mahon's "Homage to Gaia" in relation to scientist and environmentalist James Lovelock's "Gaia Theory" which proposes, in Flannery's explanation, that "the planet is intuitive and self-regulating — flexible and ruthless in its sustenance of life on earth" (31). See "Listening to the Leaves: Derek Mahon's Evolving Ecologies," in *Ireland and Ecocriticism: Literature, History and Environmental Justice*, 22–55.

51. Mahon, *Life*, 54.

52. Ibid., 55.

53. Ibid., 54.

54. Ibid., 55.

55. Ibid.

56. Ibid.

57. Ibid., 42.

4

Dorothy Molloy:
Dual Citizenship in
the Kingdom of the Sick

Ailbhe Darcy

Recently I gave a poetry reading in Liverpool with another early-career poet, Eoghan Walls. Walls and I were both born and bred in Ireland but have lived abroad for years. At question time, an audience member wondered why the event was then advertised as involving "Irish" poets since we do not live in Ireland or even write about Irish themes. The questioner seemed slightly irate about it, as though she had been hoodwinked into attending. Increasingly, we can ask the same question of Irish poetry more generally. In a preface to the third volume of the *Wake Forest Series of Irish Poetry*, Conor O'Callaghan points to a "more international perspective" exemplified by the poets represented in the volume — Colette Bryce, John McAuliffe, Maurice Riordan, Gerard Fanning, and Justin Quinn.[1] "If postmodernism means anything," declares O'Callaghan, "it means choosing one's own traditions from whatever source."[2] The Prague-based Quinn suggests a "post-nationalist" context for his own poems when he says, in an interview, that he would like to follow Joseph Brodsky in taking the English language for his context rather than any nation; Quinn's *Cambridge Introduction to Modern Irish Poetry* culminates in a chapter entitled "The Disappearance of Ireland."[3] Philip Coleman makes a similarly "post-nationalist" claim for poet Pearse Hutchinson, arguing that Hutchinson's work exemplifies the kind of "poetic transnationalism" that Jahan Ramazani has suggested "can help us both understand and imagine a world in which cultural boundaries are fluid, transient, and permeable."[4]

There are several points to be made about this insistence on a move toward post-nationalism in contemporary Irish poetry. One is that the move from a national framework to a post-national one is often inflected with a sense of liberation and even progress, as though Irish poets had previously been trapped in an idea of Irishness and are now free of it. A second point is that the Irishness in which poets were supposed to have been constrained is often framed in terms of content. The question of national and transnational poetries is not so much a question of poetic form or figure as of the proper topic for a poem. The audience member who rejected our Irishness in Liverpool was disappointed because we wrote poems about immigrant shell-pickers, silverfish, and airplanes, not because we had departed from bardic syllabic verse, Yeatsian stanzas, or self-inwoven similes. A third point is that if it is true that recent generations of Irish poets have been able to transcend Irishness and now move through a "world in which cultural boundaries are fluid, transient, and permeable," then we, as writers, occupy a position of almost unbearable privilege. Our position mirrors that of the latest generation of Irish emigrants, who have been able to use their white skin, English language, and European passport to move through the world *as though* borders were permeable, while others are stopped and turned back. One might begin to wonder if this rare and heady combination of a privileged speaking position with a colonized past is precisely what now makes our poetry "Irish."

None of us, however, writes in a language wholly free of ideology; none of us is entirely free to choose our traditions from "whatever" source. Our language — and, as a result, our thought — is inflected by our origins, our upbringing, our familial and social history, and our present location.

This assertion holds true for all writing, but it is especially pertinent to lyric poetry, because lyric is above all tasked with proving — in both senses of the word "proving" — the boundary between the individual and the linguistic community out of which the individual emerges and in which the individual operates. As Susan Stewart puts it, "[a]s metered language, language that retains and projects the force of individual sense experience and yet reaches towards intersubjective meaning, poetry sustains and transforms the threshold between individual and social existence."[5] Irish poetry that speaks from outside Ireland, that speaks of matters not particularly Irish, is no less interested than other poetry in testing this boundary between the individual (formed out of Irish society) and the (Irish or non-Irish) linguistic community in which the individual must operate. In other words, to read a poet born in Ireland but living elsewhere, or writing about not very Irish things, as merely a post-national English-language poet would be to miss the opportunity to fully tease out the different forces that meet, collide, and negotiate in that poet's language.

The poet Dorothy Molloy was born in Ireland, spent time in France, and lived for a number of years in Barcelona before moving back to Ireland, where she died. Her poetry is strongly influenced by the visual trappings and rituals of European Catholicism and frequently makes reference to locations on the European continent. Its Irishness is rarely obvious. But in her work, Molloy never allows us to lose sight of how individual experience is socially inflected through language or might even be constructed out of language in the first place. Molloy's first remarkable collection, *Hare Soup* (2004), uses Catholic kitsch and ritual to unravel oppressive ideas about gender bequeathed by that same Catholicism to post-Catholic Ireland.[6] In her second collection, *Gethsemane Day* (2006), Molloy pits older European and Irish traditions around illness and death against newer ideas arising out of the United States and taking hold in Ireland today. Molloy died of cancer while *Hare Soup* was still in production at Faber; her husband, Andrew Carpenter, assembled this second collection out of unpublished poems among her papers. *Gethsemane Day* is, as reviewer Robert Potts notes, "necessarily" dominated by Molloy's illness,[7] with Carpenter describing the change in Molloy's writing across the two collections by saying that Molloy "was never an autobiographical writer, except," that is, "for the poems she wrote when she was dying."[8] This turn toward the autobiographical does not mean that *Gethsemane Day* is any less sophisticated and complex than *Hare Soup*. When Molloy explores illness, pain, and death in her work, she is unfailingly attentive to, and often suspicious of, the workings of vocabulary and poetic form. Molloy's posthumous poems present themselves as little theatrical productions concerned with conveying something about the subjective experience of terminal illness, but also with how illness and death are staged. In *Gethsemane Day*, Molloy uses lyric to reflect upon the collision and negotiation of different social discourses — some from within Ireland, some from without — in the experience of a single individual. It is partly the poetry's position within an Irish tradition that gives it force, as Molloy pointedly breaks with conventions around control and mastery native to that tradition in her exploration of illness and pointedly sets her use of the journey metaphor against the use of it in other Irish poems. In other words, reading Molloy with attention to the transnational currents duking it out in her poetry is fruitful. But to give the poetry its full due, we must also attend to its context within Irish literary traditions.

Molloy's poem "Cast Out" illustrates Molloy's own thinking about language.[9] Language is not, for her, a space in which we can operate freely. In this she follows linguists who stress the metaphoricity of language: the idea that we understand most concepts, particularly abstract or complex concepts, in terms of other concepts.[10] The metaphors we choose in order to help our comprehension affect, in their turn, the reality through which we move. As Reisfield and Wilson put it, "When metaphors enter our conceptual system, they alter that system and the knowledge, attitudes, and behaviors to which the system gives rise."[11] Illness is as prone to this process as anything else. Since our understanding of an illness affects how we respond to it, metaphors, for all practical purposes, structure a cancer patient's everyday reality.

"Cast Out," which is set in the medieval past, is not about cancer but leprosy. It captures vividly the fear and guilt provoked by an illness poorly understood and the experience this fear and guilt produces. It invites us to think about contagion, both literal and metaphorical. The poem's speaker will give food to a leper, throw alms, bear witness, but wants desperately to stay separate from the suffering sick. The real-life ceremony to repeat and preserve such a separation by declaring lepers dead to the world and removing them from "the company of persons," developed at the behest of an 1179 ecumenical council, varied from place to place.[12] It sometimes involved the sick person climbing into an actual grave and having soil poured on her head to symbolize the sick person's death to the world — as it does in Molloy's poem.[13] "Cast Out" makes use of this grim ceremony to reap some classic horror twists. Its leper dies and is buried, but still will not leave the poem's speaker in peace:

> The priests call out
>
> 'Leviticus, Leviticus'; perform her funeral rite,
> as it behoves, beside the fresh-dug pit. The coffin waits;
>
> the winding-sheet, the spices and the spade; the carrion crow.
> I sprinkle her with clay, ignore her cries. I turn away
>
> to ring the Requiem bell. She joins the living dead.
> At Mass I see her lean into a leper-squint [...]

As Molloy's poem knows, the original "living dead" were not George Romero's zombies, but these medieval sufferers of leprosy, who lived neither within a society nor entirely without it. They lived in a kind of purgatory, where all that remained to do was to wait for death. As Miller and Nesbitt describe it, leprosy's "special place in the history of contagious diseases" is due in part to the fact that it can be so "terrifyingly visual."[14] Molloy's poem is peppered with little hints of that terror: the missing eyebrows, the "leper-squint," the "running sores." The poem is relentlessly nasty, teasing us with the promise of closure but never paying out. Its short sentences create a constant sense that it might at any moment stop; its irregular full- and half-rhymes seem to ensure its continuation. Its irregularity robs us of any sense of a predictable poetic form, one that we might expect to be a certain length or to guarantee some kind of poetic closure. Halfway through the poem, its speaker cries out, "Oh let it end. Enough!" but there are still another five couplets to go. And when the poem suddenly stops — throws its final twist at us — it ends on only the weak assonance of "House" and "face" so that even as we turn the page to the next poem, we are robbed of the comfortable sense of completion that a full rhyme might bestow.

In "Cast Out," we see Molloy thinking about how the self is affected, or infected, by language. The poem explores the idea that the religious association of leprosy with morality — and, more broadly, of disease with morality — "allows the healthy to abandon the sick because it allows them to believe that the sick brought it on themselves."[15] Molloy's poem shows how this legitimation is never complete: her speaker is ambivalent, haunted by guilt, and ultimately becomes infected herself. By the end, we are not sure whether the woman speaking has ever been separate from the leper about whom she speaks or whether they were the same person all along. The poem's final horror is the reader's realization that, as the lyric "I" is, linguistically speaking, a "shifter" — is passed from person to person depending on who "speaks" the poem — I cannot even be sure that the sick woman is not *me*. The poem infects not only the speaking voice in it, but the "I" of the reader too. It takes literally the idea that language can communicate an experience from one individual to another.

Molloy's attention to how deeply language affects our experience places her in conversation with social constructivism. Particularly relevant is Miriam O'Kane Mara's work comparing the construction of reproductive cancer in recent Irish fiction and the *Irish Medical Journal*. O'Kane Mara has shown how, in fiction and medical literature alike, illness in Irish culture is associated with the female body more than the male. This association allows for a general construction of femininity as weak, passive, and still. In practical terms, this association also enables both the over-medicalization of the female body (potentially resulting, for instance, in unnecessary medical tests) and the gendering of the medical operator as inevitably male.[16] Molloy's poetry shows her to be keenly aware of how this gendered construction of illness inflects the individual's experience of it, frequently drawing attention to, and burlesquing, conventional ideas about the sick female body.

It is also clear from Molloy's poetry and visual art that her interest in the conjunction of gender and illness in language predates her own illness and is not purely autobiographical. Long before she even began to publish poetry, Molloy was a successful artist and gallery owner. Her artwork, today available for viewing by appointment at the National Library in Ireland, includes a number of female nudes combined with small creatures ordinarily thought of as pests, to disturbing effect. A female figure languishes while rats play around and even on her; in the foreground one rat contemplates her sex and seems to grin. In another piece, a female figure pulls her t-shirt up playfully to reveal and caress her own breast while mice scramble over her caressing hand. A visual connection is made in these images between the sexualized female body and the concept of "pests" and "pestilence," words with origins in the medieval conflation of literal sickness with moral and social perniciousness. The gendering of the medical establishment is an issue that comes up in Molloy's "Floating with Mr. Swan," a poem about which I have already written,[17] and in the title poem of *Gethsemane Day*, whose speaker greets a chemotherapy session with a Plathian reference to "Daddy":

> What cocktail is Daddy preparing for me?
> What ferments in pathology's sink?
> Tonight they will tell me, will proffer the cup,
> and, like it or not, I must drink.[18]

In "S.O.S." Molloy explores the disproportionate responsibility placed on women to care domestically for the sick. A female speaker chastises herself for having tidied kin away into a hospital for the mentally ill and for having been too busy with her own life to heed the sick person's cries for help:

> I never heard her gentle tap
> upon my heart
> when she slipped out.
>
> I never heard her softly wrap
> the sea around her
> like a shroud.
> My life was just too loud.[19]

This sense of shame at failing to take adequate care of an ailing friend or relative is sharply gendered in Ireland where, according to the 2011 census, women provide around two-thirds of all care.[20]

In the poems written after Molloy became ill, she burlesques the discourse of helplessness, passivity, and inevitability bound up with constructions of the sick female body by launching her speaker on strange bedridden journeys and pilgrimages. As I will discuss in more detail later, the medical establishment and media in Ireland and elsewhere have recently embraced the journey metaphor as one of the more empowering ways to speak about cancer. In Irish writing, the journey also has its legacy of literary connotations, reaching back to the *immrama*, tales of otherworldly sea voyages, but more recently appropriated by feminist poets. Sheila Conboy has shown how Eavan Boland and Eiléan Ní Chuilleanáin, for instance, appropriate the normally masculine motif of a heroic quest in their poetry to trope "the woman poet's vital experience of seeking a new language in which to frame her experience."[21] Molloy returns several times to this motif of the journey in *Gethsemane Day* but without that journey offering redemption or renewal; instead she combines the motif with intimations of stillness and even helplessness. In "The Dream-World of my Pillow," Molloy's speaker is carried out to sea as her companion is elsewhere, "below deck, looking for solutions."[22] Her home is transformed into a ship with "glass / eyes" and "smoky funnels" with "dry waves / bashing" against it. She describes herself trying to capture the storm, which is also the "billowing sheets" on her bed as she moves restlessly on it; "But the storm escapes me." Unlike in the official "journey narrative" of cancer, which stresses growth and empowerment, this poem is full of objects and men moving busily while the narrator is still, simply waiting: "I sit on my bunk or sway in my / hammock, watching my shadow on the ceiling." The poem upends the aspirational images of journeying women in Irish literature and medical literature alike, replacing them with the passive sick female body that our language has more forcefully constructed. By the strategic extravagance of her metaphor, Molloy gives full flight to the horror of existing within this experience, rather than attempting to rewrite the experience as something more palatable.

Molloy's journey/illness poems respond to the aspirational bent of literary and medical journey narratives with the medieval idea of a pilgrimage into reclusion. In the early 1980s, Molloy translated, and wrote her doctoral dissertation on, a fifteenth-century Occitan source text recounting a pilgrimage into St. Patrick's Purgatory by the Catalan noble Ramon de Perellós. Her translation of the text is collected in *The Medieval Pilgrimage to St. Patrick's Purgatory* (under the name Dorothy M. Carpenter). In it, de Perellós tells of his journey to Ireland and into the deep pit that is the entrance to purgatory. In an introduction to *The Medieval Pilgrimage*, Yolande de Pontfarcy terms this kind of pilgrimage the pilgrimage into reclusion.[23] It is distinguishable, she tells us, from the fantastical voyages of the *immrama* because it involves a period of deprivation and contemplation instead of a trip to an exotic destination. It ended only with the pilgrim's natural death.[24] The "pit" of St. Patrick's Purgatory at Lough Derg in County Donegal was a material manifestation of this version of pilgrimage, a quiet spot where one could ritually descend into a version of the afterlife to be purged of sin and gain knowledge of the "torments of the wicked and the joys of the just."[25] As part of the experience, a pilgrim would be formally discouraged from making the pilgrimage and had earth scattered on his head to symbolize his going-over into death. De Perellós's description in Molloy's translation of a sensation of being carried away to sea on the threshold of purgatory comes back to haunt us when we read poems of Molloy's in which she describes the threshold of death likewise, in sea-going terms: "I was sweating and overcome with great anguish of heart," writes the pilgrim, "as if stricken with seasickness while sailing."[26]

By inflecting the "journey" of cancer with notions gleaned from this much older tradition of pilgrimage into reclusion, Molloy disrupts the modern-day tendency to seek self-empowerment and growth in every life event. She taps into a tradition that was not afraid to contemplate resignation to larger forces or even self-abnegation. In "I Swap the Mediterranean," the speaker relinquishes, with deep reluctance, a stint of exotic travel for a stint in a radiotherapy machine. The "turquoise waves" of the Mediterranean ocean are replaced with the tap water of a hospital ward. As the poem goes on, the imagery of a beach holiday gradually segues into the cooler, shadier imagery of European Catholicism, the metaphorical location changing to a church. "I am the sacrifice at the new / Mass," writes Molloy. By the end her speaker has morphed into a blank-eyed statue in a crypt:

Half-naked, my pelvis exposed,

my hands out of the way, criss-crossed on my

chest, I endure; stare through closed

lids at nothing on earth.[27]

This figure is reminiscent of Philip Larkin's statues side-by-side in "An Arundel Tomb" which, despite the poem's final declaration that "[w]hat will survive of us is love," outlast any memory of their human predecessors or the love they may have shared.[28] The double meaning of Molloy's "nothing on earth" allows us to imagine that the sick speaker is, in some sense, already dead — is as much a member of the "living dead" as any leper. Her hands, with which she did her writing, are now "out of the way," revealed — not without irony — as merely an inconvenience, a temporary obstacle between the speaker and death.

As well as the pilgrimage into reclusion, Molloy alludes in her poetry to the related tradition of "commutations" a nun or priest might perform in the Middle Ages to do penance. Among the commutations "proper for clerics and nuns who have not slain a man" was spending a night in a cold church while "praying without respite."[29] In her poem "I spend the night," Molloy makes of the church a lover: in the poem's opening line she does not spend the night *in* the cathedral but *with* the cathedral.[30] She stretches out along the cathedral's length as along the length of a lover's body. The pay-off for her act of penance is not transcendence but sensuality:

[…] I listen to the inward

hesitation of its bells, the angel voices

rising from the choir behind the screen;

the organ music pumping through my bones.[31]

The "screen" and the curative music "pumping through" the "fevered body" keep us in mind of a hospital setting even while the poem imagines this other, more fanciful treatment for cancer, which has less to do with a cure than with an experience.

The recent focus in the medical profession on choosing the appropriate metaphors for discussing an illness — replacing the frightening, old-fashioned battle narrative of cancer with the empowering metaphor of a journey, for example — is a discussion prompted largely by the American writer Susan Sontag.[32] Sontag was diagnosed with breast cancer in 1975. On that occasion she outlived the illness, and in its aftermath she wrote her famous polemic "Illness as Metaphor," which has drastically affected the way we speak about and experience cancer, in Ireland as in the United States. Sontag rails against our use of metaphors to characterize certain illnesses as somehow more fearful, more degrading, more brimming with meaning than other illnesses that can leave us just as dead. She compares cancer with tuberculosis, an illness that was once as vivid in the public imagination as cancer is today. Her comparison shows that, as a result of the metaphorical associations congregating around each illness, "tuberculosis had often been regarded sentimentally, as an enhancement of identity," whereas cancer is "regarded with irrational revulsion, as a diminution of the self."[33] Sontag fears that our use of metaphor will affect both our treatment and our experience of cancer. Using a battle metaphor for cancer may lead us to choose unnecessarily violent and grueling treatments; using a journey metaphor may hide or belittle the true nature of a patient's experience. "My point," Sontag concludes, "is that illness is not a metaphor, and that the most truthful way of regarding illness — and the healthiest way of being ill — is one most purified of, most resistant to, metaphorical thinking."[34]

As Sontag concedes in a later essay, it is almost impossible to talk about illness *without* resorting to metaphor. Rather than prompting a turn away from metaphor in medical discourse as she intended, her polemic has instead prompted keen attention to how metaphor might be instrumental in producing desired results. In Ireland, as elsewhere, a positive metaphor of "journey" is now being promoted over the more negative metaphor of "battle" that had widely been used to talk about cancer. In 2014 the Irish Cancer Society announced an advertising campaign that would "capture some of the positivity and optimism that can now be part of a cancer journey."[35] The national newspaper, *The Irish Times*, has published pieces from various medical commentators and practitioners advising doctors and the media to stop using battlefield terminology when writing about cancer.[36] The Irish Cancer Society offers an optimistically-named "Journey Journal" to cancer sufferers to record the specifics of their cancer experience.[37]

If Sontag's tactical approach to cancer is to staunch the proliferation of metaphor around it, Molloy's approach is the opposite. Her poems run riot over these attempts by the medical profession to tame cancer and to make it seem benign and explicable through metaphor. Luz Mar Gonzáles-Ariaz shows in her essay "A Pedigree Bitch, Like Myself" how poems like Molloy's "Moult" use unconventional imagery to rival conventional cancer metaphors. By speaking about mastectomy in terms of moulting, she observes, Molloy portrays the body as "a fluid entity constantly *becoming* and transforming itself."[38] But at other moments, Molloy's poems disrupt any comfort we may take in metaphor at all. They do justice to the surreal, the polymorphous, the horrible, and even the darkly funny aspects of terminal illness. Her mortal body in them is a Barbie doll, a scarecrow, an empty house with a vacant lot, a winter bird, a statue on a tombstone, or a "great white whale."[39] Her poems' bedridden speaker is aboard a ship, or back in school, or praying before an altar, or actually *on* an altar, or lost and crawling on a desert island; or she is Christ awaiting His betrayal; or she is Christ the infant in a manger; or she takes off "through the roof."[40] Cancer treatment is elephant trumpets, birds of prey, jackrabbits, lunatics, and waterfalls.[41] It is a cup of poison or of eternal life, or it is a sacrificial mass.[42] It is Men at Work.[43]

Molloy flouts the careful control of a poetic image that is supposed to be the hallmark of an Irish poet who has mastered his or her craft. When he identifies the new Irish poets as postmodern in his *Wake Forest* preface, O'Callaghan suggests that the increased formalism of the *Metre* generation was an extension of the formalism simultaneously burgeoning in the United Kingdom. He remarks that the formalism of a poet such as Quinn "seems to owe more to American exemplars such as Richard Wilbur and Anthony Hecht than any Irish predecessors."[44] But what this narrative of internationalism understates is how comfortably the new formalism slotted into the modern Irish literary tradition as it already stood without troubling it in the slightest, since, as Peter Sirr describes, lyric poetry in the Irish context has always been judged in terms of authorial "mastery," "craft," and "control."[45] The modern Irish tradition presents poetry as a bardic craft to be mastered. At the heart of this modern tradition is W. B. Yeats, whose example of complete control over his poetic world is crystallized in his poem

"A Prayer for my Daughter," a poem which in turn has been rewritten by many Irish poets in poems *about* control or the loss of it, including Quinn himself, Eavan Boland, and Paul Muldoon.[46]

In this modern Irish tradition of craft and mastery, carefully controlled extended metaphor is supposed to evince some rigor of thought, a consciousness concentrating, reaching after a truth that can be grasped. In many of Molloy's poems in *Gethesemane Day*, the world of the poem is instead turned topsy-turvy. The metaphors never solidify and extend. The opening lines of "Dream" are as surreal and confusing as a real fever dream:

> Mittens on your breasts, those shrines where tossing hands
> cold as bottles, rattle pectorals in pockets of loose skin.
>
> Your body hair wound round me like a scarf, I nest,
> a winter bird; and beg the duvet's benediction on cold feet.
>
> The cradle rocks. The knitting-needles click. Toes press
> upon the pedalos: the tides of feet that push me out to sea.[47]

Mittens become shrines where, oddly, bottles toss; but they as soon become pockets. Body hair becomes a scarf, an odd sort of scarf wound around a bird. Suddenly a cradle appears; knitting needles. Or we are at sea. The reasonable image of two feet pedaling a boat just as quickly becomes the surreal image of whole "tides of feet" pushing. The constant changeability of things is here part of the point. The experience the poem captures cannot be confined to one metaphor. "The indoor shoes of dream / caress my head like a school beret," turns the poem's own speaker upside-down in the space of a sentence. The verbs are dramatic: "roar" and "whip" and "rip." Baldy nuns come marching comically-terrifyingly out of mists; we catch a glimpse of Larkin's stone lovers; and when the poem settles, it is into a place and a time heady with emotion: the speaker is a child, back in her school uniform, kneeling in a church.

In "Fruits of the Womb," Molloy takes on the common metaphor of cancer as an alien growth or even, by extension, a malign fetus and employs mixed metaphor to unnerving effect.[48] As Sontag writes, some turns of speech imagine that "[a cancerous] lump is alive, a foetus with its own will … Cancer is a demonic pregnancy."[49] Sontag quotes Novalis, as long ago as 1798, defining cancer along with gangrene as "fully-fledged *parasites* — they grow, are engendered, engender, have their structure, secrete, eat."[50] In eight lines with a mock-religious title, "Fruits of the Womb" mixes its metaphors to produce a tiny gem of grotesquerie. The removal of fibroids described in the poem takes place "along the bikini-line," connoting a part of the body that doesn't exist in those terms until we start thinking of the bikini, an item designed to showcase the sexual female body. As the surgical procedure continues, we're invited to think about melons — the fibroids, that is, are as "big as melons," a turn of phrase that makes us (I know I am not alone in this) think of breasts, conceived as comical and oversized. What are breasts doing "along the bikini-line"? The grotesquerie continues with "appendages," which conjures more dangly body parts turning up where they don't belong. Finally, the poem returns us to a metaphor of childbirth by a deadpan reporting of the weight of the fibroids: "nine pounds nine," the size of a nice big baby, but not before we have been roundly revolted by our own imaginations. "Fruits of the Womb" is anything but comforting.

"Illness is the night-side of life," Sontag writes: a place of "punitive or sentimental fantasies."[51] Each of us experiences our suffering as subjective — we have very little idea how our suffering compares with the suffering of others — and it seems to us an experience to which language is hopelessly inadequate. And yet, each of us *does* experience suffering: we share that. "Everyone who is born holds dual citizenship," writes Sontag, in her much-quoted opening paragraph, "in the kingdom of the well and the kingdom of the sick. Although we all prefer to use only the good passport, sooner or later each of us is obliged, at least for a spell, to identify ourselves as citizens of that other place."[52] This kingdom of illness, the space of an intense experience that seems unspeakable yet must be spoken about, is a place where lyric poetry feels at home. It is the space which Molloy's cancer poems enter and test. As citizens of the kingdom of the sick, we can understand and appreciate the poems without reference to any more literal nationality. But acknowledging Molloy's Irishness allows us to see how sharply the poems speak back to a literary tradition that values control and intellectual rigor by showing precisely what can be achieved when poetry abandons control and intellectual rigor. And, perhaps more importantly, acknowledging Molloy's Irishness allows her poems to speak back to a society that needs to hear about how it has constructed, and is constructing, illness and gender. For if language affects our ideas and experience as deeply as Molloy's poems suggest, then the discourse constructed within Irish boundaries makes things happen, not only within those boundaries but also in all the little Irelands who have gone to live overseas.

NOTES

1. Conor O'Callaghan, preface to *The Wake Forest Series of Irish Poetry*, Vol. 3, ed. Conor O'Callaghan (Winston-Salem, NC: Wake Forest UP, 2013), xv.

2. Ibid., xvi.

3. Justin Quinn, unpublished interview with this author, Dublin 2013; Justin Quinn, *The Cambridge Introduction to Modern Irish Poetry, 1800–2000* (Cambridge: Cambridge UP, 2008).

4. Jahan Ramazani, quoted in Philip Coleman, "At ease with elsewhere," review of *Collected Poems* and *At Least for a While* by Pearse Hutchinson, *Dublin Review of Books* 1, no. 5 (2009), http://www.drb.ie/essays/at-ease-with-elsewhere.

5. Susan Stewart, *Poetry and the Fate of the Senses* (Chicago: The University of Chicago Press, 2002), 2.

6. Ailbhe Darcy, "Dorothy Molloy's Gurlesque Poetics," *Contemporary Women's Writing* 8, no. 3 (2014): 319–38.

7. Robert Potts, "Daddy's Growling Girl," *The Guardian*, May 27, 2006, http://www.theguardian.com/books/2006/may/27/featuresreviews.guardianreview17.

8. Pilar Villar-Argáiz, "The Female Body in Pain: Feminist Re-Enactments of Sexual and Physical Violence in Dorothy Molloy's Poetry," *Contemporary Women's Writing* 4, no. 2 (2010): 135.

9. Dorothy Molloy, *Hare Soup* (London: Faber and Faber, 2004), 34.

10. Lakoff and Johnson demonstrate in their study of metaphor in everyday language, *Metaphors We Live By*, that we are deeply inclined to think metaphorically. Their study is almost invariably cited in discussion of metaphor.

11. Gary M. Reisfield and George R. Wilson, "Use of Metaphor in the Discourse on Cancer," *Journal of Clinical Oncology* 22, no. 9 (2004): 4024.

12. Byron Lee Grigsby, *Pestilence in Medieval and Early Modern English Literature* (New York: Routledge, 2003), 39.

13. Ibid., 40.

14. Timothy S. Miller and John W. Nesbitt, *Walking Corpses: Leprosy in Byzantium and the Medieval West* (Ithaca, NY: Cornell UP, 2014), 1.

15. Grigsby, *Pestilence*, 14. Although Grigsby's is the most in-depth elaboration of leprosy's medieval history, Saul Brody's influential 1974 study *The Disease of the Soul* was the first to offer the insight that leprosy was once considered an outward manifestation of sin in Christian Europe, through an analysis of medieval romances. Brody showed, to use Grigsby's phrase, that "medieval medical practitioners considered medicine to be a part of theology" (3). Sontag's *Illness as Metaphor* extends this idea into the modern era when she shows that epidemic diseases whose means of transmission are unknown, or not fully understood, are always prone to moral associations. She points out that the practice of blaming the victim of illness for his or her own plight continued into the nineteenth century with tuberculosis and into the twentieth with cancer and AIDS. Philip Roth's 2010 novel *Nemesis* explores similar ideas in the context of the mid-century polio epidemic, whose means of transmission was little understood. Roth's protagonist is tormented by the idea that the polio epidemic is worsened by his attempt to flee it, an act he perceives as a moral failure because it means abandoning his post as playground director in a Newark neighborhood. Various characters in the novel suggest, at various points, that the sufferers of polio may have brought illness on themselves by being Jewish, by eating at fast-food joints, by shaking hands with a handicapped man, or by playing ball too vigorously in hot sun.

16. Miriam O'Kane Mara, "Reproductive Cancer: Female Autonomy and Border Crossing in Medical Discourse and Fiction," *Irish Studies Review* 17, no. 4 (2009): 468.

17. Darcy, "Gurlesque," 16.

18. Dorothy Molloy, *Gethsemane Day* (London: Faber and Faber, 2006), 37.

19. Ibid., 33.

20. Care is defined as "regular, unpaid personal help for a friend or family member with a long-term illness, health problem or disability (including problems which are due to old age)," according to the Central Statistics Office, *Census 2011 — Profile 8 — Our Bill of Health* (Dublin: Stationary Office, 2011).

21. Sheila Conboy, "What You Have Seen is Beyond Speech: Female Journeys in the Poetry of Eavan Boland and Eiléan Ní Chuilleanáin," *The Canadian Journal of Irish Studies* 16, no. 1 (1990): 66.

22. Molloy, *Gethsemane*, 45.

23. Yolande de Pontfarcy, "The Historical Background to the Pilgrimage to Lough Derg," in *The Medieval Pilgrimage to St. Patrick's Purgatory: Lough Derg and the European Tradition*, ed. Michael Haren and Yolande de Pontfarcy (Enniskillen: Clogher Historical Society, 1988), 9.

24. Ibid., 10–11.

25. Ibid., 8.

26. Dorothy M. Carpenter, "The Pilgrim from Catalonia / Aragon: Ramon de Perellós, 1397," in *The Medieval Pilgrimage to St. Patrick's Purgatory: Lough Derg and the European Tradition*, ed. Michael Haren and Yolande de Pontfarcy (Enniskillen: Clogher Historical Society, 1988), 114.

27. Molloy, *Gethsemane*, 46.

28. Philip Larkin, *The Whitsun Weddings* (New York: Random House, 1964), 21.

29. de Pontfarcy, "Lough Derg," 9.

30. Molloy, *Gethsemane*, 23.

31. Ibid.

32. See for instance Reisfield and Wilson, "Use of Metaphor in the Discourse of Cancer," *Journal of Clinical Oncology*; Christine Harrington, "The Use of Metaphor in Discourse about Cancer: A Review of the Literature," *Clinical Journal of Oncology Nursing* 16, no. 4 (2012): 408–12; Carlos Laranjeira, "The role of narrative and metaphor in the cancer life story: a theoretical analysis," *Medicine, Health Care and Philosophy* 16, no. 3 (2013): 469–81; Elena Semino et al., "The online use of Violence and Journey metaphors by patients with cancer, as compared with health professionals: a mixed methods study," *BMJ Supportive and Palliative Care* 10 (2014): 1136.

33. Susan Sontag, *Illness as Metaphor and AIDS and its Metaphors* (New York: Picador, 1990), 100.

34. Ibid., 3.

35. Laura Slattery, "Irish Cancer Society begins 'hopeful' campaign," *The Irish Times*, Feb. 27, 2014.

36. Muiris Houston, "Battling to Lose the Military Health Terms," *The Irish Times*,

Jan. 13, 2009; Muiris Houston, "We Need to Fight Military View of Cancer," *The Irish Times*, Sept. 11, 2012; Jacky Jones, "Don't mention the war: Cancer is not a battlefield," *The Irish Times*, Oct. 15, 2014.

37. Irish Cancer Society website, http://www.cancer.ie/publications/journey-journal#st-hash.OSpzXLUZ.dpbs.

38. Molloy, *Long-Distance Swimmer*, 17; Luz Mar Gonzáles-Ariaz, " 'A Pedigree Bitch, Like Myself': (Non)Human Illness and Death in Dorothy Molloy's Poetry," in *Animals in Irish Literature and Culture*, ed. Kathryn Kirkpatrick and Borbála Faragó (London: Palgrave Macmillan, 2015), 25.

39. Molloy, *Gethsemane*, 3, 11, 20, 42.

40. Ibid., 45, 20, 46, 27, 37, 44, 36.

41. Ibid., 40.

42. Ibid., 37, 46.

43. Ibid., 45.

44. O'Callaghan, preface to *The Wake Forest Series of Irish Poetry*, Vol. 3, xvi.

45. Peter Sirr, "How Things Begin to Happen: Notes on Eiléan Ní Chuilleanáin and Medbh McGuckian," *Southern Review* 31, no. 3 (1995): 450–68.

46. These contemporary versions of Yeats's poem employ formal and thematic strategies to undermine Yeats's vision of lyric as affording the poet control over the world. See Justin Quinn, "Non-Enclave," in *Privacy* (Manchester: Carcanet, 1999), 61; Eavan Boland, "Daphne Heard with Horror the Addresses of the God," in *Outside History* (Manchester: Carcanet, 1990), 35; Paul Muldoon, "At the Sign of the Black Horse, September 1999," in *Moy Sand and Gravel* (New York: Farrar, Straus and Giroux, 2002), 84.

47. Molloy, *Gethsemane*, 20.

48. Ibid., 39.

49. Sontag, *Illness*, 14.

50. Ibid., 13–14.

51. Ibid., 3.

52. Ibid. It feels important to note that Sontag isn't altogether correct. Some people never hold dual citizenship, being only ever unwell.

5

Seamus Heaney:
The Death of Ritual
and the Ritual
of Death

Declan Kiberd

"Wherever there is Ireland, there is the family," wrote G. K. Chesterton, "and it counts for a great deal."[1] The south Derry farm on which Seamus Heaney grew to young manhood offered a wholly secure world, in which everyone knew their place and in which every tree or flower had a meaning in the scheme of things:

> The landscape was sacramental, a system of signs that called automatically upon systems of thinking and feeling... There, if you like, was the foundation for a marvellous or magical view of the world, a foundation that sustained a diminished structure of lore and superstition and half-pagan, half-Christian thought and practice. Much of the flora of

the place had a religious force, especially if we think of the root of the word 'religious' in religare, to bind fast. The single thorn-tree bound us to a notion of the potent world of the fairies — and when the Blessed Virgin appeared in a thorn bush in Ardboe, a few miles up the country, the fairy-tree took on a new set of subliminal attributes.[2]

In May buttercups flowered and the pagan goddess gave way to altars dedicated to the Virgin Mary. Members of the community "genuflected a million times, blessed ourselves a million times, never felt ourselves alone in the universe for a second."[3] Such a sense of security was rooted also in the life of an extended family.

The intensity of religious ritual and of family living among rural Catholics in Northern Ireland was, to some degree, attributable to the fact that there was no larger social institution with which they might identify. The law, the army, the civil service, even local government itself, were all the preserve of the Unionist majority, a group never slow to proclaim its superiority from the rooftops. Against that backdrop the family was a haven, but a haven in a heartless world.

The poetry of Heaney has much to say of that childhood and of its subsequent loss. Early lyrics in *Death of a Naturalist* (1966) record the decision of a bright young scholarship boy to "dig" with his pen rather than his father's spade, to record farm life and rural crafts before they die away. Many modern poets return to scenes of childhood in their fifties or sixties, but Heaney was writing with tenderness, exactitude and lyricism about that lost world in his early twenties. The eruption of political violence in Northern Ireland after 1969 complicated this task but never wholly distracted the writer from it; and the recapturing of childhood scenes took on a new urgency in *The Spirit Level* (1996), following the ceasefire by the Irish Republican Army (IRA). While other Irish writers of the 1990s offered bitter exposés of alcoholic fathers and abusive clerics, Heaney wrote moving lyrics in memory of parents, uncles and aunts, as well as celebrations of a brother who still farmed the land. The farm had seemed to the younger writer to have been filled with a poetry not yet conscious of itself as such: and, even when reviewed by the sadder, older man, it was still capable of transforming people from prisoners of the dire political experience to possessors of it.

Like Mark Twain, Heaney looked back upon his childhood as upon a zone of radical innocence before a fall into civil strife. He understood that every child, in its phases of growth, relives the fundamental experiences of the human race. There is a distinctly evolutionary quality to many memories — of unwanted pups being drowned, of tadpoles taking the shape of complex life, of traditions passing from generation to generation. Inevitably, the adult poet will find in some childhood memories elements of that fear and loathing which led him, in some distress, to evoke them. The Wordsworth of *The Prelude* will be his guide through such moments, for he also had tried to bring the world of boyhood into alignment with that of the man he had become: "He feels like a traitor among those he knows and loves. To be true to one part of himself, he must betray the other part. The inner state of man is thus shaken and the shock waves in the consciousness reflect the upheavals in the surrounding world."[4] This is an attempt which has been made by many poets in the aftermath of a failed revolution. John Milton was the first to attempt at the level of poetic practice a transformation no longer possible in his society, and that attempt would be repeated by Blake and by Wordsworth. Each had supported a revolution in its early stages, only to be disillusioned by the cruelty later unleashed.

Born in 1939, Heaney was a beneficiary of the 1947 Education Act, like so many other supporters of the civil rights marches in Northern Ireland of the 1960s, and his subsequent experience of the "People's Park" movement in Berkeley, California, taught him that even his poetry could be "a mode of resistance."[5] By 1970 the uglier side of American radicalism had begun to manifest itself in shootings and bombings. "In contrast to the revolutionary language of America," he wrote somewhat naively in December of that year, "the revolutionary voice of Ireland still keeps a civil tongue in its head."[6] Within a short time, however, the brutality of the IRA and of British securicrats changed all that. If there was to be a revolution, it would have to happen — like Milton's, Blake's, and Wordsworth's — inside the head.

The polarities of the conflict had by then become clear to the young man in coded but troubling ways. While he was reading the writings of the anti-clerical Joyce at college, he might also find himself driving his mother to attend May devotions in the local church. He might confess to sins of impurity, yet find himself studying the novels of D. H. Lawrence. He had to relocate his Pioneer Total Abstinence medal inside his lapel before attending sherry parties at university. One effect of the divided society was to give a defiantly conservative cast to northern Catholicism. It is most unlikely that a southern student moving, say, between a Wicklow farm and Trinity College Dublin would have felt so acutely the sort of strain recalled by Heaney:

> As a northerner, my sense of religion and my sense of race or nationality or politics were inextricably twined together. If you have ever walked through a Belfast street on Ash Wednesday, your forehead badged with the mortal dust, you will know how this sense of caste is enforced by the sectarian circumstances. If you have ever blessed yourself in a city bus (or, more piercingly, not blessed yourself for fear of being noticed) you will know it too.[7]

Over the years that religious practice was eroded, partly due to "problems with some central mysteries,"[8] but the poet also recognized that the cultural conflict between Catholic ritual and secular art might be more apparent than real. Insofar as it was real, it had value as one source of poetry, but what was at stake was a crisis in the very status of ritual itself. By the mid-1970s, as political scientists pronounced Northern Ireland "a problem without a solution,"[9] some of the better-publicized explanations of the Troubles began to wear a little thin. The socialist analysis, which cast the problem in terms of the economic oppression of a minority by a majority, lost traction as the memories of the student radicalism of the previous decade faded. The purely political accounts did not seem to explain the appalling intensity of feeling on all sides. The official churches had repeatedly condemned the gunmen, to palpable effect. Against that bleak backdrop, people began to look to the poet for the sort of vatic wisdom once expected of the *filí*. For some years, Heaney had been compelled to make statements in prose as to why he was making none in poetry. Then, in 1975, he published *North*, a work of epic scope which seeks, like that of Milton, Blake, and Wordsworth, to solve an irreconcilable conflict by outgrowing it, by developing a "new level of consciousness."[10]

Previous volumes of his had contained the usual accumulations of poems over a three- or four-year period. *North* was shaped, however, around a set of linked themes. Throughout the volume, central if never directly expressed, was a diagnosis so surprising that it was not noticed by those commentators calling for a solution: to the effect that the death of rituals in modern life had led to rituals of death. Marxists might complain that such analysis attempts to solve at the level of ritual problems which can only be treated in the body politic: but it was his application of the methods of comparative anthropology which permitted Heaney to take the longer view, which "solved" the question not so much by changing it as by extending it right back in time. He excavated the meaning of the present not by going back twenty years but by two thousand.

The poet suggested that to understand the strange clash, the 1600s were scarcely more helpful than the morning newspapers: better to re-read Tacitus. The mythical was reasserting itself in a world stripped of useful ritual. Such an analysis shocked left-wing Nationalists, able to quote hard-and-fast statistics of discrimination on housing and jobs. To them it seemed like a culturalist over-interpretation rather than a true account of the psychology of the killers, most of whom were lapsed members of their respective Christian churches. But Heaney could see that those who thought of themselves as having stripped away all pointless rituals were submitting, unconsciously, to a repetition of some of the oldest rituals of all. Such a diagnosis had much appeal for anti-materialist intellectuals, since it secured their role in any ensuing debate — and in any possible solution. Many overseas intellectuals found Ireland fascinating, because (in the words of Bernard Shaw) the laws of economics seemed to stop at Holyhead (the embarkation point for the sea journey to the island).[11]

In *North* a line of anthropological writing about Ireland that began with Edmund Spenser and continued through Swift comes full circle. Such a writing asked (in Spenser's case) where the ferocity of rebels came from and (in Swift's) what the cruelty of the official response told the planters about themselves. The main focus in *North*, however, is on the sufferings and sins of those on the Nationalist side. Whether through courtesy or a decent reticence in the face of the unknown, the poet has surprisingly little to say about the Unionists.

It begins with a domestic scene: the poet's aunt Mary baking in the farm kitchen, a gesture of creativity in a broken, breaking world. Yet a companion piece, "The Seed Cutters," suggests a violence even in domestic ritual. The aunt dusts the floor with a goose's wing and the cutters bisect every root. Like those seeds split in half, *North* is divided into two parts. The first is mythical and ancient-seeming, concerned with the meaning of bodies dug out of old bogs. The second is documentary and apparently contemporary, about the challenges that current affairs pose for language. Splitting might seem a fitting response to a divided society, but the artist's real concern is to align mythical and mundane, a technique derived from Joyce's *Ulysses*. In that book a Homeric grid was brought down on the characters from above, its arbitrariness being part of its point, a contraption which in its attempt to impose order on the chaos of modernity might seem more real than the experiences on which it was being imposed. Heaney's bog myth is, by comparison, overt and earned and slowly evolved in response to the pressure of experience.

The woods had once marked the frontier between native and planter, and so became an image of the Unconscious, as in American culture. But now they were gone, and so the earth itself became a symbol of a world once populous and noisy, to be contemplated by the silent poet-archaeologist, striking in and down.[12] These zones would, like the American frontier, be a place where the theory of original innocence and the facts of human corruption are confronted. The pioneers celebrated in Heaney's bog poems, unlike the Americans, were less interested in subduing the land than in studying it, in learning from it rather than in measuring it out. Unlike the American frontier, the bogs could never disappear. Far from being erased by an encroaching civilization, they were augmented by each development. Ever since the time of Spenser, the Irish had been depicted as bogmen, dwelling in softlands and luring imperial soldiers clothed in heavy armor into such terrain. For centuries "bogman" had been a term of racist abuse but it was now occupied by Heaney as a term of defiance, complication, and resistance not just to colonialism but to the effects of time itself. In Berkeley he had seen black radicals say "black is beautiful," and he was doing no less with the bog. The man had been taken out of the bog but he had no desire to let the bog be taken out of the man, for the bog preserves not only bodies and objects but also consciousness.

A strong suggestion all through *North* is that the dead themselves may not recognize that they are dead and think of themselves as translated into a new dimension. The emphasis, however, is steadfastly on the community which unites at a wake rather than on the departed: hence the rather stately, dignified diction. The grave honor done to the dead at wakes attended by the teenaged boy contrasts utterly with the randomness of contemporary slaughter in the north:

> I shouldered a kind of manhood
> stepping in to lift the coffins
> of dead relations.
> They had been laid out ...[13]

For a young man in an unjust state there will always be a question as to where "manhood" is to be found. This will be exacerbated if he chooses a career as a writer, since (in the words of an Italian proverb) words are feminine, deeds masculine. Heaney's own frequent characterization of Unionists as masculine and the colonized Catholics as feminine suggests that a degree of sexual anxiety attended a literary career in a place where Protestant schools took pride in their profile in the sciences (leaving Catholic ones to stake claims in arts). Hence the occasional assertions by Heaney of a masculinity which the very act of becoming a writer may have thrown into question.[14] Newsreel footage through the 1970s featured teenage boys (less likely than older men to be arrested) shouldering the coffins of dead IRA comrades; and he knew that many Nationalist males, emasculated by decades of unemployment, were turning to the IRA to assert a jeopardized virility. Writing, however, was Heaney's alternative to violence, his way of taking power.

Nothing in Heaney's world seems as remote as the recent past, and his language deliberately distances funerals of corpses with "dough-white hands" and "igloo brows" until they seem like glaciers moving into pre-history. The long-familiar is presented as the ever-distant:

> Now as news comes in
> of each neighbourly murder

we pine for ceremony,

customary rhythms …[15]

The problem is acute. Between the 1950s and 1970s the world around the Derry farm has been disenchanted and its ceremonial elements all but lost; and this has happened all over Europe — Bologna has its car-bombs as well as Belfast. What little ritual remains has been stripped down to the level of routine. Even the flag-draped, glove-topped coffins at IRA funerals — so patently modeled on those of the British army — are a belated attempt to restore that sense of ceremonial dignity lacking in the lives of those mourned. Deprived of ritual, people had grown disillusioned with political leaders, whom nevertheless they accused of acting all the time. Northern Ireland, far from being aberrational, simply poses an intense version of the common problem.

So the poet proposes a healing ritual, a funeral to end all other funerals, a pilgrimage of forgiveness in which past grudges will be buried in the Neolithic chamber of Newgrange. Standing by the Boyne, a river sacred in memory to Loyalists whose ancestors triumphed there in 1690, the poet sees a locale which transcends such divisive moments with an appeal to a shared pre-history. The great house of the Celtic dead is also the vault into which the winter sun shines every solstice on December 21, the shortest day of the year. The old imagery of Loyalist marching or of Nationalist martyrs will be subsumed into a pilgrimage affirming a common life. The appeal made to a pre-Christian, pagan bedrock of values by W. B. Yeats is now amplified by Heaney, who emulates his predecessor by using painfully paradoxical phrases ("neighbourly murder"), in order to show that sacrifice is not at all remote in a community at war with itself. In doing this, Heaney also follows in the tracks of Synge, who went to Aran in the poet's account "to put on the armour of an authentic pre-Christian vision which was a salvation from the fallen world of Unionism and Nationalism, Catholicism and Protestantism, Anglo and Irish, Celtic and Saxon — all those bedeviling abstractions and circumstances."[16] The objective embodiment of a subjective consciousness which Synge found among the stones of Aran was discovered by Heaney amid the boulders of Newgrange:

Now I would restore

the great chambers of Boyne,
prepare a sepulchre
under the cup-marked stones.
Out of side-streets and bye-roads

purring family cars
nose into line.
The whole country tunes
to the muffled drumming

of ten thousand engines.
Somnambulist women,
left behind, move
through emptied kitchens

imagining our slow triumph
towards the mounds.
Quiet as a serpent
in its grassy boulevard

the procession drags its tail
out of the Gap of the North
as its head already enters
the megalithic doorway.[17]

The resolution is merely imagined, but the search is for a ceremony equal to the suffering of "each blinded home" (blinded by grief, even more than prejudice, with its curtains down). The image of the old is of the *péist* of Gaelic mythology, one serpent not yet banished by St. Patrick from the nearby hill of Slane; and the vaguely threatening animal recalls Yeats's own rough beast slouching to a holy place as another ceremony of innocence is annulled.

But Heaney knows that he can never be a Yeats. Facing the collapse of ceremony, Yeats called for its renewal, but went further and created in *A Vision* an entire philosophical and religious system that would give it a claim on people's attention. It is possible, of course, to laugh at this as the "southern Californian" in Yeats,[18] but at least it offered a positive theory of the world and not just a diagnosis of its limitations. Heaney, born over seven decades later (in fact, in the year of Yeats's death), is too honest to simulate belief when he feels none, and so he is at the mercy of the finality of early death. The terrorism takes away the only life which many members of the community believe that they will ever have. There is here no Yeatsian faith that can look through death; rather, the funeral offers a way of controlling grief until it is slowly purged in this life.

The model for such renewal is Gunnar of *Njal's Saga*: a warrior who managed to smile and sing of ancient heroes in his burial vault, even as his own killing went unavenged. If the first part of "Funeral Rites" made the familiar farm-world seem remote, this third and final section makes that ancient saga-world seem familiar. The restoration of a true sense of community demands fortitude and forgiveness, as well as the dismantling of current names (always insisted on by recent winners) down to their source meanings ("Strang and Carling fjords"). Gunnar is himself literally re-membered, a warrior whose body did not rot. So he is transformed into a sort of saint, who learned how to praise the world as he found it:

> Men said that he was chanting
> verses about honour
> and that four lights burned
>
> in corners of the chamber:
> which opened then, as he turned
> with a joyful face
> to look at the moon.[19]

Despite his sweetness of temper, the old warrior sickness (chanting verses about honor) asserts itself, but on this occasion is cured by the four votive lights that turn the verses into a prayer to the moon, symbol of love and beauty. The corpse which sings is an ancient motif, from Gaelic lore to the poetry of Blake: but rarely has it such poignant force.

"Viking Dublin: Trial Pieces" considers objects taken from the bog and displayed in the National Museum in Dublin, itself a Viking settlement. On the bones of dead people artists doodled, in search of a convincing line (much like the poet himself, who wonders whether a child attempted to trace on just the sort of longship out of which the relics came). The longship drawn by the ancient child "enters my longhand" in an act which is at once repetition and translation of the original impulse into a new element. The subtle calligraphy has to be "magnified on display," like the poet's tabulating, noun-centered art; and he is amazed that it is on the jaws and ribs of the dead that images of vibrant life, "foliage, bestiaries," are inscribed.[20] The process is both reassuring and barbarous (rather like the cuff-links made of "genuine human molars" worn by a businessman in *The Great Gatsby*).

Thoughts of Scandinavian founders lead to that Denmark which produced not only the bog-preserved corpses, on which many poems here focus, but also the tale of Hamlet, the intellectual unfitted for a bloody act in the rotten state. The implication seems unavoidable:

> I follow into the mud.
> I am Hamlet the Dane,
> skull-handler, parablist,
> smeller of rot
>
> in the state, infused
> with its poisons,
> pinioned by ghosts
> and affections,
>
> murders and pieties,
> coming to consciousness
> by jumping in graves,
> dithering, blathering.[21]

Yeats, in "Meditations in Time of Civil War," had turned upon the stairs of his tower to ask whether he could have proved his worth in a direct action "that all others understand or share." By the end he had settled for "the half-read wisdom of daemonic images."[22] So does Heaney. By his day Percy Shelley's definition of the poet as unacknowledged legislator of the world had been reversed in a famous quip by W. H. Auden that "such a description better fits the secret police."[23] *North* will record injunctions by admirers to "be the poet of your people," but when the Royal Ulster Constabulary (RUC) fire at his former schoolmates in Derry in 1969, Heaney will find himself suffering "only the bullying sun of Madrid" outside the Prado, which houses Goya's painting of a revolution bringing forth monsters.[24]

Hamlet is a figure in whom many Irish writers have seen a version of themselves. Yeats's Hamlet was a deployer of masks, feigning madness; Joyce's a man intent on becoming his own father; and Heaney's a man who stands in graves, dithering and blathering. There is more than barren self-accusation or self-justification at work, for Hamlet, like Heaney, expended his greatest energy in trying to realize the state of being dead. His jump into Ophelia's grave is a logical part of that investigation. The analogy is quite pressing: a man in his thirties who, after a protracted education, is about to come into his proper inheritance but then is confronted by a ghost and must thereafter defer that moment when he would have become his destined self. The role of people's avenger is one to which Heaney is ill-suited by temperament, and so he becomes instead a troubled soliloquist, obsessed with ritual, role-play and acting. Hamlet coaches Polonius and the players in the actor's art, he tells the queen to assume those virtues which she does not have, he punctures the facile disguises of others, and he develops a boundless gift for mimicry, until in the end he can play virtually every part except his own. When he appears among the graves in act 5 of the play, following a period of withdrawal (much like Heaney's move from Belfast to Wicklow in the 1970s), he is a sort of revenant, back from the death intended for him, but expected to simplify himself for the sake of a revenge tragedy. Heaney, of course, will deviate from the ur-plot as Shakespeare's hero could not do: and he will seek instead a line of escape in the figure of Sweeney, the visionary man-bird who fled the field of battle to live among the trees.

For he knows just how little words of his can do but how vitally important it is that they do it: soothe a community's pain by describing it so well. In doing as much and as little, he may raise the consciousness of some people to a level of understanding at which the currently irreconcilable positions seem ill-conceived, even meaningless. If you cannot solve a question, that may be because of the silliness in which its terms are put: and your words can at least discredit those terms.

There is no pretense of superiority or objectivity. If there is poison in the state, the poet also is "infused" with it. He knows that his is a carrion art. The word "blathering" is borrowed from Synge, who never forgot the bones beneath the skin and who insisted that "before verse can be human again it must learn to be brutal."[25] Living in the gate-lodge of the Synge family estate in Glanmore must have reminded Heaney of that duty to record the violence at the heart of man's sense of beauty. One section, indeed, ends with a quotation from Synge's *Playboy of the Western World* — "Did you ever hear tell of the skulls they have in the city of Dublin?" Synge often reminded himself, as he held the actress Molly Allgood in his arms, that one day she would be whitened bone; he was as excited as Webster by thoughts of "the skull beneath the skinne."[26] In "Bone Dreams," however, the gesture goes beyond mere frisson to a slow, steady consideration of such ossification:

> Come back past
> philosophy and kennings,
> re-enter memory
> where the bone's lair
>
> is a love-nest
> in the grass.
> I hold my lady's head
> like a crystal
>
> and ossify myself
> by gazing: I am screes
> on her escarpments,
> a chalk giant

carved upon her downs.
Soon my hands, on the sunken
fosse of her spine
move towards the passes.[27]

The word "ossify" suggests drunkenness as well as a measurement of bones; and the hint of necrophilia is deliberate, for the poet knows that the pornographic imagination may in extremity seek the ultimate fulfillment in death. Synge had said that all poetry, though a tender flower, has strong roots among clay and worms.[28] The necrophilia is invoked here in the attempt to achieve a fuller understanding of tradition, for the bog preserves not just bodies but consciousness; it is not only a graveyard but a house of love:

And we end up
cradling each other
between the hips
of an earthwork.[29]

Many of these themes achieve a most complex articulation in "The Bog Queen." Up until this moment in his bog poems, Heaney had been willing the dead bodies to speak, and now at last one does. Unlike the Tollund and Grauballe Man, this one is feminine, dug out of an Irish rather than a Danish bog:

I lay waiting
between turf-face and demesne wall,
between heathery levels
and glass-toothed stone.[30]

Caught between the native boglands and the compounds of the Ascendancy, this queen bore the cultural history of the island on the shorthand of her body.

The opening line will be repeated, as if to echo the old Republican motto (*éireoimid arís*, "we will rise again"), but also as an emblem of that condition known by the destitute tramps of Samuel Beckett — "My body was braille / for the creeping influences"[31] — because the bog has preserved not only her body but her consciousness. Every level of earth has a particular history, translated into the facts of a geography; and, like all who make the desperate bargain to live in a culture, she has been preserved by the sheer weight of that earth which also suffocated her:

> the illiterate roots
>
> pondered and died
> in the cavings
> of stomach and socket.
> I lay waiting
>
> On the gravel bottom
> My brain darkening ...[32]

She is assimilated back to nature from culture, yet some recessed part of her causes her to resist and persist, as in the case of Beckett's protagonists, the more her body fades, the more defiantly active is the mind which records that fading. Here is an inversion of the sky-woman or *spéirbhean* of Gaelic tradition, now found not on high but deep in the earth, as a reminder of how a tradition will always be reborn in the lament for its disappearance. The dead, though forgotten, are never truly gone, and since they do not recognize death, they must be just wintering out:

> My skull hibernated
> in the wet nest of my hair,
>
> which they robbed.
> I was barbered
> and stripped
> by a turfcutter's spade,
>
> who veiled me again
> and packed coomb softly

between the stone jambs
at my head and at my feet.[33]

Literally, the kind turf-cutter (who accidentally dug her out) re-membered her, reassembling her bones in proper order before the discreet "veiling." This was the very moment for which, all along, she had been waiting, that instant when she would re-enter human minds and come forth as a challenge.

The facts, however, record otherwise: that when she was dug out on Lord Moira's estate in 1781, her body was not accorded the dignity deserved by such patient, prayerful waiting. The cutter was given cash and Lady Moira plundered the corpse, which might better have been respectfully restored to its resting-place:

Till a pier's wife bribed him.
The plait of my hair,
a slimy birth-cord
of bog, had been cut

and I rose from the dark,
hacked bone, skull-wave,
frayed stitches, tufts,
small gleams on the bank.[34]

The grave decorum of the earlier stanzas is turbo-charged at the close: and some readers hear in its defiant rhythms an echo of Sylvia Plath's "Lady Lazarus": the rocking, metronomic movement of a reborn with, back from the dead, protesting the insult to a body reduced to mere exhibit. Deeper still is the sense of the anonymity of pain, as suffering erases all trace of the individual, while past wars are waged in new ways in the present. Even the dead, as Walter Benjamin warned, may not be safe from an enemy who wins.[35]

Yet, by contrast with some earlier bog poems, there are no suggestions here that a pornographic imagination might find its ultimate satisfaction in the extinction of the other party. Nor does the Bog Queen resemble Plath in experiencing her own slow-motion disintegration as the ultimate aesthetic experience. There is no sense of the vengefulness to be found in Plath's closure:

> Out of the ash
> I rise with my red hair
> And I eat men like air.[36]

Rather what is asserted, more in the rhythms than in the statement ("I rose"), is a dignified margin of possible hope. This Cathleen Ni Houlihan is not the "bitch" with a "surly gob" lamented by Sean O'Casey,[37] but a figure of perfect poise and patience. The greater the humiliation of her body, the surer her mind's recovery from it. Although she feels violated by the planter's wife, even in this abjection she finds a sweet vindication of all her waiting, sure in the knowledge that she would rise. Her plight may be similar to that of the later Plath, but her thought is closer to the later Yeats:

> A brief parting from those dear
> Is the worst man has to fear.
> Though grave-digger's toil is long,
> Sharp their spades, their muscles strong,
> They but thrust their buried men
> Back in the human mind again.[38]

A good lesson also carries warnings, as do these lyrics. The figures of Bog Queen and others are made available for contemplation by their status as prized exhibits in museums, but the very principle of museumization is discredited in the poetic enactment. Denying the Bog Queen's fixity as an exhibit, Heaney prefers to return her to a world of process and transformation. The imagining of the fuller details of her story is a refusal to connive in the common curatorial desire to present everything old as an art-work. That curatorial effect is usually achieved by removing objects or human remains from their proper context, estrangement and defamiliarization seem to confer on these the arbitrary qualities of a modern work of art. The danger here is that a discourse of connoisseurship (such as Lady Moira's) will take the place of the turf-cutter's honest workings. The impulse to adore may carry an undertow of prurient curiosity and titillation (as Heaney had conceded in "Punishment" by dubbing himself an "artful voyeur").[39] There is indeed something savage at the heart of some acts of apparent veneration. Better by far to return such objects to the bog which will preserve them better than any museum. The primary forces of nature in Ireland seemed to conspire in such a natural process, providing the wood for making works of art and the rains which dissolve them. As Chinua Achebe has observed of somewhat similar issues in Africa: "When the product is preserved or venerated, the impulse to repeat the process is compromised."[40]

The "melancholy of the collector" is a phenomenon well known among modernists and among Irish Revivalists. Collection is one way to bolster and ratify a self felt to be in jeopardy, and that self may respond with demonstrations of its power to tabulate "numbered bones." But that is a one-way transaction, affording the dead no chance to answer back. In *North* that unilinear anthropology is disrupted by a poet who warns repeatedly against fetishism and who refuses to possess objects, which seem instead to possess him. The personation of the dead in the politics of Northern Ireland had always been legendary and continued so into the years covered by *North*. After a narrow victory by a very few votes in the 1969 election in Belfast, the socialist MP Gerry Fitt received a telegram: "Congratulations Gerry. Can only quote Pearse: the fools, the fools, the fools — they have left us our Fenian dead."[41]

The anthropologist in Heaney sees the crisis in cultural rather than economic terms, as the vestige of an ancient battle between devotees of a goddess and a god. Protestantism is male, imperial, English; Catholicism female, Nationalist, Irish. Some might consider the division vulgar for such a subtle poet, but it was hardly of his making. "I think that the Hail Mary is more of a poem than the Our Father," he told an interviewer: "Our Father is between chaps, but there's something faintly amorous about the Hail Mary."[42] In a benchmark lecture written during the work on *North*, Heaney offered the Royal Society of Literature a completely cultural explanation of the northern wars:

> There is an indigenous territorial numen, a tutelar of the whole island,
> call her Mother Ireland, Kathleen ni Houlihan, the poor old woman,

the Shan Van Vocht, whatever; and her sovereignty has been temporarily usurped or infringed by a new male cult whose founding fathers were Cromwell, William of Orange or Edward Carson, and whose godhead is incarnate in a Rex or Caesar resident in a palace in London. What we have is the tail-end of struggle in a province between territorial piety and imperial power.[43]

So in poems he explores analogies between the male victim of an ancient fertility rite and those modern youths who sacrifice lives to appease Mother Ireland — or between a sacrificed Scandinavian woman and the tarring-and-feathering of a woman who mixed with British soldiers. The typology, however, is never quite as pat as that makes it seem — the deeper analogy in "Punishment," for instance, is with the poet who pursues his own instinctual desires above and beyond the code of his tribe. The poems summon up feeling for the ancient victims, which flows like a tributary back into the flood of emotion felt for current sufferers.

If present horrors seem too much and journalism inadequate, then one way of realizing current atrocity is through ancient experience, to measure what Helen Vendler has tellingly called "the insult of the actual."[44] That technique may (again) owe something to Synge, who wrote that the profoundest moments in poetry are achieved when the dreamer is reaching out to reality. Each lyric here protects itself from sounding too pleased with its own conclusions by raising the essential criticisms of the code to which it adheres. Lest ancient image seem beguiling, the poet weighs it against

the actual weight
of each hooded victim,
slashed and dumped.[45]

Yet, along with the ethical need to make an inventory of the present is a desire to remember the future: as the ancient victims seem to us, so shall we seem to people two thousand years from now.

"*Tout comprendre, c'est tout pardonner*"? Not quite. The risk is that culturalist explanations might seem to absolve murderous activities, and even one of Heaney's staunchest admirers worried that the method might accord "sectarian killing in Ulster a historical respectability which it is not usually given in day-to-day journalism."[46] It is a measure of how dreadfully the IRA campaign and British army response impinged on even the most intrepid minds that such speculations could even be entertained.[47] For many decades, what had been lacking from most Irish cultural debate was the sort of comparative dimension which Heaney applied. A Revivalist myth of national exceptionalism had left generations of political scientists, folklorists and literary critics indifferent to (or unaware of) analogies with the outside world. In later decades Heaney would multiply the comparisons, with eastern Europe, rural England, St. Lucia, as part of his "nostalgia for world culture;" and others like Brian Friel would do the same. It would, however, be difficult to overstate its liberating effect on young Irish readers in 1975, exhausted by the conflict yet anxious to make sense of it in terms of a wider Europe which suffered its share of car bombs, street disturbance, and police atrocity. The method was not wholly new, since Joyce had used Homer to suggest a mythic parallel. What was new was that a sponsor of such an analysis might be accused of conniving with the very chaos which his myth sought to bring to order and control. It may seem banal to repeat the point: *North*, in seeking to understand sacrificial myth, does not propose its reenactment. Heaney's implicit allegation against the killers is that they have degraded sacred ritual to the level of a killing routine and so done the work of the colonizers in further disenchanting the land.

Heaney's focus may be on his own side, but he is hardly a doctrinal adherent. Its codes shaped him but he in turn reshaped them:

> I grew out of all this
> like a weeping willow
> inclined to
> the appetites of gravity.[48]

If Catholics over time had tended to impatriate through memories of history (all those lost battles, rebel songs, and so on), Protestants in search of their Irish identity had found it most often in geography (landscape, the lore of place). The bog poems, however, offer a point at which history and geography meet. The attainment of a higher level of consciousness, beyond the terms of current conflict, is to be found at the lowest levels of the earth.

The final poem of Part One might easily but glibly be read as a celebration of Hercules's holding-aloft of the body of Antaeus, a way of preparing for the more discursive, willed, and pragmatic poems of Part Two. Heaney had long contended that there were two kinds of poems: the one given and received by sheer instinct, and the sort knowingly shaped by force of will. Antaeus, with his feeling for the artesian wells beneath, is a sponsor of the first kind; and Hercules, impelled by an urge to order and control, seems to phase in the second. The poet had been wary of becoming excessively self-analytical, lest the element of risk and surprise which bless any creative process be lost, as will exceeded imagination: "A poem always has elements of accident about it, which can be made the subject of inquest afterwards, but there is always a risk in conducting your own inquest: you might begin to believe the coroner in yourself rather than put your trust in the man in you who is capable of accident."[49] There has been a tendency to see the sections in *North* as replicating that dualism; but the structuring is not so straightforward. The first section will, of course, expose the shallowness of many journalistic clichés about the conflict in the second section, yet many of those clichés will repeat earlier points. The very looseness of some of the poems in the follow-up section suggests an ease, an instinctual element in the writing, whereas Part One, though filled with depth and suggestion, is arguably the most knowingly assembled of all of Heaney's poetic sequences.

Part Two is less dense and difficult. Much of it is slack and conversational in the ad-lib manner favored by Patrick Kavanagh. Confronted by journalists seeking views on "the Irish thing" (a phrase Kavanagh often used to disparage Yeats and the Revivalists), the poet considers the various languages by which people evade a full awareness of current atrocities. Journalists with their talk of "polarization" and "long-standing hate" may be no worse than cautious neighbors:

'Oh, it's disgraceful, surely, I agree',
'Where's it going to end?' 'It's getting worse'.
'They're murderers'. 'Internment, understandably…'
The voice of sanity is getting hoarse.[50]

Against these clichés, heartfelt but threadbare, must be pitted the unanswer-able facts: "Men die at hand. In blasted street and home / The gelignite's a common sound-effect …"[51] And the poet seeks the "right line" to expose the bigotry beneath sham platitudes.

The impulse here is Orwellian in the good sense: based on the con-viction that an inadequate language reflects a prior corruption in politics, which can only feed off it. The "famous Northern reticence" may be just an excuse for refusing to referee between two sides, one of which may actually be worse than the other:

Of the "wee six" I sing
Where to be saved, you only must save face
And whatever you say, you say nothing.[52]

The childhood idyll is now thrown into question, with memories of a "land of password, handgrip, wink and nod," by which names and addresses revealed sectarian affiliations. In "The Ministry of Fear," Heaney recalls his early experiments as a secondary-school poet with his friend at St. Columb's College, Seamus Deane:

I tried to write about the sycamores
And invented a South Derry rhyme
With 'hushed' and 'bulled' full rhymes for 'pushed' and 'pulled'.
Those hobnailed boots from beyond the mountain
Were walking, by God, all over the fine
Lawns of elocution.[53]

The same sense of being invaders of an "English" space might be felt in later years at a police road-block, where the very name "Seamus" was enough to prompt the constable to read the letters sent by his poetic collaborator:

Ulster was British, but with no rights on
The English lyric: all around us, though
We hadn't named it, the ministry of fear.[54]

The poetic problem mirrored the wider social one: somehow the rights of British freemen to jobs, housing, and "one man, one vote" had not been extended to Nationalists. "A Constable Calls" honestly locates this troubled recognition back in the beloved farmhouse in which Heaney's aunt Mary did the baking in the opening poem, but now it is darkened in memory by the presence of a policeman, suspicious that the tillage returns might be incomplete. Only as the constable cycles away does the full menace of state power become apparent: "And the bicycle ticked, ticked, ticked."[55]

Yet that experience which left Heaney the poet of two traditions was what would in time bring him global fame as a representative instance of the postcolonial poet. It would explain and enrich his collaboration with Derek Walcott, a native of St. Lucia, who would write in a similar vein: "Mongrel as I am, something prickles in me when I see the word ASHANTI as with the word WARWICKSHIRE, both separately indicating my grandfather's roots, both baptizing this neither proud nor ashamed bastard, this hybrid, this West Indian."[56] The double structure of Walcott's *The Arkansas Testament*, dedicated to Heaney, with its division between Here and Elsewhere, is an homage to *North*,[57] and so also is its determination to embrace the language of Shakespeare, Wordsworth, and Auden as of right:

In the rivulet's gravel
light gutturals begin,
in the valley, a mongrel,
a black vowel barking.[58]

"Even the most imposed-upon colonial," Heaney would say years later in one of his Oxford Lectures on poetry, "will discern in the clear element of Herbert's 'The Pulley' a true paradigm of the shape of things,"[59] and his nostalgia for world culture will lead him to imagine a free space "where one will never have to think twice about the cultural and linguistic expression of one's own world on its own since nobody else's terms will be imposed as normative or official."[60]

The affinities between Heaney and Walcott are a useful reminder that theirs is a vernacular modernism, quite different from that of a Proust or an Eliot writing at the metropolitan center, and that what looks like pastoralism or archaism in their works is usually framed by some more radical, modern consciousness. "Act of Union" by Heaney is not just a traditional Gaelic attempt to imagine the Anglo-Irish relation in terms of a marriage which has come under dire strain, it is also an account of a New-Age father apprehensively watching over the birth of a child who will bring unprecedented challenges into the world.

The closing poem of *North*, "Exposure," places the book's two modes, the mythical and the documentary, into a dynamic equilibrium. Written in his new exile in County Wicklow, it shows a poet surrounded by woods into which Irish rebels traditionally retreated for cover until the next fight. He has made a separate peace, like previous exiles through literary history from Ovid ("weighing / my responsible tristia") to Mandelstam ("an inner exile").[61] The old temptation to be the people's hero has been passed up: but the writer is not wholly satisfied with his Yeatsian choice, fearing that he may have missed a potentially defining moment. The title is ironic, for the poet, fled from the Northern violence, must expose himself to a different set of dangers, the quarrel with himself. He had followed the example of the mad king Sweeney in seeking an exposure to nature, away from the noise of battle, a line of flight made possible to those who abandon the territorial imperative and take to the air:

> I am neither internee nor informer;
> An inner émigré, grown long-haired
> And thoughtful; a wood-kerne
>
> Escaped from the massacre,
> Taking protective colouring
> From bole and bark, feeling
> Every wind that blows;
>
> Who, blowing up these sparks
> For their meager heat, have missed
> The once-in-a-lifetime portent,
> The comet's pulsing rose.[62]

The wood-kernes had been described by Edmund Spenser emerging from the trees famine-stricken, on hands and knees, "like anatomies of death, they spake like ghosts crying out of their graves."[63] But, akin to the Bog Queen and to Yeats's buried men they had already found in poetry a force "analogous to the immunity system of the human body," and so, like all of them, the speaker, denied illumination but expecting aurora borealis, can lie patiently, waiting for his next moment to arrive, ensuring that there will be a life before death.

NOTES

1. G. K. Chesterton, *The Autobiography of G. K. Chesterton* (New York: Sheed and Ward, Inc., 1936), 139. I am grateful to Emily Hershman for much assistance in preparing this essay for publication.

2. Seamus Heaney, "The Poet as a Christian," *The Furrow* 29, no. 10 (1978): 604–5.

3. Ibid., 606.

4. Seamus Heaney, *Place and Displacement* (Cumbria, UK: Frank Peters, 1984), 3.

5. James Randall, "An Interview with Seamus Heaney," *Ploughshares* 5, no. 3 (1979): 20.

6. Seamus Heaney, "View," *The Listener*, Dec. 31, 1970, 102.

7. Heaney, "Poet as a Christian," 603.

8. Ibid., 604.

9. Richard Rose, *Governing Without Consensus: An Irish Perspective* (London: Faber and Faber, 1971), passim.

10. Heaney, *Place and Displacement*, 1.

11. Richard Kearney, "The IRA's Strategy of Failure," in *The Crane Bag Book of Irish Studies*, eds. Mark Patrick Hederman and Richard Kearney (Dublin: Blackwater Press, 1982), 699–707; also Richard Kearney, *Myth and Motherland* (Derry: Field Day Publications, 1984).

12. Seamus Heaney, "Prairies," in *Door into the Dark* (London: Faber and Faber, 1969), 55.

13. Seamus Heaney, *North* (London: Faber and Faber, 1975), 15.

14. On this see Elmer Andrews, *The Poetry of Seamus Heaney: All the Realms of Whisper* (London: Macmillan, 1988), 105ff.

15. Heaney, *North*, 16.

16. Seamus Heaney, "A Tale of Two Islands: Reflections on the Irish Literary Revival," in *Irish Studies 1*, ed. P. J. Drudy (Cambridge: Cambridge UP, 1980), 9.

17. Heaney, *North*, 16–17.

18. The phrase was first used of Yeats by W. H. Auden: "The Public v. the Late Mr William Butler Yeats," in *The Complete Works of W. H. Auden, Prose: Vol. II, 1939–1948*, ed. Edward Mendelson (Princeton: Princeton UP, 2002).

19. Heaney, *North*, 18.

20. Ibid., 22.

21. Ibid., 23.

22. W. B. Yeats, *Collected Poems* (London: Macmillan, 1952), 232.

23. Auden, "The Public v. the Late Mr William Butler Yeats."

24. Heaney, *North*, 69.

25. J. M. Synge, preface to *Poems*, ed. Robin Skelton (London: Oxford UP, 1962), xxxvi.

26. J. M. Synge, *Letters to Molly: John Millington Synge to Maire O'Neill, 1906–1909*, ed. Ann Saddlemyer (Cambridge, MA: Harvard UP, 1971), passim.

27. Heaney, *North*, 29.

28. Synge, preface to *Poems*, xxxvi.

29. Heaney, *North*, 29.

30. Ibid., 32.

31. Ibid.

32. Ibid.

33. Ibid., 33.

34. Ibid., 34.

35. Walter Benjamin, *One-Way Street and Other Writings*, trans. J. A. Underwood (London: Harcourt Brace, 1979), 107.

36. Geoffrey Moore, ed., *The Penguin Book of American Verse* (London: Penguin Books, 1977), 575.

37. Sean O'Casey, *Drums Under the Windows*, vol. 3 of *Autobiography* (London: Macmillan, 1972), 164.

38. W. B. Yeats, *Collected Poems*, 398.

39. For an analysis of "Punishment," see my *Inventing Ireland: The Literature of a Modern Nation* (London: Jonathan Cape, 1995), 593ff.

40. Cited in James Clifford, *The Predicament of Culture: Twentieth-Century Ethnography, Literature, and Art* (Cambridge, MA: Harvard UP, 1988), 207.

41. Gerry Fitt, lecture to College Historical Society (Trinity College, Dublin, Feb. 12, 1973).

42. John Haffenden, *Viewpoints: Poets in Conversation with John Haffenden* (London: Faber and Faber, 1981), 61.

43. Seamus Heaney, *Preoccupations: Selected Prose, 1968–1978* (London: Faber and Faber, 1984), 57.

44. Helen Vendler, *Seamus Heaney* (Cambridge, MA: Harvard UP, 1998), 45.

45. Heaney, *North*, 36.

46. Blake Morrison, "Speech and Reticence: Seamus Heaney's *North*," in *British Poetry Since 1970: A Critical Survey*, eds. Peter Jones and Michael Schmidt (Manchester, UK: Carcanet Press, 1980), 110.

47. For even harsher analyses, see Edna Longley, "*North*: 'Inner Émigré' or 'Artful Voyeur'?" in *The Art of Seamus Heaney*, ed. Tony Curtis (Dublin: Wolfhound, 1994), 78; and Ciaran Carson, review of *North*, *The Honest Ulsterman* 50 (Winter 1975): 184ff. For a more positive and convincing analysis, see Henry Hart, *Seamus Heaney: Poet of Contrary Progressions* (Syracuse, NY: Syracuse UP, 1992), 88ff.

48. Heaney, *North*, 43.

49. Heaney, *Preoccupations*, 52.

50. Heaney, *North*, 58.

51. Ibid.

52. Ibid., 59.

53. Ibid., 63–64.

54. Ibid., 65.

55. Ibid.

56. Derek Walcott, "The Muse of History" (lecture, South Bank, London, Mar. 3, 1995).

57. Derek Walcott, *The Arkansas Testament* (London: Faber and Faber, 1987), passim.

58. Ibid., 21.

59. Seamus Heaney, *The Redress of Poetry: Oxford Lectures* (London: Faber and Faber, 1995), 9–10.

60. Ibid., 82.

61. Heaney, *North*, 73.

62. Ibid., 73.

63. Cited by Heaney, *Preoccupations*, 34.

6

Writing by Night: Nuala Ní Dhomhnaill's Dream Notebooks

John Dillon

When Nuala Ní Dhomhnaill was four or five years old and having trouble sleeping, her mother would tell her to "think of a black spot" as a tactic for falling asleep.[1] Since then, and before then, Ní Dhomhnaill has been a vivid and frequent dreamer. She remembers in the 1980s even having a pen with a light on the end so that when she would wake up in the middle of the night, she could scribble down her dreams without waking her husband, Dogan Leflef. Although dreams have been an important part of Ní Dhomhnaill's creative imagination, as far as I know, none of the past or recent scholarship on her work has discussed, in detail, her dream records.

It seems, however, that poetry and dreaming go hand in hand. The Austrian philosopher Ludwig Wittgenstein, in a 1949 observation published after his death in *Culture and Value*, compares the language of dreaming with the language of aesthetics: "… if Shakespeare is great, his greatness is displayed only in the whole *corpus* of his plays, which create their *own* language and world. In other words it is completely unrealistic. (Like a dream)."[2] Relying to a large extent on Wittgenstein, this essay argues that there are striking similarities between the dream and the lyric, and that by juxtaposing dream against lyric we reach clearer understandings of how aesthetic opacity works in each. By aesthetic opacity, I mean those elements, such as images or settings or characters, in either lyric or dream, which elicit an emotional response that cannot be logically justified or explained. I first provide an overview of Ní Dhomhnaill's dream writings especially from the mid- to late 1970s, during which time she was living abroad in Turkey and starting to write poetry in a more rigorous and systematic fashion. I then press ahead to suggest that Ní Dhomhnaill writes at least some of her poems out of her dreams and that this method illuminates how opacity, and even creativity, work in the lyric. This essay, in line with the overarching thrust of this collection, highlights the capaciousness of Ní Dhomhnaill's poetic imagination and dream space and her talent to make poetry which is indebted to both tradition and innovation, to both the most local and the far reaching.

In the Burns Library at Boston College, there are thirty-three (and counting) "Writing Journals" by Ní Dhomhnaill.[3] These journals begin in May 1976 and end in June 1992. Many of these entries were written while Ní Dhomhnaill was living abroad in Turkey, and they constitute both a new and burgeoning imaginative landscape. These notebooks are invaluable to Ní Dhomhnaill's poetic process — "If I do not have paper near me I'd write on the walls."[4] The notebooks range in size and color and for the most part are made up of primarily two things — drafts of poems and dreams. Many of the entries, for instance, begin by referring to a dream: "Bhí taibhreamh uafásach agam aréir." ("I had a terrible dream last night.") / "Dreams that I have to write down." / "Bhí taibhreamh ait agam aréir ..." ("A strange dream last night ...") / "Dhá thaibhreamh aréir." ("Two dreams last night.") / "Taibhreamh." ("Dream").[5] Without exaggeration, Ní Dhomhnaill has recorded at least hundreds and, most likely, thousands of her dreams. It appears that she first writes down her dreams by hand, in Irish and/or English, and then occasionally types up these records.[6] Initially, Ní Dhomhnaill intended to bring together all of her dreams into a long poem tentatively titled after a piece of Turkish classical music, "An Bóthar go Baghdat" (The Road to Bagdad).[7] Some of these dreams are of very local places such as her family home in Nenagh, a train station in Tralee, or Newcastle West where she is looking for Michael Hartnett.[8] Other dream topologies are more pseudo-exotic à la dream adventures: the Congo, India, Saudi Arabia, Zurich, Indonesia, or the British Embassy.[9] And many of the dreams do have the feel of sensational fiction in the making: "Strange dream about a plot of a detective novel."[10] Or take for instance the start of a dream in November 1979: "The beginning of the dream is not entirely clear anymore but it has to do with these aliens from outer space who are double people and they kidnap humans and take their place and the only way you can protect yourself against them is by wearing a magnetized metal bracelet — as if they were the perpetrators of rheumatism."[11] Notice the way that the sentence bears the style of a dream. And in this case, there is a strange and poetic play between art and life — Ní Dhomhnaill remarks later that the "magnetized metal bracelet" refers indirectly to the kind of metal bracelet her father would wear as a treatment for rheumatism in his wrist.[12]

Then there are the more ostensibly personal dreams about recurrent anxieties from boarding school or Ní Dhomhnaill's fraught relationship with her mother. For instance, one dream recorded in November 1979 begins with Ní Dhomhnaill and her parents in the kitchen of a house in Nenagh. Her father is reading the paper when,

> … thosaigh Mam ag gabháilt orm nó rud éigin agus don chéad uair i mo bheathaidh labhras léi ar an tslí theastaigh uaim riamh — firm, controlled, totally straight from the hip. Bhí deacaireacht agam é seo a dhéanamh — is cuimhin liom bheith ag breith ar an ráille ós comhair an oighinn AGA is é á dhéanamh agam — ach d'éirigh liom é a dhéanamh agus ansin bhíos ana-sásta liom féin.

> (Mam started giving out to me or something and for the first time in my life I spoke to her as I always needed to — firm, controlled, totally straight from the hip. It was difficult to do and I remember leaning on the rail of the AGA oven for support while I was speaking. But I did it, and was glad I did …)[13]

Notice, as well, the detail and vividness of the dream: "I remember leaning on the rail of the AGA oven for support …" This specificity is in part what makes Ní Dhomhnaill's dreams grist for the poetic mill. Even a short dream record in May 1978 exemplifies this vividness: "Taibhreamh in an-áit i dtaobh sméara dubha is subh craobh" ("A dream in a place where there were blackberries and raspberries").[14] There is an aesthetic aspect to these early dreams which is subsequently carried over into Ní Dhomhnaill's poetry.

Notebook One begins in May 1976 and has a blue, green, and orange paisley cover. At this point Ní Dhomhnaill is married to Dogan Leflef, and they are living abroad in Ankara, Turkey. Their first child, Timucin, is nearly one year old, and their second child, Melissa, is not yet born. And in Ankara, Ní Dhomhnaill begins writing down her dreams. In this regard, Declan Kiberd was perhaps right when he noted that, "If Seferis and the Greeks lie on the shelves of Seán Ó Tuama, or the love-poets of France on the mantelpiece of Máire Mhac an tSaoi, then John Berryman lies alongside the collection of local folklore which animate the muse of Nuala Ní Dhomhnaill,"[15] for in this first notebook there are Irish-language versions of some of Berryman's dream songs, such as number 54, "No Visitors," or in Irish, "Cosc ar Chuairteoirí."[16] And tellingly, at the top corner of one of the first few pages of the second notebook, there is a note-to-self that reads "Type Berryman's Poetry."[17] As Adam Kirsch and others have observed, Berryman in 1954 begins recording and analyzing his dreams out of which he would eventually write his *Dream Songs*. In one letter, Berryman exclaims of his dreams, "38 in two months would be *228 a year!* intolerable."[18] Perhaps Berryman's *Dream Songs* is where Ní Dhomhnaill learns the art of writing by night. Regardless of the source of the method, on June 8, 1976 we find one of the first dream entries, written in English, entitled, "A Dream I had last night":

> Dogan and I were looking at the land that Hoaja was selling and behind
> it we found a valley and if we built a house there, in the plot facing
> the road our garden would have a wonderful view of the valley. And
> we went into a house there where there were 2 old women, typically
> old-fashioned Turkish, but nice old women. One of them could speak

very reasonable English and said that the first four months Ros had come to Turkey she had stayed with her. Then I don't remember any more, I think that I woke up.[19]

This dream has the feel of both dream and lyric. The specificity of the location and the familiarity of some of the people in the dream ("Ros," for instance, is Ní Dhomhnaill's neighbor and friend in Ankara) is contrasted with the "2 old women" with whom there is a feeling of recognition, but the exact affiliation is unclear. This opacity or resistance to interpretation is part and parcel of both dream and lyric. If we stretch this argument a bit, it may even be the case that this opacity constitutes and defines the lyric aesthetic. "What is intriguing about a dream," Wittgenstein remarks, "is not its *causal* connection with events in my life, etc., but rather the impression it gives of being a fragment of a story — a very *vivid* fragment to be sure — the rest of which remains obscure."[20] In the following point, Wittgenstein notes how when we describe our dreams to other people and point out the opacity of certain aspects of the dream (in this case the two old women), no explanation is satisfying. In other words, certain elements, such as images or impressions, of both dream and lyric only make sense autochthonously (i.e., in the lived context of dream or lyric). In the vein of Cleanth Brooks's *The Well Wrought Urn* or Friedrich Schlegel's understanding of aphorism, these elements resist translation and elucidation — aesthetic and dream space do not obey the same rules and conditions of more sober scrutiny.

In Notebook One, Ní Dhomhnaill recognizes this aesthetic affinity between dream and lyric. For instance, she writes in a things-to-do list: "Write fox dream into poem" or "Write dreams into novel, esp. dreams about my mother and fox dream."[21] This "fox dream" appears to be the seed for the poem "An Sionnach" ("The Fox"), which is in the last section of Ní Dhomhnaill's first collection, *An Dealg Droighin* (1981).[22] And as we read through the records, these notes-to-self persist: "Píosa scríobhnoireachta bunaithe ar thaibhreamh" ("a piece of writing based on a dream") / "Taibhreamh mar gheall ar dhán" ("a dream like a poem") / "bunaithe ar thaibhreamh" ("based on a dream").[23] It isn't long before any stable divide between a "real" poetic sphere and the dream records blurs and things like source text or target text seem irrelevant. Ní Dhomhnaill even dreams of writing and reading poetry: "Bhí dán á scríobh fhéin i mo thaibhreamh, n'fheadar an rud maith é sin, ná seans go dtiocfaidh dán mór éigin as" ("A poem was writing itself in my dream, though I don't know if that was a good thing or if there's any chance that some great poem will come out of it").[24] The remarkable aspects of these notes and observations is that Ní Dhomhnaill recognizes the affinity between a dream space and a poetic space. What is especially notable is that the creative processes between dreaming and writing blur and that there isn't a clear linearity between what comes first and what comes second. In other words, and to balance some of the observations I make toward the end of this chapter, Ní Dhomhnaill's dreams draw from her poetic work and her poetic work draws from her dreams. And it almost seems as if the final "version" of a certain poem may not be printed in Ní Dhomhnaill's collection, but that it too is re-processed into dream material. In this sense, Ní Dhomhnaill's dream-lyric process, or dream-lyric-dream process, is similar to an Irish oral tradition where the idea of a definitive and final version of a text may not exist.

For Ní Dhomhnaill there is a productive and poetic overlap between dreaming and writing that develops in the late 1970s as she begins to write poetry on a regular and habitual basis. But what does this shift from dream to poem look like at a more granular, case-by-case level? Throughout the notebooks, there are drafts of poems spliced between dream entries. I want to look at two early poems from *An Dealg Droighin*. These two poems come from a small cluster dated, "Bealtaine 1979" ("May 1979"). The first poem, "Turas Oíche" ("Night Journey"), most likely began as a dream that Ní Dhomhnaill recorded on April 3, 1979:

B'fhear mé agus Seapánach agus tomadóir, ach ní do phéarlaí ach d'éisc. Bhíodh mála fada plaisteach againn agus do shnámh na héisc isteach ann. Bhíos ag obair do chomhlucht mór agus d'úsáidíst bithe-olaithe chun an gnó seo seachas aon sort innealtóirí eile toisc gur againn ab fhearr fios na hiasc a thabharfadh praghas maith ar an mar-gadh. Ní raibh aon mhaith ins na héisc mhóra. Ansan theastaigh uaim dul abhaile ar thuras go dtí mo bhean, nó mo mháthair agus bhíos ag ullmhú i gcóir an turais. Thugas liom samplaí dena héisc a bhí á marú againn, go háirithe samplaí dena héisc sliogánacha, muiríní óga, oisrí. Chuimhníos gur mhór an trua gur cailleadh mo mháthair gan oisrí a bhlaiseadh. Thugas liom sampla amháin d'iasc beag eile — iasc beag gleoite deadhathach a d'fhéach an-chosúil le broiste agus cloch luachmhar ina lár.

(I was a man, a Japanese diver, diving not for pearls but for fish. We'd have a long plastic bag and the fish would swim inside. I was working for a big company which employed biologists and not any sort of engineers since we knew who would give the best price at the market. The big fish weren't the good ones. Then I had to go home on a trip to my wife or my mother and I was preparing for the journey. I took with me samples of the fish which we had killed, especially samples of the shellfish, scallops, and oysters. I remembered what a great pity it was that my mother had died without tasting an oyster. I also took with me one sample of a small fish, a lovely tiny two-colored fish similar to a broach with a valuable stone in it. …)[25]

And here is the subsequent poem, aptly titled "Turas Oíche":

Cuimhníonn an tomadóir Seapánach
Ag dul síos dó faoi bhun na dtonnta glasa
Gur mhór an trua cailleadh a mháthair
Gan oisrí a bhlaiseadh

Scinneann an slua éisc
Isteach ina mháilín plaisteach
Is cuardaíonn sé sliogáin
Le tabhairt abhaile,
Muiríní, sceana mara
Is iasc beag eile ar chuma bháirnigh
A bhfuil cloch luachmhar i lár a bhrollaigh.

Ní phiocann sé ach ceann amháin díobh seo
Ar mhaithe le caomhnú na dúlra.

(The Japanese diver remembers
while going beneath the grey waves
that it is a real pity that his mother died
without ever tasting oysters

The shoal darts
Into a small plastic bag
as he searches for shellfish
to bring home
scallops, razor clams
and other small fish like a limpet
with a valuable stone in its breast.

He only picks one of these
for the sake of nature.)[26]

So much hangs on the first word of the poem, "Cuimhníonn," which gestures both back toward the source-dream and also locates the lyric in a space of memory that is akin to dream in its imperfection and imprecision. There are differences, however, between the dream and the poem: The poem is obviously more distilled and pared-back than the dream, and some details and backstory are left out as unnecessary. Nevertheless, despite these minor changes, the key elements remain intact. The event which strikes us as poetic in both the dream and the subsequent poem is the experience of eating an oyster. In the dream, Ní Dhomhnaill discovers that this image or experience of eating an oyster has lyric and aesthetic value. We are reminded of Umberto Eco's *Foucault's Pendulum* and the epiphany, "When I bit into the peach I understood the Kingdom and was one with it. The rest is only cleverness."[27] So what is it about an oyster or the experience of eating an oyster that matters?

The point is that at the foundation of every lyric there is a black spot. This epistemological cul-de-sac is like the soporific black spot that Ní Dhomhnaill's mother suggested she use to help fall asleep. These are images or experiences or settings or moods or colors that are describable but not explainable. If such a thing can exist, perhaps it exists in the lyric. In "Turas Oíche," the black spot is the experience of eating an oyster — why is it that the diver should regret that his mother never tasted an oyster? And, more importantly, why is it that a description of eating an oyster also elicits regret in the reader? First, to dispense with the obvious: Despite Freud's insistence that "the very great majority of symbols in dreams are sexual symbols," as well as the fact that oysters are an aphrodisiac, a Freudian reading of oysters does not satisfactorily explain the aesthetic effect of the dream or poem.[28] Instead, if we think of our reaction to "Why?" it may also be, "*Well* — have you ever tasted an oyster?" Here we are using the phenomenon as justification for the poetic phenomenon and sticking close to Wittgenstein, who notes canonically that "explanations come to an end somewhere."[29] Dream images for Wittgenstein, unlike for Freud, are not necessarily codes to be cracked.[30] Wittgenstein and Jung are in accord on this point, contra Freud, i.e., dreams are not "invariably concealing the unacceptable," nor is there "a 'manifest content' cloaking a 'latent content.'"[31] In short, there is something about the experience of eating an oyster that is both unique and non-trivial.

What about, though, the distance and dissimilarity between dreaming and the lyric? After all, it is usually the case that when we wake up from a dream and logic kicks in, what once seemed to have great importance, now that we are awake seems completely irrelevant. Wittgenstein, however, draws our attention to an opposite case: "Words occurring in the dream can strike us as having the greatest significance. Can't we be subject to the same illusion when awake? I have the impression that *I* am sometimes liable to this nowadays. The insane often seem like this."[32] Here again is an affinity between dream and lyric. The difference between the poet and the insane is that the poet is attuned to how these opacities resonate among an audience, or, to put it another way, which motifs are transferable from dream to lyric. Unlike Septimus in Woolf's *Mrs. Dalloway*, for whom every aspect of the world has a significant significance, the poet is able to discern that eating an oyster is a very different phenomenological experience from eating a hamburger.

To take a second example, the next poem in *An Dealg Droighin* comes straight out of a dream which Ní Dhomhnaill records in June 1979:

… Ansan bhíos i dtigh éigin sa Daingean agus bhí mo leanaí ag labhairt Gaeilge, teanga nach raibh ag an tseanbhean sa teach. Ansan bhí duine éigin ag teaspáint pictiúir dom, péintéireachta a lá Velázquez de rí na Spáinne agus cé nach bhféadfainn an pictiúr go léir a fheiscint bhí a fhios agam cad a bhí ann. Bhí an rí ina shuí ag bun boird, agus bhí gíománach leis taobh an bhoird agus trádaire airgid ar iompar aige. Bhí a fhios agam go raibh litir ar an tádaire seo, cé nach bhféadfainn é a fheiscint go rí-shoileár ag an nóiméad sin. Laistigh de dhoras an tseomra gné le feiscint ag an rí, bhí fear gléasta in éadaí dubha. Ní raibh aon pheirbhic air seo seachas na beirte eile. An t-ealaíontóir féin a bhí ann, ní foláir.

(Then I was in some house in Dingle town and my children were speaking Irish, which the old woman in the house did not understand. Then there was a person showing me a picture — like a painting by Velázquez of the king of Spain and although I was not able to see the whole picture, I knew what it was. The king was seated at a table, and he had a yeoman at the side of the table holding a silver tray. I knew that there was a letter on this tray, even though I couldn't see it very clearly at that moment. Inside the door of the room there was a man all dressed in black. He was not wearing a periwig like the other two. The artist himself, no doubt.)[33]

The poem which Ní Dhomhnaill writes out of this dream is called "Aghaidh an Photadóra" ("The Face of the Potter"), and it begins by following the dream record quite closely. It begins exactly as does the dream, in Dingle with "Is mo bheirt leanbh ag labhairt Gaeilge" ("my two children speaking Irish") and "Nár thuig an tseanabhean sa tigh" ("the old woman in the house not understanding it").[34] *So far so good.* Then, however, both dream and poem move away from straightforward representation:

[t]aispeánadh pictiúr dom a dhein Velasquez
de Rí na Spáinne ag suí chun boird
is clúdach litreach á shíneadh chuige
ag searbhónta, ar thrádaire óir.

(I was shown a picture by Velázquez
of the King of Spain sitting forward at a table
and an envelope outstretched towards him
by a servant, on a gold tray.)

The painting is likely Diego Velázquez's "Las Meninas" (The Maids of Honor) which is a maze of reflection and trans-mediation, of representation and illusion. So there is a recycling between art and dream — Ní Dhomhnaill's poem is based on a dream in which she sees Velázquez's masterpiece. And in the second and third stanzas, as artistic divisions between dream, painting, and poem are crisscrossed, aesthetic opacity is introduced. In both dream and poem, the arresting aspect and uncertainty are created by a layering of representation that makes it unclear who is the artist of what. This effect is appropriately introduced in Irish with the word "Taispeánadh," which is the past autonomous form of the verb and here literally and appropriately means, "It was shown."[35]

Both poem and dream gradually move from the house in Dingle to the painting by Velázquez to an "alcove" in the bedroom of the painting which is "hidden inside the door."[36] Notice the way the mind and poem search, as if through a method of distancing and appraising, *to see* the fundamental uncertainty. The poem persists:

tá fear ard tanaí
gléasta ar fad in éadaí dubha;
níl púdar air ná peireabhaic
dála na beirte eile,
is ní foláir nó is é
an t-ealaíontóir é
ach a aghaidh a bheith casta uainn.

(there is a tall thin man
dressed entirely in black
he isn't wearing any powder or periwig
like the other two
and he must be

the artist

with his face turned away from us.)

At last we arrive at the uncertainty that is the face of the artist. This critical aspect of recognition and identification is "casta uainn" or "turned away." The poem concludes by returning to the dream records: "táim ag súil le taibhreamh eile / ina iompóidh an potadóir orm / a haghaidh" ("I am looking forward to another dream / in which the potter will show me / his face").[37]

This figure dressed in black is not limited to one dream record or poem. Nor is it limited to a single collection — Ní Dhomhnaill returns to this theme in "Mo Mháistir Dorcha" ("My Dark Master") in her collection *The Fifty Minute Mermaid* (2007). Or to take another dream from January 1978, there is a similar "fear go raibh aghaidh ban [illegible] air agus é gléasta i leathar dubh" ("man with a white face who is dressed in black leather").[38] Or just a few days later, Ní Dhomhnaill writes, "Ansan tháinig straonséar ar an bhfód, fear go raibh aghaidh chomh bán le cailc air agus é gléasta ó bhun go barr i leathar dubh" ("Then a strange person came into the field, a man with a face as white as chalk who was dressed from head to toe in black leather").[39] Similarly, this figure is also extended in Ní Dhomhnaill's most recent collection, *The Fifty Minute Mermaid*, in "Mo Mháistir Dorcha" ("My Dark Master").[40] In other words, and this is the key point, it isn't uncertainty as such which holds our attention. No one would necessarily mistake an uncertain number of beans in a jar as aesthetically arresting. Rather, specific dreams or poetic images hold our attention.[41] Again, questions such as "Why?" or "How?" certain phenomena elicit this kind of aesthetic response seem to be irrelevant and their plausible answers unsatisfying. These types of images or moods thoroughly resist translation from a lyric or dream space into more transparent and logical systems. Furthermore, the attraction and opacity that attends these images create the aesthetic space and allow the lyric room to breath in a non-logical fashion.[42]

These dream images which create the aesthetic feel in both dream and poetry are not unique occurrences but preoccupations. Another Irish-language poet, Seán Ó Ríordáin, once described the act of writing poetry as "… gnó seachas scríbhneoireacht nó ceapadóireacht, gnó a bhí níos cóngaraí do ghlanadh. Measaim go rabhas i riocht duine a bheadh ag glanadh meirge nó clúimh léith d'íomha agus ag lorg agus ag athnuachaint na bundeilbhe — ag lorg grinnealldromchla"[43] ("an unusual task — an activity which isn't writing or shaping, but is closer to cleaning. I'd say that I was like someone who was cleaning rust or mildew off of a statue, searching for and renewing the basic image — searching for bedrock").[44] The same could be said for Ní Dhomhnaill's poetic process. Among her dream note-books we find lists of dream images and motifs. Here is one, for instance, for "snow" and "frost":

The dates, of course, refer to the dream records which deal with snow and frost, both of which are hostile forces in Ní Dhomhnaill's poetic mythol-ogy. And there are similar dream record inventories for other motifs such as "trains" or "phantom/fairy lovers." Poems such as "An Traein Dubh" ("The Black Train"), "An Poll sa Staighre" ("The Crack in the Stairs"), or "Banríon an tSneachta" ("Snow Queen") depend on these dream images, which Ní Dhomhnaill has been crafting and refining by night over many years.[45] With this kind of practice, it is not surprising that Ní Dhomhnaill has suggested that she writes almost entirely by instinct.

Past and recent scholarship of Ní Dhomhnaill's poetry has recognized the creative debt she owes to both Celtic mythology and a living oral tra-dition.[46] It may be the case, however, that her method of writing poetry, which seems to be a heady cocktail of folklore, dreams, and habit, indicates that deep-rooted cultural transmission occurs at a subconscious level and out of some sort of necessity. For instance, Bo Almqvist has traced some of Ní Dhomhnaill's poems to folktales that she heard from the West Kerry storyteller Bab Feiritéar.[47] Ní Dhomhnaill has noted that when she returned to West Kerry from Turkey and recorded these source folktales from Bab Feiritéar, she would listen to the recordings as she was going to sleep. It is little surprise that these folktales from Feiritéar have made their way into poems such as "An Dealg Droighin" and "Féar Suaithinseach," as well as "Na Trí Shraoth." So far, however, I have not found the dream records between folktale and these poems. But I have looked through only a very small fraction of the dream notebooks in detail. The corpus is vast, and there is substantial work to be done in comparing Ní Dhomhnaill's published oeuvre with her dream records. One payoff of such a large-scale archival comparison may reveal not only how the poet reinvents and preserves traditions such as "An Mhaighdean Mhara" ("The Mermaid") or the "Bean an Leasa" ("The Fairywoman"), but also, and equally fascinating, how she crafts new aesthetic scaffolding and images which have the force of tradition.

Illegibility, silence, nonsense, noise, ineffability, absence — these are some of the other ways theorists of the lyric have approached concepts akin to the strange phenomenon that I have been calling lyric opacity.[48] Given that we are dealing with concepts that are difficult to articulate, the challenge of this kind of work is to find a way to be less theoretical, less abstract. A large-scale archival comparison of Ní Dhomhnaill's oeuvre and dream records may illuminate in a more concrete fashion how the aesthetic core (i.e., the image) of the lyric is made. A full-scale archival study of the immediate contexts surrounding Ní Dhomhnaill's poetry may give us a better sense of the coordinates of creativity. We may even be able to trace, in some cases, the trajectory of creativity from the National Folklore Collection to Ní Dhomhnaill's notebooks to her dream records and finally into a finished poem. In this sense, Ní Dhomhnaill is one of the few contemporary poets who has managed, like many Modernists, to blend a pre-modernist and contemporary lyric process. From Milton to Coleridge to Berryman to contemporary poets like Ní Dhomhnaill, dreaming and writing seem to be kindred activities. With Ní Dhomhnaill we have a detailed and vast record of her dreams. This archival fieldwork — like the research that led to the Parry/Lord thesis, which described how oral epic poetry is composed — may reveal the creative process beneath the lyric.

NOTES

1.   John Dillon, Interview with Nuala Ní Dhomhnaill, Aug. 7, 2014.

2.   Ludwig Wittgenstein, *Culture and Value* (Chicago: The University of Chicago Press, 1980), 83e.

3.   I am grateful to the Nuala Ní Dhomhnaill "Archives and Manuscript Department Finding Aid" by Carolyn Farnoli et al., which has made this research a great deal easier.

4.   *A Catalogue of the Manuscripts, Typescripts, and Correspondences of Nuala Ní Dhomhnaill* (Dublin: Kennys Bookshop & Art Gallery, 1994).

5.   (May 8, 1978) Box 8, Folder 1, Nuala Ní Dhomhnaill Papers, 1974–2000, (MS1997-12) John J. Burns Library, Boston College; (Mar. 7, 1978) Box 8, Folder 1; (Jan. 11, 1979) Box 8, Folder 1; (Apr. 19, 1979) Box 8, Folder 1; (Mar. 30, 1979) Box 8, Folder 1. I would like to thank all of the research support, especially Christian Dupont and Andrew Isidoro, at the Burns Library, without whom this research would not have been possible.

6.   Because of the difficulty of reading Ní Dhomhnaill's handwriting, I have, for most of this chapter, depended on the typed copies of her dream records. Also, I have partially standardized some of the non-standard spelling and variation in transcribing sections of the dream records.

7.   (No date) Box 9, Folder 3, Nuala Ní Dhomhnaill Papers.

8.   (Mar. 30, 1983) Box 8, Folder 2; (Aug. 30, 1979) Box 8, Folder 2; (Dec. 2, 1982) Box 8, Folder 2.

9.   (Sept. 13, 1979) Box 8, Folder 2; (Mar. 7, 1983) Box 8, Folder 2; (Sept. 3, 1979) Box 8, Folder 2; (Apr. 19, 1979) Box 8, Folder 1; (May 10, 1979) Box 8, Folder 1; (Mar. 7, 1978) Box 8, Folder 1.

10.   (Oct. 6, 1979) Box 8, Folder 2.

11.   (Nov. 10, 1979) Box 8, Folder 1.

12.   Dillon, Interview, Aug. 7, 2014.

13.   (Nov. 14, 1979) Box 8, Folder 1.

14.   (May 7, 1978) Box 8, Folder 1.

15.   Declan Kiberd, *The Irish Writer and the World* (Cambridge: Cambridge UP, 2005), 120.

16.   (Oct. 21, 1977), Box 20, Folder 1.

17.   (No date) Box 20, Folder 2.

18.   Adam Kirsch, *The Wounded Surgeon: Confession and Transformation in Six American Poets* (New York: W. W. Norton & Company, 2005), 122.

19.   (June or July 1976) Box 20, Folder 1.

20. Wittgenstein, *Culture and Value*, 68e.

21. (1977) Box 20, Folder 1.

22. Nuala Ní Dhomhnaill, *An Dealg Droighin* (Dublin: Cló Mercier, 1981). A type-script dated Apr. 20, 1979 begins, "An maidrín rua rua rua rua rua a eitlíonn trí lár na stoirme, a thagann mar splanc gorm trasna an tseomra chugam is gur nimh dom…" Box 8, Folder 1.

23. (Jan. 9, 1979) Box 8, Folder 1; (Apr. 11, 1981) Box 8, Folder 1; (Dec. 10, 1978) Box 8, Folder 1.

24. (Apr. 11, 1981) Box 8, Folder 1.

25. (Apr. 23, 1979) Box 8, Folder 1.

26. Ní Dhomhnaill, *An Dealg Droighin*, 52.

27. Umberto Eco, *Foucault's Pendulum* (San Diego: Harcourt Brace Jovanovich, 1989), 622. I initially encountered this quote from Richard Rorty's *Philosophy and Social Hope* (London and New York: Penguin, 1999), 132. Like Rorty in many ways, the following reading is concerned with a poetic sphere which operates at a pre- or post-logical plane.

28. Sigmund Freud, *Standard Edition of the Complete Psychological Works of Sigmund Freud*, vol. 15, trans. and ed. James Strachey (London: Hogarth Press, 1953–1974), 153. I am indebted to my friend and colleague Darragh Greene for this reference and reference 31.

29. Ludwig Wittgenstein, *Philosophical Investigations* (Chichester, West Sussex, UK: Wiley-Blackwell, 2009), 6e. This move of delimiting reference is trademark Wittgenstein, and it is the same philosophical move which Wittgenstein makes in *Remarks on Frazer's Golden Bough* (Newark: Brynmill, 1991) where Frazer's "explanations" of religious and cultural practice are rejected in the same way Wittgenstein rejects Freud's "explanations."

30. For a description of Freud's understanding of "dream work" as in part obfuscating, see Anthony Storr, *Freud* (Oxford: Oxford UP, 2001), 45.

31. Anthony Storr, *Jung* (London: Fontana, 1973/1995), 109.

32. Wittgenstein, *Culture and Value*, 65e.

33. (June 1, 1979) Box 8, Folder 2.

34. Ní Dhomhnaill, *An Dealg Droighin*, 53.

35. "duine éigin ag teaspáint pictiúr domh." (June 1, 1979) Box 8, Folder 2.

36. "I bhfolach laistigh den doras / i gcailleach shúgáin," Ní Dhomhnaill, *An Dealg Droighin*, 53.

37. Ibid.

38. (Jan. 21, 1978) Box 8, Folder 1.

39. (Jan. 15, 1978) Box 8, Folder 1; (Jan. 21, 1978) Box 8, Folder 1.

40. Nuala Ní Dhomhnaill, *The Fifty Minute Mermaid* (Loughcrew, County Meath: The Gallery Press, 1993).

41. I'm using here the perhaps slightly outdated idea of "dream images" to describe these phenomena because it provides a degree of descriptive concreteness. It is not the case that every aspect of any poem elicits an aesthetic reaction, and this discretion is important. Marjorie Perloff in *The Poetics of Indeterminacy* alternatively attends to process instead of product when she notes of a similar phenomenon in Ashbery, "Not *what* one dreams but *how* — this is Ashbery's subject" (Princeton: Princeton UP, 1981), 252.

42. We are flirting here with circularity — the argument hinges on knowing the aesthetic image when we see it and then defining the aesthetic image by having seen it. For an in-depth discussion on this point, see Terry Eagleton's *The Event of Literature* (New Haven and London: Yale UP, 2012), especially chapter 2, "What is Literature? (1)," which also begins with Wittgenstein.

43. Seán Ó Ríordáin, *Eireaball Spideoige* (Dublin: Sáirséal / Ó Marcaigh, 1952), 12.

44. Seán Ó Ríordáin, *Selected Poems*, ed. Frank Sewell (New Haven & London: Yale UP and Cló Iar-Chonnacht, 2014), 233.

45. Nuala Ní Dhomhnaill, *The Astrakhan Cloak* (Winston-Salem: Wake Forest UP, 1993), 28, 34; *The Water Horse* (Winston-Salem: Wake Forest UP, 2000), 86.

46. For recent examples see Michaela Schrage-Früh's *Emerging Identities: Myth, Nation and Gender in the Poetry of Eavan Boland, Nuala Ní Dhomhnaill and Medbh McGuckian* (Trier: WVT, 2004), or Cary A. Shay's *Of Mermaids and Others: An Introduction to the Poetry of Nuala Ní Dhomhnaill* (Bern: Peter Lang, 2014).

47. Bo Almqvist and Roibeard Ó Cathasaigh, eds. *Ó Bhéal an Bhab: Cnuas-Scéalta Bhab Feiritéar* (Indreabhán: Cló Iar-Chonnact, 2002). See also, Bo Almqvist, "Of Mermaids and Marriages: Seamus Heaney's 'Maighdean Mara' and Nuala Ní Dhomhnaill's 'An Mhaighdean Mhara' in the Light of Folk Tradition," *Béaloideas* 58 (1990): 1–74.

48. For example see Craig Dworkin's *Reading the Illegible* (Evanston: Northwestern UP, 2003) or Philippe Lacoue-Labarthe's *Poetry as Experience* (Stanford: Stanford UP, 1999).

7

Reconfigurations in Colette Bryce's Poetry

Ailbhe McDaid

Colette Bryce's early collections suggest an urge to withdraw from and transcend the bodily, cultural, and political constructs of her native city of Derry. Her latest volume, *The Whole and Rain-domed Universe* (2014), overturns this impulse to return to Northern Ireland and to childhood, albeit through the tentative strands of memory. This essay explores Bryce's tensions of appearing and disappearing in her poetry of Derry and proposes that anxieties of identity and an emergent ethic of responsibility conduct a creative tension in her work.[1] In 2011, Bryce commented on her anxieties of identity:

> I see myself as a poet of "the UK and Ireland" but very much as an Irish poet within that. It's strange. I've been away now for longer than I lived in Derry, yet when my work wasn't represented in a recent anthology of my Northern Irish peers I was surprised at how hurt I felt. It was as though I was being edited out of the story.[2]

In addition to the complex frames of belonging inherent in a Northern Irish identity, Bryce has resided outside of Derry — in Scotland, in Spain, and long-term in England — for almost all of her adult life. If, in 2011, an anthology-maker might have seen fit to exclude Bryce on the basis of physical, imaginative, or thematic non-residence of Northern Ireland, her most recent collection, *The Whole and Rain-domed Universe*, leaves little doubt about the significance of Bryce's relationship with her native city of Derry. From her first collection, *The Heel of Bernadette* (2000), however, Bryce has engaged with her home city, albeit in a poetic mode that embeds, rather than exposes, the context of the Troubles. This essay traces the ways Bryce's poetry is preoccupied with varieties of escaping and inhabiting the city and then turns to examine how the past is confronted and controlled in her latest collection.

Given her upbringing in a city riven by division, it is unsurprising that Bryce's poetry is preoccupied with the politics and prejudices of space. Bryce was born in Derry in 1970, and her childhood in a society inscribed with actual and ideological boundaries lays the contours for a nuanced poetic engagement with the various ways structures of power are transferred within these symbolic demarcations of inclusion and exclusion. In her impetus to map her personal identity within those pre-defined spaces, Colette Bryce engages poetic strategies of escape, erasure, and invisibility in poems such as "The Full Indian Rope Trick," "Form," and "Car Wash." These poems carefully balance normative political, cultural, and sexual expectations against the societal backdrop from which Bryce longs to escape and yet is charged to represent.

The interplay of public and private spheres underpins Bryce's key poetic motif of borders and boundaries to probe questions of enclosure and exclusion. These questions are located in spatial and political allusions, and they reach into cultural and sexual aspects less overtly delineated but similarly entrenched. Across her collections, Colette Bryce constructs the city of her childhood along the lines of separation that defined the streets, both physically and metaphorically, during the Troubles. An early poem from *The Heel of Bernadette* entitled "Line"[3] deals explicitly with the scored flesh of Derry's city center, "the criss-crossed heart of the city" marked by the so-called "peace lines" constructed at the interface of Republican and

Loyalist neighborhoods. Likewise, the city's ancient walls demarcate social boundaries in "Stones"[4] from *The Full Indian Rope Trick* (2005), a version of Spender's "My Parents Kept Me from Children who were Rough" that reinvents the original poem in terms of the social class prejudices of her youth.[5] Bryce's "Stones" opens with "We kept ourselves from children who were rich," placing herself as one of Spender's children "who threw words like stones." Watching the privileged children "strapped in the backs of foreign cars / whose quick electric windows rose / effortlessly," Bryce and her peers observe from the physical divisions that carve up the city:

> From walls we saw them come and go.
> War-daubed faces, feathers in our hair, wild,
> we never smiled.

As well as being marked by material and social divides, Bryce's Derry is constructed with imagery of a "twisted, stricken" cityscape warped by violence, as in "Last Night's Fires":

> The street lamp by the gutted bus
> soft-ticks, watches us from the stuck
> joint of its neck. There's windscreen
> shattered on the ground like jewels,
> diamonds, amethysts, on the school
> walk.[6]

The street-lamp watching "from the stuck joint of its neck" is like a trapped animal or a deer in the jaws of a lion, helpless and resigned. Searching for beauty in the devastation, the smashed windscreen is transformed into something precious, the poignancy of which is amplified when the setting is clarified as "the school walk."

"Last Night's Fires" forms a triptych of poems with "Device" and "1981" in *The Full Indian Rope Trick* that address, without attributing, cause and effect in the cycles of suffering during the Troubles. "1981"[7] alludes to the public/private events of the hunger strikes and traces the corrosive effect on the public psyche of the display of "[a] makeshift notice in the square / … with numbers, each day higher." While the poem shies away from explicit identification with the hunger strikers and the Nationalist community, "1981" nevertheless demands questions of power and expression, culminating in the icy observation of the final lines:

> heads are bowed, as mute as theirs,
> that will find a voice in the darker hours,
> say it with stones, say it with fire.

The question of articulation and how a section of the community can express itself when it is reduced to the mute humiliation of a "makeshift notice" leads into "Device,"[8] which challenges those standards of communication. The matter-of-factness in the way Bryce presents the construction of the "device" is characteristic of Bryce's Troubles poetry prior to *The Whole and Rain-domed Universe*, tending toward detached allusive language punctuated by graphic detail. *The Whole and Rain-domed Universe* maintains the explicit detail but occupies a personal space within the telling, opting for domestic settings rather than public squares and anonymous bombings.

"Device" elucidates Bryce's early technique, with its titular euphemism lending a delicacy that balances the bluntness of the ensuing lines. The opening statement — "Some express themselves like this" — is a neutralized acknowledgment of how certain segments of society choose to communicate, and it follows directly from the closing lines of "1981" of how to "say it with fire." The dull litany that follows is similarly drained of color:

> circuit kit; 4 double-A batteries, 1 9-volt,
> 1 SPDT mini-relay, 1 M-80
> rocket engine, a solar ignitor,
> a pair of contacts, 1 connector […]

While the Irish literary tradition is familiar with poets and playwrights incanting a litany of place-names to invoke their native locations, Bryce's subversive recitation twists the *dinnseanchas* tradition to a darker purpose. The paraphernalia of a car bomb is reeled off with the ease and familiarity of a prayer, but these utterances, while bland on their own, compile a sinister mass. The precision of the recitation reflects the process of assembling the device: "wired, / coiled and crafted together, care / taken over positives and negatives." A suggestion of responsibility and consequence is brought up by the reference to "positives and negatives" but these remain, finally, issues of electrical rather than moral imperative.

The representation of the device as a gift over which its creator has toiled implies the extent to which this society is monstrously misshapen. In this place, the act of destruction becomes a gesture of creativity in which devastation bequeaths immortality. The gentleness of the closing stanza enshrines the disjunction between the depicted act and its inevitable effect:

> Dawn or before, the artist's hour,
> it is placed, delicately as a gift,
> under a car in a street that will flare
> to a gallery in the memory,
> cordoned off and spotlit for eternity.

There is no hint of violence here; only the word "flare" suggests an explosion, while the reference to "under a car in a street" is subtly constructed as the installation of an artwork. The destruction it will cause is alluded to only in its impact on the collective memory where it will be "spotlit for eternity." That destruction is made explicit in "Last Night's Fires," which completes Bryce's triptych of violence and suffering.

This boundary between destruction and creation is also courted in the poem "Form"[9] which similarly considers an unconventional act of creativity. Ostensibly about hunger artistry, the poem flows with undercurrents of gender, politics, and art that surface during the narrative. The imprint of growing up during politically fraught times is perceptible here in the unspoken allusion to the Long Kesh hunger strikes, already addressed in "1981." In "Form," those events remain as a presence outside of the poem but cast their shadow across the work: a method of addressing a trauma without ever mentioning it. Bryce inhabits the persona of a hunger artist and conveys the act of self-starvation as a creative act, as valuable (or pointless) as any other artistic gesture. The purpose is pure — "because it is something to do / and I do it well." The undertaking is religious, like a "vocation," and an enabling experience — "the hunger isn't a sacrifice / but a tool."

The sense of liberation through self-denial parallels with the creative/ destructive binary that troubles much of Bryce's work and also speaks to the need "to find a voice in the darker hours." Whether through "stones" and "fire," a "device" or "hunger," the search for a mode of expression is a theme Bryce explores with empathy but also with detachment. It is difficult to place the poet herself in these poems and harder still to perceive her position around these Troubles poems, which might indeed be a deliberate strategy.

> I'm writing this as my only witness
> has been the glass on the wall.
> Someone must know what I've done
> and there's no one to tell.

The urge to share is curiously depersonalized by this disassociation from the reader who becomes incidental to the performative act. The use of the first-person in "Form" contrives a certain intimacy that is contradicted in this stanza by the speaker's justification for the poem's existence. In constructing an isolated, incarcerated space, Bryce approximates a prison of sorts, and her reference to the wall suggests an image of a prisoner scratching out his/her final words. The prison wall also calls up the so-called "dirty" protests that preceded the hunger strikes, reinforcing the unstated external framework of "Form." Within the poem, form itself is the binding goal of the hunger artist's act as she revels in the steady revelation of smooth lines and contours on the body.

> Or would lie, supine, stomach shrinking,
> contracting, perfecting its concave line.

> Each day gave a little more: depth to the shallows
> of the temples, definition to the cheek,
> contrast to the clavicle, the ankle bone, the rib,
> the raised X-ray perception of my feet.

Hard consonant sounds, deliberate assonance, and strong internal rhymes ("supine"/"line"; "shrinking"/"contracting"/"perfecting"; "temples"/"clavicles"/"ankle"; "raised"/"ray") reiterate the poem's thematic emphasis on the body shedding flesh. This careful poetic reconstruction builds another dimension to the poem's title, "Form," which is also an analysis of the private/public act of creativity and exposure. In private, the artwork is molded and made to "conform to my critical eye," but once out on the street, the speaker (and by extension the artwork) is exposed to "a latent contamination of eyes / from windows and cars."

In her delineation of threatening and safe spaces, Bryce recognizes the codes of behavior dictated through inherited structures. By reinventing spatial configuration within her poetry, space itself is turned into a tool to acknowledge and question those very boundaries. Migration is a version of disappearance that challenges the societal expectations laid out in public space, while memory works as a form of reappearance in the way it revisits and reconstructs the past and the self. Bryce's poetry enacts a sharp tension between an imagistic desire to disappear and narratological and thematic urges to reappear in poems set in childhood and in Northern Ireland. "Form" is a poem about artistry and politics but it is also a poem of self-erasure; likewise "Car Wash" and "The Full Indian Rope Trick" conspire toward vanished and concealed selves. Contrastingly, "The Search" and "The Analyst's Couch" from *The Whole and Rain-domed Universe* reach for restitutions that remain, like damaged memory, marginally beyond grasp, and the potential of the poem as a mode of retrieval is complicated by the instabilities and conflicts of memory.

The individual in the title poem of *The Full Indian Rope Trick* reaches for liberation into the infinite space of "thin air" enabled by the sleight of hand of the magic trick. The trick itself sees a *fakir*, or Hindu ascetic, toss a coiled rope into the sky where it remains, levitating, while his assistant (a young boy) ascends it. Some accounts have the boy disappear into the sky and reappear on the ground; others claim the *fakir* climbs after the boy, slashing at the sky with a knife until the boy's bloodied limbs fall to the ground. Bryce's poem is purposefully located in the delineated space of Guildhall Square, a setting that foregrounds the desire to transcend the constructed parameters of societal behavior. The location also lends a political angle to the poem, particularly given the historically-charged setting of Guildhall Square which was, of course, the destination for the Civil Rights march on Bloody Sunday 1972. Within the poem, the paraphernalia of the rope and the square hint at public hangings; contrastingly, the protagonist's feat in "The Full Indian Rope Trick"[10] is entirely voluntary and self-motivated. The speaker makes careful avowals of independence from the outset — "[t]here was no secret / murmured down through a long line / of elect" — and any hint of assistance ("no dark fakir, no flutter / of notes from a pipe") is dismissed. The communal space of the square is emphasized by the detail: "walls" to delineate (and enclose) the area, "bells" to call attention, and "passers-by" to observe. Even the time of day suggests a "high noon"–style confrontation. The scene set by Bryce conjures an arena, primed for public performance:

> Guildhall Square, noon,
> in front of everyone.
> There were walls, bells, passers-by;
> then a rope, thrown, caught by the sky
> and me, young, up and away,
> goodbye.

The gentle lilt to the rhyming of "by," "sky," "away," and "goodbye" allows the act to take place with ease within the poem, and that rhyme continues into the next stanza: "Goodbye, goodbye. / Thin air. First try. / A crowd hushed, squinting eyes." The speaker's marginality is encoded in her performance that is, essentially, an attempt to refute the dominant parameters of social behavior.

In Bryce's version of her "one-off trick," there is, however, no possibility of return, no miraculous reappearance. The act of disappearing is irreversible, a "one-off trick / unique, unequalled since." There is "no proof, no footage of it" nor, implicitly, of the woman herself — erasure is the realization of the trick's ambition. Having disappeared, the difficulties of reappearance are immediately made clear in the final lines of the poem. Striving if not to undo the performance, then to at least reassert the self, the speaker reaches from her place above the rope to try to reconnect with the public she left below. She asks, "what would I tell them / given the chance?" constructing the permanence of the trick's consequence through the absence implied by the phrase "given the chance." Even the self-evidence of the poem does not suffice as a statement of existence as the speaker is still at pains to state her presence:

It was painful; it took years.
I'm my own witness,
guardian of the fact
that I'm still here.

The poem speaks to the transition from childhood to adulthood, from co- to independence, to coming out or distinguishing oneself from the mass, and to emigration as a means of escape.

The process of dissolving and realizing the self is "painful" but is a necessary act of self-determination that allows the speaker to declare in that final sentence "I'm still here." Bryce invests in the poem as the only "proof" that the trick happened, and in this way, the poem is also an analogy of artistic purpose and value — to capture events for which there remains "no proof, no footage" and to speak for those who have vanished or been erased from the public narrative formed within the walls of a city square. "Hide-and-Seek" from *The Whole and Rain-domed Universe* picks up the theme of disappearance as it appears to caution against "hiding" too well, particularly in migration: "Watch out, / if you're too clever you might not ever / be found. England, say. Or adult life."[11] Along with her expressed anxieties about her anthological presence, the personal dimension of hiding in migration is exposed in the way Bryce's poetry finds its way back to Northern Ireland in her most recent collection.

Disappearing through migration means having to continually reappear on return; furthermore, it requires renegotiation of the terms of public space. "Car Wash"[12] from *The Full Indian Rope Trick* centers conflicted structures of identity in the innocuous setting of the forecourt of a petrol station. Like Elizabeth Bishop's "Filling Station" and Martina Evans's *Petrol*, the garage is a shared space of social regulation, itself a microcosm of society that conceals hidden private lives. Ed Madden suggests that in "queer narratives [...], home must be negotiated as a site of estrangement and nostalgia, complex (dis)affiliations and (dis)identifications, especially since 'home' (domestic space or place of origin) is linked to heterosexuality."[13] "Car Wash" opens with an assertion of the dominant heterosexual structures of the immediate and social context: "This business of driving / reminds us of our fathers" the poem declares, evoking particular familial and patriarchal structures, and the speaker and her partner, in returning to Northern Ireland, find themselves "two / women in our thirties, / [in] this strange pass, / a car wash in Belfast." The "strange pass" of the petrol station becomes a kind of portal through which Bryce realizes an alternate space in which her reappearance and her sexuality are accommodated.

The sub-space of the car in the carwash exists both within and beyond the visible public sphere where all acts are scrutinized and, once the machine begins, the car itself becomes a private, enclosed space, a heterotopia, which cannot be observed or invaded.

> [...] and find ourselves
> delighted by a wholly
> unexpected privacy
> of soap suds pouring, no,
> cascading in velvety waves.

The heterotopic space, realized here within the car going through the carwash is, according to Foucault's construction, a "counter-site."[14] Highly localized, it is a space of marginality and alterity that is simultaneously improvised and actual. The counter-site occupies a physical presence as well as a space of imaginative disruption; it is "a kind of effectively enacted utopia in which the real sites, all the other real sites that can be found within the culture, are simultaneously represented, contested, and inverted."[15] Society's norms are reinforced by the association of "driving" with "fathers" but in this heterotopia, that expectation is challenged and overturned through the female drivers. Requirements are observed (they "have minded / the instructions to wind up / our windows and sit / tight") but in obeying the rules, the heterotopia is fully realized in "a wholly unexpected privacy."

The erotic tincture of the "soap suds pouring, no, / cascading in velvety waves" brings the poem to its inevitable climax, a private act snatched in a normally public space. The crucial sentence begins as a plea to the reader but soon turns its question into a statement. The initial appeal to a shared sense of human connection is retracted as the narrator remembers her own outsiderness, even within this temporarily safe zone. Bryce's deft phrasing carries the weight of the image's allusions lightly:

> what can we do
> but engage in a kiss
> in a world where to do so
> can still stop the traffic.

The construction and collision of gendered sites in "Car Wash" is another manipulation of space by Bryce. The domain of the car and the act of driving is recalled as masculine — "this business of driving / reminds us of our fathers" — and the aural, visual and olfactory detail of the "low purr of fifth gear, / the sharp fumes, the biscuity / interior" reinforces the embedded, almost subconscious association of the car with a male figure of power. The repossession by these "two women in our thirties" of patriarchal control through the occupation of the car is, thus, an act of rebellion against that gendered discourse. Within the space created by "spinning blue brushes / of implausible dimensions," a creation myth of violence that belies the calm affection of the kiss, the heteronormative expectations of society are dissolved. Emerging from the car wash, those expectations are restored as the machine dictates how the car is presented and when it can progress.

> we are polished and finished
> and (following instructions)
> start the ignition (which
> reminds us of our fathers)
> and get into gear
> and we're off
> at the green light.

In "Car Wash," enclosure within the heterotopic space is a liberating experience that enables the motorists but it is a temporary, concealed space that is dissolved upon re-exposure to society, insinuated by the reminder "of our fathers." Bryce's sexuality problematizes her identity formation in the strictly heteronormative society of her youth, as depicted in "The Full Indian Rope Trick," and indeed, of the present. "A Clan Gathering"[16] from *The Whole and Rain-domed Universe* insists on its contemporaneity in its subtitle "*Dublin, 2009*" and analogizes familial and societal attitudes toward the speaker's lifestyle:

> I don't mention my lover
> how we have to invent
> for ourselves a blank, unscripted
> future; her guaranteed absence
> from the diagram, the great
> genetic military campaign,
> and no one asks,
> sensing a difference.

The poet's relationship is excluded from "the family chart," an "excitable flow of births, / deaths, accidents, marriages," by virtue of its homosexuality. The doubly othered conditions of her relationship — as a migrant and as a lesbian — maintain her exclusion from the conventional family structures inscribed through the family tree. In "*Cé Leis Tú?* Queering Irish Migrant Literature," Tina O'Toole considers the ways LGBT diasporic identities trouble established migrant narratives, arguing that "queer kinship and migrant affinities unsettle the fixities of family and place in Irish culture."[17] In seeking alternate spaces in her poetry, Bryce pursues and, through migration, finds a mode of realizing and representing the self.

This dialogue of personal representation is carried out alongside analogies of political responsibilities. The sectarianism and violence of her youth are mostly adverted to through detached imagistic and formal references in her early work; her fourth collection, contrastingly, is an explicit engagement with personal and community experiences of the Troubles, as well as addressing public events including the murder of Jean

McConville. *The Whole and Rain-domed Universe* demonstrates a sense of ethical responsibility toward the past that Bryce's poetry carries in personal lyrics. Bryce makes the past reappear by remembering personal and familial events in poems with provocative titles, including the colloquial "Don't speak to the Brits, just pretend they don't exist," "The Republicans," and the ekphrastic "Positions Prior to the Arrival of the Military." The motif of disappearance and reappearance, established in *The Full Indian Rope Trick*, is sustained in *The Whole and Rain-domed Universe* and directly presented in the confronting poem "The Search."[18] Subtitled *"i.m. Jean McConville,"* "The Search" extends Bryce's key trope of presence/absence to address the historical truth of "the disappeared" during the Troubles. The eponymous "search" pictures a crowd of children scouring the sand for the lost wedding ring of a family member, and it is only in the dedication that the poem's underlying subject is articulated. The language of erasure and irretrievability as well as the familiar imagery of failed digs definitively locates "The Search" in its historical context as Bryce's poem allusively speaks of the hidden past:

> Close to the dunes,
> we sifted, dug. One
> patch of sand soon merged
> with another. Not a land
> mark, not a post or rock,
> the script of the beach
> erased by the weather.
> Our shadows loomed
> on the lit strand,
> conducting their own
> investigation.

The recovery of McConville's body on Shelling Hill Beach in 2003 finds its way into the poem in the quiet dignity of the final stanza's opening lines: "Thirty years. / The coolness of that sand; / just coarse enough / to hold itself together / in the wind." In trying to recover the past, memory is as fragile and as insistent as the "cloudy gems / of greenish glass" turned up by the children, and the poem itself is a tentative gesture toward salvaging the fragments.

Despite Bryce's concern about being excluded from the story of Northern Irish poetry, *The Whole and Rain-domed Universe* leaves no doubt about her personal and poetic lineage. Her assertive reappearance as a Northern Irish poet is an effort to exorcise the erasures of migration, and she expressly rewrites herself into Northern Irish poetry by constructing a dialogue with Louis MacNeice. Similar to how fellow Northern Irish poet Sinéad Morrissey's "In Belfast" converses with MacNeice's "Valediction," Bryce's "Derry"[19] reworks MacNeice's "Carrickfergus" into a coming-of-age poem during the Troubles.[20]

> I was born between the Creggan and the Bogside
> to the sounds of crowds and smashing glass
> by the river Foyle with its suicides and riptides.
> I thought that city was nothing less
>
> than the whole and rain-domed universe.
> A teacher's daughter, I was one of nine
> faces afloat in the looking-glass
> fixed in the hall, but which was mine?

Like her earlier evocation of Spender's "My Parents Kept Me from Children who were Rough," Bryce's "Derry" conjures a childhood marked by the "ancient walls with their huge graffiti, / arms that encircled the city" in an unrelenting embrace. While MacNeice's poem also recollects military presence, the calm distance of the "dummies hanging from gibbets for bayonet practice"[21] is transformed into the reality of "another explosion, / windows buckling in their frames"[22] in Bryce's unstinting representation of the Troubles in "Derry."

The poems' return to childhood and, by implication, to its traumatic events, carry an emotional intensity in the way they square up to the past. The visceral brutality of the Troubles is seen through a child's eyes, as depicted in "The Analyst's Couch."[23] The Troubles are made to reappear, although the speaker's admittedly borrowed memories complicate the veracity of her narrative: "I was not there when the soldier was shot, so I didn't see him / carried up the street," the opening sentence announces, yet the poem continues with detailed recollection of his suffering.

> Blood, seeping into the cushions, dark brown stuff
> like HP sauce, soaking thoroughly into the foam, the worn
> upholstery of the enemy.

The fabric of memory, like the material of the couch, is stained by events absorbed through cultural and collective experiences as well as through individual observation. The interjection — "Am I making this up? Its animalness" — doubts the memory, but the repetition of bestial imagery that characterizes Bryce's depiction of victims of the Trouble asserts its validity, if not necessarily its truth, through its association.

In returning her poetry to Derry, Bryce configures memory as flawed and subjective; similar to the map in "North to the South," it is "like a kite, a barely controllable thing / to be wrestled."[24] This negotiation for control over difficult subject matter is enacted through distancing techniques, such as the way Bryce relinquishes jurisdiction of perspective in "Helicopters," leaving the reader to decide, or as in "The Analyst's Couch," which doubly removes the narrative through memory, hearsay, and repetition. In "Re-entering the Egg,"[25] memory takes on spatial configurations in a grotesque version of a Fabergé egg that, once opened, reveals overwhelming detail.

> A tiny family fills the rooms.
> [...]
> In one, first floor, a spangled girl
> enters in her diary: *I am headed for a fall.*
> In one, girl-twins, conjoined
> at the skull, freak themselves
> to a pitch of shrieks.

Bryce acknowledges Anne Sexton's influence on this poem in the appended notes, which recognize the intertextuality of many of her poems. The opening lines rephrase the initial sentences of Sexton's "The House," taking

Sexton's third line — "Like some gigantic German toy, / the house has been rebuilt / upon its kelly-green lawn" — and recasting it in a more recognizable location.[26] Bryce's version reinvents the detail but retains the image: "Like some magnificent Swiss clock, the house has been rebuilt / in the same position, in that Georgian street." This notion of reconstruction locates the poem in Derry during the Troubles but it also signals the artificial memory-space to which "Re-entering the Egg" alludes.

Reflecting on how her "recent poems seem to want to examine that place, and time, more closely," Bryce recognizes the house as a site of symbolic consciousness and of childhood.[27] "Re-entering the Egg" pauses to scrutinize this family home that is bizarre, and yet entirely domestic; the ordinary paraphernalia of an Irish Catholic home is made *unheimlich*:

> and turfs collapse in the grate
> beneath the glowing coal
> in the ruptured chest
> of the Sacred Heart.

The poem's final lines recoil from the intensities of memory, and demand that "the egg" of the past be set aside: "Close it up. That's enough for now."

Approaching the past through frames that contain and can be set aside, Bryce engages precautionary modes — such as the Fabergé egg or the snow globe of "The theatrical death of my maternal grandmother as revealed in a 1960s glitter globe" of *The Whole and Rain-domed Universe* — and distancing devices, including the hunger artistry of "Form" and the sleight of hand in the eponymous poem of *The Full Indian Rope Trick*. She places memory in carefully configured spaces over which the poet and narrator maintains strict control; like Adrienne Rich's use of formalism as a pair of "asbestos gloves," Bryce's strategies of detachment similarly enable her to "handle materials [she] couldn't pick up barehanded."[28] The bank of memories encased in her grandmother's glitter globe draw Bryce's poetry back to childhood and the Troubles, but there is a furtive, cautious quality found in the constructed distance of her formal approach. "I give it a shake and look again," the narrator announces in "The theatrical death of my maternal grandmother [...]", a snatched glimpse of the many agitations of memory and space that make up Bryce's poetry of Derry.

NOTES

1. Colette Bryce, *The Heel of Bernadette* (London: Picador, 2000); *The Full Indian Rope Trick* (London: Picador, 2005); *Self-Portrait in the Dark* (London: Picador, 2008); *The Whole and Rain-domed Universe* (London: Picador, 2014).

2. Rosita Boland, "What Daffodils Were to Wordsworth, Drains and Backstreet Pubs Are to Me," *The Irish Times*, Mar. 12, 2011. The anthology to which Bryce refers is presumably Chris Agee's 2008 anthology *The New North: Contemporary Poetry from Northern Ireland* (Winston-Salem, NC: Wake Forest UP, 2008; London: Salt Publishing, 2011), which includes four women poets born after 1955: Jean Bleakney, Moyra Donaldson, Leontia Flynn, and Sinéad Morrissey. For more on the fate of women poets in Northern Irish anthologies, see Alex Pryce, "Ambiguous Silences? Women in Anthologies of Contemporary Northern Irish Poetry," *Peer English* 9, *Time and Space In Contemporary Women's Writing* (2014): 57–73.

3. Bryce, *The Heel of Bernadette*, 11.

4. Bryce, *The Full Indian Rope Trick*, 3.

5. Stephen Spender, *New Collected Poems* (London: Faber and Faber, 2004), 110.

6. Bryce, *The Full Indian Rope Trick*, 13.

7. Ibid., 11.

8. Ibid., 12.

9. Bryce, *The Heel of Bernadette*, 17–18.

10. Bryce, *The Full Indian Rope Trick*, 17–18.

11. Bryce, *The Whole and Rain-domed Universe*, 8.

12. Bryce, *The Full Indian Rope Trick*, 6–7.

13. Ed Madden, "Queering the Irish Diaspora: David Rees and Padraig Rooney," *Éire-Ireland* 47, nos. 1 & 2 (Earrach/Samhradh [Spring/Summer] 2012): 177.

14. Michel Foucault, "Of Other Spaces: Utopias and Heterotopias," *Architecture/Mouvement/Continuité* (Oct. 1984): 20.

15. Ibid.

16. Bryce, *The Whole and Rain-domed Universe*, 29–31.

17. Tina O'Toole, *"Cé Leis Tú?* Queering Irish Migrant Literature," *Irish University Review* 43, no. 1 (2013): 132.

18. Bryce, *The Whole and Rain-domed Universe,* 19–20.

19. Ibid., 2–5.

20. Sinéad Morrissey, *Between Here and There* (Manchester: Carcanet Press, 2002); *Louis MacNeice, Collected Poems* (London: Faber and Faber, 2007; Winston-Salem, NC: Wake Forest UP, 2013).

21. MacNeice, *Collected Poems,* 55.

22. Bryce, *The Whole and Rain-domed Universe,* 5.

23. Ibid., 15.

24. Ibid., 17.

25. Ibid., 6–7.

26. Anne Sexton, *The Complete Poems* (Boston: Houghton Mifflin, 1981), 72.

27. Colette Bryce, "Omphalos," *The Poetry Review* 103, no. 3 (Autumn 2013), accessed online Aug. 15, 2016, http://poetrysociety.org.uk.gridhosted.co.uk/wp-content/uploads/2014/12/1033-Bryce.pdf.

28. Rich, Adrienne, "When We Dead Awaken: Writing as Re-Vision," *College English* 34, no. 1 (1972): 22. I am grateful to Bríona Nic Dhiarmada for this observation.

8

Contemporary Irish-Language Poetry: After *Innti*

Brian Ó Conchubhair

The late 1960s heralded not only political and social turbulence but also witnessed a generation coming to adulthood. A new vitality marked these decades, a will to change dominant belief systems and challenge the perceived sages. Across the globe, young people openly and publically defied existing power structures. This cohort, driven by an optimistic idealism, no longer accepted the status quo and actively sought to overthrow established patterns, social formulas, and civic configurations. They expressed themselves and their values by living in communes, sharing resources, listening to psychedelic music, growing their own foods, and behaving in socially permissive fashions. This counterculture, which was spawned in the 1960s and flourished in the 1970s, was "local, homemade, entrepreneurial the alternative to mainstream.... It was a very artisan approach to making food and clothes and new tastes and attitudes ... the beginning of gender fluidity, open-air festivals, yoga and meditation."[1] The freedom offered by a psychedelic drug culture — whether LSD, cannabis, peyote, or magic mushrooms — offered a stark contrast to the bland conformity of the postwar years of the 1950s in the United States, Canada, France, and Britain, as well as Ireland. Many of the divisive issues that now dominate contemporary public discourse — environmentalism, globalization, individualism, and mass communication — originated as social concerns in the 1960s. That Bob Dylan, the unofficial spokesperson for the 1960s counterculture movement who articulated and publicized injustices within American society, received the 2016 Nobel Prize for literature demonstrates how mainstream that counter-revolution became. And many of the gray old men who now govern twenty-first-century Irish politics were then dashing student radicals: bitchin', twitchin', and leading protests on Irish university campuses.

In the 1960s, Ireland pulsed with a new energy, fresh optimism, and a hunger for liberation that would initiate the culture wars of the 1970s and 1980s. These years of relative affluence witnessed a marked decline in emigration and a recurrence of violence in Northern Ireland. In sculpture, modern expressionism with its minimalist, almost skeletal, approach conveyed empathy for the subject that reflected both egalitarianism and a new sense of confidence. In music, Seán Ó Riada's innovative fusion of classical and traditional brought vernacular music out of pubs and private dwellings, putting it centerstage in theatres and hotels. Groups like Ceoltóirí Chualann and later the Bothy Band, Planxty, and the Chieftains, transformed the nature, arrangement, and performance of the traditional. Within Irish-language discourse, the 1960s counterculture empowered the rising generation of Irish-speakers to organize and coalesce around the popular protest organization Gluaiseacht Cearta Sibhialta na Gaeltachta to demand equal rights for those living in Irish-speaking districts. In literary terms, the counterculture was instrumental and integral to the emergence of *Innti*.[2] Poets Ciaran Carson and Gabriel Rosenstock suggested that the arc of Irish-language poetry veered dramatically in the 1960s:

> Irish-language poetry, especially in the post-Jacobite era, has been more concerned with geography than history. Certainly some of the defining movements in European thought and art, whether the Enlightenment,

the Reformation, the Industrial Revolution, Impressionism, Expressionism, Psychology, Orientalism, Existentialism, Dadaism, Surrealism,
Feminism — few such influences colored the consciousness of the
gael, and then in the 1960s everything seemed to arrive together like a
colourfully wrapped parcel waiting to be opened.[3]

Innti's emergence marked that critical moment in twentieth-century Irish-language poetry. Yet to describe it as marking the introduction
of modernist and modern concerns is more than unfair to Máire Mhac
an tSaoi, Máirtín Ó Direáin, Seán Ó Ríordáin, Brendan Behan, Caitlín
Maude, and Eoghan Ó Tuairisc — "whose *Aifreann na Marbh* (1964) stands
with Kavanagh's *The Great Hunger* (1942) as one of the more remarkable
achievements of Irish-poetry at mid-century"[4] — amongst others. Equally
inaccurate are descriptions that present it solely as focusing on "sex, drugs,
and rock n' roll." *Innti*, a literary magazine that began life as a broadside
(one large page printed on one side only), was first published in March 1970
by a group of undergraduates attending University College Cork. The core
poets — Michael Davitt (1950–2005), Nuala Ní Dhomhnaill (1952–), Gabriel
Rosenstock (1949–), and Liam Ó Muirthile (1950–) — were students of Seán
Ó Tuama (1926–2006), Chair of Modern Irish at UCC and an accomplished
critic, poet, and dramatist.[5] The fifth member of the famous five is Cathal
Ó Searcaigh, an undergraduate at the nearby National Institute for Higher
Education, Limerick (later the University of Limerick), who attended Ó
Tuama's writing workshops. Not only did the annual poetry journal that
sprang from the initial broadsheet become a prestigious journal for poetry,
essays, interviews, and artwork, but it also provided a critical vehicle for
the young cohort of poets, offering them a platform and an identity. It both
raised the profile of Irish-language poetry and branded it. Such was the
power of the Innti brand that now, some forty-five years after the first *Innti*
appeared, it marks the great divide: a watershed moment clearly dividing
all that went before from the present.

    Ó Tuama and de Paor's 1991 *Coiscéim na hAoise Seo* — a landmark
anthology encompassing the period 1900–1990 and containing seventeen
poets — didn't merely announce a new elite in Irish-language poetry. It was a
public coronation of the Innti group.[6] Controversially, the volume not only

omitted Rosenstock, one of the core five, but also placed Ní Dhomhnaill on par with Seán Ó Ríordáin, the doyen of Irish-language poets and arguably the most important modernist poet to emerge in twentieth-century Ireland.[7] Subsequent anthologies have largely reinforced the hierarchy established by *Coiscéim na hAoise*.[8] Minor discrepancies aside, Ní Dhomhnaill,[9] Ó Searcaigh,[10] Davitt,[11] and Ó Muirthile[12] are entrenched as the major Irish-language poets at the start of the twenty-first century, within and beyond the Irish-language canon. Of the four, Ní Dhomhnaill and Ó Searcaigh have the broadest appeal and strongest international reputations: their work is more widely translated and anthologized in translation. In tandem with their intrinsic merits, their poems lent themselves to the theoretical bent that swept Irish Studies in the 1980s and 1990s when decentering the center and writing back from the margins dominated literary and cultural discussions in academia. Both poets' works were successfully co-opted and quarried with great profit and insight for gender studies, feminism, gay rights, psychoanalysis, postcolonialism, and translation studies.

The core Innti poets, other than Davitt who died suddenly on June 19, 2005, are still alive. Yet Ó Searcaigh is much less in the public or critical eye since *Fairytale of Kathmandu*, a 2007 television documentary which alleged the sexual abuse of underage boys in Nepal. Never charged and never convicted, a presumption of guilt has nevertheless rendered his subsequent volumes almost invisible to institutional review and scholarly criticism.[13] He rarely receives invitations to read outside Ireland. Nuala Ní Dhomhnaill's most recent volume in Irish appeared in 1999. In terms of translated work, her collaboration with Medbh McGuckian and Eiléan Ní Chuilleanáin resulted in *The Water Horse* in 2000, and 2007 witnessed her latest collaboration with Paul Muldoon, *The Fifty Minute Mermaid*. Gabriel Rosenstock, described as "one of the world's foremost writers and translators of the haiku,"[14] has maintained his prodigious output in the twenty-first century with multiple volumes, including *Syójó* (2001), *Eachtraí Krishnamurphy* (2003), *Forgotten Whispers / Cogair dhearúdta* (2003), *Krishnamurphy Ambaist* (2004), *Hymn to the Earth* (2004), *Rogha Dánta / Selected Poems* (2005), *Bliain an Bhandé / Year of the Goddess* (2007), *Margadh na Míol in Valparaíso / The Flea Market in Valparaíso: new and selected poems* (2014), *Cuach ó Aois Eile ag Glaoch* (2014), and *Sasquatch* (2014).[15] His translations of Bob Dylan's songs received rare praise in Maria Johnson's otherwise sobering critique of Irish poetry in 2000–2009 as published in *Poetry Ireland Review*.[16] Ironically, in light of Máirtín Ó Cadhain's infamous condemnation that Irish-language poets published too little and even then, too many "liricí beaga deasa" ("pretty little lyrics"), Rosenstock stands open to accusations of publishing too well rather than wisely. Such is his productivity that few critics can engage with his work before the next volume appears. Of the original Innti members, Liam Ó Muirthile has, perhaps, best stayed the course. The greatest stylist of his generation, his collected poems in translation, *An Fuíoll Feá — Rogha Dánta/Wood Cuttings — New and Selected Poems*, only appeared in 2013. Critic Clíona Ní Ríordáin described it as a "volume of great scope and beauty.... It allows the reader to grasp the varied palette and multiple preoccupations of the poet...."[17] His output continues to be considerable, including novels, plays, and poetry.[18] Arguably the least well-known Irish-language poet in the Anglo-American world, Ó Muirthile writes sensitive and technical accomplished verse that draws on his French and Irish experiences. "In many ways," Bernard O'Donoghue contends, "Ó Muirthile carries forward the lyric tradition of Ó Ríordáin more faithfully than his fellow-members of the group."[19] Time may well lead to a reconsideration of his place in the Innti hierarchy.

Opinion is divided on whether the Innti cohort constitutes a poetic school or a collection of individual poets with differing styles, themes, techniques, and concerns. Theo Dorgan writes that "the INNTI poets were essentially unruly and individual as much as they were ever a school. Their education helped shape but does not explain them."[20] What links them is less their similarities and more their common rejection of existing poetics:

> Formally and thematically, they were ripping through received forms and received wisdom in unprecedented ways; perhaps only Paul Durcan, at that time, was doing in English what these poets were doing in Irish. This cleavage with the past, especially with the immediate past, was so shocking that, in effect, the shock anaesthetised itself. They were out and through into a new, unexpected re-appropriation of the past almost before they, themselves, realised what was going on.[21]

Ó Dúill, an accomplished poet and critic,[22] argues that the majority of poems and poetry produced by the Ó Tuama-inspired undergraduates share certain qualities and traits and contends that Ní Dhomhnaill, Rosenstock, and Ó Searcaigh "share an explicit sensuality, a degree of mysticism; their best work is exciting, lambent, liberating, achieves real liberties … Sound is, if not quite all, nearly all."[23] This focus on sound repeats in Ní Dhomhnaill's 1993 statement that "in English we write for the interior eye, but in Irish we write for the ear … there are codes of sound stored in our bodies and when we hear certain sounds of poetry those codes are awoken."[24] And again, in a 1985 lecture, Ní Dhomhnaill noted that "Agus sin againn croí-lar na ceiste — i mBéarla is don tsúil inmheánach a bhímid ag scríobh faid is don gcluais a bhímid ag scríobh i nGaeilge" ("And that is the heart of the matter — in English we write for the internal eye while in Irish we write for the ear").[25] Similarly, Ní Dhomhnaill stresses that poetry differs from other forms of writing in the degree it honestly reveals the deepest emotions in the heart: "Nochtadh macánta ar na mothúcháin is doimhne i gcroí an duine an rud is mó a thugann dimeinsiún breise don bhfilíocht that gach sort eile scríbhneoireachta."[26] Ó Dúill traces this favoring of sound and privileging of poetry that rejoices and exults — rather than poetry that rigorously interrogates and scrupulously examines — to Ó Tuama's influence. If the absence of a rival academic of similar stature and standing, working in contemporary literature, allowed him to shape the literary canon as he saw fit, "the problem," as Ó Dúill sees it, is two-part. Firstly, "Ó Tuama's insistence that poetry should celebrate rather than interrogate or analyse, and by a resulting concentration on sound rather than on sense, on feeling rather than on reason"[27] contributed to a constricting definition of Irish-language poetry. Secondly, there was a focus on sound and sensory experience at the expense of intellectual and critical analysis:

> An overt, well-articulated claim that one's concentration is on sound and on other sensory and extrasensory fields sabotages all critical efforts to come to grips with the poetry. It not only shifts the goal-posts, it metamorphises the pitch into a swimming pool, and the critic is not wholly convinced he should play water-polo. So the condition of literary criticism is dire.[28]

Ó Dúill provocatively argues that the following poets lie outside the accepted area of what constitutes Irish-language poetry: "The philosophy of Ó Maolfabhail, the investigation of Mac Síomóin, the perfectionism of O'Siadhail, the painstaking professionalism of Hartnett, the internationalism of Hutchinson, the intelligence of Jenkinson."[29] As a result, the excitement and attention devoted to *Innti*'s poetic flowering was less than universally beneficial. In fact, it created an artificial expectation of what poetry in Irish was and should be, and was possibly marginalizing.[30]

> There was a downside. Poets such as Caitlín Maude and Mícheál Ó Cuaig[31] from Conamara, Con Ellis and Seán Ó Leocháin from the midlands, Pádraig Ó Croiligh and Réamonn Ó Muireadhaigh and Diarmaid Ó Doibhlin and Pascal Mac Gabhann from Ulster and even Art Ó Maolfabhail, Micheal O'Siadhail and Michael Hartnett found what little attention was available for Irish poetry — allocated in the major media and the cultural establishment by people whose own grip on the language was often slight — tended to go to the new groups.[32]

No critic accuses the Innti poets of siphoning attention. Far from it, as Ó Dúill stresses: they willingly shared their reading opportunities with their peers. But the periodization, as currently understood, of Irish-language poetry is unhelpful at best and misleading at worst. It risks privileging certain poets and marginalizing others. More critically it presents a false image that there is a uniformity of sorts to be detected amongst Irish-language poetry when the opposite is clearly the case.

Salon des refusés

Periodization continues to be among the most problematic issues in literary studies. As Marshall Brown observed, "Periods are entities we love to hate. Yet we cannot do without them."[33] The problem with periodization is not just who belongs to the Innti group and who belongs to the post-Innti generation; the problem is much greater and more complex. Máire Mhac an tSaoi is a case in point: born in 1922, she predates the Innti group but is still alive and active. Her novella *A Bhean Óg Ón* appeared in 2001, her autobiography *The Same Age as the State* appeared in 2003. *Marbhnaí Duino*, her translation of Rainer Maria Rilke's *Duineser Elegien*, appeared in 2013. She is both a contemporary poet and a key member of the post-WWII group, but she also contributed poems to the *Innti* journal. She defies easy periodization and exemplifies the challenges and shortcomings of those who seek easy periodization and chronological groupings. Similarly Seán Ó Leocháin, born in 1943 in Athlone, has produced a number of publications: *Bláth an Fhéir* (1968), *An Dara Cloch* (1969), *Saol na bhFuíoll* (1973), *Idir Ord agus Inneoin* (1977), *In Absentia* (1980), *Aithrí Thoirní* (1986), *Bindealáin Shalaithe* (1989), *Traein na bPúcaí* (1993), *Oiread na Fríde* (1998), *Soupe du Jour* (2003), *Cloch Nirt* (2011), *Scannán gan Fuaim* (2011), and *Obair Bhaile* (2013). A scrupulously scholarly poet who draws heavily on the older literary tradition and mines classical and old Irish for linguistic gems, his work — an important precursor to Aifric Mac Aodha's — bears scant resemblance to the Innti group's.

Áine Ní Ghlinn, born 1955, is the author of *An Chéim Bhriste* (1984), *Gáirdín Pharthais* (1988), *Deora Nár Caoineadh/Unshed Tears* (1996), *Tostanna* (2006), and *An Guth Baineann* (2013). If nothing else, her terrifying "An Chéim Bhriste" is certainly one of the Irish-language poems of the twentieth century. Bríd Ní Mhóráin, born in 1951, in Camp, Kerry, is the author of several volumes: *Ceiliúradh Cré* (1992), *Fé Bhrat Bhríde* (2002), *Síolta an Iomais* (2006), *An Cosán Bán/The White Path* (2008), and *Pietas* (2010). A 1975 graduate of University College Cork, her precise and controlled lyrics explore loss, death, and childlessness. Another case is "that most logophilic and mysterious of Irish-language writers,"[34] Biddy Jenkinson. Born in 1949, she is clearly a contemporary of the Innti Five but her first collection didn't appear until the late 1980s. Her works include *Baisteadh Gintlí* (1987), *Uiscí Beatha* (1988), *Dán na hUidhre* (1991), *Amhras Neimhe* (1997), *An Grá Riabhach* (1999), *Mis* (2001), *Rogha Dánta* (1999), and *Oíche Bhealtaine* (2005).[35] The partner of a career diplomat, Jenkinson — like Mac Síomóin and O'Sullivan — has lived outside Ireland for a considerable portion of her adult life and consequently her poetry displays a "dizzyingly broad frame of reference spanning everything from Cú Chulainn to fossilised faeces … it is extravagant in grief and exults in bawdiness. Sex, for once, is hilarious and bizarre, with the poet jealously marvelling at gastropods who don't have to stop canoodling for a post-coital pee. The body is revelled in, marvelled at, and occasionally dismembered without a hint of sentimentality."[36] Pádraig Mac Fhearghusa, born in 1947, is the author of *Faoi Léigear* (1980), *Mear-cair* (1996), and *An Dara Bás* (2002). As befits the author of *Tóraíocht an Mhíshonais* (*The Pursuit of Unhappiness*), a study of Freud and Jung, his poetry is intellectual and philosophical and bears the marks of deep thought, scholarly introspection, and rigorous self-scrutiny. Denied membership of the Innti group, they are poetic refugees belonging to no literary period, no literary journal, no aesthetic movement. It would be possible to extend this list of poets further and list example after example after example of poets who pre-date the emergence of the Innti group but who share few if any literary, ideological, philosophical, and aesthetic traits with them other than a common language. These poets, their approaches, and their poems represent a "hidden Ireland" of Irish-language poetry: those occluded by the aesthetic and perceptual revolution wrought by Innti.

Multilingual Migrants and Vagrant Versifiers?

While the "haunting" of poetry written in English by the older languages is widely acknowledged, the issue of bilingual poets receives less, if any, consideration.[37] The tradition of bilingual poets publishing and alternating between languages is a tradition dating back to P. H. Pearse, Brendan Behan, and Críostóir Ó Floinn.[38] Michael Hartnett, born in 1941, is arguably Ireland's most famous bilingual poet, but one who rarely features in discussions of Irish-language poetry. His decision in 1975, announced in *A Farewell to English*, to renounce English in favor of Irish led to three volumes in Irish: *Adharca Broic* (1978), *An Phurgóid* (1983), and *Do Nuala: Foighne Chrainn* (1984). Despite returning to writing in English in 1985, he produced some of the most popular translations of classic seventeenth-century and eighteenth-century Irish poems in *Dáibhí Ó Bruadair* (1985), *Haicéad: Translations from the Irish* (1993), and *Ó Rathaille: The Poems of Aodhaghán Ó Rathaille* (1999). He also published *An Lia Nocht* (Coiscéim 1985) and *A Necklace of Wrens: Poems in Irish and English* (The Gallery Press 1987). His *Collected Poems* appeared posthumously, but bizarrely without his Irish-language poems.

Hartnett is, perhaps, the most famous example of an Irish poet moving between languages, publishing in both languages and alternating between them. But he is neither an outlier nor the exception. When contemplating the future of Irish poetry after Seamus Heaney, of the five contemporary poets considered likely "to shine in the sunlight," two — Paul Muldoon and Ciaran Carson — were bilingual.[39] Micheal O'Siadhail, born in 1947, has sixteen collections of poetry to his name, but as a bilingual poet fits neatly into no existing schema other than urban bilingual poet or scholar-poet. Eithne Strong (1923–1999) is a similar case. Born a year after Mhac an tSaoi, she was a bilingual poet, lacking "conventional discretion and decorum,"[40] who published volumes initially in English but from the 1990s onwards in Irish, including *Cirt Oibre* (1980), *Fuil agus Fallaí* (1983), *Aoife faoi Ghlas* (1990), *An Sagart Pinc* (1990), and *Nobel* (1999). And a final case is Celia de Fréine, born in 1948, who is older than any of the famous Innti five. Her eight collections of poetry[41] are marked by a "controlled, fluent anger … directed against the state and its agents,"[42] — especially her narrative poem *Fiacha Fola*, translated as *Blood Debts*, which focuses on the Hepatitis C scandal that blighted the lives of more than 1,500 Irish women. This volume represents poetry as social criticism and the poet as social critic, as arbitrator and seer, of whom Mhac an tSaoi wrote: "I don't think anything has yet been composed in modern Irish as powerful as those lines … For me, the whole revival movement has been worth it, so that its like could be provided."[43] Conleth Ellis, born in Carlow in 1937, is yet another bilingual poet of merit who published several volumes in both Irish and English.[44]

Not all exposure between Irish-language poetry and the wider world is mediated through English. Born in 1938, Tomás Mac Síomóin, a doctoral graduate of biology at Cornell University, overlaps with the emergence of *Innti*. His first volume, *Damhna agus Dánta eile*, appeared in 1974 and was followed by *Codarsnaí* (1981) and *Cré agus Cláirseach* (1983). *Scian* appeared in 1991, and more recently in 2010, *21 dán/poemes/poemas*, a tri-lingual collection of poems in Irish, Catalan, and Spanish. And Dorgan has suggested that Mac Síomóin is "productively indebted to a Continental sensibility which owes more to Pasolini than to Pearse."[45] Among other poets who complicate easy periodization and categorization is Derry O'Sullivan, born in 1944, and living in Paris since 1969. His publications include *Cá bhfuil do Iudás?* (1987), *Cá bhfuil Tiarna Talún l'Univers?* (1994), *An Lá go dTáinig Siad* (2005) — a long poem about the Nazi occupation of Paris — and *An bhfuil cead agam dul amach, más é do thoil é?* (2009). Translations of his work into English as *The King's English* (1987) and into French as *En Mal de Fleurs* (1988) have also appeared. Kaarina Hollo's English-language translation of O'Sullivan's "Marbhghin 1943: Glaoch ar Liombó" ("Stillborn 1943: Calling Limbo") — "one of the most achingly beautiful Irish poems of the twentieth century"[46] — received the 2012 *Times* Stephen Spender Prize for poetry translation.[47] Other poets who have worked in two or more languages include Pól Breathnach, Dairena Ní Chinnéide,[48] Pearse Hutchinson,[49] Collette Nic Aodha,[50] Rita Kelly,[51] and Deirdre Brennan.[52] Doireann Ní Ghríofa enriches and extends this tradition with collections such as *Résheoid* (2011), *Dúlasair* (2012), the bilingual chapbook *Dordéan, do Chroí/A Hummingbird, your Heart* (2014), *Clasp* (2015), and *Oighear* (2017). Another contemporary poet who works in three languages is Diarmuid Johnson, a poet and scholar who has authored *Súil Saoir (The Trained Eye)* (2004); *Another Language, poems in Irish, English and Welsh* (2009); *The Birth of Tristan and Other Poems* (2010); *A Young Sun/Un Soare Tânăr* (2012); *The Woods are Growing Younger* (2013); and *An tÉan agus Dánta Eile/Der Vogel und andere Gedichte* (2013). He, too, is a poet deserving of critical attention. Where do such poets fit: pre-Innti, Innti, or post-Innti? How constructive is "Innti" as a term to understanding the broader strokes and varied milieu of Irish-language poetry?

Irish-language poetry retains its diverse, multilingual, idiosyncratic nature. Alert and alive to the local as to the global, to the past influences and present instances, it draws on and reimagines the wider world as perceived and understood by the individual poet. None of this should surprise or shock. As David Wheatley (1970–) — a poet who plays off "traditional models from Irish folklore and Gaelic poetry with a welcome playfulness and emotional accessibility"[53] — noted with regards to the "Irish" poem: "Tá teorainn ann, b'fhéidir, ach cad is dán Éireannach ann inniu? Tá dánta Éireannacha ann a scríobhadh i Laidin agus i nGréigis agus sa todhchaí is cosúil go scríobhfar i bPolainnis nó i Seicis iad freisin.… Is iad an deoraíocht agus an t-ilteangachas na téamaí bunúsacha againn, pé an fhoirm a aimsímid dóibh." ("There is a limit, maybe, but what is an Irish poem today? Irish poems have been written in Latin and Greek and in the future it appears that they will be written in Polish or Czech also ... Exile and plurilingualism are our basic themes, whichever form we find for them.")[54] The Irish literary canon, both prose and poetry, has since its inception been multilingual and polyglot, including works in monkish Latin and Norman French as well as Irish and English.[55] Irish-language poets of the late-twentieth century have certainly traveled extensively but, as Edna Longley correctly observes, looking outward or abroad is not in itself a literary value: "Contemporary poets seem to overlook the fact that a true poet can travel and move the reader from anywhere, but that if the poem lacks imaginative and artistic force then its setting or backdrop is of little consequence; whether that is rural Ireland or the streets of Singapore."[56]

Post-Innti: Millennials and the Poetry of the Future?

Critics often caper on the brink of a crisis of confidence about the future of Irish-language poetry with the result that any emerging poet is invariably critiqued in terms of the Innti group. This litmus test was regularly, and unfairly, applied to Louis de Paor,[57] Colm Breathnach[58] — both daubed the *iar*-Innti (post-Innti) generation — and Gearóid Mac Lochlainn, and in many ways obscured what was original, innovative, and distinctive about their verse.[59] Rather than assess them on their own merits, they were often hastily judged against the mature work of the established Innti poets and, unsurprisingly, found lacking. Consequently, Irish poetry is often seen as entering a fallow period: a period lacking a great poet, a creative voice, a poet laureate, based on the public profile, at home and abroad, of the Innti poets.[60] Now that the Innti apogee has passed, are the standards set, and expectations raised, still valid? For all the merits and positives of the Innti phenomenon, the term's use as a critical tool and periodic category may prove not only unhelpful but restrictive and limiting to a wider understanding and more nuanced appreciation of contemporary poetry in Irish.

Some shared characteristics are observed among the emerging millennial poet, including a thematic seriousness — perhaps due to the marginalization of poetry and literature in contemporary society — and a reluctance to discuss the language itself other than in an occasional poem.[61] Such traits chime with Justin Quinn's observation: "More recent poets do not move in concert with a larger nationalist objective, as the poets of a century before did. Rather they bear witness to the multitudes the island contains, and have extended its borders to include a fair piece of the known world."[62] What then is the defining characteristic of the Millennials, Generation Y, the Peter Pan generation of Irish-language poets, and what, if anything, is the Irish-language poem?

In a discussion among Na Scríbhneoirí Úra — a voluntary group to assist and promote new voices writing in Irish established by Ríona Nic Congáil in July 2007 based on a similar Catalan model — Proinsias Mac a'Bhaird, from Árainn Mhór in Donegal, lamented the absence of traditional formal and technical aspects of the poetic tradition:

> Sílimse go bhfuilimid ag déanamh dearmaid ar an reacaireacht, ar an cheol sa chúlra, ar Fhilíocht na mBard agus ar na traidisiúin sin, san fhilíocht. Tá barraíocht béime sa lá atá inniu ann ar an fhocal scríofa agus b'fhéidir nach bhfuil go leor béime curtha ar an cheol agus ar struchtúr an amhráin, mar shampla, cúrsaí rithime, cúrsaí ríme. Táimid iontach tógtha leis an tsaorvéarsaíocht, leis an ghontacht … Tá an tsúil tábhachtach fosta, ach domsa go pearsanta, nuair atá leabhar filíochta agamsa, is maith liom é a léamh amach os ard. Tuigim an bhfuil sé go maith nó nach bhfuil sé go maith nuair a léim os ard é.[63]

Such concerns echo calls by Biddy Jenkinson for "a plea for a higher quantity of 'fixed forms'"[64] and similar critiques by Johnson, who laments that:

> There is, in the poetry published throughout this decade, a severe want of technical dexterity, of ingenuity, imaginative pressure, metaphorical energy, linguistic vitality, formal possibility and intellectual play. So many of the poems are devoid of any vivifying elements of surprise or disturbance, of dialectical force, from beginning to end. There is little or no attentiveness to the line-break — the feature that distinguishes poetry from prose — no feeling for the sound and movement of works and their syntactical arrangement. Visually, aurally, at every level, words fail to spark off each other to ignite and lift off the page.[65]

Of the current millennials with at least one volume in print, the following are noteworthy and appear to be forming the core of the latest generation of Irish-language poets as we look to the fiftieth anniversary of the publication of Frank O'Brien's *Filíocht Ghaeilge na Linne Seo*, first published in 1968, and the seventy-fifth anniversary of Ó Direáin's *Coinnle Geala*.

Born in Dublin in 1973, Simon Ó Faoláin grew up in west Kerry and trained as an archaeologist prior to publishing *Anam Mhadra* (*A Dog's Soul*) in 2008 followed by *As Gaineamh* (*From Sand*) in 2011. Ó Dúill detects in *Anam Mhadra*, a "strangely assured voice ... unafraid of both formal learning and experimentation" while *As Gaineamh* marked "the widening of his intellectual, cultural and social reference points: no other poet could compare the small irregular hillside fields with cancerous cells on a screen."[66]

Born in Tralee, Kerry, in 1984, Ailbhe Ní Ghearbhuigh's 2008 collection *Péacadh* led to her being perceived "as among the most urban and outward-looking of her generation, she is not immune to traditional concerns, among them the issue of the Irish language itself ... acutely aware of the challenges faced by the language in 21st-century Ireland and in an increasingly globalised world."[67] Her poem "Filleadh ar an gCathair" served as Ireland's 2013 EU presidential poem and was shortlisted for RTÉ's 2015 A Poem for Ireland, and "unapologetically celebrates the immediacy, the liveliness and the buzz of city life."[68] Her poems "display an affinity for the clandestine character of minority languages while managing the trick of making Irish-speaking Ireland appear metropolitan, even decadent..."[69] Despite drawing on and paying homage to Ó Ríordáin and Ó Direáin, sensuality and eroticism abound here, and her poems, writes Wheatley, "have legs and bite, and use them to forage all manner of new territories for the tradition."[70] A second collection, *Tost agus Allagar* (2016), concerns various modes of communication: verbal, physical, symbolic, and other.[71] While clearly applicable to Irish, she stresses that the poems address issues beyond the immediate and the national.[72]

Born in Gortmoney, Emyvale, Monaghan in 1978, Caitríona Ní Cléirchín's first collection *Crithloinnir* (2010) contains poems that Liam Carson considered "delicate, airy constructions, sparse, intimate. This is a world of *amour fou*, of passion, of sensuality.... Her best love poems are those which contain notes of tension and darkness, the sense that love might be fleeting or deceptive."[73] Influenced by "French écriture feminine and the poststructuralist distrust of language itself,"[74] those poems set in the seventeenth century fuse tradition, modernity, and postmodernism. In poems such as "Scaradh na gCompánach," she attempts "to repossess the tradition by giving a voice to a voice that was never heard in previous poems."[75] Such efforts mirror Doireann Ní Ghríofa's "The Horse under the Hearth" in that they refocus the narrative as perceived from a tangential perspective. Born in Galway in 1981, Doireann Ní Ghríofa published her first two collections in Irish — *Résheoid* (2011) and *Dúlasair* (2012) — before a bilingual chapbook appeared in 2014 entitled *Dordéan, do Chroí/A Hummingbird, your Heart*. The publication of *Clasp* in English in 2015, however, was "a huge change for me, as it was a turning to a different language…"[76] and earned her critical attention and the 2016 Rooney award. A significant concern in her verse to date "is the sense of palimpsest, how the events of the past lurk always just below the surface, a persistent influence on our days, whether we perceive it or not."[77] Her poems "explore a diverse array of absences in order to examine how we choose to accept or deny absence as a presence in our lives … how we respond to the things that disappear — the erasures, the deletions, the missing things — our resilience, our grief, and the ways in which we collapse or persist when something or someone has suddenly vanished from our days."[78] "The Horse under the Hearth" in *Clasp* offers a different take on *Caoineadh Airt Uí Laoghaire*[79] where the poet rewinds "to that liminal moment, when she and Art's horse were still locked in momentum, suspended between suspicion and discovery, 'galloping / and galloping and never reaching him.'"[80]

Beatha Dhónaill Dhuibh is the first book by London-born Séamus Barra Ó Súilleabháin (1992–). Raised in Listowel, Kerry, this rap artist won the 2011–12 All-Ireland Poetry Slam Championship in Derry where the adjudicators praised "the fluidity and passion of his performance and his natural ability to make poetry in the Irish language as melodious as music." Prior to the publication of *Beatha Dhónaill Dhuibh*, his work was widely available on YouTube. Explaining the difference between a poet and a rapper, Ó Súilleabháin stresses the rapper's autonomy and ability to connect with his immediate audience, while the poet is beset with doubts, introspection and self-examination rather than focusing on the act of telling, narrating and communication with the immediate audience.[81] In some ways this approach marks a return of the barántas tradition and the narrative style of "amhráin na ndaoine" and mock-heroic songs of the eighteenth and nineteenth centuries. It also breaks down the walls between traditional vernacular art forms such as *agallaimh beirte* and *lúibíní*, traditional arts performed in real-time to live audiences and the lonely act of reading poetry in isolation.

Predicting the future is a fool's errand. Prior to the emergence of *Innti*, there was little to indicate that a literary revolution was on the horizon. When contemplating the future of Irish-language poetry in 1977, Ó Tuama speculated that future poets would return to older, classical forms of literary language as had the Scots: "Braithim go gcasfaidh filí agus lucht liteartha na Gaeilge amach anseo níos mo ar an seanteanga liteartha, agus go mbainfidh siad leas nua comhachtach aisti mar a dheineann Mac Gill Eathain."[82] If Irish poetry is to survive, let alone thrive, it must revisit its roots and explore forms, themes, and aspects beyond those embraced and practiced by the Innti poets. Musing on the future of Irish-language poetry, Alan Titley wrote "[t]he *Innti* phenomenon was probably an exception which gave us an explosion of poetry the likes of which we never had before since the first half of the 17th century. One suspects the future will belong again to the single individual talents who will always be with us and from whom we make our collective traditions."[83] That observation parallels Conor O'Callaghan's view that direct correlations between social forces and good poetry are tenuous at best and that poetry is the product of silence and solitude.[84] Such views offer some succor to those concerned at the distressing figures of the rate, quantity, and quality of Irish as spoken in the traditional heartlands. As John McAuliffe wrote recently, "Where are we? Somewhere we might not have seen elsewhere in contemporary Irish literature, somewhere these poets take us in their inventive modes, escaping from a name, creatures of desire, alone, for whom poems are compensatory spaces or newly invented safe rooms, places we might not have noticed until they were shown to us."[85] Irish-language poets have recourse to different and distinct modes of writing. As they learn their trade and sing whatever is well made, they may benefit from bearing in mind that tradition in which they trade is tantalizingly diverse, teeming with different approaches and aesthetics.

1. Liz Hoggard, "The revolutionary artists of the 60s' colourful counterculture," *The Observer*, Sept. 4, 2016.

2. The Gaeltacht Civil Rights Movement's campaign for greater civil rights for Irish speakers demanded access to services, broadcasting, and an elected assembly. See Jerry White, "Place, Dialect, and Broadcasting in Irish: Plus ça change ..." *Éire-Ireland* 50, nos. 1 & 2 (Spring/Summer 2015): 113–36.

3. Gabriel Rosenstock and Ciaran Carson, "Aspects of Irish-language Poetry and Its Miraculous Survival," *Poetry Ireland Review* 105 (Dec. 2011): 23.

4. Thomas Dillon Redshaw, "The Living Voice," *Poetry Ireland Review* 104 (Sept. 2011): 129

5. Séamus Blake, "Seán Ó Tuama and Irish Gaelic in the Twentieth Century," *American Journal of Irish Studies* 8 (2011): 117–36.

6. For Ó Tuama's robust response to criticism of the selection, see his article "Coiscéim na hAoise seo - agus duanairí eile," *Comhar* 51, no. 5 (May 1992): 68–74. For an alternative selection, see Ciarán Ó Coigligh, *An Fhilíocht Chomhaimseartha 1975–1985* (Dublin: Coiscéim, 1987); Cathal Póirtéir, *Éigse an Aeir* (Dublin: Coiscéim, 1998); Greagóir Ó Dúill, *Fearann Pinn: Filíocht ó 1900–1999* (Dublin: Coiscéim, 2000); Clíodhna Cussen and Micheál Ó Ruairc, *Síoda ar Shíoda* (Dublin: Coiscéim, 2008).

7. The repercussions of this decision still reverberate in various reviews and essays some twenty-five years later.

8. For instance, Louis de Paor's recent *Leabhar Na hAthghabhála: Poems of Repossession* (Northumberland, UK: Bloodaxe Books, 2016).

9. Collections include *An Dealg Droighin* (1981), *Féar Suaithinseach* (1984), *Selected Poems/Rogha Danta*, (1986), *Feis* (1991), *Pharaoh's Daughter* (1990), *The Astrakhan Cloak* (1992), *Cead Aighnis* (1998), and *The Water Horse* (1999).

10. Collections include *Homecoming/An Bealach 'na Bhaile* (1993), *Na Buachaillí Bána* (1995), *An Tnúth leis an tSolas* (2001), *An tAm Marfach ina Mairimid* (2010), *Aimsir Ársa* (2014), and *Fear Glas: The Green Man* (2014).

11. Collections include *Gleann ar Ghleann* (1982), *Bligeard Sráide* (1983), *Selected Poems/Rogha Dánta* (1987), *An Tost a Scagadh* (1993), *Scuais* (1998), *Freacnairc Mhearcair/The Oomph of Quicksilver* (2000), and *Fardoras* (2003).

12. Born in Cork city in 1950, his collections include *Tine Cnámh* (1984), *Dialann Bóthair* (1992), *Walking Time agus Dánta eile* (2000), *Dánta Déanta* (2005), *An*

Seileitleán agus véarsaí seilí eilí (2005), and *An Fuíoll Feá: Rogha Dánta/Wood Cuttings: New and Selected Poems* (2013).

13. Jody Allen Randolph, "Cathal Ó Searcaigh, January 2010," in *Close to the Next Moment: Interviews from a Changing Ireland* (Manchester, UK: Carcanet, 2010).

14. Liam Carson, "Taking literature in Irish out of the Gaelic ghetto," *The Irish Times*, Oct. 6, 2014. Rosenstock's preference may be linked to the form's links with the early Irish lyric which privileged "economy of words and deftly outlined images." See Proinseas Ní Chatháin, "Themes in Early Irish Lyric Poetry," *Irish University Review* 22, no. 1 (1992): 4. See also Gabriel Rosenstock, "How I Discovered Irish *or* How Irish Discovered Me," in *'Who Needs Irish?' Reflections on the Importance of the Irish Language Today*, ed. Ciarán Mac Murchaidh (Dublin: Veritas Publications, 2004), 83–93; and Pádraig de Paor, *Na Buachaillí Dána: Cathal O Searcaigh, Gabriel Rosenstock agus ról comhaimseartha an fhile sa Ghaeilge* (Dublin: An Clóchomhar, 2005).

15. See Liam Ó Muirthile, "Offshore on Land—Poetry in Irish Now," in *A New View of the Irish Language*, eds. Caoilfhionn Nic Pháidín and Seán Ó Cearnaigh (Dublin: Cois Life, 2008), 145–46.

16. "Highly enjoyable were witty renderings into Irish of two Bob Dylan hits by Colm Breathnach and Gabriel Rosenstock in *PIR* 99 which must have got every reader singing along: 'Ó, ó, ó, a Áilteoir' ('Jokerman')." Maria Johnson, "Reading Irish poetry in the New Century: *Poetry Ireland Review* 2000–2009," *Poetry Ireland Review* 100 (Mar. 2010): 44.

17. Clíona Ní Ríordáin, "Liam Ó Muirthile, *An Fuíoll Feá—Rogha Dánta/Wood Cuttings—New and Selected Poems*," *Études Irlandaises* 39, no. 1 (2014): 223. See also Tadhg Ó Dúshláine, *Anois Tacht an Eala: Fili Chorcaí INNTI agus an Réabhlóid Chultúrtha* (An Daingean: An Sagart, 2011), 155–226.

18. See note 12.

19. *Modern Poetry in Translation* 3, no. 1 (2004): 51–52. http://poetrymagazines.org.uk/magazine/record.asp?id=16711.

20. Theo Dorgan, "Twentieth Century Irish-Language Poetry," *Archipelago* 7, no. 3, accessed online, http://www.archipelago.org/vol7-3/dorgan.htm.

21. Ibid.

22. *Innilt Bhóthair* (1981), *Dubhthrian* (1985), *Blaoscoileán* (1988), *Crannóg agus Carn* (1991), *Saothrú an Ghoirt* (1994), *Traverse* (1998), *New Room Windows* (2008), and *Outward and Return* (2012).

23. Greagóir Ó Dúill, "Infinite Grounds for Hope?: Poetry in Irish Today," *Poetry Ireland Review* 39 (Autumn 1993): 16. His most recent collection is *Ag dul Anonn* (2016).

24. Ibid.

25. Nuala Ní Dhomhnaill, "Filíocht a cumadh: Ceardlann Filíochta," *Leachtaí Chomh Cille* XVII (1986): 170. She continues: "Tá aon dainséar amháin ann áfach—sé sin go dtosnófar ag scríobh filíochta i nGaeilge amhail is dá mba Béarla í. Ciallaíonn san go mbeadh níos mó béime ar an íomhá, níos mó luach á thabhairt di agus b'fhéidir lios lua suime i gcúrsaí rime, rithime agus fuaime" (179).

26. Ibid., 170.

27. Ó Dúill, "Infinite Grounds," 16.

28. Ibid., 17.

29. Ibid., 13.

30. Ibid., 15.

31. See Lillis Ó Laoire, "Sean Ó Curraoin agus Mícheál Ó Cuaig," *Filíocht Chomhaimseartha na Gaeilge*, ed. Ríóna Ní Fhrighil (Dublin: Cois Life, 2010), 205–31.

32. Ó Dúill, "Infinite Grounds," 14–15.

33. Marshall Brown, "Periods and Resistances," *Modern Language Quarterly* 62, no. 4 (2001): 309.

34. http://www.poetryinternationalweb.net/pi/site/poet/item/18333/30/Ailbhe-Ni-Ghearbhuigh.

35. Caitríona Ní Chléirchín, "Abjection and Disorderly Elements of Corporeal Existence in the Irish-Language Poetry of Nuala Ní Dhomhnaill and Biddy Jenkinson," *Proceedings of the Harvard Celtic Colloquium* 30 (2010): 157–74.

36. Caitlín Nic Íomhair, "In praise of Biddy Jenkinson," *The Irish Times*, Aug. 4, 2015. Peggy O'Brien comments that it was "purely for want of enough good translations that Biddy Jenkinson, Caitlín Maude, and Áine Ni Ghlinn, all poets in Irish, were not considered for inclusion" in *The Wake Forest Book of Irish Women's Poetry* (2011), xxxix.

37. See Robert Archambeau, "Postnational Ireland," *Contemporary Literature* 50, no. 3 (2009): 616–17.

38. Born in 1927, Criostóir Ó Floinn's poetry publications include *Ó Fhás go hAois* (1969), *Banana* (1979), *Aisling Dhá Abhainn* (1977), *Hunger Strike* (1984), *A Poet in Rome* (1992), *The Obelisk Year* (1993), and *Seacláidí Van Gogh* (1996).

39. Philip Cummings, "Who can now be considered Ireland's leading poets in the aftermath of Seamus Heaney's passing? Five contemporary Irish poets everyone should read." *The Irish Post*, Sept. 28, 2013. The five poets identified were Muldoon,

Carson, Paula Meehan, Conor O'Callaghan, and Peter Sirr. Sirr has "translated" Old and Middle Irish poems in "Edge Songs."

40. Tadhg Ó Dúshláine, "The Magnanimous Poetry of Eithne Strong," *SouthWord* 2, no. 1 (Winter 1999): n.p.

41. *A Lesson in Can't* (2014), *Blood Debts* (2014), *Cuir amach seo dom: riddle me this* (2014), *Aibítir Aoise: Alphabet of an Age* (2011); *imram: odyssey* (2010), *Scarecrows at Newtownards* (2005), *Fiacha Fola* (2004), and *Faoi Chabáistí is Ríonacha* (2001).

42. Lia Mills, "Hidden Irelands," *Dublin Review of Books* (Mar. 2014), accessed online, http://www.drb.ie/essays/hidden-irelands#.

43. De Fréine herself has stated that "the themes of pregnancy, childbirth and mother-hood—in the context of a national scandal—may have gone against *Fiacha Fola* in Irish-language circles. Another factor that could work against it is the fact that it has an urban setting and is written in urban Irish." See Lia Mills, "Hidden Irelands."

44. His collections include *This Ripening Time* (1966), *Under the Stone* (1971), *Fómhar na nGéanna* (1975), *Aimsir Fháistineach* (1981), *Nead Lán Sneachta* (1982), *After Doomsday* (1982), *Táin* (1983), *Seabhac ag Guairdeall* (1985), *Age of Exploration* (1985), *Darkness Blossoming* (1989), and *Selected Poems* (2005).

45. Theo Dorgan, "Twentieth Century Irish-Language Poetry."

46. Louis de Paor, "Contemporary Poetry in Irish: 1940–2000," in *The Cambridge History of Irish Literature*, Vol. 2 (Cambridge: Cambridge UP, 2006), 349.

47. For criticism, see Pádraig de Paor, "Cúpla Samoineamh i dtaobh na nuafhilíochta agus i dtaobh *An Lá go dTáinig Siad* (2005) le Derry O'Sullivan," *Leachtaí Cholm Cille XLI*, (2011): 112–24. See also Louis de Paor, "Contemporary Poetry in Irish," 317–56.

48. Her published collections include *An Trodaí agus Dánta Eile/The Warrior and Other Poems* (2006), *Máthair an Fhiaigh/The Raven's Mother* (2008), and *An tEachtran-nach/Das Fremde/The Stranger* (2008), a trilingual publication in German, Irish, and English. *Poll na mBabies* (2008) and *Bleachtaire na Seirce* (2011) appeared in Irish only. *Fé Gheasa/Spellbound* appeared in 2016.

49. See Philip Coleman and Maria Johnston, *Reading Pearse Hutchinson: From Findrum to Fisterra* (Dublin: Irish Academic Press, 2011).

50. Born in Shrule, Mayo in 1967, Colette Nic Aodha's collections include: *Baill Seirce* (1998), *Faoi Chrann Cnó Capaill* (2000), *Gallúnach-Ar-Rópa* (2003), *Sundial* (2005), *Between Curses/Baine Géar* (2007), and *Scéal ón Oirthir* (2009).

51. Born in Galway in 1953, Rita E. Kelly's collections include: *Further Thoughts in a Garden* (2013), *Travelling West* (2000), *Fare Well/Beir Beannacht* (1990), *An Bealach Éadóigh* (1984), and *Dialann sa Díseart* (with Eoghan Ó Tuairisc, 1981).

52. Deirdre Brennan was born in Dublin in 1934, and her collections include *Reilig na mBan Rialta* (1974); *Scothanna Geala* (1989); *Thar Cholba na Mara* (1993); *Ag Mealladh Réalta* (2000); *The Hen Party* (2001); *Beneath Castles Of White Sail* (2003); *Swimming With Pelicans/Ag Eitilt Fara Condair* (2007); *Hidden Places/Scáthán Eile* (2011); *As Trunc* (2015), a selection of poems by Portuguese poet, Fernando Pessoa (1888–1935); and *Coiscéim Cuislí Allta* (2016).

53. Richard Tillinghast, "The Future of Irish Poetry?" *Poetry Ireland Review* 89 (2007): 89.

54. David Wheatley and Ailbhe Ní Ghearbhuigh, "Ní hAnsa," *Comhar* 72, no. 8 (Sept. 2012): 24–25.

55. Archambeau, 611.

56. Johnson, 41.

57. See Tadhg Ó Dúshláine, *Anois Tacht an Eala: Fili Chorcaí INNTI agus an Réabhlóid Chultúrtha* (An Daingean: An Sagart, 2011), 228–342.

58. Ibid., 344–88. See Louis De Paor, 317–56. See also Máirín Nic Eoin, "Colm Breathnach," *Filíocht Chomhaimseartha na Gaeilge*, ed. Ríóna Ní Fhrighil (Dublin: Cois Life, 2010), 232–53.

59. See Liam Ó Muirthile, "Offshore on Land." See also Fionntán de Brún, "Gearóid Mac Lochlainn," *Filíocht Chomhaimseartha na Gaeilge*, ed. Ríóna Ní Fhrighil (Dublin: Cois Life, 2010), 271–88.

60. See Louis de Paor, *Leabhar na hAthghabhála: Poems of Repossession*: "While there is an impression of lost ground toward the close of the millennium in terms of audience and the audibility of poetry in Irish in a more congested literary marketplace dominated by the novel, the original Innti poets continued their development in the final decade of the twentieth century, with Biddy Jenkinson and Colm Breathnach establishing themselves as the most impressive successors of the first wave associated with the journal" (27). De Paor's modesty aside, he undeniably belongs in the same category as Jenkinson and Breathnach in the above description. See his recent collection *Grá Fiar* (2016). See Caoimhín Mac Giolla Léith, "Louis de Paor," *Filíocht Chomhaimseartha na Gaeilge*, ed. Ríóna Ní Fhrighil (Dublin: Cois Life, 2010), 254–70.

61. Caitríona Ní Chléirchín, "Todhchaí na Scríbhneoireachta Gaeilge: bláthú, péacadh agus dóchas," *Comhar* 70, no. 6 (June 2010): 7.

62. Justin Quinn, "The Disappearance of Ireland," in *The Cambridge Introduction to Modern Irish Poetry, 1800–2000* (Cambridge: Cambridge UP, 2008), 210. Ironically, Siniša Malešević argues that nationalism has increased in Ireland: "Consequently nationalist ideology and practice has actually intensified over the last several decades and today's nationalism is much more powerful and socially embedded than that present in de Valera's era." See Siniša Malešević , "Irishness and nationalisms," in *Are the Irish different?* ed. Tom Inglis (Manchester: Manchester UP, 2014), 11. The question needs to be asked, however, in relation to Irish-language poetry, which poet was so moved? Since WWII Irish-language poets have, by and large, turned away from cultural touchstones and nationalist pieties and concentrated their gaze inward to mine poetry from silence and solitude and physiological and emotional introspection. The Innti generation celebrated the urban experience, delighted in unrestrained emotional and intellectual freedom, and freely confessed their inner thoughts, secrets, and desires.

63. Ríona Nic Congáil et al., "An Lucht Fileata," *Comhar* 70, no. 9 (Sept. 2010): 13–14. (I believe that we are forgetting the [art of] reciting, the music in the background, the Bardic Poetry and those traditions in poetry. There is too much emphasis today on the written word and perhaps not enough stress on music, on the structure of the song, for example rhyme and rhythm. We're enthralled with free-verse, with brevity … The eye is still critical, but for me, when I read a book of poetry, I like to read it aloud. I know if it is good or isn't when I read it aloud.) Some aspects of this attitude resonate with Tomás Ó Floinn as expressed in a 1987 essay on Art Ó Maolfabhail, see Liam Prút, ed. *Cion Fir: Aistí Thomáis Uí Fhoinn in Comhar* (Dublin: LeabharComhar, 1997), 411–16.

64. Johnson, 45.

65. Ibid.

66. Gréagóir Ó Dúill, "Simon Ó Faoláin," *Poetry International Rotterdam*, accessed online, http://www.poetryinternationalweb.net/pi/site/poet/item/22528/30/Simon-O-Faolain.

67. Livia Brennan, "Ailbhe Ní Ghearbhuigh," *Poetry Ireland Rotterdam*, accessed online, http://www.poetryinternationalweb.net/pi/site/poet/item/18333/30/Ailbhe-Ni-Ghearbhuigh.

68. A Poem for Ireland website, http://apoemforireland.rte.ie/shortlist/filleadh-ar-an-gcathair/.

69. See David Wheatley, "Ailbhe Ní Ghearbhuigh and the Buntús Cainte ('Rudiments of Language')," in *The Wake Forest Series of Irish Poetry*, Vol. 4 (Winston-Salem, NC: Wake Forest UP, 2017).

70. Ibid.

71. Simon Ó Faoláin, "Ailbhe faoi Agallamh: Márta 31ú, 2016," NÓS, accessed online, http://nos.ie/cultur/leabhair/ailbhe-faoi-agallamh/.

72. Ibid.

73. Liam Carson, "Silent Cities," *Poetry Ireland Review*, 104 (2011): 139.

74. Ibid.

75. "Caitríona Ní Chléirchín—Poetry," *Connotation Press*, Issue II, Vol. VIII: Nov. 2016, accessed online, http://www.connotationpress.com/featured-guest-editor/december-2011/1159-caitriona-ni-chleirchin-poetry.

76. Alvy Carragher, "Meet the Poet," *HeadStuff* website, Apr. 17, 2015, http://www.headstuff.org/2015/04/doireann_ni_ghriofa/.

77. "Poet Doireann Ní Ghríofa on writing *Clasp*," *The Irish Times*, Apr. 23, 2015.

78. Ibid.

79. Ibid.

80. Ibid.

81. Robert McMillen, "Agallamh: Véarsaí ón mbreacGhalltacht le Séamus Barra Ó Súilleabháin," *Tuairisic.ie*, Deireadh Fómhair 11, 2016, http://tuairisc.ie/agallamh-vearsai-on-mbreacghalltacht-le-seamus-barra-o-suilleabhain/.

"An difríocht idir file agus rapper, bíonn fios ag an rapper, bíonn cumhacht aige nó aici, níl aon laigí, níl aon smál ar a ndeir sé. Tá sé ag reacaireacht agus ag rá amach agus tugann sin cumhacht do na daoine a éisteann leis. Géaraíonn sé an coinsias, léiríonn sé cé chomh mór is chomh fuinniúil is atá an coinsias agus cuireann sé ag gluaiseacht é. An difear idir an rap agus an fhilíocht ná go mbíonn amhras ar na filí, is dócha, seachas a bheith ag rá rud éigin—'seo é mar atá sé' nó 'seo an rud a tharla'. Leis an bhfile cuireann an file ceist, bíonn próiseas féinfhiosraithe ann agus osclaítear bealaí eile tuisceana ar an dóigh sin. Uaireanta, tagann an rap agus an fhilíocht le chéile."

82. (I feel that the Irish-language poets and literary people will turn more in the future to the old literary language and will manipulate it powerfully as Somhairle Mac

Gill-Eathain does.) Seán Ó Tuama, "Pádraig Ó Mileadha agus Traidisiún Filíochta an Gaeilge," *Aguisíní* (Dublin: Coiscéim, 2008), 55.

83. Alan Titley, *Nailing Theses: Selected Essays* (Belfast: Lagan Press, 2011), 332.

84. Conor O'Callaghan, preface to *The Wake Forest Series of Irish Poetry*, Vol. 3 (Winston-Salem, NC: Wake Forest UP, 2013), xiv.

85. John McAuliffe, "Contemporary Irish poetry impresses in inventive mode," *The Irish Times*, Jan. 2, 2016.

9

Original in Translation: The Poetry of Aifric Mac Aodha

Daniela Theinová

In *Government of the Tongue*, Seamus Heaney reminds us how poets confronted with an oppressive doctrine, linguistic system, or ideology often give themselves over to the power of language. Osip Mandelstam, he remarks, believed that "it was the poet's responsibility to allow poems to form in language inside him, the way crystals formed in a chemical solution. He was the vessel of language."[1] Besides its crystallizing function in poetry, however, language is instrumental in not simply confirming but also interrogating one's sense of belonging and status as a communal being. If, as T. S. Eliot writes, poetry is "stubbornly national" in having more relevance than any other art to the language of the poet's race,[2] the language issue is impossible to disregard in a discussion of Irish poetry, in which the notion of a linguistic community is ridden with complex oppositions and where many have tried to elegize the Irish language itself out of existence.

Indeed, writing in Irish has for a long time been associated with the idea of the lost past. In the inevitably dichotomized concept of "Irish poetry," it stands for two kinds of fissure: one is linguistic (between Irish and English, Standard English and Hiberno-English), the other is chronological (oral tradition vs. written literature, Old Irish vs. modern Irish). Consequently, the distinction between Irish as the language of the dead past and English as the language of the living present has been a vital part of the often heated polemics surrounding the topic of poetic translation from Irish into English. Due to the linguistic imbalance in Ireland, translating from Irish into English has frequently been perceived as a problematic intervention. Much of the Irish-language criticism of the 1980s and 1990s, when poetic translations from Irish began to be published on a large scale, objected to the "excessive," "domineering" fluency of the English versions. Critics called for an approach that would stress the "difference" of the Irish source text rather than attempt its assimilation.[3]

Poets of Irish that were active at the time mostly complained about unequal publication opportunities and critical reception, but they also rejected the popular notion of the language as dead material. If Nuala Ní Dhomhnaill has been termed the "most visible" of the modern Irish-language poets,[4] it is due to the fact that most of her work has appeared in bilingual editions, especially since the publication in 1990 of *Pharaoh's Daughter* which comprised translations by thirteen different Irish poets, including Seamus Heaney, Paul Muldoon, Medbh McGuckian, and John Montague. To Ní Dhomhnaill, writing in Irish feels like being a "corpse" which nevertheless "sits up and talks back."[5] Biddy Jenkinson, on the contrary, has opposed the notion of Irish-language poetry as a talking specter. Like many other poets of her generation, she is not a native speaker of Irish. Yet, she refuses to be praised on account of working in "a fast dying minority language": "I write in a living language for living friends."[6] Accordingly, as "a small rude gesture to those who think that everything can be harvested and stored without loss in an English-speaking Ireland,"[7] she has placed translations of her work in Ireland under taboo.

A different strategy has been employed by Aifric Mac Aodha (b. 1979) who not only translates her own work, but has acknowledged translation as part of her linguistic situation and adopted it as a determining element in her poetry. The practice of producing one's own English versions is no new thing — it can be said to have started with Patrick Pearse — but it has shown a growing tendency in the last ten or fifteen years. Gearóid Mac Lochlainn's English "Freestyle Rap" versions of his own verse[8] or Ailbhe Ní Ghearbhuigh's co-authoring translations of some of her poems can be seen as part of the current trend in Irish poetry to dispense with clear-cut distinctions. This confident inhabiting of the unclaimed zone between the two languages and the increasing acceptance of translation as part of the process take place in a world where English and Irish appear to have grown further apart but which is also increasingly pluralistic and less marked by division. The very heterogeneity of the poets just mentioned seems to contradict the concept of a national language based on linguistic uniformity. Most of the current theoretical debates on the future of the Irish language as a creative tool are indeed based on the supposition that Irish has been successfully extricated from its role as a token national language and that it might benefit from the growing cultural diversity of Irish society and the changing linguistic context.[9]

While she is unquestionably part of this development, Mac Aodha's case is particular in her embrace of the translation issue as both a polemic stance and an enabling factor in her writing. This essay looks into poems from her poetic debut, *Gabháil Syrinx* (2010), and some of her recently published work and argues that her proposal to "act as a translator for the language of my forebears into a vibrant living version of their Irish"[10] is a strategic move with political, creative, and theoretical implications. Questions concerning what constitutes the "Irishness" of Irish poetry and its tradition are a natural part of this exploration. I want to show that Mac Aodha's decision to write in Irish is simultaneously a statement of affiliation and a way to accommodate differences. She seeks to secure the continuance of the tradition but insists at the same time that it is unattainable. The gulf is too wide. Yet the very brokenness of the tradition and the lack of continuity also bring with them unforeseen freedoms. If she has adopted dissimilarity and change as the main drives of her poetry, this allows her to engage in as well as distance herself from the ongoing, if slackening, linguistic disputes. Irish is at once the language for which this poetry becomes a vessel and a language which threatens to become a (self-imposed) delimiting code.

A sense of outer composure checked by tensions within pervades the poems in Mac Aodha's first collection, *Gabháil Syrinx* (The Capture of Syrinx). Although this volume includes poems from over a period of almost ten years, it is compact in terms of form, expression, and subject matter. Still, the initial impression of solidity, supported by the strong rhythm of her verse, gives way to a more careful reading of the idea of fractured temporality based on the mixing of the old with the new. The anachronistic features which follow from the poet's investigation of older poetic meters are countered by her unconventional use of Irish syntax and lexis. For Mac Aodha, writing in Irish always entails recovery of a language which *is* dead.

An outright confrontation of the legacy informs the opening epigram "File" ("Poet").

> Ní iarrann sé de chothú
> Ach conablach an chait:
> Guíonn go mbeadh a ghoile
> Á chnaí ag fiacla bioracha [...]

> (For sustenance he wants
> only a cat's cadaver:
> prays that its scything
> teeth rend his stomach [...])[11]

This satirical account of an idiosyncratic inspiration ritual functions as the volume's epigraph or overture; its sly, appalling curtness is in tune with the prevalent self-mocking tone of Mac Aodha's poetry. The reference to the oral tradition in the subheading ("De bhéaloideas na hÉireann é go n-itheadh an file amhfheoil an chait roimh dhul i mbun pinn dó" ["Irish folklore records that the poet would eat the raw flesh of a cat before composing"]) combines with Mac Aodha's compact, contemporary tone to telescope the tradition as it were. The notion of a nexus between the literary past and present, between what is borrowed and what is new, is even stronger if we consider the poem as a sarcastic response to the famous eighth-century Irish lyric about fruitful alliance between a scholar and his faithful cat, "Pangur Bán."[12] In "Pangur Bán," the scholar and the cat practice their respective crafts in harmony: "bíth a menma-sam fri seilgg, / mu menma céin im saincheirdd" (his mind is set on hunting, / my mind on my special craft).[13] While the reverse arrangement and mood of the two poems is self-evident, it is also interesting to take into account the popular practice of translating "Pangur Bán" into English. Having translated his own version of "Pangur Bán," Heaney concedes that it is a poem which "Irish writers like to try their hand at, not in order to outdo the previous versions, but simply to get a more exact and intimate grip on the canonical goods."[14] While she did not write her poem with "Pangur Bán" in mind, Mac Aodha has remarked that when she approached Paul Muldoon for an opinion, he replied by saying that "File" makes you think twice about "Pangur Bán."[15] What most likely made her send the poem to Muldoon in the first place was his own poignant grip on the Old-Irish classic and his version of the mouse-hunting/scholarly-endeavor parable: "so long as there's some crucial point / with which we might […] // yet grapple, into which yet sink / our teeth."[16] If Mac Aodha's lyric with its sybaritic roughness stands in contrast to the donnish style of the Old-Irish poem, there is an obvious connection in the shared topic: the hard-to-come-by fruits of the "stealthy art" of concentration.[17] Although not strictly a "translation," Mac Aodha's "File" is the first exposition of the slipperiness of poetic inspiration that comes up throughout the book. Many of the poems in the volume adhere to the pattern of introducing a literary or mythological "source" followed by a modern "version" or a personal commentary.

Translation or transposition is the basic mode not only of this first collection but also of Mac Aodha's general concept of poetic creation. In her contribution to the blog of the American literary journal *Columbia*, she remarks that working on poetry in Irish "forces you to think about translation, for practical reasons as well as artistic ones."[18] She is aware that her poems will mostly be published with a translation and that the majority of her readers will not have read her poems in the original. Reasoning of this kind, however, poses more questions than it clarifies. The first uncertainty bears on the idea of her audience. While she knows that it would be pointless to "yearn for the ideal Irish reader," Mac Aodha's "translations" are triggered by something other than concern for the generic, ignorant anglophone, and it is thus possible that she has no reader in mind at all. Her lyric "I" speaks to itself or to nobody in particular, engrossed in its attempts to reveal the self to the self.

Further uncertainties relate to the indeterminate nature of her "source." If translation is the underlying principle of her approach, Mac Aodha's "original" is her very medium that is loaded with ambiguities. Arising on the border between the Irish of historical literary tradition and modern usage, her poetic language is innovative and extremely supple. Her reliance on the old meters can be detected in her frequent use of alliteration, assonance, and consonance. Still, besides these nonspecific formal characteristics, it is the fluid, multi-layered quality of her poetic narratives and the absence of all explanation which makes them sound ancient. Mac Aodha's poetry is remindful of the associative wisdom of the Irish triads and legends not so much through its thematics and imagery as in its combination of pedestrian tone and contemporary lexis with the sense that much is being held back. Despite occasional allusions to established tropes, like "an chailleach / Le cniotáil an bhrait" (the hag [...] / knitting her cloak) in "La Tricoteuse,"[19] and to old-time rituals and seanfhocail, such as the traditional rules of heritage touched upon and breached in "Briseadh an Dúchais,"[20] the obvious truth is that were it written in English, Mac Aodha's poetry would be much trickier to localize. Yet, if it might seem that her language choice is meant to sustain the Irishness of her poetry, she constantly disrupts this image by unorthodox Irish usage, mixing archaisms with coinages, colloquialisms, and equivocal syntax.

Moreover, not a native speaker, she describes herself as a "linguistic tourist" and consciously disregards the requirements of caint na ndaoine, i.e., to employ one of the recognized dialects of contemporary Irish, championed by the older schools of criticism. Her method can thus be aligned with Walter Benjamin's description of the purpose of translation as "merely a preliminary way of coming to terms with the foreignness of languages to each other,"[21] as well as with his insistence on its curative possibilities. Reconciled with the obvious fact that translation cannot have any influence on the original, she is happy to operate in a sphere that proceeds from the original. Thus her poems, which she describes as "translations," secure the continuance of the original. If her source is a language that is "technically" dead, her work, in Benjamin's terms, constitutes its "survival" (Überleben).[22]

While I have concentrated on the moment of anachronism in Mac Aodha's writing, her straddling of the border between English and Irish is equally important. This aspect of her situation indeed does come into play when she — or others — translate her work into English.[23] Commenting on the collaboration between Ní Dhomhnaill and Muldoon and what she terms their "fruitful poetic team," she argues that: "[t]he poetry resides not simply in the original poem, nor can it be located in the translation. It exists between them in a kind of dynamic tension [...] between the Irish way of expressing an idea conceived in Irish and in that idea's translated equivalent."[24] Her work aspires to "translation" in both the aforementioned senses. But while Irish is in part the "source," it can hardly be considered the "target language," for "target" implies finality and completeness. Asserting, like Ní Dhomhnaill, that she is unable to write poetry in English, she calls Irish her "literary home," admitting in the same breath that for all its familiarity, she finds it "full of exotic delights."[25] The language with which her poetic voice identifies is also something that she can explore from the outside. This ambiguous, forked position is due not only to the liberating detachment following from the use of a language which is not one's own but to the fact that — in Mac Aodha's case — it is a language which has lost continuity with its historical development and a community that would be exclusively defined by it. While this is emblematic of her idea of Irish as defunct, in her work the language often escapes characterization as doomed and becomes a source of inspiration in its own right.

Consider the title sequence of the book, "Scéal Syrinx" ("Syrinx Story"), in which language, its opaqueness but also its outward, transcendental thrust, figures as an inspiring factor. The premise of "Scéal Syrinx" is the Greek myth of the god Pan who, unsuccessful in his courtship and pursuit of the nymph, transformed her into the famous reed flute. Yet, the poem — a sequence of three non-symmetrically organized poems loosely based on the nymph's fate — is no simple retelling of the myth: it is as much a reflection on the theme of inspiration as it is a tribute to nature's endless transformations. There are several ways in which Syrinx, in her metamorphosed reed shape, can be attributed with the role of the muse. The most obvious one, of course, is to see her as inspiring Pan's song. But it is more interesting, I suggest, to examine her bearing on the poet herself. If, at first, it might seem that Mac Aodha identifies with the nymph as she is about to be captured through the imagery of constantly shifting light, the moving leaves and wings, and the fleeting shapes of waves, it gradually becomes apparent that she has made Syrinx *her* muse. The ephemerality of the natural world is closely linked with the elusiveness of the runaway nymph. But although she stands for the fleetingness of inspiration, the poem with its flowing imagery, veiled contours, and indecipherable causality serves as its perfect embodiment. Indeed, almost every image in the three-part sequence is received through a liminal point or state of being: "Spágfaidh an eala aníos / Ó mhínshruth a scátha" ("The swan flip-flops its way / out of its shade's smooth flow"); "Scarfaidh cúr coipthe / De chraiceann an uisce" ("The frothy foam will part / along the water's skin"); "Critheann an solas / Ar chothrom an locha" ("The light shakes slightly / flush with the lake").[26] Though clumsy-footed (*spágach*), the swan's exit at the very beginning of the sequence signals quiet triumph. Free of the doomful clamor of the multiple take-off in "The Wild Swans at Coole,"[27] these images of transmutation are remedial to Yeats's elegiac complaint that "All's changed." Instead of "great broken rings" rippling the water at Coole, in "Scéal Syrinx" we get the moon run "rings / by far too perfect" ("Ritheann an ghealach / Den chiorcal róchumtha"). Ultimately all is cohesion:

> Feileann an t-iomlán
> Do theorainn na luachra.
> Ceileann an chiumhsóg
> Tosach an bhruacha.
>
> (The belt of reeds
> hoops all this in.
> That edge hides where
> the banks begin.)[28]

The latter, self-enclosed image anticipates the final two stanzas of the sequence with their meta-poetic material and the sudden revelation of the speaking "I."

Ligim uaim le haimsir
Pictiúr seo na bruinnille:
Ní ghéilleann sí d'éinfhear
Ná ní sheasann ina choinne.

Anáil mhná, ní scaoileann
Ach eadarghlór ar tinneall:
I láthair na gabhála,
Ceiliúrann sí is critheann.

(In time I let it go,
the likeness of this maiden.
She yields to no one man
nor stands in his way.

A woman's breath. She readies
a half-voice that will sing.
It's time: her body shaken,
abandon as she's taken.)[29]

This "epilogue" not only sums up the whole sequence, but also brings together several of the historical theories of artistic inspiration — from the trope of the desirable yet unattainable female muse through the perception of creative genius as a life-giving breath to the localization of the source of inspiration in the composing mind. But if the poet can be identified with the nymph and yet Syrinx is her muse, what does it mean if she now wants to let her go? Obviously we are experiencing neither the denouement of the Syrinx story nor a series of beautiful natural images, but a parable of Mac Aodha's poetic maturing. The final message is that she will sing her song, not in spite of anyone, but despite every attempt to stop her. She readies a half-voice, and, pretending to let it be seized, she sets it free.

Mac Aodha's poetry illustrates that there is rarely a single, coherent identity and, indeed, just one other involved when a lyric "I" is speaking. Her poetic oneness always involves at least two others — that is English and Irish. The latter, of course, can split into a long chain of possible compound identities such as the Irish in which she writes and the Irish that she speaks, the language of older Irish writings and the Irish that she views as a viable poetic idiom. Ambivalences of that kind are probably common to most poets of different languages, yet in relation to Irish they have special urgency. One of the possible ways to read the closing section of "Scéal Syrinx," then, is to associate the seemingly subdued half-voice with the Irish language. But if Irish is her muse, the latter's dismissal at the end of the poem does not mean the poet is taking leave of or giving up on Gaelic. Rather, her resolute settling between English and Irish and her adoption of the outsider's perspective positions her at the beneficial threshold (represented throughout the poem by the images of the invisible banks and the churned surface of the lake) through which inspiration emerges.

The elusiveness of the muse and the corresponding motif of randomness imply other binding characteristics, among them the prevalent moment of secrecy. In "X agus O-anna" ("X and O's") from the "Athar agus Iníon" sequence, we come upon "Father and Daughter" as they "marked their boxes on the steamed-up board of the screen" in an afternoon traffic jam ("Bhreacadar a mboscaí ar cheochlár na gloine"), the girl wondering how "it was a mystery to her childhood self. / The way he always failed to gain the line / and how easy it was for her to win" ("Ba rúndiamhair dise i bhfíorthús a hóige, / An tslí go dteipeadh air an líne a ghnóthú / Is gurb aicise an bua gan dícheall, gan dua").[30] In the three-line "Buaine" ("Permanence") from the same sequence, this non-representational tone combines with the idea of the unattainability yet irreversibility of human bonds. The father's love for his child endures "Mar shnáithín uainolla, / É i bhfostú i ndriseog" ("Like a yarn of lamb wool / caught up in bramble").[31]

In this poetry, both images and events seem transient inasmuch as they represent no more than a fraction of time captured in words. They bear on, nevertheless, thanks to the intensity of feeling and their place on the page. Still, autobiographical motifs, identifiable through the poems' titles and occasional dedications, elucidate nothing. The ubiquitous snatches of stories and personal histories are mere cover for what takes place under the surface: what determines the content and the form of these poems is the prevailing tone of abstruseness which connotes utterance. Semantic indeterminacy based on sparse syntax and contextual ellipsis is the nexus of Mac

Aodha's writing. In this concept, words and images can be mere pointers to meaning. They are elusive cicerones, often misleading, and always only followed from afar: "Ní féidir gur uaimse / An teachta sin romham" ("that messenger sent out / ahead can't be from me");[32] "Ach an glór a mheall anuas mé, / Táim ag brath air ó shinibh" ("But the voice which beguiled me from above — / I'm looking at it from afar").[33]

The acceptance of the moment of mystery is an essential part of belief. As the poet claims in "Focal Faoisimh" ("The Soothing Word"), the opening image of "thousands and thousands of mice / streaming in and out / of the railway sleepers" in the poem "commands belief" ("Creidtear san íomhá thosaigh: / Na mílte is na mílte luchóg / Ag rith isteach is amach / I measc ráillí iarnróid"). This is how the lyric concludes:

Achar sula ligtear aon fhead,
Airítear í faoina gcnámha.
Tagadh an traein, sa deireadh
Ach roimhe sin, asláithriú.

(Waiting for the whistle to sound
we feel it under their bones.
Let the train come, in the end but
before that: displacement.)[34]

"Focal Faoisimh" testifies to the poet's persuasion that the efficacy of art is dependent on a belief in its communicative and transforming power. Yet, it is also a parable of the instant of "removal" (another equivalent of "asláithriú") which completes the act of translation, that most profound but ultimately most reductive mode of reading, when myriads of other guessed-at meanings are effaced just as an equivalent is chosen. Still, Mac Aodha's baffling referentiality and occasional hermeticism serve to prolong this moment charged with conceptual possibility just before the whistle blows. As it perpetuates uncertainty by linguistically ambiguous expression, Mac Aodha's poetry bespeaks a joyous acceptance of the notion that — as George Steiner points out — "a major portion of language is enclosure and willed opaqueness."[35] As it undergoes constant change, language itself is translation.

Mac Aodha believes that language, like poetry, develops and functions by way of analogy. If language is translation, then translation can be poetry. In an earlier version of the *Columbia* blog, she points out that due to the fact that Irish as a language had been excluded from various aspects of public life and modern usage, writing about twenty-first-century life "absolutely necessitates" finding new words for new phenomena. The poet thus becomes an etymologist as well as a coiner of new expressions and meanings. Lexicographers in Irish, she points out, have "a more active role in the forging of the language than their counterparts in English [...] To my mind that wilful renewing of the language at the most basic level of vocabulary is an act of poetry."[36] Mac Aodha's penchant for dictionaries is at the base of the purposeful ambivalence of her verse. Derived from the wealth of connotations and poetic possibilities behind individual words, it can be aligned with Muldoon's concept of poetry and its intricacies as an attempt "to be equal to the variousness and complexity of the world."[37]

Indeed, Muldoon's style, with its baffling etymological digressions, brilliantly buffoonish neologies, and revelatory lexical and cultural transpositions, has been a major influence on Mac Aodha's writing. The slight touching of poetics we saw in Muldoon's comment on Mac Aodha's "File" is played out in full in her latest work, a serial poem entitled "Sop Préacháin" ("A Crow's Wisp"). Riddled with esoteric lexis, possible sexual innuendos, and puzzling turns of narrative, the poem addresses Muldoon as "leath-chéile na cuilte" (literally "one of the spouses of the quilt"), rendered asymmetrically by David Wheatley as "Pillow-talker,"[38] with a nod to the opening lines of the central epic of the Ulster Cycle, *Táin Bó Cuailnge*.[39] As it identifies two of the four central lyrics as "Ath-Quoof I" and "Ath-Quoof II" ("Quoof: Slight Return I and II"), Mac Aodha's sequence points to Muldoon's "Quoof" as one of its sources. While, in terms of verbal and anecdotal reference, Mac Aodha's poem seems to be modeled on *Shining Brow*, Muldoon's libretto for Daron Hagen's opera about the architect Frank Lloyd Wright, further — albeit more furtive — allusions to various strata of "Quoof" (and other of his poems) are equally important.

Like so many occasions in Muldoon, "Sop Préacháin" starts *in medias res* as a casual address to an unidentified group of listeners. A seemingly public statement, it actually urges reticence:

Ba cheart bhur gcur ó aithne,
tá an tír róbheag, teanga
níos stuama a chleachtadh
nó seasamh siar ón tús.

(Wipe your memory: the country's
too small, practice
holding your tongue
or stand back from the thing.)[40]

The title of the opening lyric, "Stuaim," (shifted by Wheatley shrewdly as "Cant") indicates ironic dismissal of the requirements of "prudence," "steadiness," and the "patient skill" of "self-control" (in women) which Ó Dónaill's dictionary lists as equivalents of "stuaim," together with the illustrative phrase "bean na céille agus na stuaime" ("a woman of sense and prudence").[41] This interpretation of "Stuaim," however, only proposes itself in the closing "Iarfhocal" ("Afterword") ("Is d'admhódh de chogar claon / gur fhadaigh tost an béaldath" ["and beyond that she knew / how silence improves lipstick"]), before the conclusion circles back to the title of the whole sequence, "Sop Préacháin," offering an explanation:

Sop préacháin a deirtí
le bean a chaitheadh fear uaidh,
píosa tuí a d'ardaigh an ghaoth
nuair nár oir go beacht don éinín.

(A woman a man drops
is called a crow's wisp:
something the wind takes
when a bird lets it slip.)[42]

Shining Brow, explains Muldoon, seeks to show how Wright's alleged obsession with Native American traditions[43] and his libertine behavior rendered him shallow as a person and artist. The impulse behind the libretto, he adds, was to remind himself that he too may have gone "overboard" in his plentiful references to Native America — a qualm he would do little to settle in the future.[44] Yet, although it sounds like an Indian appellative, "Shining Brow" comes from the name of the house designed by Wright in South Wisconsin where the plot is partly situated, which in turn is based on the name of the Early Welsh bard Taliesin and refers to the Welsh origins of Wright's maternal family who owned the estate. "Sop Préacháin" is suchlike protean gesture, and one suspects that "crow's wisp" might have its source halfway between the Amerindian folklore and the Irish oral tradition. A neologism, possibly based on obscure local or family lore,[45] it provides Mac Aodha's language and narrative with new impulses. As such, it is her answer to Muldoon's "Quoof": "[an]other shy beast / that has yet to enter the language."[46] Indeed, those impulses are as sundry here as elsewhere in Muldoon, and they produce images just as inscrutable and full of dark humor. At one point, we are reminded of Muldoon's father in "Quoof" as he would "juggle a red-hot half-brick / in an old sock"[47] when another father and son set about heating their carrier pigeons' eggshells in order to "strengthen the bird's beaks" ("go ndéanaidís blaoscanna uibhe a théamh / chun gob an éin a neartú").[48] Until it goes awry, of course, and the eggs start bursting in the oven. The boy sits up watching, caught in a daze, and will not "rest until / the train whistle blows" ("Níorbh fhéidir a shuaimhniú / go gcloiseadh fead na traenach"). Again, the train whistle is heard. This time, however, its sound is loaded with countless new connotations of guilty memories which should not have been brought to light ("nach ligtear as do cheann iad, na cuimhní cinn / a roinntear");[49] of the lunchtime whistle in Shining Brow;[50] of the Crow Indians' traditional bowing contest involving "clay pigeons" of wisps of grass thrown over the archer's head,[51] which Muldoon alludes to in "Tell" (who of course is William Tell, alias Muldoon's father crossed with a "Crow, or Comanche" Indian).[52] The sound of the whistle thus seems to be ameliorative to the one heard in "Focal Faoisimh": rather than signalling displacement and restraint, translation as an act of naming increases the potentiality of language.

In response to Muldoon's poems in Horse Latitudes, Michael Schmidt observes: "Such poems don't just say things. We read them for what they do with and to language, how they engage and transform clichés, how they subvert genres not in a mere spirit of play, but to make them serviceable in new ways."[53] Indeed, he might have been speaking of Mac Aodha's poetry which, by doing things to and with language, also manages to say quite a few things, not least about the language. With Muldoon, she seems to share his artistic credo, "the impulse not to belong, not to fit in,"[54] which keeps coming up also in his perpetually bemused reluctance to answer questions as to whether he should be considered an Irish or an American poet. In Mac Aodha, this ambivalence is played out on the level of language. On the one hand, writing in Irish allows her to declare herself undeniably an Irish poet. On the other hand, it provides a template for encompassing and thematizing the complexities of a linguistic, poetic, or any other form of identity.

NOTES

1. Seamus Heaney, *Government of the Tongue* (London: Faber and Faber, 1989), xix.

2. T. S. Eliot, "The Social Function of Poetry," in *On Poetry and Poets*, 4th ed. (London: Faber and Faber, 1965), 18–19.

3. See Brian Ó Conchubhair, "The Right of Cows and the Rite of Copy; an Overview of Translation from Irish to English," *Éire-Ireland* 35, no. 1/2 (2000): 104.

4. Peter Denman, "Rude Gestures? Contemporary Women's Poetry in Irish," *Colby Quarterly* 28, no. 4 (1992): 253.

5. Nuala Ní Dhomhnaill, *Selected Essays* (Dublin: New Island, 2005), 13.

6. Biddy Jenkinson, "Máire Mhac an tSaoi: The Clerisy and the Folk (P.I.R. 24): A Reply," *The Poetry Ireland Review* 25 (Spring 1989): 80.

7. Jenkinson, "A Letter to an Editor," *Irish University Review* 21, no. 1 (Spring/Summer 1991): 27–34.

8. Gearóid Mac Lochlainn, *Sruth Teangacha / Stream of Tongues* (Indreabhán: Cló Iar-Chonnacht, 2002), 188.

9. See for example Michael Cronin, *An Ghaeilge san Aois Nua / Irish in the New Century* (Dún Laoghaire: Cois Life, 2005), 49.

10. Aifric Mac Aodha, "'A Talkative Corpse': The Joys of Writing Poetry in Irish," *Columbia: A Journal of Literature and Art*, Oct. 25, 2011, http://columbiajournal.org/902.

11. Mac Aodha, *Gabháil Syrinx* (Maynooth: An Sagart, 2010), 11. Trans. David Wheatley, "Poet," *The Stinging Fly* 20, no. 2 (Winter 2011/2012): 80.

12. The Old-Irish poem is preserved on the margin of a Latin primer by an Irish monk, originally compiled at a monastery in South Germany and now preserved in St. Paul's Abbey in Lavanttal, Austria.

13. "Pangur Bán," in *Old Irish Reader*, ed. Rudolf Thurneysen (Dublin: Institute for Advanced Studies, 1981), 40. "'White Pangur': A Scholar and His Cat," in *Early Irish Lyrics*, ed. and trans. Gerard Murphy (Oxford: Oxford UP, 1956), 3.

14. Heaney, "Translator's Note," *Poetry* 188, no. 1 (Apr. 2006): 4–5.

15. Interview with the poet, Prague, Nov. 2, 2011.

16. Paul Muldoon, "Anonymous: Myself and Pangur," in *Poems 1968–1998* (New York: Farrar, Straus and Giroux, 2001), 436.

17. "Pangur Bán," *Poetry* 188, no. 1 (Apr. 2006): 4. Trans. Seamus Heaney.

18. Mac Aodha, "A Talkative Corpse."

19. Mac Aodha, *Gabháil Syrinx*, 38. Trans. Wheatley.

20. Ibid., 43.

21. Walter Benjamin, "The Translator's Task," trans. Steven Rendall, *TTR: Traduction, Terminologie, Rédaction* 10, no. 2 (1997): 157.

22. Benjamin, 153.

23. Although she translated some of her early verse, since the publication of *Gabháil Syrinx* her main translators have been David Wheatley and Justin Quinn. Some of the translations by Wheatley have appeared in *Poetry*, *The Stinging Fly*, and on the *Poetry International* website (see Bibliography).

24. Mac Aodha, "A Talkative Corpse."

25. Ibid.

26. Mac Aodha, *Gabháil Syrinx*, 12–14. Trans. Quinn.

27. W. B. Yeats, *The Poems*, ed. Daniel Albright (London: J. M. Dent, 1994), 180.

28. Mac Aodha, *Gabháil Syrinx*, 12–14. Trans. Quinn.

29. Ibid.

30. Mac Aodha, *Gabháil Syrinx*, 35. Trans. mine. (Unless otherwise indicated, all translations are mine.)

31. Ibid., 37.

32. Ibid., 38. Trans. Wheatley.

33. Ibid., 41.

34. Ibid., 16. Trans. Wheatley, "The Soothing Word," *Poetry International* (Oct. 2, 2015), http://www.poetryinternationalweb.net/pi/site/poem/item/24202/auto/0/The-Soothing-Word.

35. George Steiner, *After Babel: Aspects of Language and Translation*, 3rd ed. (Oxford: Oxford UP, 1998), 300.

36. E-mail to the author, Nov. 15, 2011. For several years, Mac Aodha was part of the team of translators working on the *New English-Irish Dictionary* launched by Foras na Gaeilge in January 2013. Until recently, she was an Assistant Editor for An Gúm, the largest publisher of Irish language books in Ireland, responsible, among others, for the publication of *The New Irish-English Dictionary*.

37. James S. F. Wilson, "The Art of Poetry No. 87," an interview with Paul Muldoon, *The Paris Review* 169 (Spring 2004), http://www.theparisreview.org/interviews/30/the-art-of-poetry-no-87-paul-muldoon.

38. Mac Aodha, "Sop Préacháin"; Trans. Wheatley, "A Crow's Wisp," *Poetry* (Sept. 2015), http://www.poetryfoundation.org/poetrymagazine/poem/250798.

39. See Thomas Kinsella, *The Táin* (Oxford: Oxford UP, 2002), 52.

40. Mac Aodha, "Sop Préacháin"; Trans. Wheatley, "A Crow's Wisp," *Poetry* (Sept. 2015).

41. See Niall Ó Dónaill, *Foclóir Gaeilge-Béarla* (Baile Átha Cliath: An Gúm, 1977).

42. Mac Aodha, "Sop Préacháin"; Trans. Wheatley, "A Crow's Wisp," *Poetry* (Sept. 2015).

43. In his quest for a specifically American iconography, Wright frequently referred to the indigenous American culture. See for example Anthony Alofsin, *Frank Lloyd Wright — the Lost Years 1910–1922: A Study of Influence* (Chicago: The University of Chicago Press, 1993), 229–35.

44. Wilson, "The Art of Poetry."

45. In conversation Mac Aodha told me that she heard the expression from a friend who claimed to have heard it from a neighbor in the Connemara Gaeltacht.

46. Muldoon, *Poems*, 112.

47. Ibid.

48. Mac Aodha, "Sop Préacháin."

49. Ibid.

50. See Muldoon, *Shining Brow*, act 1, scene 2.

51. See Stewart Culin, *Games of the North American Indians: Games of Skill*, vol. 2 (Lincoln: University of Nebraska Press, 1992), 391.

52. See Muldoon, *Moy Sand and Gravel* (New York: Farrar, Straus and Giroux, 2002), 19.

53. Michael Schmidt, "A Jester in the Earnest World," *PN Review* 173 33, no. 3 (Jan./Feb. 2007), http://www.pnreview.co.uk/cgi-bin/scribe?item_id=2914.

54. Wilson, "The Art of Poetry."

10

End Rhymes and End-Rhymes: Paul Muldoon's Echoic Elegies

Nathaniel Myers

Among Paul Muldoon's most acclaimed poems are his elegies.[1] That this is the case, however, might give the reader pause. How would Muldoon, whose poetry is generally characterized as ludic, erudite, and often opaque, find critical favor for his work in a genre that often demands a certain gravitas and emotional transparency from its poet? Why is it that his elegy "Incantata" — no short poem — has been anthologized in multiple volumes, and yet, as Helen Vendler once famously noted, his poetry has "a hole in the middle where the feeling should be"?[2] Several potential answers to this apparent conundrum present themselves in the critical literature on Muldoon. Some scholars have suggested, for example, that the elegiac genre itself has become capacious enough to accommodate Muldoon's style — that, in fact, the poet fits snugly within the larger trajectory of the elegy in the twentieth century as Jahan Ramazani has mapped it, in which elegists more frequently employ the kinds of ironic stance and parodic mode that befit Muldoon's work.[3] Other scholars argue, conversely, that it is Muldoon's style that has changed, that his style now better accommodates the genre. This latter perspective is shared by Vendler in her review of Muldoon's collection *Horse Latitudes* (2006); she remarks, after having spent considerable space unpacking two elegies from the volume, that "Paul Muldoon seems to me a more convincing poet now than he was ten or fifteen years ago," that "age has deepened Muldoon's poetry," and that he is now able to "bear aloft both grief and playfulness."[4] Time has brought Muldoon a great deal of loss, and in grappling with that loss, Vendler argues, he has plumbed new emotional depths.

Both arguments — that is, on the one hand, that the genre of elegy has changed, and, on the other hand, that Muldoon's style has changed — have merit, and, in fact, together they speak to the linguistic, tonal, and affective complexity of his elegies. These poems *are* simultaneously somber and ludic, opaque and direct, ironic and sincere, as well as many other things. It is these very complexities of language, tone, and emotion that provide the central focus of this article. In his elegies, and in particular through his now infamous use of the same ninety rhyme sounds that he employs across multiple poems, Muldoon plots the linguistic coordinates of his grief, charting what amounts to both a map of that grief and a key to reading that map.

As seen in and across poems like "Incantata," "Yarrow," and "Sillyhow Stride," this distinctive practice of plotting grief produces a kind of affective echo-chamber. Through an accumulation of affect generated by his repeated use of the same language and rhyme, Muldoon's elegies hold the promise of a shared emotional intimacy between poet and reader. In returning time and again to the same end-rhymes, his language continually echoes its own sonic and affective history, even as it generates new points along that history. And for the dedicated reader of Muldoon, the accumulating complexities of that history only deepen the bond (however imperfect, if no less compelling) between the reader and the poet. Ultimately, in a poem like "Turkey Buzzards," Muldoon thematizes and reflects on his poetic techniques — what I call his end-rhyme aesthetic of affective accumulation — and in doing so considers not only the untenable nature of that promise of emotional intimacy but also the problematic aestheticization of loss and grief that is a consequence of those techniques. And while it is surely a fool's errand to seek an answer to the question that opens this article — why Muldoon's elegies in particular should be critically lauded — in its examination of the linguistic and affective work of these poems, this essay nevertheless offers a few potential reasons.

In likening Muldoon's elegiac strategies to the charting of a map, I also wish to point to the suggestive parallels between the changing shape of his elegies and the poet's move from Ireland to America — from one point on the map, that is, to another. Muldoon's early volumes include a number of elegies, but it is not until *Meeting the British* in 1987 — the same year as his transatlantic relocation — that elegy becomes a primary poetic mode for Muldoon. Nor is it until that time that he begins to employ his more complex, expansive elegiac strategies. The poet's move to America occurs in the year following his father's death, and it is only some years after that move, with *The Annals of Chile* in 1994, that Muldoon begins to elegize his mother, who had passed away more than twenty years before in 1973. The reasons for the twenty-year gap between his mother's death and his elegizing of her are not clear,[5] but it would be hard not to consider the role distance might play — the distance, say, achieved by permanently moving across the Atlantic — in allowing the poet to finally confront that death. And yet, even despite what might be gained by distance, and as these elegies will demonstrate, there is clearly an impulse for Muldoon to anchor his elegies in the past, to close the gap between his life in Ireland and his life in America; and it is only through this anchoring that Muldoon can generate an affective map of his grief, that he can lead the reader from point A to point B through and across his elegies.

So while several elegies prior to or in the midst of Muldoon's move to America thus gesture to the elegiac work that is the primary focus of this article — for example, "The Mirror," Muldoon's translation of Michael Davitt's "An Scáthán," exhibits the morbid and macabre characteristics of these later elegies, and "The Coney" has drastic tonal shifts similar to the elegies featured here — nevertheless, I begin with an examination of "Cauliflowers," from his second post-relocation collection, *Madoc: A*

Mystery (1990). "Cauliflowers" is, as Tim Kendall notes, Muldoon's first formally published attempt at a sestina,[6] a specific poetic form that will become significant for an elegy like "Yarrow," which Muldoon famously described in an interview as a "very complex poem involving nine or ten intercut exploded sestinas."[7] More importantly, however, it is the sestina form's general ability to play with and complicate the relationship between sound and affective meaning that make it central to understanding Muldoon's elegies more broadly.[8] The complex affective charge of the sestina's end-words accumulate when their sounds bring their diverse individual contexts into conversation with each other. The potential, then, to stretch and accrue meaning through rhyme and sound is vast, and Muldoon's "Cauliflowers" is particularly suggestive of this vastness.

"Cauliflowers" is an elegy for Muldoon's father. It is also a poem that twists and turns, moving not only from image to image, but from tonality to tonality. As the poet sits in an Oregon motel, he recalls various memories of his father and uncle over the course of several stanzas until those recollections are interrupted by two lovers in the room next door, which is then interrupted, for example, by the thought of Magritte's pipe, which is then interrupted again by an image of pipe-bombs that recall the Northern Irish conflict. In other words, and in terms of tone, the introspective abuts the erotic abuts the surrealistic abuts the violent.[9] These tonal fluctuations and tensions — wrought by association — are seeded in more meticulous ways through the sestina's various end-words and end-rhymes that, over the course of the poem, accrue greater and more complex meaning. Following, for example, the poem's end-rhyme phrase "going down" as it appears variously throughout the elegy, the reader finds it not only refers to the price of cauliflowers that "goes down" as well as to a memory of Muldoon's father "going down / the primrose path" but also to the "lovers / repeatedly going down / on each other."[10] This phrase "going down" thus *goes down* its own windy path; but within the sestina, it also cannot help but turn back on itself again and again, recalling, through rhyme, where it originated and has since been.

Arguably more complicated is the end-rhyme that begins, in the first stanza, as "Belfast market," where the price of cauliflower is going down. What follows in the second stanza is the memory of a platoon that

Muldoon can just "make out"; following that, it is the "mud-guard" of a lorry he remembers his uncle leaning against; then, the "scorch-marked" pocket into which his father slips his pipe; then "Magritte's" own pipe that is not a pipe; then "Margaret," of whom the poet asks, "are you grieving?"[11] thus recalling Gerard Manley Hopkins's "Spring and All"; and finally, the "unmarked" pit where the cauliflowers are harvested. It is worth noting that there is no discernible end-*word* in these rhymes, only end-*sounds*. And even then, it is not clear what those sounds are: "m-r-k-t," "m-k-t," "m-g-r-d," "m-r-k-d," "m-g-r-t," "m-r-g-r-t"? Not only are we faced with varying letter combinations in which these consonants are ordered, but we must also contend with the question of whether the consonants are voiced or unvoiced. These sounds thus signal both their relative closeness as well as their ultimate differences: within their various contextual meanings in their lines and in their stanzas, they remain distinct, and yet through sound they continue to echo each other. The reader can hear "Magritte" in "Margaret," but the relatively playful surrealism of Magritte starkly contrasts the soberness of Muldoon's reference to Margaret, which, in recalling Hopkins's poem — about a child who, in mourning the falling of leaves, mourns for herself — gestures to the self-elegiac nature of Muldoon's poem. Indeed, this poem seems more interested in Muldoon than in his father; or, more accurately, this poem — as with many of these elegies — is more interested in the nature of Muldoon's own mourning, and the relationship of grief to language consequent of that mourning.

This poetic self-reflexivity is no less clear than in the central metaphor of the poem, the titular cauliflowers. As the poem concludes, and as the poet has returned to thinking about the passing of his father and uncle, the tornada reads, "All gone down / the original pipe. And the cauliflowers / in an unmarked pit, that were harvested by their own light."[12] The cauliflowers are, on initial reading, a proxy for the poet's father, who was a farmer of, among other things, cauliflowers. But, as Falci notes, if the cauliflowers are, as the poem says, "harvested by their own light," they are no cauliflowers of Patrick Muldoon, whose economic woes surrounding the crop are evident in its declining prices "on the Belfast market" mentioned at the poem's beginning.[13] The sestina's end-rhymes, however, behave much like the cauliflowers, flourishing and accruing meaning and affective resonance

throughout the poem by echoing each other, by reflecting and refracting — to use the poem's visual metaphor — their own light. The reader is
presented, once again, with an elegiac aesthetic in which the poem sets
the stage for its own unfolding, for which language is in dynamic relationship to grief. Whereas the poem begins by depicting a "static" memory of
the elegized, the further we proceed into the poem, the more it begins to
uproot itself, to progress through association. On the one hand, this associative, accumulative aesthetic seems to lose track of its central figure(s),
Muldoon's father (and uncle); and in this way, the poem could very well
validate Vendler's concern that Muldoon's poetry has a "hole in the middle
where the feeling should be." In other words, in the associative head-game
of the poem, we lose, as it were, its heart. It is a concern articulated by the
poem itself, beginning as it does with an epigraph that describes the science
behind the cauliflower's self-generating light, but which is a quotation
attributed to that most untrustworthy source, *The National Inquirer*, thereby
suggesting that "Cauliflowers," too, is all false artifice. And yet, on the other
hand, this associative, accumulative aesthetic keeps at the foreground its
other central figure, the mourning poet. The poem meanders, it twists;
but so, too, does grief twist, and sometimes through thoughts unbefitting
of solemn mourning.

What the sestina form gives to Muldoon, then, is a fixed poetic structure in which linguistic and affective complexity can arise. As he famously
described (almost a decade before writing "Cauliflowers"):

> I've become very interested in structures that can be fixed like mirrors
> at angles to each other — it relates to narrative form — so that new
> images can emerge from the setting up of poems in relation to each
> other: further ironies are possible, further mischief is possible. I hope
> the mischief I make is of a rewarding kind, not that of a practical joker,
> and will outline the complexities of being here.[14]

The end-rhymes of the sestina create these kinds of complex, rewarding
ironies. What "Cauliflowers" does specifically is demonstrate the close
relationship between the complexities created by the sestina form and
the complexities also already inherent in grief. If, through its end-words,

the sestina records its own history, linguistic grief is similarly defined by history — by which I mean the elegy not only marks the history of a person who has died but also records the history of grief that continues in the wake of that person's life. Muldoon's follow-up volume to *Madoc*, *The Annals of Chile*, marks the poet's further elaboration (and complication) of the relationship between poetic form and history, affective echo and linguistic mourning, which he achieves not only through the aforementioned "explosion" of the sonnet form in "Yarrow" but also through his establishment of the ninety end-rhyme sounds that make up both "Yarrow" and "Incantata" in this collection.

If we read *The Annals of Chile* sequentially, then "Incantata" is the first poem to use these ninety rhyme-sounds, though the poem already has its own (sonic) history in the form of his poem "Mary Farl Powers: *Pink Spotted Torso*" from *Quoof* (1983). "Incantata" is Muldoon's elegy for the American artist (and his former long-term partner) of the earlier poem's title; *Pink Spotted Torso* is the name of one of her paintings. Their relationship ended in the early 1980s, and Farl Powers died in 1992 from cancer. While we learn much about both her and her relationship with Muldoon in "Incantata" — or, at least, we learn what Muldoon offers us, whether truthful or not — "*Pink Spotted Torso*" offers an initial, fleeting glimpse of the artist, and "Incantata" seems to build itself on the stage that the other poem has set. For example, "Incantata" begins:

> I thought of you tonight, *a leanbh*, lying there in your long barrow
> colder and dumber than a fish by Francisco de Herrera,
> as I X-Actoed from a spud the Inca
> glyph for a mouth: thought of the first time I saw your pink
> spotted torso, distant-near as a nautilus,
> when you undid your portfolio, yes indeedy,
> and held the print of what looked like a cankered potato
> at arm's length — your arms being longer, it seemed, than Lugh's.[15]

The rhyme scheme of the stanza — though perhaps not immediately apparent due to Muldoon's fast and loose rhyming — is *aabbcddc*, the stanza's end-rhymes being (in some shape or other) "-arrow," "-ink," "-lus," and

"-dada." A reader of "Mary Farl Powers: *Pink Spotted Torso*," however, will have seen the images from this stanza before; they will have heard some of its rhymes already. The "pink spotted torso" may certainly be Farl Powers's sexualized body (with the thinly veiled expression of arousal, "when you undid your portfolio, yes indeedy") but that earlier poem also has already introduced the knife, the hieroglyph, and the potato. More importantly, the poem's opening lines — "She turns from the sink / potato in hand. A Kerr's Pink"[16] — introduces the "-ink" end-rhyme that will find later iterations not only in "Incantata" but also in "Yarrow," and then again in other, later poems. It is as if Muldoon anchors the beginning of his elegy by recalling the images and sounds of his earlier poem, by giving us a reference point he has already provided. The affective work of rhyme carried out within a sestina like "Cauliflowers" develops, at this juncture in Muldoon's poetic output, beyond one self-contained poem and, instead, extends across multiple poems.

As the two poems in which Muldoon first incorporates the same ninety end-rhymes, "Incantata" and "Yarrow" are fundamental to the claims I am making here about the relationship between grief and language in Muldoon's elegies. But they are also expansive, unwieldy poems, and the complicated affective entanglements wrought by the very ninety end-rhymes in which I am interested resist paraphrase — at least in the space provided here.[17] For that reason, I have limited myself to following the trail of one and only one of the end-rhymes Muldoon uses in these two long elegies: that of "-arrow," echoed, as it is, in "Yarrow." By tracing the development of this end-rhyme through these two poems (and then beyond), I will suggest the import of the many affective complexities that accrue over the end-rhyme's repeated use, in which Muldoon plots a comprehensive history of his own grief.

While abstracting the end-rhyme from its original stanzaic context strips that end-rhyme of much of its meaning (if not comprehensibility), I have listed below each instance of the use of "-arrow" in both "Incantata" and "Yarrow" to offer at least some semblance of its tonal and affective variety. Next to each line, I have noted the poem and stanza number in which the end-rhyme is used ("I" means "Incantata"; "Y," ""Yarrow"; "t" for "Yarrow's" tornada); and I have included in brackets those words or phrases that immediately precede or follow the end-rhyme, in order to clarify context:

> I thought of you tonight, *a leanbh*, lying there in your long barrow (I 1)
> colder and dumber than a fish by Francisco de Herrera (I 1)
> on which you've etched the row upon row (I 45)
> of army-worms, than that you might reach out, arrah, (I 45)
> Little by little it dawned on us that the row (Y 1)
> the Spanish *Lear*; the umpteenth *Broken Arrow*; (Y 9)
> [Harp-]er and Row (Y 18)
> in which he'd dash off a couple of 'sparrow-[songs]' (Y 27)
> as a two-edged sword, as the arrow [that flieth by day] (Y 36)
> The day S— came back with the arrow [through a heart tattooed] (Y 46)
> 'parsnips', 'swedes', and, I guess, 'vegetable marrow'; (Y 57)
> That must have been the year I stood by the wheel-barrow (Y 58)
> The magical toad entrusted to me by Francisco Pizarro (Y 75)
> The storm blew over, of course, and with the help of Arrow (Y 92)
> but (this chilled me to the marrow) (Y 93)
> As we neared Armagh, she'd dipped the tip of each little arrow (Y 103)
> bird that she is, feeds on the corpse from *Run of the Arrow*, (Y 112)
> now her tattoo of a heart and arrow (Y 121)
> my da would have said — while the Cathedral of Ero-[tic Misery] (Y 130)
> bird while the scald crow (Y 139)
> 'I am the arrow that flieth by day. I am the arrow.' (Y 147)
> In a conventional tornada, the strains of her '*Che sera, sera*' (Y t)
> to a bath resplendent with yarrow (Y t)
> it has to do with a trireme, laden with ravensara (Y t)[18]

A quick glance through this list helps illuminate the difficulty of unpacking the development of even one end-rhyme, let alone all end-rhymes in their entirety. In "Incantata," the "barrow" of Farl Powers's gravesite is echoed in the Spanish painter Francisco de Herrera, known as the "Spaniard of the Fish" for his masterful still lifes; this juxtaposition of "barrow" and "Herrera" manifests, tonally, in the comically morbid tone that we have seen in Muldoon's earlier elegies — not every poet would compare their deceased ex-lover to a fish — and yet that juxtaposition also reinforces Farl Powers's relationship to her own artistic life, even in her cold death. This relation to her painterly life is reinforced later in stanza 45 with the row (upon row) of "army-worms" — the name the poet gives to the squiggly figures of Mary Farl Powers's painting *Emblements*. And in "-arrow's" final iteration in "Incantata," the rhyme resonates in "arrah," the Anglo-Irish expression of thrill, or excitement, which, in its original context, *seems* to articulate a hope in the consolatory power of art that ends the poem: "that you might reach out, arrah, / and take in your ink-stained hands my own hands stained in ink."[19]

I say "seems" because, even while the image of Farl Powers's hands in Muldoon's hands — and the chiasmus that frames that image — suggests resolution and closure, the inkiness of the image contrastingly *stains* the sentiment. Does the "arrah," then, signal not compensatory thrill but unresolved frustration? Can it do both? What affective charge is consolidated in the end-rhyme at this point? The answer is unclear, and thus, too, is our understanding of how the end-rhyme "-arrow" develops. It is possible to read this ambiguity as a failure of the work of end-rhyme in the poem, especially if, as I have been arguing, part of that work is to make legible (for both Muldoon and his reader) the poet's grief. But if so, it is a failure that is already registered in the poem in various other ways. To clarify: as I have been arguing, yes, in the affectively-charged aesthetic of end-rhyme, Muldoon locates and establishes his grief in sound and echo; however, as he does in "Cauliflowers," so, too, in "Incantata" does Muldoon include a critique of that aesthetic, an awareness of its limitations. For example, the poem comes to a close only after a long catalogue — beginning in the middle of the poem and lasting some twenty stanzas — of memories and artifacts that remain in Farl Powers's wake. These memories, like affect in the poem, accumulate in an act of poetic monument-building. But this act is one that can also only ever signal Muldoon's inability to capture it all — to capture the life of Mary Farl Powers and Muldoon's relationship to her in their entirety, to capture the full dimensionality of Muldoon's grief at her passing.[20] And in one of the elegy's most oft-quoted passages, Muldoon makes his signature self-critical move, noting that Mary Farl Powers "detected in me a tendency to put / on too much artificiality, both as man and poet, / which is why you [Farl Powers] called me 'Polyester' or 'Polyurethane.'"[21] To be sure, in the poem's use of ninety end-rhymes deployed through an intricate rhyme scheme, the complaint of artifice and artificiality that Farl Powers voices (through Muldoon) in this particular passage is not unfounded. The end-rhyme aesthetic smacks of cold virtuosity and detached calculation. But that doesn't stop Muldoon from returning it.

Indeed, "Yarrow" once again employs the ninety-rhyme aesthetic of affective accumulation and does so through an even more intricate rhyme scheme; but it, too, comes prepackaged with its own critique of that aesthetic. "Yarrow" is a sprawling elegy that interweaves many narratives and intertextual sources together — the yarrow that threatens to overwhelm the Muldoon farm's kale (and just about everything else in the poem) encounters the death of Muldoon's mother, which encounters the picaresque novels of his youth, which encounters the poet channel-surfing, which encounters Sylvia Plath's suicide, which encounters *King Lear* and Nabokov's *Ada*, which encounters the figure of S——, a drug-addicted, fictional lover of the poet who is at times the antithesis of and at other times conflated with his mother. Many of these encounters can be deduced from "-arrow's" various iterations listed above: the "row" in stanza 1 is that row of kale about to be overwhelmed. In stanza 9, as Muldoon flips through television stations, he comes across (yet another) episode of the late-1950s television series, *Broken Arrow*. By stanza 36, that *Arrow* (having, in the meantime, also become "sparrow" and "marrow") summons the "arrow that flieth by day" of Psalm 91:5, the arrow from which, in its Biblical context, God protects us. By stanza 147, however, this Biblical phrase is echoed in Sylvia Plath's suicidal proclamation, "I am the arrow," from her poem "Ariel" — a poem whose title itself evokes the "-arrow" rhyme. This short catalogue of the poem's references fails to unpack "-arrow's" many other iterations, like S——'s tattoo (an arrow through the heart), or the Cathedral of "Ero"-tic Misery, another of Muldoon's gestures to the art world, this time to German artist Kurt Schwitters's Dadaist art installation, bombed during the Second World War. From television series to suicide to S—— to surrealism, the sound of "-arrow" becomes cacophonous with meaning, affectively pulling the reader in innumerable directions, to such degree as to resist paraphrase. Too much is compacted into one rhyme to be fully unpacked, to be fully articulated — hence language actually *activates* grief in Muldoon's end-rhyme aesthetic. The end-rhymes and their affect *must* be experienced. Language activates grief because rhyme can shoulder accumulating paradoxes, it can draw out similarities while accommodating difference, and thus it can contain the full complexities of mourning and make it alive (if overwhelming) to both the mourner and his readers. The poet gives life to rhyme, but rhyme eventually speaks back; and the reader, if he or she is willing to follow, can hear it too.

The reader can hear rhyme speak because Muldoon, by anchoring meaning and affect repeatedly and so thoroughly in rhyme, imbues rhyme with history, an affective history of his grief that lives in language and rhyme and thus can be read, studied, and potentially understood. In history is legibility. And yet, the method is not infallible, and of this fallibility Muldoon is, as always, aware. If rhyme can speak independently of its author, then it can also speak beyond him or her. I am not merely voicing some death-of-the-author stance; if anything, the elegy as a genre reasserts authorship, insists on the subject who locates grief in language. On the contrary, what makes Muldoon's elegiac end-rhyme aesthetic so robust is the tension between author and echo: the poet may localize his overwhelming grief in, for one, the "-arrow" end-rhyme, but by the poem's tornada, "-arrow" speaks beyond itself by echoing another of the poem's end-rhymes, an end-rhyme I have designated "-sara."[22] Thus the poem signals the very slipperiness of the end-rhyme aesthetic, the inability of rhyme to contain its own echoes. As the compiled list above illustrates, the final three articulations of "-arrow" (all located in the tornada) swing from the muddled strains of "*Che sera, sera*" — a mishmash of the 1950s American tune "*Que sera, sera*" and the 1970s Italian song "*Che sará*" — to the poet's (imagined?) memory of a bath teeming with yarrow, and then finally to the image of a ship decorated in ravensara, a plant, like yarrow, believed to have medicinal qualities. Before the reader advances too far in interpreting the ravensara as a kind of doubling-down of yarrow as metaphor for healing (and thus gesturing to the poem's potential consolatory power), it should be noted that the end-rhyme "-sara" of ravensara also recalls from earlier in the poem, among other things, "Assaroe" in stanza 122 — Assaroe being the waterfall in Donegal named after the legendary figure Aodh Ruadh, who, as tale tells, drowned in its waters — and *Writing Degree Zero* in stanza 104 — or what is the first full-length book of Roland Barthes. Both of these earlier articulations of the "-sara" end-rhyme throw into question the credibility of the healing power of ravensara, whether by recalling death in Irish legend or by referencing the work of a writer responsible for proclaiming dead the very figure of the author. That "-arrow" echoes "-sara" more generally through the poem further implicates the slippery instability of the end-rhyme aesthetic, its capacity to speak beyond itself, to echo boundlessly, to gather interminable affective charge. Yarrow may heal, but it may also suffocate all in its path. It may give shape to Muldoon's grief, but it may also drown him in that grief. It may provide his reader with a map to follow his grief, but it may also lead that reader astray.

Muldoon uses his set of ninety end-rhymes in a handful of poems following the two collected in *The Annals of Chile*; and by way of conclusion, I would like to examine one of these poems alongside another poem which, for reasons that will become clear, does not use the end-rhymes. In "Sillyhow Stride" and "Turkey Buzzards," both collected in *Horse Latitudes*, Muldoon mourns the passing of two people who, like Mary Farl Powers and like his mother, fell victim to cancer: the poet's sister, Maureen, and his friend and sometimes collaborator, the rock musician Warren Zevon. In these poems, Muldoon thematizes once again this aesthetic of accumulation, but instead of cauliflowers or yarrow, he employs the central metaphor of the turkey buzzard.[23] Through this metaphor, the poet lodges a further critique of that aesthetic, the ethical import of which makes for a particularly scathing occasion for self-reproach, arguably more trenchant than those presented in his earlier elegies.

In "Sillyhow Stride," Muldoon doubles down on that effort to make the biographical historical, to make the personal public. His use of the end-rhyme aesthetic is, in the case of this poem, just the cherry on top; in addition to these end-rhymes, Muldoon packs the poem with allusions and references to his own work, the work of Zevon, their collaborative work, as well as the work of one unlikely if not irrelevant source, John Donne. Buttressed by these numerous sources, "Sillyhow Stride" is Muldoon's most ambitious effort to make an increasingly complex grief legible, to rhyme that grief in a past that is his own but that might be shared with others.

As "Incantata" picks up specific elements from his earlier poem "Mary Farl Powers: *Pink Spotted Torso*," "Sillyhow Stride" picks up elements of an earlier Muldoon poem about Zevon, the poem titled "Warren Zevon: *Excitable Boy*," from the "Sleeve Notes" section of his collection *Hay* (1998). During the time of "Warren Zevon: *Excitable Boy*," Muldoon and his wife — at least as the poem describes — were particularly unfaithful to each other, and one of her lovers introduced the poet to Zevon's album, whose songs "to booty, to beasts, to bimbo, boom boom / are inextricably part of the warp and woof / of the wild and wicked poems in *Quoof*."[24] The poem thus suggests the deep influence of Zevon's style on Muldoon from early on. More importantly, lines from "Sillyhow Stride" rhyme with those of "Warren Zevon: *Excitable Boy*," most conspicuously the "zoom zoom" and "vroom vroom" of the latter poem that echo the "boom boom" quoted in the lines just above.[25] "Boom boom" *also* gestures to another Zevon song, "Boom Boom Mancini," a song that takes as its subject the real-world boxing champion from the early 1980s, Ray Mancini. So, Muldoon once again anchors his elegy with earlier material from his oeuvre; and in doing so, he also begins to anchor his work in material from Zevon's oeuvre. Such is the porousness of their styles.

To be sure, if Zevon's *Excitable Boy* was truly a significant influence on Muldoon's poetry, that influence may be no more clearly discernible than in the tonal dissonance of Muldoon's elegies. Zevon's album, of which there are many references in "Sillyhow Stride,"[26] is full of the kind of macabre ironies seen in Muldoon's elegies, which are no more conspicuous than in the album's title song. "Excitable Boy" tells the story of a teenaged sociopath who rapes and kills his prom date and keeps her bones as a souvenir many years later. But while the story is very dark, the song parades as a light pop song, with an upbeat saxophone melody leading the charge, and a band of pop singers "ooh-wah-oohing" their way through the horrific narrative. The dissonance of musical style and narrative make for the kind of macabre tone that occurs, as in Muldoon's poetry, when death encounters the comical and the sexual. "Sillyhow Stride" is thus not merely the kind of emulation of the style and theme that Jahan Ramazani has argued is true of, for instance, Auden's elegies, which "represent a symbolic interfusion between poet and deceased" through stylistic imitation[27]; rather, Muldoon's style was already deeply indebted to, more firmly rooted in, Zevon's style.

Muldoon and Zevon's eventual collaboration is, for these reasons, not entirely surprising, and their song "My Ride's Here" exhibits many of the stylistic traits shared by the two. Tara Christie Kinsey's piece "Rave on, John Donne: Paul Muldoon and Warren Zevon" already terrifically examines Muldoon and Zevon's collaboration and friendship, and so I wish only to draw out two other features of the song for my analysis.[28] The first is that the song provides a future line for "Sillyhow Stride" — that of the sky "full of carrion," a line that speaks to one of the poem's central metaphors in the turkey buzzard.[29] But the song also, in a line ultimately omitted from the recorded version, introduces another key figure in the poem "Sillyhow Stride," that of "the Reverend Donne / strik[ing] up his organ."[30]

John Donne's poetry is pervasive in "Sillyhow Stride," his work not so much alluded to in the elegy as it is heavily quoted throughout the poem. From Donne highlights such as "Valediction: Forbidding Mourning" and "The Sun Rising," to material pulled from his sermons, to references to texts *about* the poet — like, for example, Coleridge's "On Donne's Poetry" — Muldoon ventriloquizes the metaphysical poet again and again. Midway through "Sillyhow Stride," for example, the poet turns momentarily from Zevon to the image of his dying sister, sitting in her hospital bed. The poet remarks, "I thought of how the wrangling schools / need look no further than her bed / to find what fire shall burn this world."[31] These lines originate from Donne's poem "A Fever," in which the speaker looks on a dying woman and imagines the heat of her fever as a metaphor for the heat of her passions — sexual included. The conflation of death with passion is by no means unusual for Donne, nor, as has been established, is it for Muldoon. Certainly, in this specific instance of the poem, the "fever" refers to Zevon's passions — his music, but also his alcohol and sometimes drug abuse — as well as the fever of Muldoon's sister in her hospital bed, oxygen mask on, "drowning in her own spit."[32] The frequent summoning of Donne's words creates, in this way, yet another connection to an aesthetic of tonal dissonance. Kinsey has suggested that Donne's presence suits the poem because, like Zevon, he was one who thought often and deeply about his own mortality;[33] this is true (and true, too, of Muldoon), but I would argue further that Donne functions as a stylistic predecessor to both Zevon and Muldoon, one who discovers in death its strange and jarring associations. He was also a poet of biographical importance to the two friends: in Zevon's final months, after inquiring about Donne's work, Muldoon emailed the rock star the text of Donne's "Death be not proud." Zevon wrote back saying, "It's an honor to receive the Donne lines from your fingers. To look for those lines and have them come from you. What a shining life."[34]

The personal significance of Donne's poetry in Muldoon and Zevon's relationship cannot be understated; Donne may have been a stylistic forebear, but he was also at the emotional center of that relationship, and thus of Muldoon's grief. "Sillyhow Stride" thus plots a history of his grief thematically, even as it continues that plotting through the ninety end-rhyme technique. And of those ninety end-rhymes, the poem, of course, also gives new meanings: the "-arrow" end-rhyme, for example, returns once again in the elegy's terza-rima final lines:

> lies belly-up on a Space Lab scaffold where the turkey buzzards pink
> Matsuhisa-san's seared *toro,*
> turkey buzzards waiting for you to eclipse and cloud them with a wink
>
> as they hold out their wings and of the sun his working vigor borrow
> before they parascend through the Viper Room or the Whisky a Go Go,
> each within its own "cleansing breeze," its own *Cathartes aura.*[35]

The "-arrow" end-rhyme begins in this excerpt as the sushi cut of *"toro,"* or tuna, picked at by a group of turkey buzzards. The rhyme is picked up again two lines later in another quotation from Donne, from his poem, "Love's Growth." In Donne's poem, the speaker comes to the realization that love is not an abstract, unchanging thing, but a feeling that grows and suffers and is influenced by, among other things, the increased "vigor" of springtime's sun. In Muldoon's poem, it is the buzzards whose flight appears to be invigorated by the sun. The rhyme is picked up a third and final time in the Latin name for the turkey buzzard, *"Cathartes aura,"* which literally means, as the poem states, "cleansing breeze."

What to make of the "-arrow" end-rhyme at this point? On the one hand, the poem's final gesture to the "cathartic," the "cleansing breeze," would suggest a kind of consolatory purification in the form of a breeze, the "aura," that blows away Muldoon's suffering. If the buzzards "borrow" the sun's vigor and take flight, it is also possible to read here that Muldoon similarly *borrows* Donne's invigorating poetry, as if for support toward consolatory ends. The poem's lines also imply a form of apotheosis befitting the elegiac genre, in which Zevon ascends to the skies with the vultures, perhaps to participate in a sky burial — a ritual for which the vulture is well-known, and which is made reference to at various times in the poem through the "Parsi Towers," the Towers of Silence, or what, in the Zoroastrian tradition of which Parsi is one, denotes the raised, tower-like structure on which the dead are placed so as to be exposed to the elements (among which are the sun and scavenging birds) as a way to clean the dead body, to rid the spirit of the pollution of the earth.[36]

But while "aura" thus implies a kind of consolatory cleansing, it also echoes, through the figure of the turkey buzzard, the poem's image of "the sky being full of carrion," a line which may be pulled from the lyrics of "My Ride's Here," but in the context of the poem is conflated with the falling bodies from the Twin Towers during the September 11 terrorist attacks.[37] This distressing and horrific image taints the sense of a redemptive consolation otherwise suggested by the end. And is it not also possible to read "-arrow" — along with the other eighty-nine end-rhymes — as themselves carrion floating in the sky, circling through association and carrying the baggage of all their previous iterations — carrying, that is, the weight of earlier death, the weight of Muldoon's former grief? To reuse the ninety end-rhymes is not to let go, not to be consoled, but to hold on to grief, to recycle mourning.

The poem "Turkey Buzzards" offers some clarification to the ambiguity of "Sillyhow Stride's" final lines, not, that is, by definitively supporting one reading or the other — either the consolatory or the melancholic — but by clarifying the double-nature of the turkey buzzard metaphor. "Turkey Buzzards" is a challenging poem in that it progresses much the way the latter half of "Cauliflowers" progresses, from association to association, seemingly suspended in the air, not unlike the buzzards who "seem to stall in the[ir] kettle" at poem's start.[38] The central elegized figure in the poem is Muldoon's sister, whose cancer eats away at her insides much the way the buzzard eats away at the insides of its carrion meal. If this image seems to incriminate the buzzard, it thus also incriminates the elegist himself, who, in his way, feeds off of the cancer of his sister (among many others) in order to write his poetry. The implication is, of course, that cancer is, and has been, for Muldoon, a means by which to profit, both aesthetically and commercially.

But the poem complicates this image of the vulture further. As the poet notes, buzzards habitually defecate on themselves, an act the reader might find unpleasant, but which is a protective measure for the birds, "their poop containing an enzyme / that's known to boost / their immune systems" in the chance they might accidentally cut themselves on a bone, "at no small cost / to their well-being."[39] Does Muldoon's end-rhyme technique not similarly immunize the poet by recycling the material of his historical grief in order to create enzymes that stave off suffering in the present? The poet conditions himself by locating his grief in the aesthetic, in the rhyme that, through sound, spreads that grief across his oeuvre.[40] Here the metaphor of the turkey buzzard takes on a positive spin; perhaps it is the thing that allows him to withstand grief.

And yet, Muldoon complicates the figure of the buzzard even further. By the poem's end, the vultures have failed to return to the surface to feed and defecate, and thus have failed to immunize themselves; they suffer "their command of the vortex / while having lost / their common touch, they've been so long / above it all."[41] In this final passage, the poet lodges a critique on the artist who ultimately stands at a distance, through artifice, of the grim realities of death, who suffers *because* he is caught up in rhyme and echo, in his own poetic mourning, rather than in mourning in the guts of the living. The self-recrimination of "Polyester" that Muldoon voiced in "Incantata" finds new articulation in the shape of the turkey buzzard who flies above it all; but in this latter poem, the self-critique seems all the more scathing. The critique of artifice in the earlier poem has become a critique of one who floats at a distance in the aesthetic, who comes down only to feed off the dead, and who returns to the sky not to shape a history of the elegized but a history of the poet's own grief. Some twelve years after initiating the end-rhyme aesthetic, "Turkey Buzzards" condemns the aesthetic for, like a kettle of vultures, circling around itself.

Or, at least, that is half the story. As I have shown, "Sillyhow Stride" and "Turkey Buzzards" — like "Incantata" and "Yarrow" before them — articulate not one but *both* sides of Muldoon's elegiac aesthetic and his ambivalent attitude toward it. The "-arrow" is both a cleansing breeze and a lofty and distant buzzard; and so, in these later elegies of *Horse Latitudes*, the poet holds out hope that his grief might come to some consolation, that he might find some catharsis, even as he recognizes the dangerous game of aestheticization that a poetic technique like the end-rhyme aesthetic presents. This article has by no means been an exhaustive account of Muldoon's elegies. There are many impressive elegies that do not use these ninety rhyme sounds, just as there are many poems that use these ninety rhyme sounds that are not elegies.[42] And yet, Muldoon's project — if we can call it a project — as demonstrated in these particular elegies deserves special attention. Not only does the end-rhyme aesthetic of affective accumulation speak more broadly to the tonal dissonances of Muldoon's elegiac work, but it has also been for Muldoon a unique means by which to articulate the hopes and failures of writing, an aesthetic that, on the one hand, potentially captures the complexities of grief and activates that grief, giving it a history and a potential legibility, but that, on the other hand, can often speak beyond the poet's intentions, a means through which the poet ultimately can lose sight of the elegized figure, aestheticizing grief such that it removes mourning from its object and makes the mourner its solipsistic focus. Muldoon holds these distinct potentialities — one cathartic, one condemnatory — in tension; and he can do so, in part, through rhyme, which holds such tensions in suspension. Wallace Stevens famously wrote, "The poem is the cry of its occasion, / part of the *res* itself and not about it."[43] Muldoon's elegies are cries that echo themselves, that through rhyme give the poet (and reader) the very means by which grief can be sounded and experienced, and ultimately puzzled over by poet and reader alike.

1. For one example, in his review of Muldoon's *Horse Latitudes*, James Longenbach begins, "Whatever else he is (rhymester, punster, taster, prankster), Paul Muldoon is an elegist." See "Paul Muldoon: The Poet of Giddiness," *Slate*, Nov. 28, 2006, http://www.slate.com/articles/arts/books/2006/11/paul_muldoon.html.

2. Helen Vendler, "Anglo-Celtic Attitudes," *New York Review of Books*, Nov. 6, 1997, 59.

3. See Jahan Ramazani, *Poetry of Mourning: The Modern Elegy from Hardy to Heaney* (Chicago: The University of Chicago Press, 1994). Most recently, Stephen Regan has noted the aptness of Muldoon's work within Ramazani's historical arc; see Regan, "Irish Elegy after Yeats," in *The Oxford Handbook to Modern Irish Poetry*, eds. Fran Brearton and Alan Gillis (Oxford: Oxford UP, 2012), 603. See also Iain Twiddy, "Cancer and the Ethics of Representation in Paul Muldoon's *Horse Latitudes*," *New Hibernia Review* 16, no. 4 (Winter 2012): 19.

4. Helen Vendler, "Fanciness and Fatality," review of *Horse Latitudes* by Paul Muldoon, *The New Republic* 235 (Nov. 9, 2006): 26–33. Jefferson Holdridge has similarly noted this change in Vendler's stance, though it is worth adding that, even in her earlier review for the *New York Review of Books*, she was already backing down from her claim that Muldoon's poetry lacked feeling — a retraction based on her reading of none other than "Incantata"; see Holdridge, *The Poetry of Paul Muldoon* (Dublin: The Liffey Press, 2008), 174. Tim Kendall has also remarked, with regards to Muldoon's elegy "Yarrow" from his earlier collection *The Annals of Chile* (1994), that the poem "is as emotionally charged as anything Muldoon has ever written," similarly suggesting that the elegy is an exceptional (in both senses) genre for Muldoon; see Kendall, *Paul Muldoon* (Chester Springs: Dufour, 1996), 226.

5. One potential explanation is the apparently fraught relationship between Muldoon and his mother, which are evident in poems (if we take them by their word) like "Brazil," "They That Wash on Thursday," and "Yarrow." Muldoon has also been quoted as remarking that "I'm sure we [he and his mother] had some unfinished business." See Robert Potts, "The Poet at Play," *The Guardian*, May 11, 2001, http://www.theguardian.com/books/2001/may/12/poetry.artsandhumanities. Jefferson Holdridge suggests the death (also by cancer) in 1992 of Muldoon's partner Mary Farl Powers, who is elegized in both "Yarrow" and "Incantata" in *Annals*, may have reignited the poet's grief for his mother. See Holdridge, *The Poetry of Paul Muldoon*, 130.

6. Kendall, *Paul Muldoon*, 154.

7. Originally in Paul Muldoon, "An Interview with Paul Muldoon," interview by Lynn Keller, *Contemporary Literature* 35, no. 1 (Spring 1994): 9. See also, among others, Kendall, *Paul Muldoon*, 227.

8. In similar regard, Muldoon further notes of "Yarrow" that it "uses repetition in a way that wouldn't have occurred to me before *Shining Brow*," the first of his select opera librettos. Again, it is the relationship of repetition and sound that most intrigues me here. See Muldoon, "An Interview," 9.

9. Eric Falci remarks that the poem, at the point we encounter the lovers, turns "from narration to association (both sonic and intertextual)"; I agree. In this article, I wish to bring this notion of sonic and intertextual association into direct conversation with Muldoon's elegiac aesthetics. See Falci, *Continuity and Change in Irish Poetry, 1966–2010* (Cambridge: Cambridge UP, 2012), 67.

10. Paul Muldoon, "Cauliflowers," *Poems 1968–1998* (New York: Farrar, Straus and Giroux, 2002), 200–201.

11. Ibid., 201.

12. Ibid.

13. Falci, *Continuity and Change*, 69.

14. John Haffenden, *Viewpoints: Poets in Conversation* (London: Faber and Faber, 1981), 136. Quoted in, among others, Falci, *Continuity and Change*, 70.

15. Paul Muldoon, "Incantata," *Poems 1968–1998*, 331.

16. See Muldoon, "Mary Farl Powers: *Pink Spotted Torso*," *Poems 1968–1998*, 113.

17. Though see the following for excellent, comprehensive (if not exhaustive) readings of these poems: Clair Wills, *Reading Paul Muldoon*, 157–185; Kendall, *Paul Muldoon*, 209–39; Holdridge, *Poetry of Paul Muldoon*, 119–136; and Iain Twiddy, *Pastoral Elegy in Contemporary British and Irish Elegy* (London and New York: Bloomsbury Academic, 2012), 201–28.

18. Tim Kendall also lists many of the end-rhyme variants of "-arrow" in "Yarrow," and he includes some variants I have not listed here. The reasons for this discrepancy will be made clear during my analysis of "Yarrow" below. See Kendall, *Paul Muldoon*, 228.

19. Muldoon, "Incantata," *Poems 1968–1998*, 341.

20. For an excellent reading of the role of monument and objects that remain in Muldoon's elegies, see Matthew Campbell, "Muldoon's Remains," in *Paul Muldoon: Critical Essays*, eds. Tim Kendall and Peter McDonald (Liverpool: Liverpool UP, 2004), 170–88.

21. Muldoon, "Incantata," *Poems 1968–1998*, 334.

22. The end-rhymes "-arrow" and "-sara" are clearly distinct, as can be deduced from careful study of Muldoon's rhyme scheme, which helps distinguish the two according to placement of rhyme and its use of ninety (as opposed to eighty-nine) rhymes. For more about the intricacies of "Yarrow's" rhyme scheme, see Twiddy, *Pastoral Elegy*, 208–19.

23. The other central metaphor of many of these poems is that of cancer, that which has killed so many of his loved ones, and which, like the yarrow, spreads beyond control. Iain Twiddy has done impressive work considering cancer's role in Muldoon's elegies in two pieces: his chapter "Grief Brought to Numbers: Paul Muldoon's Circular Elegies" in *Pastoral Elegy*, 201–28; and "Cancer and the Ethics of Representation," *New Hibernia Review*. His claim in the latter that "the structural principles of the disease — replication, invasion, and metastasis — elicited mimetic correlatives" clearly speaks to my own work; see "Cancer and the Ethics of Representation," 18. While my emphasis is on the performative and generative work of rhyme rather than the strictly mimetic, Twiddy's influence on my article is nevertheless profound, and it should be read in close dialogue with his important work.

24. Paul Muldoon, "Warren Zevon: *Excitable Boy*," *Poems 1968–1998*, 413.

25. See "Sillyhow Stride," *Horse Latitudes* (New York: Farrar, Straus and Giroux, 2006), 105–6. Interestingly, "zoom zoom" and "vroom vroom" also rhyme with two *different* end-rhymes in Muldoon's batch of ninety end-rhymes, the former with an end-rhyme I have designated "-eam," and the latter with one designated "-arm." By this point, the reader can clearly deduce the slipperiness of Muldoon's rhyming.

26. "Werewolves of London" makes its return, as do the African mercenaries of Zevon's "Roland the Headless Thompson Gunner." (Roland, too, makes frequent appearances — as he does, it is worth noting, earlier in "Yarrow," another instance of Zevon's earlier presence in Muldoon's work.) See Muldoon, "Sillyhow Stride," *Horse Latitudes*, 96, for the first of many allusions to Zevon's album and life. Special thanks to colleague Lindsay Haney for first directing me to some of these references to Zevon's work.

27. Ramazani, *Poetry of Mourning*, 176.

28. My article also owes a debt to Kinsey's unpacking of the source material of "Sillyhow Stride," especially with regard to Donne's role in the poem. See Kinsey, "Rave on, John Donne: Paul Muldoon and Warren Zevon," *The Yellow Nib* 8 (Spring 2013): 33–51.

29. Muldoon, "Sillyhow Stride," *Horse Latitudes*, 98.

30. The omitted line can be found in Muldoon's correspondence with Zevon, located in Emory University's MARBL library. Here, I quote from Kinsey's article; see "Rave On, John Donne," 38.

31. Muldoon, "Sillyhow Stride," *Horse Latitudes*, 99.

32. Ibid.

33. Kinsey, "Rave On, John Donne," 39.

34. Quoted in ibid., 38.

35. Muldoon, "Sillyhow Stride," *Horse Latitudes*, 106.

36. See ibid., 95, 101.

37. Ibid., 98.

38. Paul Muldoon, "Turkey Buzzards," *Horse Latitudes*, 78. A "kettle" is what bird enthusiasts term the circling in the air often associated with hawks and, of course, vultures.

39. Ibid., 81.

40. This reading chimes with Twiddy's reading of the poem, in which the poet's grief is purged by "achieving an analogue" in the multifarious meanings of the turkey buzzard. See Twiddy, "Cancer and the Ethics of Representation," 32–34. Jefferson Holdridge, however, reads the poem in less consolatory terms, emphasizing the trenchant self-critique that I explore in the following paragraph; see Holdridge, *The Poetry of Paul Muldoon*, 185–87. Ultimately, my point is that the poem is doing both, and thus represents yet another articulation of the double-sidedness of Muldoon's elegiac aesthetic and, in particular, in his end-rhyme technique.

41. Muldoon, "Turkey Buzzards," *Horse Latitudes*, 81.

42. Though, admittedly, many of poems that use these ninety rhyme sounds are often, at least, *elegiac*. Those not addressed here include "The Mudroom," "Third Epistle to Timothy," "The Bangle (Slight Return)," "At the Sign of the Black Horse, September 1999," and "The Humors of Hakone." Other brilliant elegies include "The Soap-pig," "The Breather," and "White," each of which is considerably different in tone than those elegies discussed here.

43. Both Twiddy and Campbell have noted the importance of this line in Stevens for understanding the elegy; this essay has been one attempt to unpack why this might be so. See Wallace Stevens, *The Collected Poems of Wallace Stevens* (New York: Vintage, 1990), 473; Twiddy, *Pastoral Elegy*, 8; and Campbell, "Muldoon's Remains," 177.

11

Writing Ireland: Seamus Heaney, Classics, and Twentieth-Century Irish Literature

Florence Impens

In "Mossbawn," a lecture first published in *Education Times* in 1973, Seamus Heaney evokes the farm on which he grew up:

> I would begin with the Greek word, *omphalos*, meaning the navel, and hence the stone that marked the centre of the world, and repeat it, *omphalos, omphalos, omphalos*, until its blunt and falling music becomes the music of somebody pumping water at the pump outside our back door. It is Co. Derry in the early 1940s. [...] There the pump stands, a slender, iron idol, snouted, helmeted, dressed down with a sweeping handle, painted a dark green and set on a concrete plinth, marking the centre of another world. [...] The horses came home to

it in those first lengthening evenings of spring, and in a single draught
emptied one bucket and then another as the man pumped and pumped,
the plunger slugging up and down, *omphalos, omphalos, omphalos*.[1]

Vividly recapturing the place central to the life of the small rural community
in which he was born, Heaney transforms the pump into a magical character. A "helmeted" "iron idol," it brings to mind the statues to Terminus that
the Romans erected on their land and at crossroads. But the classical association which the poet chooses, and underlines many times at the beginning
of his essay, is another one, inspired by ancient Greece: the pump is the
omphalos, the heart (or literally, the navel) of the locality, a word chosen
for its musicality and mimetic qualities, but also for its association with
Greek mythology. In a region where place-names illustrate the colonial
history of Northern Ireland, "in the mixture of Scots and Irish and English
etymologies,"[2] the word brings together a complex and sometimes divisive
cultural heritage by reaching into the universal. Calling the pump the
omphalos of his world is thus a way for Heaney in "Mossbawn" to transcend
the particularism of his local experience. It is also a means to include the
place he "had always considered to be below or beyond books" into the
literary sphere.[3] The Greek word, by virtue of its associations with one of
the civilizations which have shaped the western world, endows Mossbawn
with literary qualities, giving it an existence in the world of letters and of
high-brow culture. As Heaney developed an *ars poetica* rooted in his locale
and in the Irish landscape in the late 1960s and early 70s, the Classics often
played a similar role in his poetry, giving literary credentials to the world he
had chosen as his main subject matter. As we will see in this essay, his classical representations of his homeland and of Ireland helped him throughout
his career to define his position within the modern Irish literary tradition,
revealing a shift in his perception of his Irish poetic heritage.[4]

"Personal Helicon," which concludes his first full-length collection,
Death of a Naturalist (1966), is one of those texts in which Heaney rewrites
Greek mythology as an allegory of his artistic mission. Dedicated to Michael
Longley, by then one of his friends and a graduate of the Department of
Classics at Trinity College, Dublin, it is in some ways an answer to early crit-
icisms of his poetic voice by members and associates of the Belfast Group,

as well as an introduction to his personal vision of poetry. A poem-manifesto based on a material with which his poet-friend and "rival" is familiar, it reads County Derry, and his childhood farm, as Mount Helicon. The pump, which in "Mossbawn" was described as the *omphalos*, is now a spring, from which the shepherds of lyric poetry drink and, literally, the source of their inspiration. Mount Helicon is also the place where Narcissus is said to have admired his own beauty in the reflection of pools, and Heaney combines the two sets of myths in his rewriting: he is both the poet and shepherd drinking from the wells at Mossbawn and finding inspiration in his County Derry origins, as well as "big-eyed Narcissus" gazing at his reflection, and defining his poetic endeavors as a means to "see himself, to set the darkness echoing."[5] In "Personal Helicon," Heaney re-appropriates the classical myth into the Irish landscape, and reminds the reader of the rural origins of lyric poetry in ancient Greece. At the very end of the collection, he defends the right to literary existence of many of the poems in *Death of a Naturalist*, a collection centered on life at the countryside. "Digging," "Blackberry-Picking," "Churning Day," and "The Barn," among others, all have an indirect but illustrious precedent in the history of world literature, and, in their connection with one of the most famous poetic traditions, are justified against those who may have resented Heaney's early success and the favor he enjoyed with Philip Hobsbaum. For instance, Michael Longley was, in Heaney's own words, "marked down because of his stylishness," and was "aesthetically too 'paleface' for Philip."[6]

"Antaeus," written in 1966, derives from the same impetus that had prompted Heaney to justify his *ars poetica* using the Classics in "Personal Helicon." In the mythological figure, Heaney found another image of his poetic voice, and in his struggle with Hercules, a metaphor of the evolution of his style. The poet himself stressed his identification with the character several times over the years. For instance, in his seventieth birthday speech at the Royal Hospital in Kilmainham, Dublin on April 13, 2009, he told his audience, "I identified with this earth man because I saw myself as some-thing of an earth man. [...] I therefore regarded Antaeus as something of a guardian spirit, something who could sponsor whatever poetic gift I might have."[7] The dramatic monologue sees the giant of Libya, and son of Gaia, explain how he takes his strength from contact with the earth, and if contrary to "Personal Helicon," the poem is not set in County Derry or any specific Irish landscape, it can nonetheless be read as an allegory of the importance Heaney attached to the local in his poetry, thus echoing his association of the source of inspiration with the well of his childhood. It is usually not the interpretation put forward by scholars, who have often read it in terms of postcolonial struggle, in conjunction with a slightly later rewriting of the same myth, "Hercules and Antaeus."[8] And indeed, this paired reading is encouraged by their joint publication in *North* (1975), and by the many images which the two poems share: the phrases "sky-born and royal" and "river-veins" are repeated from one text to another, and the image of the "cradling dark" in "Hercules and Antaeus" is directly inspired by the line in the previous poem, "I am cradled in the dark that wombed me." It is therefore very tempting to read "Antaeus" as a previous version of the later "Hercules and Antaeus," and as some sort of a draft for the second rewriting which connects Greek mythology with Irish and American history in the line "Balor will die / and Byrthnoth and Sitting Bull."[9] In this reading, both poems become allegories of the defeats of indigenous populations invaded by a colonizer, and from there on, metaphors of Ireland's history.

But to interpret them so, and only so, would be to obliterate the differences between the two poems — Antaeus in the first one remains defiant, and adopts an almost provocative stance. It would also be to forget that "Antaeus" was written *before* the onset of the Troubles, and later published at the beginning of the first part of *North* in the mid-1970s, perhaps thereby inviting a reading that highlights the changes created by the pressure of history in the rewriting of classical mythology. While "Hercules and Antaeus" might suggest the possibility of a historical reading, the repositioning of "Antaeus" right after the selection of poems from *Death of a Naturalist* in *Opened Ground* in 1998 tends to reaffirm Heaney's intention of using the myth not as a metaphor of colonialism, but as an image of his poetic voice. The poet himself was conscious of the ambiguity in his re-appropriation of the classical figure and insisted in 1979 on the fact that, even though "Hercules and Antaeus" echoed Ireland's past, *both* rewritings were reflections on creativity and inspiration:

One of Pound's 'A Few Don'ts' is 'Go in fear of abstraction', and I think that perhaps I took that too literally for a long time. I also have no gift for it, but whatever poetic success I've had has come from staying within the realm of my own imaginative country and my own voice, which is not an abstract thinking voice at all. So that has confirmed my belief in Pound's advice, but at the same time, for a kind of growth, you have to be prepared to extend your voice. That is what I had in mind at the end of the first section of *North* in 'Hercules and Antaeus', and to me Hercules represents another voice, another possibility [...]. The image that came into my mind [...] was of me being a dark soil and him being a kind of bright-pronged fork that was digging it up and going through it. I got these notions of two kinds of intelligence... The Hercules-Antaeus thing came to seem like a myth of colonisation almost — that Antaeus is a native, earth-grubber, in touch with the ground, and you get this intelligent and superior interloper who debilitates the native by raising him, taking him out of his culture, his element, and leaving him without force. You can think about Ireland in those terms...

When it comes to writing, Hercules represents the possibility of the play of intelligence, that kind of satisfaction you get from Borges, the play and pattern, which is so different from the pleasures of Neruda, who's more of an Antaeus figure.[10]

In this reading, and in Heaney's reading, Antaeus becomes an image for the poet who, being rooted, writes good poetry from the local and his origins. He also represents the man whose imagination has been nourished by regular contacts with the soil, a fitting image for the young Heaney whose early experiences on the farm inspired many poems. In many ways, like "Personal Helicon," "Antaeus" makes a representation for the writer whose material comes from the rural world. Both poems, hence, and despite differences in their tone, reveal how the young Heaney saw in the Classics a repository of tales and myths, which could help define and defend the nature of his poetic project. Those were well-known narratives, with which he had become familiar at school. They were *exempla* of cultural material rooted in the local that had survived across millennia and were still valued in the West. As such, they indirectly supported his decision to write about the rural world he knew, by providing successful literary precedents.

Heaney's choice of classical material, however, was not only guided by his personal appreciation of the Classics and owes much to previous treatments of similar sources by other Irish poets; in his early classical poems, Heaney seems in fact to write into the Irish poetic tradition almost as much as he rewrites Greek mythology. The poet is particularly indebted to William Butler Yeats and Patrick Kavanagh, both of whom he had read intimately. Although the authors of very different oeuvres, both Yeats and Kavanagh had indeed used classical (and especially Greek) mythology to defend their aesthetics, and the prime importance that they gave to Ireland and the local in their work. For Yeats in the early twentieth century, the Irish and ancient Greek civilizations were very similar, especially for their democratic roots, and the peasants of Ireland were, in his own words, "in their beliefs, and in their emotions, many years nearer to that Greek old world, that set beauty beside the fountain of things, than are our men of learning."[11] As a consequence, the success of ancient Greek literature, as a body of work rooted in the oral tradition before being transmitted as written artifacts across centuries, could be used as a powerful model guiding the development of modern Irish literature in English, and Yeats invited his contemporaries to join his claim that "we Irish poets, modern men also, reject every folk art that does not go back to Olympus."[12] While Kavanagh criticized what he saw as Yeats's idealization and manipulation of rural Ireland, he too identified in ancient Greece the exemplum of a literature rooted in the local and true to its origins. As he argued in "Epic," a poem defending his vision of parochialism, Homer, after all, had "made the *Iliad* from […] a local row."[13] Using the Greek poet's precedent, Kavanagh argues in essence in the poem that what happens around "Ballyrush and Gortin" matters as much as the first warning signs of the Second World War, allowing him to consider local conflicts as the "great events" that could nourish his imagination. In his vision, the classical poem had become the *Ur*-parochial text taking its universality from being rooted in the local, and a powerful validation of his challenging assertion of the importance of the poet's origins in his representation of the world.

Both Yeats's and Kavanagh's readings of Greek culture and literature in defense of their own poetic visions deeply shape Heaney's early classical poems. Despite the absence of a direct genealogy between the latter and texts written by his predecessors, reading "Antaeus" and "Personal Helicon" in the light of Yeats and Kavanagh respectively, helps us understand how Heaney's poems need to be considered for their original treatment of the Classics, as well as texts in which the poet is trying to find a place within the Irish poetic tradition. Re-appropriating Greek mythology in the late 1960s, Heaney reworked classical material at the same time as he established an Irish literary filiation for his work.

The choice of Antaeus as a figure to represent the rooted poet is in this perspective not only an appropriate choice of symbol for the young Heaney wanting to write about the rural North, but also an allusion to W. B. Yeats. In "The Municipal Gallery Revisited" (1938), Yeats had described his work as well as that of Lady Gregory and John Millington Synge as follows:

> John Synge, I and Augusta Gregory thought
> All that we did, all that we said or sang
> Must come from contact with the soil, from that
> Contact everything Antaeus-like grew strong.[14]

While Yeats's poem and "Antaeus" are arguably very different, revealing the somewhat limited influence the former had on Heaney in the 1960s,[15] the mention of Antaeus by Heaney in 1966 seems far from coincidental, and might in fact be best read as a veiled allusion to his illustrious predecessor's literary project. The mythological character was for Yeats in 1938 a figure embodying the Celtic Twilight, when he and his companions had looked toward folklore and the peasant tradition to build a new national Irish literature. Some thirty years later, Heaney used Antaeus to discreetly hint at the Revival, when looking to define his own poetic voice and material, as the time when Irish literature in English had considered the countryside as a source of inspiration. Rewriting classical mythology, he also — and maybe most importantly — retraced connections with a period of Irish history that had promoted the Irish landscape as a literary subject matter.

If "Antaeus" can be read in a Yeatsian light, "Personal Helicon," on the other hand, carries echoes of Patrick Kavanagh's re-appropriations of Homer, and of his use of Greek material to defend a parochial vision of poetry. Contrary to "Antaeus," the poem is not textually related to Kavanagh's work, and the influence is more diffuse. As has been well documented, Kavanagh is a central figure in the literary landscape of the early Heaney, who many times acknowledged his importance, not least in "The Placeless Heaven," where he wrote in 1985:

> 'Epic' appeared in the volume called *Come Dance with Kitty Stobbling*, published in 1960 and reprinted three times within the next year. My own copy is one of the fourth impression, and I have dated it 3 July 1963. I did not have many copies of books by living poets at that time and it is hard now to retrieve the sense of being on the outside of things, far away from 'the City of Kings/ Where art music, letters are the real thing'. [...]
>
> When I found 'Spraying the Potatoes' in the old *Oxford Book of Irish Verse*, I was excited to find details of a life which I knew intimately [...] being presented in a book. The barrels of the blue potato spray which had stood in my own childhood like holidays of pure colour in an otherwise grey field-life — there they were, standing their ground in print. And there too was the word 'headland', which I guessed was to Kavanagh as local a word as 'headrig' was to me. [...] I had been hungry for this kind of thing without knowing what it was I was hungering after.
>
> [...] Kavanagh's genius had achieved singlehandedly what I and my grammar-schooled, arts-degreed generation were badly in need of — a poetry that linked the small-farm life which had produced us to the slim-volume world we were now supposed to be fit for. He brought us back to what we came from.[16]

Establishing connections between the Greek springs and the pump of Mossbawn in "Personal Helicon," Heaney, like Kavanagh in the 1950s in "On Looking into E. V. Rieu's Homer" and "Epic," puts both worlds on the same level. As his predecessor, he too rereads the classical hypotext in a local and rural context, the former lending some of its literary properties to a region otherwise felt to be neglected in literature, and often deemed unworthy of inclusion in poetry. Revisiting Greek mythology once again, Heaney adopts a very similar approach to that of his forebear, inviting the reader not only to appreciate his poem for its treatment of the classical source, but also for its faint reworking of twentieth-century Irish poetry.

Re-appropriating Greek narratives, the poet, in the early years of his career, thus reworked classical representations previously modelled by other Irish writers, who had used them in their efforts to define the originality of their voice, and foregrounded, each in their own way, the importance of staying true to one's cultural origins. Not only were the myths Heaney chose relevant in his own defense of a poetics rooted in the belief in the literary value of his rural experience, but also, with those poems, he obliquely recreated an Irish genealogy for his work, which adapted the concerns of his predecessors to his own moment.

Contrasting those early classical poems with Heaney's Virgilian rewritings in the last fifteen years of his life reveals the extent to which the poet's perception of his position in the Irish literary tradition evolved over the course of his career, and how his work came to embrace other Irish models promoting a more transnational outlook. The thirty-year gap that separates "Antaeus" and "Personal Helicon" from Heaney's eclogues in *Electric Light* (2001) and his *The Riverbank Field* (2007) saw many changes in the poet's circumstances, many of which he reflected on in classical rewritings. Two crises are of particular note: the death of his parents, and the onset and development of the Troubles, both of which he captured in reworkings of, respectively, Book 6 of the *Aeneid* and Greek tragedy in the late 1980s and early 1990s. Heaney had also moved to the Republic in 1972, and had in the meantime become a poet of truly international reputation, working in the United States and receiving in 1995 the Nobel Prize for Literature, all of which contributed as well to the evolution of his relationship with his homeland. When Heaney began to re-write classical poems celebrating the Irish countryside and his locale in the years of the peace process, those changes would affect not only his choice of classical narrative, but also the ways in which he alluded to the Irish poetic tradition in his work.

Heaney first re-appropriated Virgil's eclogues in an Irish setting in the collection he published in 2001, *Electric Light*. If the poems differ widely in their relationship with the source-text, one among them, "Glanmore Eclogue,"[17] is particularly interesting for the ways in which it articulates Ireland, Classics, and the Irish literary tradition. "Glanmore Eclogue" abounds with allusions to Heaney's move to County Wicklow in the 1970s and follows many of the conventions of the classical genre. Evoking the rapid transformation of rural Ireland in the twentieth century, the poem is a conversation dramatizing the opinions of two characters: Myles, the local countryman pressured by economic changes and the modern counterpart of Moeris; and the "Poet," an outsider to this world and a learned man by the name of "Mr. Honey," a transmogrification of "Heaney." But if it most obviously reworks pastoral tropes, "Glanmore Eclogue," like Heaney's early classical poems from the 1960s, also faintly alludes to modern Irish literature in several places — in particular in the mentions of Augusta and Meliboeus. The first one, whom the Poet describes as "a woman [who] changed [his] life," indeed evokes not only Virgil's patron Augustus, but also Lady Gregory, thus creating a discreet filiation between Virgil, Yeats, and Heaney himself. As for Meliboeus, described by Myles as "tramping the roads" and "pick[ing] up" the local dialect, "listening in a loft / To servant girls colloguing in the kitchen,"[18] his characterization as a wandering poet with a keen interest in orality is certainly reminiscent of John Millington Synge and of the well-known anecdote of the playwright eavesdropping on conversations in the west of Ireland to find inspiration for his recreation of Hiberno-English in his work. The correspondence between the classical and Irish figures is further textually reinforced by a quotation from *In the Shadow of the Glen* (1903) shortly thereafter, when the Poet calls Meliboeus "a stranger on a wild night, *out in the rain falling*,"[19] in a direct reference to the first scene of the play in which Nora tells the man who has knocked on her door: "Good evening, kindly stranger, it's a wild night, God help you, to be out in the rain falling."[20] Using italics in his poem, Heaney underlines the existence of the quotation, thereby inviting his reader to explore the meaning of his choice of hypotext.

The presence in the poem of Synge and Lady Gregory, as well as the shadow of Yeats lurking in the background might seem at first to signal a return to his early classical poetry, connecting the Classics and the period of the Irish Literary Revival, and insisting on the importance of listening to the countryside and being inspired by one's origins. The allusion to Synge at the beginning of the twenty-first century in Heaney's classical poetry, however, might discreetly also herald a shift in his perception of his position within the Irish literary tradition. It is worth noting at this stage that "Glanmore Eclogue" also makes reference to a medieval English lyric, "Sumer is Icumen In," in the song the Poet offers at the end. Heaney creates a threefold genealogy for his poem, posed between English and Irish literatures, both in turn subsumed in the classical text, as a cultural resource informing the two national cultures. If the complex intertextual nature of the poem already indicates a change in Heaney's perception of the role the Classics might play in his work, from *argumenta ad verecundiam* in his *ars poetica* to a means to subsume his double cultural heritage as an Irish writer in the English language, Synge can also be read as a figure accompanying this transition. A member of the Revival, Synge had first gone to Europe and Paris, and his years abroad, as well as his intellectual training, had influenced his writing. He had returned home to focus his creative energy on Ireland, and in this respect, he could be seen at the turn of the millennium as an attractive tutelary figure for Heaney, who in the years of the peace process imaginatively rediscovered the possibilities of writing his homeland after decades of violence during which he had felt dislocated.

"Glanmore Eclogue," under the guise of a classical rewriting, is thus a complex poem in its recreation of a literary genealogy. Far from his earlier models — the Yeats of the early twentieth century and Kavanagh, who had both advocated the importance of "Irishness," albeit each with a different definition thereof — Heaney uses Virgil to bring together on an equal par both the English and Irish literary traditions, as branches growing from the same *Ur*-European root. Acknowledging the influence of both literatures on his writing, he also chooses as the main Irish intertextual figure for his poem a writer — Synge — who tried to balance foreign elements with a desire to contribute to the development of a new Irish literature, thus pointing to the transnational outlook which his poetry had in the meantime taken.

The evolution in Heaney's sense of his literary heritage is confirmed by the publication, some six years later, of *The Riverbank Field*. In the chapbook released by The Gallery Press in 2007, Heaney returns to Virgil, this time to Book 6 of the *Aeneid*. Heralded with "The Riverbank Field," a translation playing with the notion of transposition both in linguistic and geographical terms, "Route 110" is a series of twelve poems rewriting Aeneas's journey in the underworld in Northern Ireland. The classical narrative structures Heaney's poem, each section of which is modelled on a Virgilian episode, and as Michael Parker illuminatingly explains in "Back to the Heartland,"[21] "Route 110" borrows the motif of the journey to make us travel through the countryside of Heaney's childhood in the company of his neighbors, through the darker lands of the Troubles, and toward a brighter future with the birth of Heaney's grand-daughter Anna Rose in the last poem of the sequence.

If Virgil's *Aeneid* is undoubtedly the primary hypotext of "Route 110," Heaney's poem is also indebted to James Joyce's treatment of the *Odyssey* in *Ulysses*. This is an influence which Heaney himself acknowledged many times, including in a radio interview with Gerald Dawe in 2009, when he described the poem as the "mythic method [...] reduced to County Derry dimensions."[22] If Heaney's broadcast remark sounds somewhat tongue-in-cheek, the poet in "Route 110" nonetheless does the same work for County Derry as Joyce did for Dublin a century earlier when, as Heaney himself put it, Joyce imagined "a day in [the city] with *The Odyssey* in the background."[23] Like Joyce, Heaney chooses to "build a continuous parallel between con-temporaneity and antiquity,"[24] and uses the structure of a classical epic to organize his narrative set in a region of Ireland. Rewriting Virgil, Heaney also indirectly rewrites Joyce and one of the most famous texts of modern Irish literature and of the modernist period.

The Irish literary model Heaney chose in 2007 is thus very different from the ones which his first classical representations of his homeland evoke. With James Joyce, he alludes to a text which challenges the literary representations of Ireland as a rural space. Setting his novel in Dublin, and giving pride of place to the city, Joyce reacted against the importance Revivalists had attributed to the Irish countryside as the true essence of Ireland's cultural identity. He also offered an alternative to those writers who had presented a different portrait of Ireland but still of rural life, like Kavanagh in the poems which had influenced the young Heaney. For Pascale Casanova in *La République Mondiale des Lettres*, Joyce's work questions both Yeats's and Kavanagh's:

> Les moyens stylistiques et le parti pris esthétique [de Joyce] sont en rupture totale avec les présupposés littéraires qui fondent à la fois le

symbolisme de Yeats et le réalisme rural qui s'y oppose. L'attention exclusive que Joyce porte à la ville et à l'urbanité marque d'emblée son refus de suivre la voie liée à la tradition du folklore paysan et sa volonté de faire entrer la littérature irlandaise dans la "modernité" européenne.

(Joyce's stylistic techniques and his aesthetic choices radically depart from the literary premises at the root both of rural realism and of Yeats's symbolism, which the latter challenged. Joyce's exclusive attention to the city and urbanity at once signals his refusal to follow the traditional path of peasant folklore as well as his will to bring Irish literature into European "modernity.") [25]

For Heaney to re-appropriate Virgil with a Joycean method is highly significant. First of all, it might simply be a sign of the poet's confidence in his subject matter, easily explained by the trajectory to fame of his career. After all, it was also Joyce who, at the end of "Station Island" in 1984, had told Heaney to "strike [his own] note."[26] Following his predecessor's advice, Heaney has stopped using the classical element to defend a poetic decision, and both the classical and the Irish worlds are now on a par. As Paul Muldoon puts it in "A Grand Tour," written to celebrate the award of the Cunningham Medal by the Royal Irish Academy to Seamus Heaney in 2008, Heaney now teaches poets "to entertain Rathsharkin as Rome, Toome as Tomis, / the Bann itself as the Bosphorus."[27]

But more to the point, Heaney's classical poems have moved from a framework influenced by the Revival and parochialism to one encompassing modernism, thereby putting the transnational dimension of his poetry to the fore. The Irish poet, however, has not simply replaced one influence with another and become Joycean in his reading of the Classics and of his homeland. Set in the countryside of County Derry, his "Route 110" *fuses* Joyce's modernist concerns with the European heritage of Ireland, with the insistence of Yeats and Kavanagh on the importance of writing Ireland and being true to one's origins. As Synge's shadow had already obliquely indicated in 2001, the Irish countryside no longer has to be defended as an appropriate subject matter for poetry; rather it belongs to a transnational and European literary space.

Reading those classical poems written by Seamus Heaney at different stages of his career, one is struck by the ways in which twentieth-century Irish literature mediates the poet's reading of what are essentially famous classical texts and tales. As Sarah Annes Brown remarks in her study of Ovidian presences in English literature, "it is difficult […] for a modern reading of the poem to be uninfluenced by previous preferences for certain stories over others — we are likely to dwell with particular interest on those narratives which have been most imitated by later writers."[28] But Heaney's case, as this essay has shown, goes much further than that of the mere unconscious influence over a reader; the poet over the course of his life often used the Classics to reflect on his relationship with Irish literature, and on the nature of his poetic voice. The classical poems studied here are deliberate and careful reconstructions of a personal Irish literary genealogy and reveal the complex evolution of a poet's sense of cultural heritage.

NOTES

1. Seamus Heaney, *Finders Keepers: Selected Prose 1971–2001* (London: Faber and Faber, 2002), 3.

2. Ibid., 7.

3. Ibid., 138.

4. It should be made clear at this early stage that this is only one aspect of Heaney's proteiform use of the Classics in his work. For a more general overview thereof, see Florence Impens, "Classical Roots," in *Seamus Heaney in Context*, ed. Geraldine Higgins (Cambridge: Cambridge UP, forthcoming 2017/2018). Similarly, Heaney is one among many poets of his generation to have been attracted to such material, and his classical work sometimes carries echoes of that of his contemporaries. For more information on classical reception in contemporary Irish poetry and literature, see, for instance, Brian Arkins, *Hellenising Ireland: Greek and Roman Themes in Modern Irish Literature* (Newbridge: The Goldsmith Press, 2005); Robert Crawford, "The Classics in Modern Irish and Scottish Poetry," in *Modern Irish and Scottish Poetry*, eds. Peter Mackay, Edna Longley, and Fran Brearton (Cambridge: Cambridge UP, 2011), 131–46; Lorna Hardwick, "'Murmurs in the Cathedral': The Impact of Translations from Greek Poetry and Drama on Modern Work in English by Michael Longley and Seamus Heaney," *Yearbook of English Studies* 36, no. 1 (2006): 204–15; Florence Impens, "Classics and Irish Poetry after 1960," in *The Oxford History of Classical Reception in English Literature*, vol. 5, ed. Kenneth Haynes (Oxford: Oxford UP, forthcoming, 2017/2018); Oliver Taplin, "The Homeric Convergences and Divergences of Seamus Heaney and Michael Longley," in *Living Classics*, ed. S. J. Harrison (Oxford: Oxford UP, 2009), 163–71.

5. Seamus Heaney, *Death of a Naturalist* (London: Faber and Faber, 1966), 44.

6. Seamus Heaney, in Dennis O'Driscoll, *Stepping Stones: Interviews with Seamus Heaney* (London: Faber and Faber, 2008), 76.

7. Seamus Heaney, interview by Seán Rocks, *Arts Show Special*, radio broadcast, Dublin: RTÉ Radio 1, Apr. 13, 2009. Last accessed Oct. 19, 2015, http://www.rte.ie/heaneyat70/radio.html.

8. See, for instance, Brian Arkins's and Patrick F. Sheeran's reading in "Coloniser and Colonised: The Myth of Hercules and Antaeus in Seamus Heaney's *North*," *Classical and Modern Literature* 10, no. 2 (1990): 127–34.

9. Seamus Heaney, *North* (London: Faber and Faber, 1975), 46.

10. Seamus Heaney, interviewed in *Viewpoints: Poets in Conversation with John Haffenden*, ed. John Haffenden (London: Faber and Faber, 1981), 69–70.

11. W. B. Yeats, "Dust hath closed Helen's Eye," in *The Major Works*, ed. Edward Larrissy (Oxford: Oxford UP, 1997), 406.

12. Ibid., 383.

13. Patrick Kavanagh, *Collected Poems*, ed. Antoinette Quinn (London: Penguin Classics, 2005), 184.

14. W. B. Yeats, *The Major Works*, 164.

15. It was in Heaney's words, not until the 70s that he "did his serious reading of Yeats, […] which was when [he] needed him most." (O'Driscoll, *Stepping Stones*, 192).

16. Seamus Heaney, *Finders Keepers*, 137, 138, 139.

17. Seamus Heaney, *Electric Light* (London: Faber and Faber, 2001), 35–37.

18. Ibid., 35.

19. Ibid., 36.

20. John Millington Synge, *In the Shadow of the Glen*, 1.1, *The Playboy of the Western World and Other Plays* (New York: Signet Classics, 2006), 7.

21. Michael Parker, "Back to the Heartland: Seamus Heaney's 'Route 110' sequence in *Human Chain*," *Irish Studies Review* 21, no. 4 (2013): 374–86.

22. Seamus Heaney, interview by Gerald Dawe, *The Poetry Programme*, RTÉ Radio 1, Jan. 31, 2009.

23. Ibid.

24. T. S. Eliot, "*Ulysses*, Order and Myth," *The Dial* 75 (Nov. 1923): 480.

25. Pascale Casanova, *La République Mondiale des Lettres* (Paris: Seuil, 1999), 428. My translation.

26. Seamus Heaney, *Station Island* (London: Faber and Faber, 1984), 93.

27. Paul Muldoon, "A Grand Tour," in Seamus Heaney, *Articulations: Poetry, Philosophy and the Shaping of Culture* (Dublin: Royal Irish Academy, 2008), 1.

28. Sarah Annes Brown, *The Metamorphosis of Ovid: from Chaucer to Ted Hughes* (London: Gerald Duckworth, 1999), 3.

12

The Autonomous Tear: Caitríona O'Reilly's *Geis* and Conor O'Callaghan's *The Sun King*

Jefferson Holdridge

There are two quotations from Dante's *Paradiso* that outline poetry's attempt
to give the most profound ideas satisfactory expression. The first from the
very beginning of the book describes the enormity of the task:

> For when our intellect is drawing close
> To its desire, its paths are so profound
> That memory cannot follow where it goes [...]¹

The second from near the end of the book points to the metaphorical reach
of language that speaks to us through the senses, through the physical nature

of speech, through quite literally how we learn and understand our mother tongue, even if we fail to adequately reproduce its deepest meanings:

> Now, even what I recall will be exprest
> More feebly than if I could wield no more
> Than a babe's tongue, yet milky from the breast.[2]

Many poets mark this relationship in their work. For them poetry remains a bridge between such poles as the abstract and concrete, history and myth, inwardness and identity, religion and philosophy, science and art, and, if I may make a sweeping statement, in so doing verifies the enduring relevance of the humanities. But for poets of the generation of Caitríona O'Reilly and Conor O'Callaghan, as discussed in the introduction to this collection and in a number of the essays, the epithet "Irish poet" sits uneasily with them. Both O'Reilly and O'Callaghan currently live in England to begin with, but more importantly their Irishness registers with them in ways that have fewer connections to their aspirations to be poets than seemed to be the case in previous generations.

Along with other poets of their generation,[3] Caitríona O'Reilly and Conor O'Callaghan view questions of Irish identity with less urgency than many of their predecessors, and often with real diffidence. Their views often highlight those "imaginative transformations," to which John McAuliffe alludes, which "can access particular moments that offer a way out of pre-dicaments."[4] The focus of this essay will be on the ways that O'Reilly investigates our sense-experiences of the natural world and her belief that the human finds its image reflected perhaps most startlingly in the encounter with the non-human. O'Callaghan's poetry is concerned with how memory relies on sensual images and their slippery, often opaque capacity to "mean" as well as to "be." The fundamental premise beneath this consideration of both poets is that poetry has its own ways of producing theoretical vision and philosophical knowledge, in ways that are at once metaphorical, trans-cultural, and even transhistorical. The aesthetic forged in the eye, as Joseph Brodsky writes, is only less autonomous than a tear.[5]

Poetry provides its own structures for access to meaning, if not to ethics. As Susan Stewart writes of Vico in her book *Poetry and the Fate of the Senses*:

In Vico's thought, poetry serves human ends in the expression of the corporeal senses, in the imaginative reconfiguration of nature through such devices as onomatopoeia, personification, and other modes of projection, and as the coordination of various modes of temporal experience necessarily *preceding* any narrative forms. Following Vico, one could claim that poetry cannot be the subject of history, for poetry is necessarily *prior* to history. Poetry expresses the passage from not-knowing to knowing through which we represent the world, including the perspectives of others, to ourselves and those around us.[6]

Now *that* is a large concept of the place of poetry, in that it gives birth to history. It runs counter to Muldoon's famous dictum that "… history's a twisted root / with art its small, translucent fruit / and never the other way round."[7] Yet Muldoon also counters that idea in the same poem with poetry's ability to make things happen, that ultimately it *must* make things happen, and that a painting of an oyster can be a political gesture. This last image takes us back to Stewart's tensions and interrelations between the senses and abstraction, the "formal drive"[8] she derives from Schiller's *Aesthetic Education*. These are primal sympathies that take us even further back to Aristotle's *De Anima*, where "the eye is associated with water, which can absorb light; hearing is associated with air; smell with fire; and touch with earth," with taste and touch as senses that can combine with the others.[9] Both poets considered here, like most other poets, in fact, rely on the original inventory of sensual experience, as I hope to make clear.

Stewart, however, very late in her study notes of Vico's ideas of poetry how memory has three different aspects: it remembers, its imaginative capacity alters or imitates what is remembered, and sometimes it invents by giving "a new turn or … relationship."[10] This tripartite conception of memory emphasizes the poetic mythmaking origins of historical thought. One can see this in the line from Herodotus to Thucydides, where we see the mythmaking of the former become historical analysis of the latter. History and biography have shaped the critical discussion of many writers in recent decades, with varying advantages and disadvantages. Some writers, and Yeats is certainly one of them, benefit from biographical and historical contextualization; others, such as Beckett, seem to insist on more formally attentive criticism, though even for Beckett a consideration of the life and times serves to remind us of the importance of the real world. One does wonder, however, if the critical role of history and biography — or of racial, national, or any other type of identity for that matter — is of less importance in the discussion of poetry. Stewart then summarizes Vico's position by noting the relationship of "memory to historical and poetic thought." Memory is the method of history, but it is only intelligible through the imagination's determination and organization of its elements. She concludes: "… history, shaped by processes of memory informed by imag-ination, becomes a consequence of poetic activity."[11] Yeats writes similarly in *Explorations*: "History is necessity until it takes fire in someone's head and becomes freedom or virtue."[12]

If the above sentences sound like just so much Romantic rhetoric, we must ask ourselves if it is possible to ever move *entirely* away from that origin of history in poetic activity as Stewart describes it. From W. B. Yeats to Caitríona O'Reilly, an inhuman force underlies all human endeavor and makes us puppets of its will, forces us to act as if, to paraphrase Yeats's poem "A Bronze Head," "a sterner eye looked through [our] eye."[13] He chooses the inhuman landscape of "bare hills and stunted trees" (from "Hound Voice") to be his matrix, where Becoming is on the hunt for Being. Nature to O'Reilly is a "labyrinthine Gospel."[14] In "Ariadne," the non-human (which I will use for animals, reserving the inhuman for the divine and the uncon-scious) functions as a similarly disruptive force. The poem is based on the myth of Pasiphae's desire for the bull, Theseus's slaying of the Minotaur, child of that union, and Ariadne's role in providing the golden thread to allow the hero to find his way out of the labyrinth:

> Some beast
> left ample evidence
> on the sheets —
>
> stains
> hymenal or menstrual,
> underwear scattered

across the floor.
It will take me a lifetime
to unpick this,

finding the right thread
to pull and unravel,
pull and unravel.[15]

Her feeling toward nature, particularly animals and our animal nature, displays a subtle understanding of the place of predation (qualifying all attempts to view nature in simple ethical terms). Yet finally, all efforts and demands come down to scrutinizing the fall from grace. The mark of the beast, above, infects even the most intimate "erotic" aspects of our lives. Still, for O'Reilly, animal instinct is also aligned with the sacred, as in "Amanita Virosa":

To be brushed by the least wing-
tip, the feathered edge of a gill,
ignites in the cell's
integument the sacred fire.
It is her silent spreading gift,
tiny destroyer:
her colourlessness, her bone-white chrism.[16]

It is helpful to note that *Amanita Virosa* is the Latin name for a fungus that is commonly known as the "Destroying Angel." In the immature state that O'Reilly is describing, the fungus resembles several edible species commonly consumed by humans, increasing the risk of accidental poisoning. In O'Reilly's poem, "to be brushed" becomes a baptismal rite (or the related rite of extreme unction for the sick). Either way it is something that rests on the thresholds of experience, where inhuman, non-human, and human meet.

O'Reilly seems intent on stripping away all humanist presumptions concerning the non-human or animal world. Nevertheless, she has a strongly sympathetic poetic, for the virtues and vices of human intelligence are very much her subject. The creatures inhabiting her world are at once familiar and strange to us, like those uncanny images that rise from our unconscious. In this, her training as an archaeologist has served her well,[17] even if the depths or heights she scales are often underwater or in the air as well as below the ground. She is constantly seeking the angle on the object which will make it hang fire, trying to capture some original focus or discovery of being — a first infatuation with reality, a flame burning in a secret place, an eye and a mode of seeing which is not ours, which we have only partially experienced, but which suddenly deepens our insight. One might wonder at an Irish poet who is so removed from more conventional Irish contexts such as history or politics. O'Reilly does not avoid these issues, but she does consistently relate them to the processes of perception. Her voice is consistently striking and original. Words, vital in their context, accumulate meaning, and rub against unusual scientific and naturalistic terms. Her sense of the object world as the chief method of uncovering layers of perception has deepened considerably since the publication of her first two volumes, *The Nowhere Birds* (2001) and *The Sea Cabinet* (2006). As she writes in "Blue Poles"[18] (on Jackson Pollock's method of painting as it was famously filmed from below) from her newest volume *Geis* (2015): "… there was nothing left to do / but plant blue poles … and step … into the sky / where a lens rose to meet you like a terrifying eye." The animals that move through her poems, particularly birds and fish, almost take the place of people. They also mirror the actions of the Other, of the inhuman opposite whose "terrifying eye" deeply questions our assumptions and perspectives. The best poems endeavor to reestablish consciousness in the face of what threatens its extinction.

In O'Reilly's work, the civilization that nature constitutes, instead of merely presenting the unfathomable and obscurely barbaric heart of darkness, actually holds the key to our deepest symbols. Her third volume, *Geis*, winner of the *Irish Times* Poetry Now Award, follows the critically acclaimed *The Nowhere Birds* and *The Sea Cabinet*. Her title refers to a word from Irish mythology meaning a supernatural taboo or injunction on behavior. In poems that are sometimes personal, sometimes philosophical, O'Reilly imaginatively probes our prohibitions and compulsions from psychological and moral perspectives. For the poet, the composition of this volume was a lifting of a spell, or in her own words, "it felt like a breaking of some taboo I'd placed myself under."[19] The title sequence, "Geis," vies with Nuala Ní Dhomhnaill's brilliant meditations on folklore.[20] In such poems as "The Winter Suicides"[21] she keeps a lucid eye (much like Plath or Sexton) on difficult subjects in order to reveal the insights they will offer us if we too pay attention to their grief. Such a fine first line, full of sympathy and anger ("They ask and the world gives them a stone"), and then the disturbingly unnamed question which "we" all must ask: What is the meaning of such a brief existence, haunted by the winter that is implicit in the beginning of spring, by snow that has the pallor of the stars? Influenced by the American writers John Haines and Spencer Reece,[22] O'Reilly questions our links with the natural world, with others, and even with ourselves, but these poems ultimately celebrate the richness of experience, the sense of the sacred, and the power of language. Suicide, as seriously as it's being taken, is also a rhetorical device, a vehicle of impersonal language, is the death of language or its limits. In "Riddle" (part VII of "Geis"),[23] for instance, a poem of fourteen metaphors in fourteen lines, the phrase "It is" is actually all the things it is not — a syntactical expletive in the deepest sense.

Sometimes she is haunted by the inhuman, or non-human world, which reminds her of how, in light of a lost love, her body betrays her, as in "Empty House." In "Comparative Mythography,"[24] O'Reilly compares the myths of the gods with the mythic thinking of science to show how the latter is mistaken in its conception, mistaken in its sense that the "how" of experience is more important than the "why." She states that "Knowledge means // not that it is true, but that it works," believing that fundamentally such knowledge of mere function is based on a false premise, which forgets how "souls" are "made." This critique of myth is predicated itself on the myth of mythlessness.[25] The scientific mode of thinking on its own makes us like bees, as in "Bee on Agastache": "Our calling demands we verify, verify, verify." [26] These are the many spikes of the flower on which the bees and we are supping. O'Reilly often has the eye of a scientist but refracts it through an aesthetic lens: the imaginative response to objective sensual observation. This lens is something which she feels is missing: "We have little time for aesthetics: / our schema will not permit it." "Comparative Mythography" is as much of a lament for the loss of mythic thinking or the diminishment of the aesthetic ("Once, men [... knew] their souls were made // of polished atoms") as it is a call for its return, which ends in the mythological proof that nothing exists, not even the real: "It takes the strength of sixteen horses // ... [to prove] that nothing exists." But that "nothing" is what at the beginning of the poem primitive mythmakers feared ("greatly fearing emptiness") and our etiological imaginations must fear again now that "nothing" confronts us once more. O'Reilly's gothic sensibility is ever apparent and here we see the need to believe, being stoked by a fear that there is nothing in which to believe. Or as she writes of sensing a "hint" of a wolf-spider's "intellect" in "Everything Flowers"[27] near the end of the volume:

> What was it you quoth? *Two possibilities exist:*
> *either we are alone in the universe or we are not.*
>
> *Both are equally terrifying.*
> How apposite, I thought. How *grand guignol.*

O'Reilly's use of the gothic is nuanced, however. She most certainly can be said to have a gothic sensibility but she also uses the word in its historical sense. In "Jonah" (part VIII of "Geis"), she insists on the difference between the claustrophobic space of the "ringing interior" and those gothic interiors that provide refuge from the gargoyles on the outside of the church, those cathedral groves that are based on the ancient forests. Yet, the suffering of the prophet is gothic in its own right.

In "Triptych,"[28] written at the rightfully famous cathedral in Lincoln, England, where she now lives, she meditates on the historical use of the gothic that highlighted "those leering demons at the corners of your life." In the second part, "Nave," she makes the connection between cathedral and forest explicit. She insists that they each create a sacred space which invites deities or avatars to enter, but which also threatens to remain frighteningly empty or, more worryingly, which forebodes much worse to come: "Is there a god of the gaps, and is it // of the interstices between trees / only, and of what might breathe there?" The last hope may be in those very interstices she invokes. We might read them as the interstices between religion and art, between science and the aesthetic, between holy dread and terror.

For O'Reilly, the need to believe and the curse of love are interwoven in the title poem, "Geis."[29] She writes in the first part of the poem, in which she imagines she is a bird: "It was a sickness, this love I imagined / descending in a feathered storm." The long sequential title poem is a powerful example of this combination. The poems revolve around nightmarish images of the supernatural that display an erotic and religious vision "out of Bosch," as in the second part, "Night Sweat," where she is scorched "hotter / than any bitch burned by history":

> Now I am straddled by a great night bird,
> a muscular talon to each hip bone.
> How I struggle to bear him up:
> his soaked wings hover.

Not only Bosch broods on this image, but also Yeats in "Leda and the Swan," a poem in which history burns and leads to the Trojan War. In the section itself called "Geis," the poet ends with an image of darkness that also affirms the light. As in so many poems of hers, the messenger is avian and summons a contradictory image of silencing and speech: "The wound of the mouth closes. // To perish its roots / a radiant stone is placed on the tongue." The stone is talismanic of the purification of speech: "The wound of the mouth" is the stigmata of the divinely inspired. The word "perish" is used as a transitive verb, in the British usage; it would seem the poet means benumb rather than destroy. In this reading the "radiant stone" could be read as medicinal, as cauterizing the wound of the mouth. The sequence ends first with visions of mental and emotional torment in the ward and then a type of prayer in biblical language. There is a desire in "Jonah" to be released from the whale of mental disease that has swallowed the speaker. She calls to the brethren who suffer with her, understanding both the depth of their experience in the mind's "ringing interior" and enjoining them to accept the corrosion of the self that comes with living in the world:

> Brothers, we who have gone down to the roots of the mountain,
> and have seen the worm bite the gourd's root,
> are sea-changed, and see with the light behind us,

as through a fine membrane,

a thin curtain of isinglass,

the floaters drifting in our eyes like ghosts.

Brothers, to refuse is not to live.

The world has eaten us the way the world must.

A poem like "The Gardener"[30] repeats this call for help from a barren place. The speaker must learn from the plants that "life is worth holding onto, / even at its bitterest."

For all of the despair and the inhuman coldness in O'Reilly's poetic world, there is comfort (if somewhat "cold comfort" at that) in the natural world, as "Snow"[31] emotively illustrates: "And it is a relief to feel it touch me / with its meaning, // its vast multitudinous silence, / again and again." Beholden to Louis MacNeice's "Snow," this "incorrigible plurality" of meaning shows that O'Reilly is not a univocal poet. She writes poems that both reflect an ecological concern and that also acknowledge the mythic quality of the natural world, which in the poem "Polar"[32] (in defense of polar bears) becomes symbolic of the emptiness of our myths, and the need for rituals to anoint the great being of the Bear. She writes of the polar bear as "a great absconded god of emptiness" and ends with a final question that is as much a plea as it is an interrogation: "Who will bury him like the Chukchi, / his huge head indicating true north, / amid libations and the pouring out of oil?" She also takes comfort in love, whose momentary absence by a "frozen water- / fall" takes her breath away ("Iceland").[33]

As stated earlier, O'Reilly is among the poets of the "post-Ireland" or "after Ireland" generation,[34] a description that suggests the emergence (perceived or real) of a new ethos in Ireland which is not overtly defined by the old postcolonial and religious/sectarian questions of history. Yet, this does not mean that she does not address issues related to such questions, though she certainly approaches them from her own angle. "The Servant Question" reminds us of the social realities of Irish history, namely the servitude that a history of colonization entailed. Some of the poems that follow it also meditate on history and prove that however much a generation of poets remain aloof to certain shibboleths of identity they may surface nonetheless. "Baltic Amber"[35] enlarges the historical view to include not only the ancient world of Pliny and the Greeks, but meditates on geological time. The meditation on the jewel ends with its image of "Eocene sun / between finger and thumb." O'Reilly is replacing Heaney's spade and gun with this jewel that is among the most species-rich fossils there are. Like Heaney then she is digging, but it is not so much about Ireland as the history of the non-human, even pre-human, world. Beneath even the largest conceptions of history is fate. In "Clotho,"[36] O'Reilly considers the youngest of the three Fates who is responsible for spinning the thread of human life, which gave her power over life and death. In the poem this seems hubristic. Clotho herself senses something deeper about the life source, something she "cannot reach." As in the sculpture by Camille Claudel, on which the poem is based, Clotho seems burdened by the destiny over which she has control. For Claudel and O'Reilly, she seems to share the human characteristic of being aware of immortality and divinity but not able to attain them. Humanity and divinity are connected like leaf and bole. That women are seen as determiners of fate makes sense, for as life-givers they are the threshold between the transcendental and the immanent worlds, between mortality and immortality, and often between cruel divinity and abject humanity.

Elsewhere her poetry meditates on women's relationship to language, especially in the light of atrocity. In such poems as "Marmoreal"[37] from her first volume, The Nowhere Birds, and "Autotomy"[38] from Geis, O'Reilly creates poems of an impersonal, indeed intellectual, variety. For instance, the conclusion (and even the title) of "Marmoreal" contains this uncanny difference from the familiar: "from the howling circle, we'll stare / in from our stone address. // Two eyeless statues under snow / blinded by their own bodies' whiteness." These lines move through Eiléan Ní Chuilleanáin's "Pygmalion's Image"[39] back to Mallarmé's symboliste resistance to the values of the quotidian. A line from Beckett's novel Molloy best describes the particular accomplishments of O'Reilly's poetic: "To restore silence is the role of objects."[40] "Autotomy," in the same vein, seeks to find an object, in this case "the quiver tree," that restores the role of silence, by bearing silent witness to "burning life." Female victims (Lavinia, Philomel) become objects that bear the disappearing scars of history. This objectification is an important aspect of the volume. There is a mysteriousness to the object which must be restored.

"The Airship Era"[41] sees in the object of the title an image of humanity's "ashen armature." The poem on Clint Eastwood, "The Man with No Name as Vital Principle: A Ghazal,"[42] extends the relationship between subject and object as the self is born in the eye of the other: "Under the drunken parabola of the sun he watches himself turn, / reflected in the eye of his enemy, from a speck of dust into a man." Vision in her work is one of the dominant and most meaningful senses. And the animals and scenes of nature provide the background.[43] It is not surprising then that birds in her work always seem supernatural themselves, sometimes all-seeing, sometimes harbingers of destruction, sometimes, as in "Night Sweat," symbols of a sort of divine union. Besides the title poem "Geis," one of the most potent images of a bird appears in "Bell Tower"[44] (the third part of "Triptych"). Like O'Reilly's earlier poem, "A Quartet for the Falcon,"[45] it too celebrates the life and vision of the raptor, aware of the bird's power in flight, its beauty and its deadly skills, but also its presence on top of the sacred space of the bell tower, which both announces the sacred hours, but also provides a perceptual vantage point: "All lines converge in the eye of the falcon. / Her harsh cries wreathe the bell tower / from her scrape on the high sill." The bird is agent of the vertiginous: "at its heart a precipice, a continual launching." Again O'Reilly establishes a keen visionary balance of subject and object. The bird looks down on us as we look up to see the stars, measuring "her prey from a serene angle, / the way a stargazer averts his gaze / to see the dimmer stars." Her killing is like a sacred ritual, one that either provides a transcendent sacrificial angle or brings down the deadly talons of nature: "To see is to grasp; to see is to taste — / killing an empty ceremony sealed in blood / for an act already done."

The volume ends with two poems that offer the rituals of love and art as recompense. "Potlatch" is based on the North American ceremonial exchange of gifts, used for various purposes, but in this case, it acknowledges romantic union. In this poem quotidian and verbal interactions give way to lovemaking, which provides both affirmation and renewal. More importantly, perhaps, it is an exchange of gifts that becomes a form of sacrifice in which, as O'Reilly writes, "all we have hoarded we burn." In some sense both the gesture of lovemaking and the gesture of making art provide something beyond what the verbal usually provides. The note to

"Komorebi"[46] tells us that it "is a Japanese word to describe the effect of sunlight filtering through the branches and leaves of trees" and that it "has no exact English translation." The poem exults in the gap "between the world and the word." When the poet watches the light leak through the branches and leaves, the syntax leaves it vague as to whether the light is leaking between the ideograms "tree," "escape," and "sun," or between the things they signify. The cormorant, "extending his wet wings" at the end of the poem makes a "messianic gesture" toward it "as if dazzled to absolute / by the word and the world's beauty." The volume ends with these notes to emphasize the way that even in her darkest poems O'Reilly celebrates the richness of experience, especially of the natural world. As Emily Dickinson notes: "Perception of an object costs / Precise the Object's loss." And yet she notes that "Perception [is] in itself a Gain."[47] For O'Reilly, both the cost and the gains of perception are clear.

In his preface to the third volume of *The Wake Forest Series of Irish Poetry*, Conor O'Callaghan writes of the poets he is introducing: "There is also here, I suggest, a delectation of the material surface, of bric-a-brac and brands, that is absolutely of the age." Perception of the object is the subject of much poetry of his generation. O'Callaghan continues: "Subjects that would have seemed unimaginable to their immediate predecessors — trips to IKEA, credit cards, plasma screens, and Japanese cinema — are second nature to these poets." He concludes: "Not that any of these poems are ultimately *about* any of these things. Rather, they use the data and white noise of 21st century life as subjects for coming at poetry's old enduring themes from different angles."[48] Caitríona O'Reilly and Conor O'Callaghan both endeavor to look at the changing world from different angles.

For O'Callaghan, memory relies on sensual images in its decision to mean as well as to be. The fundamental premise is that poetry does have its own theory to adhere to. In this he reiterates Dante's great claim that the paths of wisdom and desire are so profound, so difficult to follow that only the metaphorical possibilities of poetic language may suffice. In *The Sun King* (2013), Conor O'Callaghan accomplishes many things, in many places, times, and voices. In some poems, he has one foot on either side of the Atlantic; in others he straddles past and present with an eye to the future. He both invokes the glories of the sublime and refutes them.

Celebrates love and laments its loss. Bathes in the warmth of family while standing out in the cold. Sees sexuality as the blinding life force that it is and measures the pulse of betrayal with a calculated clarity that is nothing short of disarming. He can be clever in the best sense of the word regarding technique and poetic voice, handling one with virtuosity and interrogating the other with postmodern zeal; in other poems, he drops this guard and witnesses his own situation with a candor and simplicity that is made even more powerful because it has been so richly earned. All emotion is parried, tested, proved, or disproved before it is so deftly handled.

The epigraph of *The Sun King*, from Gary Snyder's "The Sweat," establishes the transatlantic nature of the volume. It also registers an awareness of dawning middle age, a consciousness that one's forties are the old age of youth, though one likes to think of them as the youth of old age. "This life," Snyder writes, "We get old enough and finally really like it!" Snyder's poem is a celebration of women growing older, of bodies growing "more tasty."[49] For O'Callaghan, this might be more equivocal given the nature of this collection's meditation on desire. Not to say that this isn't a powerful evocation of desire, just that there is as much ruefulness as pleasure in its evoking. Or as the sexually sophisticated first poem of the volume, "Lordship," puts it:

> There's no return route, is there? You sussed that too?
> The truth, much as time does, vanishes behind.
> It's not like userdata, waiting retrieval by us.[50]

This poem keeps its secret as it reveals it has one to keep, admits its sentimentality in perfectly skeptical fashion. The revelation that is also a screen, the lifting of the veil there is merely a rustling of it, is at the heart of this secretive and telling volume. The poems that follow delve inward and yet remain so interested in the outside world that they are almost driven to distraction, as we see in "Among Other Things":

> The rest have
> driven to the mall.

Any second now
will be too dark.

This close to the edge,
among other things,
I read.

Leaves rattle overhead.
Little pockets
of canned applause
sift through
the screened porch
in next door's yard.[51]

Even the title has a way of stating the issue by avoiding it. This distraction is another part of the method of the book, which revels in the sensual distractions of the everyday, often finds its metaphors there, and is driven to this distraction by the emotional turmoil that underlies its composition.

In "Wild Strawberries," the two meanings uncomfortably mingle, much as they do in poems of sexual profligacy, neglect, and deceit, like William Carlos Williams's "This is Just to Say" and "The Young Housewife." The scent of wild strawberries, like the bored neighborhood girls, reads like a metaphor for a carnal knowledge that is both profoundly desired and profoundly disturbing in a time of unease.

Saturday, late
and but for a handful
of neighbourhood girls
hanging in the street,
nothing doing.

I cut the back,
brim the yard-cart.
The air is thick

with the scent
of wild strawberries'
mown flesh.

This weather we keep
the bedroom sash ajar.
I lie to myself:
they're not metaphors.
They are not metaphors.[52]

The solitary nature of the speaker's voice, the intense self-consciousness ("I lie to myself"), seems to imply the lack of sexual congress rather than its fulfillment. The metaphor must be resisted because it cannot be enjoyed. The lyric is bodily, somatic, as it turns toward the social element. A climax that is resisted in the time of the poem is nevertheless oddly approximated in the extension of the contraction: "They're not metaphors / They are not metaphors." Yet even earlier in the poem we move from the lower senses of smell and taste (implied) to touch ("mown flesh" with its sexual double meaning, as in "moan"); touch is often seen as the mediator between the play of the senses and the externalization of the object, or its intellectual consideration. Here we may hover between entering into and refraining from the Baroque ecstasy of the poem and subsequently find that suspension delicious in and of itself.

The heat, the vegetation, the "yard-cart," and, in its simplicity, even the language is in the American grain. In some poems, such as "Lordship," the demotic tone combines American and Irish usage. In "Swell,"[53] the language veers between American usage ("swell") and objective details ("dogwood," "Y" as in YMCA) and Irish ("lovely," "gorgeous"). The poet is clearly relishing the differences and the richness these differences confer to his poetry: "April's bright stretches, the mailman says, are swell." The poet is learning to understand the elements: as the poem closes, he is learning "to swim." Yet as he embraces this life outside the fishbowl of Ireland, there are undercurrents that a change is at hand, which in retrospect, the poet knows will be difficult and deep.

In "Woodsmoke," it is a woodstove from Alabama that becomes the crucible of change, one that makes the speaker seem like a hobo around his fire, that makes the kids think he is nuts. The stove is dangerous; a fire marshal stops by. The poet realizes as the stock market ebbs, and as the dead from the war pile up, that the stove is an image of fate, which he can both feed and by which he is inexorably affected. In the end it is the image of the crucible of his own imagination ("some flame's liminal eye"), larger than he is, controlled by him yet controlling him.

> I get an odd peace
> imagining these clear nights
>   how bits of spare cash,
> Alabama, this garden,
> my son's and daughter's faces
>
>   at the sliding door,
> the market's ebbs, the stacked dead,
>   a hut placed on pause,
> its stove's words, my writing them,
> the page's threshold even,
>
>   this book in your hand,
> the bookstore open Sunday
>   in which you're reading,
> are all bound to get threaded
> through some flame's liminal eye.[54]

From this point on in the volume, the shared space is just as often one remembered from a distance as it is lived. And the distance must be explored. "Each afternoon survives your absence," O'Callaghan writes in the mildly Larkin-esque, pained but wise and sensual, "In Praise of Sprinklers."[55] The poem insists that the past is as ephemeral as the spume of water in a heat wave while the present, the now of poetry that defies physics (as Einstein commented) is waiting to pass through its cooling shower. The now is to be savored. Yet this poet of contradictions will not allow himself or us the luxury of being untroubled for long. Nor will his ironic tone long avoid the heart's pressures to give existence some meaning.

Poetry is about what cannot be expressed in language. In "Translation,"[56] the soul "for crying out loud" appears and the person in question is like a poem before it has been translated. Such belief in the metaphysical possibilities of both life and poetry may be surprising from a poet who in the opening poem writes "I could go on outsourcing what history we share / to the chum-of-a-chum third party beard above // that's kidding no one."[57] Even those simple objects that distracted him previously take on larger significance. The poem as a whole seems meant to call to mind Frost's famous definition of poetry as that which is lost in translation.[58] The intensity of this statement cannot be underestimated within the poet's corpus. *Fiction* (2005), Conor O'Callaghan's previous volume of poems, similarly uses the metanarrative of writing as its overarching theme, as it tests a web of truth and lies, reality and imagination. In "Translation," there is a similar but enlarged commitment to the creative impulse. It is not about silence but about moving beyond silence in words that can only be mouthed: *"I have a soul,* you appear to be calling. / *Make of my soul what you will."*

The title poem, "The Sun King," captures the angst at the heart of the volume perhaps most eloquently of all. There is a loss of relationship, a family, and a place. The poet sees in his sunroom a metaphor for the French King and for all the splendors of Versailles. The builder, Roy, represents both the king (*roi*) and the lore of place (this time northwestern North Carolina — "parables waiting for windows to arrive"). He is the yodeling snake handler — if the poet doesn't mind this extrapolation — who closes the circle of the divine: "and Roy joined hands in a ring that all lost rooms be filled / by a sun to which even the godless among us could say Amen." In the last stanza, when *Leaves of Grass* falls "onto the laminate," the poem has entered the space of metaphor for absence and displacement. The poet, living elsewhere now, can only pray for the sun to enter and light the room once more so that the forms of past lives are lit brightly enough to provide an outline for the emotions to fill. In the shape poem, "A Nest of Tables," we see that this cannot be done, that the laminate will not allow the leaves of grass to grow:

2

The thing about things, surfaces,
the ache ingrained in bric-a-brac,
is the way that each refuses
point blank to miss us back.

3

I could use
a sunrise.[59]

As Susan Stewart writes of shape or pattern poems: "Practices of pattern or concrete poetry remove the poetic from its attachment to particular
voices and bodies to create a poetry that is object-like or artifactual. Such
poems — in the Hellenistic age, in the Renaissance, and revived under
modernism — are the most visual and objectifying of all poetic forms. It is
indeed not surprising that the final glimpse of the experience of imagery
such a poem produces is a geometrical abstraction, a pure Platonic form
that overrides the fallen materiality of the words."[60] Yet, apropos of that
pure Platonic form, Stewart proceeds to acknowledge that modern usage
tends to emphasize the objects' resistance rather than their higher repre-
sentationality — for they "are objects that have definable and recognizable
spatial boundaries clarifying what they are from what they are not."[61] As
much as objects contain histories, public and private, in war and peace,
they cannot in their inanimate or soulless indifference return us to those
times. Their point is indeed blank and we are left trying to fill it ourselves
with the appropriate metaphor, one we have lived by.

After such concentrated grief and longing, the volume opens out
into a swirling cloud of computer information in "The Server Room," as if
to counter the stasis of indoor spaces with the vast panoply of images that
constitute virtual reality. Virtual reality is like a reservoir of the subconscious.
We may surf it, but we are too seldom able to retrieve any images we might
want to keep. Though there is some parodic disbelieving force behind this
poem, which makes the spatial quality of *Paradise Lost* seem positively solid
and defined when compared to the cascading levels of this poem, there is

also relief taken in the escape (being "on the lam") into its sensual vortex, especially when we hit "refresh." The last line of the poem is a play on the final line of Robert Frost's poem "Directive," which reads "Drink and be whole again beyond confusion." Comparing the two endings makes the play apparent. First Frost:

> I have kept hidden in the instep arch
> Of an old cedar at the waterside
> A broken drinking goblet like the Grail
> Under a spell so the wrong ones can't find it,
> So can't get saved, as Saint Mark says they mustn't.
> (I stole the goblet from the children's playhouse.)
> Here are your waters and your watering place.
> Drink and be whole again beyond confusion.[62]

And then O'Callaghan:

> Up here on the lam, the limb of oneself,
> form a cup of digits/palms and wait
> for data like rain meltwater cold
> to pool to brimming point, to cascade down.
> Drink. Be whole again beyond communication.[63]

Confusion almost being the point of this skinny-dipping in the virtual stream of information, one can see that O'Callaghan's directive is not redemption, not meant to take us beyond confusion, but to explore its "argot's luminous opacity." There is even a hint of celebration: "Such gorgeous nubless hubris! […] such sumptuous fluff, acres of the stuff." Yet, for all the celebration, the poem is seeking something on "the limb of oneself," seeking, if nothing more, to drink and slake its thirst. Here we may turn to Frost's poem to apply some counter pressure. It is also about a lost time, lost childhood, the loss of beloved wife and children[64] (either through death for Frost or through separation for O'Callaghan), and the ways to rediscover those beauties, much like many of the poems in *The Sun King*, including "The Server Room." Though it may not be the traditional Holy Grail, the poet is hoping that at the center of this server, matrix of the postmodern imagination, there might be something like that grail. As in the poem "Translation," there is a great deal that relies on what cannot be expressed; only here do we appear to be mouthing "I have a soul," only here may we be "whole again beyond communication."

The poem "Comma"[65] likewise celebrates how the computer screen itself provides a much needed pause. The next poem, "Peace," even sees that loss itself calls forth peace: "There's got to be a term in currency for this: / the debt all losses owe to sentiment / for loss that wakes in happiness." With these poems comes the ability to forget oneself in distractions of the everyday. In the poems that follow — "Bulk Collection," "The High Road," and "Emergency" — the poet finds himself well placed in borrowed spaces, but in "Emergency" there is a sense that where there is borrowed space there is borrowed time, and living on borrowed time leads only one direction, which makes the poet conclude "we are veering years from a return."[66] The jarring aspect of this poem is how it juxtaposes three places (Ireland, America, Japan) and three eras (the now, World War II, and the Edo period of the great Japanese poet Basho). Perhaps the emergency is the emotional costs of neutrality for the Irish during World War II, for the poet in his present predicament, and for Basho on his trip on the narrow road to the deep north, where few before had gone or wanted to go. The volume has begun its travels further afield to a new house in the north of England, back to Ireland (in memory in "The Pilot Light"; and in fact in "Required Fields"); and also to Italy in "Sospeso." With those travels come new love and the promise of future happiness, which the poet feels one creates with a gesture hopeful enough to carry one through such afflicted times. In this, the last poem makes a beautiful point. "Sospeso" is based on the idea of a *caffè sospeso* (Italian: suspended, as in suspended coffee), which is a cup of coffee paid for in advance as an anonymous act of charity. The tradition began in the working-class cafés of Naples, where someone who had experienced good luck would order a *sospeso*, paying the price of two coffees but receiving and consuming only one. A poor person inquiring later whether there was a *sospeso* available would then be served a coffee for free. To O'Callaghan this gesture toward the human family must counter the ache about his own personal dilemma in which his name is suspended:

we hold as we
hope to one day
one another
like family [...][67]

This is not to say that division is that easily rectified (see "Division Street")
nor is betrayal so easily forgotten (see "The Unfaithful Housewife," his
translation of García Lorca's "La Casada Infiel"). "Translation," "The Server
Room," and the translation of Lorca's poem form a crucial triangle of poems
in the volume. The poet has written of this triangulation:

> I suppose "The Unfaithful Housewife" and "Translation" could be read
> as a piece. In the former, I was trying to use the Lorca to think about
> fidelity. Does "fidelity" mean the same thing in literature that it does in
> love? I realise now that I deliberately altered the sense of Lorca's ending,
> as if acting out some paradigm of infidelity. The parallels between
> translation and marriage: the immovable need to be faithful and the
> irresistible desire to be free. The inner negotiation of the translator is
> very similar to that of the husband/wife. In "Translation" I was thinking
> too about a student at Wake [Forest University] who turned out to be
> deaf, and how translating can feel like colonization: a big rich language
> moving in on the literature of a smaller poorer language, in spite of
> being deaf to the nuances of its apparently out-moded terms of refer-
> ence, such as "soul." If I recall correctly, I got it into my head that "soul"
> had become the dirtiest word in poetry, that the Poundian suspicion of
> abstraction by which we have all worked has become a cul-de-sac. In
> "The Server Room" I use the Frost model to navigate back to a source;
> in this case the current is the electronic all around us rather than that
> of a cabin-side creek. I was trying to locate a cadence poised between
> satire and celebration. I was trying, I suppose, to suggest that the virtual
> now occupies the space once held by the spiritual; that poor defunct
> old God, indeed, effectively served as a prototype for virtual reality.[68]

In that virtual spiritual space, perhaps all that is left is the pleasure/peril
binary in all desire. As "The End of the Line" delineates, it is difficult to fit

love into the iambic pentameter of the sonnet. One finds oneself in water looming deep and black with no lifeguards around. Like the poet, we are still learning how to swim, to brave the uncertain elements.

From "Revision" to the close of the first part of the volume and before the glorious peroration of its themes in the Twitter-poem "The Pearl Works," a noticeable change occurs. Home is no longer the imagined and lost spaces, but instead has become real, lived in. The remembered roads and locales of the lost home are now deferred spaces to return to, but which cannot be revivified. In "Revision"[69] the tone is set. The poet understands now that the best revision is not the elegiac one, but is about "starting over." "There is still hope, even now, / and for all those light years shining overhead." Traveling and loss of place intensify the beauty "of being this far from home" as he states in "Borders."[70] He has learned to "Bless the elsewhere / where others are / not here or you," as he writes in "Game Night."[71] Yet there are two other contending themes among the revision of the latter poems. The storms that blow through his corner of America symbolize both his desire ("January Drought") and his present distance from that place and from the object of desire (the villanelle "Three Six Five Zero"). The other mood is the sincere, almost pure regret of "Kingdom Come" with its hope of some redemptive future to absolve the guilt that almost always attends great loss (see Matthew Campbell's essay in this book). In this, the poem contains the "imaginative transformations" alluded to at the beginning of the essay.

In the final analysis, O'Reilly's and O'Callaghan's poems help us to educate the imagination, making us more attuned to the flexibility of language and its possibilities in making sense of cognition, memory, desire, history, myth, and identity in the often contradictory conditions of displacement and attachment. Their sophisticated aesthetic forged in "silence and solitude" nevertheless keeps "social forces ... audible as background."[72] These thoughts came to mind in light of current debates on the value and place of the humanities, which has been a question since the advent of the scientific age, one which seems to resurface with a vengeance when the economy is particularly precarious. The opposing views of the humanities and sciences may be said to rest on the inwardness of the humanities versus the outward focus of the sciences. By "sciences" we might include the political and social sciences upon which much of the thinking on Irish identity rests and which often doesn't quite know what to do with Irish poetry, as it is more interested in the applied use of words than it is the poetic. But these debates over the humanities are not new. We can look back to the 1970s when Northrop Frye wrote the following in *The Educated Imagination*:

> To try to teach literature by starting with the applied use of words, or "effective communication," as it's often called, then gradually work into literature through the more documentary forms of prose fiction and finally into poetry, seems to me a futile procedure. If literature is to be properly taught, we have to start at its center, which is poetry, then work outward to literary prose, then outward from there to the applied languages of business and professions and ordinary life. Poetry is the most direct and simple means of expressing oneself in words: the most primitive nations have poetry, but only quite well developed civilizations can produce good prose. So don't think of poetry as a perverse and unnatural way of distorting ordinary prose statements: prose is a much less natural way of speaking than poetry is. If you listen to small children, and to the amount of chanting and singsong in the speech, you'll see what I mean.[73]

The date of Frye's comments reminds us of how long this debate has been enacted. It goes back to the nineteenth-century arguments between Matthew Arnold and Thomas Huxley, and took a turn for the worse in the early twentieth century with F. R. Leavis and C. P. Snow. Of course, we who are interested in poetry appreciate the central role Frye gives it. Though poetry and prose may not be as different as Frye makes it seem, there are enough differences that his argument is not lost on us. As Dante insists and Frye reiterates, there is something in the physicality of poetry, its similarities to children's use of language, that underline poetry's attempt to give the most sophisticated ideas satisfactory expression. By speaking to us through the senses, through the physical nature of speech, through quite literally how we learned and understand our mother tongue, poetry remains a bridge between several epistemologies. The inwardness of literature remains the most germane aspect in this understanding, even if it doesn't have to carry the apolitical freight it is sometimes given. In the continuation of the above passage by Frye, the critic points out, much like Susan Stewart's more recent meditation, that poetry has a sense of physical movement, that it is rooted in the senses, that is, in the aesthetic. In *Watermark*, Joseph Brodsky's contemplation on the ineluctable beauties of Venice, the Russian poet writes: "Aesthetic sense is the twin of one's instinct for self-preservation and is more reliable than ethics. Aesthetics' main tool, the eye, is absolutely autonomous." He adds poetically: "In its autonomy, it is inferior only to a tear."[74] Both O'Reilly and O'Callaghan understand this because they have been torn and mended by the autonomy of the aesthetic as well as the tear.

NOTES

1. Dante Alighieri, *The Divine Comedy* 3: *Paradise*, trans. Dorothy Sayers and Barbara Reynolds (Middlesex: Penguin, 1962), canto 1, lines 7–9, 53.

2. Ibid., canto 33, lines 106–8, 346.

3. For example, David Wheatley, Sinéad Morrissey, and Vona Groarke, and some a bit older, like Harry Clifton, the late Dennis O'Driscoll, Maurice Riordan, and Gerard Fanning.

4. John McAuliffe, "Sound, rhythm, a soft-top and a disco ball's bright distortions," review of *The Sun King* by Conor O'Callaghan, *The Irish Times*, June 15, 2013.

5. Joseph Brodsky, *Watermark* (New York: Farrar, Straus and Giroux, 1992), 109.

6. Susan Stewart, *Poetry and the Fate of the Senses* (Chicago: The University of Chicago Press, 2002), 14.

7. Paul Muldoon, "7, Middagh Street," *Poems 1968–1998* (London: Faber and Faber, 2001), 178.

8. Stewart, *Poetry and the Fate of the Senses*, 15.

9. Ibid., 20.

10. Ibid., 245–46.

11. Ibid.

12. W. B. Yeats, *Explorations* (New York: Macmillan, 1962), 336.

13. W. B. Yeats, *The Complete Poems*, ed. Daniel Albright (London: Dent, 1992), 387.

14. Caitríona O'Reilly, "Pollen," *The Sea Cabinet* (Northumberland, UK: Bloodaxe, 2006), 59.

15. O'Reilly, *Geis* (Winston Salem, NC: Wake Forest UP, 2015), 9; all quotations from *Geis* are taken from this edition.

16. Ibid., 7.

17. O'Reilly studied English and archaeology at Trinity College, Dublin.

18. O'Reilly, *Geis*, 39–40.

19. O'Reilly, "'It felt like a breaking of some taboo I'd placed myself under': Caitríona O'Reilly on writing *Geis*," by Shannon Magee and Alexander Muller, Wake Forest University Press website, Oct. 7, 2015, http://blog.wfupress.wfu.edu/2015/10/07/it-felt-like-a-breaking-of-some-taboo-id-placed-myself-under-caitriona-oreilly-on-writing-geis/.

20. O'Reilly states: "I am naturally of a deeply skeptical mindset, but I am fascinated by myth and it is partly a way of escaping my frustrations with the highly rational, highly materialistic globalized world we now live in; myths represent a compelling, entirely localized way of understanding uncontrollable phenomena, of relating to the landscape, a means of placation and reassurance, an explanatory style. I am aware of their double-edged nature — they also represent a sump of ignorance and prejudice — but I think we are the poorer psychologically for the loss of our myths." O'Reilly, "It felt like a breaking of some taboo."

21. O'Reilly, *Geis*, 23.

22. See O'Reilly, "It felt like a breaking of some taboo."

23. O'Reilly, *Geis*, 20.

24. Ibid., 12–13.

25. See Laurence Coupe, *Myth* (London and New York: Routledge, 1997), 19, for a discussion of Frazer's mythographic approach to myth that both dismisses and is nostalgic for the mythopoeic sensibility of the primitive world. Frazer believes it has become outmoded by science and yet universalizes its understanding of the world as something shared by many peoples.

26. O'Reilly, *Geis*, 52–53.

27. Ibid., 50–51.

28. Ibid., 54–59.

29. Ibid., 14–22.

30. Ibid., 29–30.

31. Ibid., 24–25.

32. Ibid., 26–27.

33. Ibid., 28.

34. The phrase "after Ireland" is the title of a poem by Harry Clifton from *The Holding Centre: Selected Poems 1974–2004* (Winston-Salem, NC: Wake Forest UP, 2014), 144; and an article by Declan Kiberd, "After Ireland?" *The Irish Times*, Aug. 29, 2009.

35. O'Reilly, *Geis*, 37–38.

36. Ibid., 41.

37. O'Reilly, *The Nowhere Birds* (Northumberland, UK: Bloodaxe, 2001), 37.

38. O'Reilly, *Geis*, 42–43.

39. Eiléan Ní Chuilleanáin, "Pygmalion's Image," *The Magdalene Sermon and Earlier Poems* (Winston-Salem, NC: Wake Forest UP, 1991), 9.

40. Samuel Beckett, *Molloy*, in *The Trilogy* (London: Picador, 1979), 14.

41. O'Reilly, *Geis*, 47–48.

42. Ibid., 44–45.

43. O'Reilly makes clear that solitude and walks in the woods near her house are a seminal part of her poetry: "I go for long solo walks in a nearby wooded park, during which time ideas often occur, and then I go back home and write them down. I suppose it is a routine of sorts." O'Reilly, "It felt like a breaking of some taboo."

44. O'Reilly, *Geis*, 58–59.

45. O'Reilly, *The Sea Cabinet*, 50.

46. O'Reilly, *Geis*, 63–64.

47. Emily Dickinson, *The Complete Poems of Emily Dickinson*, ed. Thomas H. Johnson (Boston: Little, Brown and Company, 1960), 486.

48. Conor O'Callaghan, preface to *The Wake Forest Series of Irish Poetry*, Vol. 3 (Winston-Salem, NC: Wake Forest UP, 2013), xiv–xv.

49. Gary Snyder, "The Sweat," *No Nature: New and Selected Poems* (New York: Random House, 1992), 364.

50. O'Callaghan, *The Sun King* (Winston-Salem, NC: Wake Forest UP, 2013), 3. All quotations from *The Sun King* are taken from this edition.

51. Ibid., 4.

52. Ibid., 5.

53. Ibid., 6.

54. Ibid., 13–15.

55. Ibid., 16.

56. Ibid., 17–18.

57. Ibid., 3.

58. Robert Frost, quoted in Jay Parini, *Robert Frost: A Life* (New York: Holt, 1999), 386. It is worth noting that Frost felt that prose also "tends to evaporate" when "translated."

59. O'Callaghan, *The Sun King*, 20.

60. Stewart, *Poetry and the Fate of the Senses*, 34.

61. Ibid., 38.

62. Robert Frost, *The Poetry of Robert Frost*, ed. Edward Connery Lathem (New York: St. Martin's Press, 2002), 379.

63. O'Callaghan, *The Sun King*, 25.

64. Parini, *Robert Frost: A Life*, 361–64.

65. O'Callaghan, *The Sun King*, 26.

66. Ibid., 30–31.

67. Ibid., 35.

68. Conor O'Callaghan, e-mail message to the author, July 15, 2013.

69. O'Callaghan, *The Sun King*, 41.

70. Ibid., 44.

71. Ibid., 45.

72. O'Callaghan, preface to *The Wake Forest Series*, xiv.

73. Northrop Frye, *The Educated Imagination* (Bloomington: Indiana UP, 1971), 121.

74. Brodsky, *Watermark*, 109.

13

Southern Wind

Theo Dorgan

I

It seems to this working poet that the default stance in the critical response to contemporary poetry, Irish poetry included, is all too often governed by, shaped by, the *a priori* exigencies of theory. Marxist, post-Marxist, structuralist, post-structuralist, post-modernist, and other theories have proved extraordinarily useful, helpful even, in challenging us to think about poems in fresh and productive ways, but it is the nature of poetry to be always mutating beyond the circumscriptive capacities of any one theory. That, at any rate, is the argument I will make here. There is no argument against theory *per se*, but there is perhaps an argument against hubris, against exclusion, against over-simplification, against the absurd idea that any theory can, ever, be considered adequate to all imaginable circumstances.

Cultural commentators and historians of culture are fond, perhaps over-fond, of invoking the spirit of Walter Benjamin, of conjuring up the commodification of the work of art as an explanation for everything that has happened in Western cultures since the early days of the twentieth century. Nothing wrong with that, in itself: Benjamin's insight has proved remarkably useful and applicable, and I find it helpful myself in trying to understand the lineaments of what has been happening in our art and writing in recent generations.

The paradoxical danger with all truisms, and Benjamin's proposition has become a truism, is that the more general their scope may be in the original formulation, the more narrow their application becomes with the passage of time. Great insights that should provoke and nurture a sense of open-ended wonder can easily become an instrument for the unthinking foreclosure of thought. In the case of Benjamin's great insight, when we find ourselves saying that the work of art in our time has become a commodity, we all too often mean no more than to say that the work of art has become something whose primary worth, regrettably, has become its value as a tradable commodity in the marketplace.

Benjamin, I think, meant far more than this.

In any case, one result of this foreshortening of perspective has been to situate the process of making art, literature, music, and poetry inside a larger economy of material production in a way that evades or elides Benjamin's intention — which was to characterize this phenomenon as negative and a distortion of the true situation — so that, for instance, inside a certain discourse of criticism, the term "cultural worker" acquired a kind of retro-nobility, inscribing the artists among the romanticized "toiling masses" so dear at one time to faux liberals and to far too many bourgeois intellectuals.

Consciously or not, this reductive process has the effect of taming and nullifying the grounded subjectivity and radical independence of the individual poet, composer, painter, or dancer. It is, in effect, both an apology in the face of an imagined hostility to the artist from fantasized "real" workers (a ventriloquized "who do you think you are?") and a means of reining back individuality of expression by situating the artist's work inside some imagined, abstract, theoretically constructed mass phenomenon. Economic determinism, whether in leftist or rightist ideology, demands that the individual's identity as a maker, understood as embodied in the work they do, be harnessed, reined back, chopped, and shaped so that it fits, finally, inside some expressive category of explanation.

Commodification in general, in the twentieth century, has been a working out of the industrialization of all aspects of life, not just in manufacture but also in agriculture, construction, transport, social systemics, and so on. As an inevitable consequence, a rhetoric, one might say a propositional grammar, has grown out of these apparently successful practices and spread itself into what used to be called the humanities. Once, teaching was a matter of leading the student into experiencing a text, a process grounded in a holistic dialogic process that situated the text in both its natal and its contemporary contexts. In recent decades, however, we more and more find the mass of texts produced by autonomous self-situating individuals being treated as raw material in a quasi-industrial process, and the shaping of these materials into products to be delivered to consumers inside a distribution mechanism that is always in danger of fetishizing itself.

At its best, this process allows a set of sophisticated theories to establish themselves as propositional constructs, matrices inside which and with the aid of which the individual student might gain insight. Handled with care, and a certain self-critical modesty, this way of working can and often does yield valuable insights. Predictably enough, though, the tail soon begins to wag the dog, and those texts come to be considered important and meaningful that fit best with the projective mechanism of a particular theory.

With, of course, the inevitable corollary that texts resistant to being read inside the ambit of a particular theory are quietly downgraded, discarded, or ignored.

The shift to the industrial mindset, whether under capitalism, state capitalism, fascism, or what was once called "actually existing communism," can be represented as mirroring a decisive shift in the machinery of production from the artisan/craftsman model to the worker-as-component-of-process model. From the farmer, carpenter, or metalworker, if you like, to the robotized factory worker, the anonymous man or woman trained only to operate increasingly human-proofed machinery.

The crucial component in machine-age commodification or the rhetoric of industrialization is the dehumanization of any one individual conscripted into the process. The whole point of the process, in a way, is that nobody walking out of a Ford plant, watching a car being driven away, can say: "I built that car." The worker as maker cannot identify, or identify with, the fruits of her or his labor.

Once the ancient human scale is superseded by the commodifying logic of industrial production, the individual human, as agent or victim, is conscripted into a discourse in which there is no longer a space that allows us to insist on the absolute value of individual identity.

II

In the late twentieth century, commodification re-invented itself not as a process in the material world but as an event in the imagination, a meta-language that is at once more totalizing and more alienating than simple industrialization and the ramification of the industrial thought process into all areas of life. Inevitably, inexorably, this meta-language moves into the discourse we use to critique events in the imagination.

As an example of an event in the imagination, let me propose the god Apollo, and certain phenomena that constellate in the imagination about the god's name.

Apollo in Greek mythology is the god of sun and light, of prophecy and herd-keeping; he is the patron of the nine Muses; he is the god who can bring plagues and ill-health; and he is also, of course, the god of music and poetry. In the fullest of senses, he is a god of our home place.

When the first photographs of Earth began to come back from the Apollo missions, it came home to most of us that indeed we live on a planet with finite boundaries. Light and prophecy, music and poetry, herds and plagues, health and the human imagination, all this and so much more has one home and one home only. Some were moved to wonder, many were moved to a profound understanding that all the productive land and sea, all the air and minerals we are ever going to have are right here, right now. We understood that our world and its resources are finite, and in many this awoke both a practical and a moral sense of stewardship. We understood that our home planet, the only one we are ever going to have, is absolutely confided to our care.

The commodifiers, however, were moved to a different perception. If the material reserves of the planet are finite, then open-ended and profit-oriented industry has an absolute horizon. Eventually, to put it plainly, we will run out of stuff to work and to sell and to consume. Quite a dilemma, and one solved with brutal simplicity: our owners simply redefined us as consumers, but not in the straightforward sense of people who consume by eating and using things that wear out and need to be replaced, people who make use of material things in the process of being and doing in the world. This new kind of consumer would consume not toward any practical end but as an end in itself; they would purchase not goods, not exactly, but the idea of goods, a brand, an image, a virtual experience.

A thing, from now on, for the purposes of commerce and profit, would become not just the thing in itself but also the idea of the thing. We would own not just the thing itself but the constructed idea of the thing. Then, just as industrialization spawned a ramifying discourse at the opening of the twentieth century, a new rhetoric spread itself through all areas of our life. Citizens became customers of the state and its services, students became not learners but entitled consumers of services they had paid for, and teachers became distribution nodes in an architecture of delivery. No longer educators as they might have wished to be, not human witnesses to centuries of thought and scholarship, not companions to young minds embarked on voyages of discovery, teachers came to be viewed as simply a means of delivering whatever the disembodied and ultimately unknowable market appears to demand at a given moment: content divorced from its occasion, evacuated of its singularity as witness.

This is the new hegemonic discourse of our time, and its sign in the domain of language is the ascendancy of opinion over knowledge, the displacement of a living, evolving tradition by arbitrary fashion and the attenuations of bureaucratic diktat, the decoupling of identity from responsibility to self and others, of words from their etymologies, of the moral dimension from critical discourse, and of pleasure from the appreciation of art.

Now in one of its aspects, this complex process I have been struggling to describe results in the construction of particular kinds of descriptive sets. In themselves, descriptive sets are an ancient, even an organic reflexive phenomenon — we Greeks, those Persians, my village, your family, soldiers, philosophers, Romantic poets, Cubist painters… We've always done this, and for obvious and practical reasons. Historically we have distinguished between different kinds of descriptive sets: some have absolute boundaries — my family, for instance; some are understood to have more or less fixed boundaries — my nation, for instance, is a term that becomes fuzzy around the edges when closely examined, but has a kind of rough-and-ready intelligibility. Descriptive sets in the cultural realm have tended to be more fluid, not least because the protean natures of artists, the protean and manifold varieties of art-making, tend to flow under and around and through any attempt to set boundaries. There was so much more to Picasso than cubism, and nothing much is gained by defining Miró as a surrealist, Joyce as a modernist and so on, unless we mean to limit our understanding of them to what happens in their work within the boundaries of a descriptive set.

Such descriptive sets, until very recently, were understood to be no more than temporary, fluid designations, terms that allowed us to understand an artist in relation to her times, his contemporaries, their work in relation to the work of others, instruments toward understanding the individual in his or her work, but having no more than an instrumental and in that sense temporary, evolving value.

The iron logic of brand consumerism will have none of this. The success or failure of branding depends on persuading the consumer toward brand loyalty, absolute choice, absolute categories. Crucially, brand loyalty demands not just the partisan adoption of a brand as preferred choice but also the denigration, exclusion, and nullification of other options, of what is not the brand.

The figure who comes to my mind here is Procustes, son of Poseidon, who owned an iron bed in which he would invite passers-by to spend the night. If they proved too short for the bed, he would hammer their legs until they could be stretched to fit; if they proved too tall, that is too long for the bed, he would amputate their legs.

III

Under the artificial sun of this new hegemony, descriptive sets become prescriptive sets — and it is instructive to consider how contemporary Irish poetry is dealt with in the schools in this baleful light.

"Irish poetry," as a descriptive term is usually and uncritically taken to mean poetry written by Irish poets born in Ireland. As a consequence, however, of the tendency for description to mask prescription, almost all the major surveys of Irish poetry carry the unvoiced code "written in English," and this both reflects and drives a paradoxical stance that sees Irish poetry written in Irish as being at a tangent to the main thrust of the living tradition.

It isn't, of course, that Nuala Ní Dhomhnaill or Cathal Ó Searcaigh are not seen by serious people as Irish poets writing Irish poetry, it's just that when scholars, commentators, and journalists refer to Irish poetry, they almost always have in mind Irish poetry written in English. This mindset is a reflection of the hegemonic power of English as a world language, since brand-making always aspires to operate under the aegis of the greatest power available. Reflecting commodification unconsciously, the consequence is that — with no malice at all intended — all those who deploy the signifier or brand "Irish poetry" without deliberately making it clear they mean Irish poetry in both languages are participating in the larger globalization project of standardization, a project that sometimes unconsciously, sometimes deliberately, seeks to marginalize and make redundant all but a handful of power languages in the marketplace.

You would imagine, perhaps, that it is no great problem, to say Irish poetry in English when that's what you mean, Irish poetry in Irish when that's what you mean, and to mean Irish poetry in both languages when you deploy the term "Irish poetry." Why, then, do we so rarely encounter this level of clarification? I suggest that the hegemonic discourse of branding is impatient with such fine distinctions — the niche market for poetry in Irish being too small to merit attention while Irish poetry in English is a significant component not just of poetry in the English language, but of other appreciable market segments of the present moment, such as gender studies and postcolonial studies, where market-leading courses and teachers work in English — a world language of considerable weight and power. Unsurprisingly, then, the presumptive category "English" overrides the subaltern category "Irish" (meaning here Gaelic).

Translation, one might object — are not Irish poets widely available in translation? The short answer to this is that some of them are, and many are not, but two points need to be made here: the translation is not the poem, it is a substitute for the poem, and the false equivalence of translation with original rests on a very dangerous and usually hidden proposition, that the original poem is no more than a prompt to exposition and paraphrase.

When the term "Irish poetry" is used as it normally and unquestioningly is, we are looking at the unfolding of a process that begins by defining a market segment in terms of what exists, proceeds to prescribe the parameters of inclusion in this constructed domain, and ends in the exclusion of what does not fit the criteria for inclusion.

In the study of Irish poetry, other elements also are imbricated — Irish history, Irish politics, Irish regional identities, Irish social cohorts, the land of Ireland, and so on. Because the very word "Ireland" (and thus of course also "Irish") carries such a resonance, as signifier and thus as brand in the new discourse, market synergy makes it all too easy to ring the changes on combinations of terms and phenomena — thus the proliferation of academic theses along the lines of: "Gendering Regional Identity in Rural Ireland: A Poetics of Discord," or "Regionalizing History: Eco-poetry and the Rural-Urban Divide in Five Irish Women Poets," and so on.

Now of course any one such thesis might very well be a contribution to wider understanding, a valuable specialist study in itself, an exemplary piece of elegant writing, a source of amplifying insights — I do not mean in the least to denigrate specialized scholarship, no matter how arcane. I am pointing here to the likelihood that synergy in such discourse will most likely take the form of correlation between descriptive categories that are already inherently prescriptive and exclusionary, so that what seems on the surface to be an augmentation, a widening out of critical attention, may in fact be producing the very opposite.

The descriptive categories that divide up the brand marketplace into sub-categories, the very categories that in varieties of combination appear to offer that grand illusion of the twenty-first century, infinite consumer choice, are far more unstable than they might seem to be at first sight. We have seen that the simple term "Irish poetry" cannot resist too much pressure before buckling and fragmenting. It might be said, therefore, that the existence of limiting categories is no great matter, since the categories and their imperatives are so inherently unstable. It might also be said that, as with all other marketplaces, the Irish subdivision of the general poetry marketplace is subject to the severe instabilities of whim and caprice, of the arbitrary shift of mood, the vagaries of fashion. And these are to some extent reasonable observations — in the market, as everywhere in this life, nothing is forever.

I want to suggest at this point that the problems can be thought of as constellating around a single word, and that word is "alienation."

The OED offers as its primary definition of this interesting word: "The act of estranging or state of estrangement in feeling or affection" — which sends us, perhaps somewhat puzzled, on to its definition of "estrangement," which is no help at all: "The action of estranging or becoming estranged; the state of being estranged; alienation." Well, on to "estrange" then, where we find, very much apropos: "Withhold from a person's perception or knowledge."

In the discipline of philosophy, there are many useful and provocative meditations on the concept of alienation. I want here to single out two, not because I necessarily fully agree with either but simply because they serve to keep this argument within reasonable bounds. Each concept derives in some way from Hegel, as far as I can judge, and they are sharply and succinctly expressed by Sean Sayers as follows:

> In the Marxist literature, alienation is often taken to be a concept which describes and criticises the social and economic conditions of capitalism. In existentialist writing, by contrast, the concept is used primarily to refer to a psychological, perhaps even spiritual, kind of malaise which is pervasive in modern society but not specific to it. Rather it is symptomatic of the human condition as such.[1]

Now back to the OED where, under "alienate" we find: "1 Estrange; turn away in feelings or affection… 2 Transfer to the ownership of another… 3 *gen.* Turn away, divert."

In the Marxist analytic, the worker is alienated from the product of his or her work, like the Ford worker I mentioned earlier who cannot identify, or identify with, any one car she or he has made.

In Existentialist terms, the individual has ceased to feel at home in the world, is displaced and disconnected.

Drawing on both these analytics, we observe that individuality is devalued or in extreme cases nullified and, it follows surely, that communion between individuals becomes reduced or attenuated, can even become impossible.

We might note here in passing that in its definitions of both "alienation" and "estrangement," the dictionary refers to "affection" and to "ownership."

Bearing all the foregoing in mind, and narrowing down from a series of wide-ranging propositions to a particular example of consequence, I want to propose that a very considerable number of poets from the Republic have become alienated in and by and through the habitual critical discourse of our time.

Alienated because a large cohort has been excluded from study under the brand rubric of Irish poetry.

Alienated because they write in Irish.

Alienated because Procustes has been at work, chopping and fitting a body of work to fit with a pre-ordained thesis.

Alienated because the prescriptive term "Irish poet" negates more complex transnational identities.

Alienated because they have become co-opted into descriptive sets by gender.

Alienated because they have been co-opted by tribal identity.

Alienated because their elected lineages as poets are neither identified nor respected.

Alienated because they consider themselves first poets and second Irish poets, while the critical discourse, if it refers to them at all, confines them inside the brand identity "Irish."

Alienated because, above all, their work is not studied and taught with affection, for pleasure, by other sentient beings, in a common conversation among beings struggling to make sense in and of the world in the face of mortality.

There are, of course, individual exceptions among the scholars. I mean no disrespect here to those who in severe and loving friendship have kept faith with the ancient compact of mutual respect between a poet and her critical reader. There are scholars who are loved and revered and listened to by working poets in that all-important dialectic of echoes centered upon the only thing that matters, or should matter: the poem itself, launched into community in blind faith.

I offer here, as a focus for reflection, that luminous phrase of Nuala Ní Dhomhnaill's in her poem "Ceist na Teangan":

Cuirim mo dhóchas ar snámh
i mbáidín teangan [...]

(I set my hope afloat
in a small boat of language.)[2]

I do not know a single working poet in our time who does not feel that at one level or another their work is, in one way or another, reduced to commodity in scholarship's version of the dominant rhetoric of our time.

Most poets of my acquaintance care very little whether or not they are taught in the universities, and when they are taught they pay little attention to how they are taught. Neither indifference nor misleading inscription in (or exclusion from) the brand will impede the writing of the next poem, and the next... But all the same, something is being lost here.

In assenting to the commodification of the poem, to the commodification of learning, the academy is foregoing the possibility of breaking the cycle of alienation where it is not actively perpetuating that cycle. It is a notorious charge, in our times, that the academy has seceded from the possibility of engaging with, leading and learning from, a general social culture. The charge is often unfair in the individual instance, but carries a certain persuasive weight in the general.

The fact is that every poet, and every poem, benefits from the instructed reading. More, society at large can only benefit from the humane insights into our common human predicament that can and should flow from the conversation between poet and critic.

It is an urgent need at the present moment that we reground language so that it can embody and make possible the human imagination in all its constitutive aspects, not least the moral. This is a task, it seems to me, for writers and critics alike. One can conceive of a world where poets and their professional colleagues in criticism maintain a mutually beneficial dialogue — but, and always acknowledging exceptions, it is not our world at present. In Marxian terms, while they share a common alienation as persons, they have been cast in a relationship where each contributes to the further alienation of the other. In existential terms, because the idea of meaning-in-community is not embraced, each is necessarily alienated from the other. In the terms offered by the OED, they are estranged from each other, and they are not in a relationship based in common affection.

We are all, of course, poet and critic alike, subject to profound world-constituting forces so vast and all-encompassing that it is hard to see how one might even begin to resist. We are swept onwards, it sometimes seems, by a tidal wave of unimaginable weight and power, styling itself progress, against which it seems impossible to rebel.

I remind myself here, in passing, of the late Michael Hartnett's powerful and luminous lines:

> Poets with progress
> make no peace or pact,
> the act of poetry
> is a rebel act.[3]

We live in an age saturated with information, and one consequence is that, as consumers of information, we are constantly under pressure to make rapid and often unreflective choices. It seems impossible, even perverse, to claim a personal space and time where, surveying the possibilities, one might choose to take a stand.

You might say, develop a personal, independent sensibility.

Over the past forty years, anyone disposed to study Irish poetry will likely be directed there under the bright light shone by scholars, journalists, and other commentators on recent Irish political history. The salient world-visible fact about Ireland in those four decades, particularly between the Civil Rights marches of 1968 and the Belfast Agreement of 1998, was the war in the north of our island. In those decades, considerable talents began to flower in poetry coming from the North — Heaney, of course, Montague, Mahon, Carson, Muldoon, McGuckian, Longley, together with Fiacc, Simmons, Ormsby, Newmann, a host of others — and the media market created an instant niche: Northern Irish Poets.

The academy followed.

Among the consequences of this directed attention: poets of the Republic fell into the critical shadows, and poets from Northern Ireland began to be read through the lens of the sociology of war and tribal conflict.

Journalism engaged with Northern Irish poetry as expressive of a politics of the present moment, and the politics that drew most attention was the politics that most engaged the mass media: the macro politics of war and civil unrest, the polarities of Dublin-Belfast-London.

Larger human horizons were ignored or glossed over. Again in terms of politics, the engagement among poets of the Republic with gender, class, and environmental issues passed under the radar for a long time — until the emergence of gender studies as a category in the academic marketplace prompted a considerable and welcome attention to the poetry of some women from the Republic.

That women poets from the Republic were beginning to appear in numbers, free, engaged as they themselves saw fit, and fiercely independent, was not always welcome in the then-dominant discourse.[4]

In any case, my general point here is that the solidification of a category into the comfort of its own unexamined parameters always risks misrepresenting what is subsumed into that category, not the least of which misrepresentations is the Procustean distortion of any given poet's work.

Let me put this in a particular way: in what way is it useful to say that Derek Mahon is a Northern Ireland poet?

True, he was born there. He grew up there. Then he was educated in Dublin, he spent much of his life in London and elsewhere, and in latter decades in the Republic. Some of his work refers to the landscape, tropes, and tribulations of his youth, but nobody would seriously argue that his sensibility is dominated, much less explained, by the accident of his birthplace. Subsuming Mahon into that particular category leads to a particular kind of rhetorical demand, that he remain in some way "faithful" to the North as subject matter, that he confine his worldview to what might be expected of a Protestant poet of his class and background. That Mahon is an urban sophisticate, indeed a cosmopolitan, in his influences and predilections, in stance and tone, in his subject matter, and in his affinities with the likes of, say, the Francophone Swiss Philippe Jaccottet, becomes hard to see under the smoke and fog of "Northern Irish poet." Mahon's reputation and considerable achievements as a poet have been obscured by tribalist readings and demands — most notoriously when a Northern-born critic said of him, unforgivably, that Mahon has become "infected" by the South.

By accident of history, Mahon is an Irish poet, not least because he himself elects for collegiality with other poets born in Ireland, with whom he shares elements of a linguistic and cultural common heritage. But then, technically and legally, Mahon is also a British poet, and entitled to call himself such if he should so choose. I do not see that it would advance our ultimate understanding of his work, or our estimation of that work, to read him simply under one aegis or another.

That those people with whom he most closely identifies, that particular subset of Irish who form his proto-community, were embroiled in war for decades is bound to have an effect on his sensibility, but then as a cultured man of considerable moral sensibility he is equally distressed by all forms of war, declared and undeclared.

Turning south, it would be possible, were one so inclined, to characterize Eavan Boland as a poster child for poets of the Republic — daughter of a Dublin painter and of an Irish Ambassador, brought up in London and in New York with an intense awareness of her Irishness, we might indeed be unsurprised to see her characterized as a Poet of The Republic — but, oddly enough perhaps, that designation, that brand, has not been evoked. Boland, instead, has been recruited as an object of interest in the field of gender studies, and not without reason: her exemplary public life as a poet as much as the themes and strategies of her work both entitle her to be read in that light but, alas, all too often restrict her to being read only or mainly in that light.

Boland is a fine love poet, an astute chronicler of suburban life, a laconic recorder of time passing, an elegist (as Mahon, her contemporary at Trinity, is also an elegist), but these are all too rarely categories of inquiry and elucidation under which her work is offered to us.

One might multiply examples of how poets who have been, so to speak, accepted as fit to be studied have been done a disservice through their co-option into diminished or diminishing critical categories — but there are many other Irish poets who have been unevenly, when barely or not at all, acknowledged in the work of the academy.

Curiously enough, or perhaps not, the vast majority of these are from the South. Thomas McCarthy, Michael Coady, Mary O'Malley, Tony Curtis, Peter Sirr, Gerry Murphy, Enda Wyley, Pat Boran, Leanne O'Sullivan, Macdara Woods, Gregory O'Donoghue, Michael Gorman, Maurice Riordan, Fred Johnston, Pearse Hutchinson, Moya Cannon, Caitríona O'Reilly, Harry Clifton — I am choosing here more or less at random from a very considerable number — are all poets of the Republic, and their work has been interwoven with the complex emergence of civil society in the Republic. The same could be said of Biddy Jenkinson, Gabriel Rosenstock, Liam Ó Muirthile, Nuala Ní Dhomhnaill, Tomás Mac Siomóin, Cathal Ó Searcaigh, Gearóid Mac Lochlainn, and others writing in Irish — although some of these have indeed received critical attention.

All Irish poets. All poets of the Irish Republic — but, so what?

There are of course cross references between them, shared preoccupations, shared inheritances, conversations of all kinds in a kind of local shorthand. Some have soldiered together on political, environmental, and social issues, and have the scars to show for it. All have to some degree or another engaged directly or obliquely with the society they share, and there is something to be learned about each of them by a scholar directing his or attention to that common context they both share and are in the business of co-creating.

But, and it is a large but, when you have said of any one of them that he or she is a poet of the Irish Republic you will almost always have said the least interesting thing about them, you will almost always have situated them in a context that does far less than you might imagine to lead us into the heart of the work.

The poet, like every one of us, is born and must die alone. Not one of us is fully or even adequately explained by inscription in a category, whether that category be gender, class, family, or nation. When we come to consciousness, when we embark on the long and difficult process of leading an examined life, all that we do and say and think and feel is in the light that flashes between two voids — the darkness before birth, the darkness that follows life. That is a primary determinant in how we compose our stance toward the world. All lives are particular in the light of this terrible and inescapable knowledge, and it has always seemed to me that by far the most interesting aspect of a poet's work is to be found in her or his gestures and witness in the face of this knowledge.

If alienation is the great wound, and moreover a wound in the affections, every good poem is a refusal of that alienation, a rebel act, a declaration that community is possible. When I read Thomas McCarthy I am heartened and strengthened by his humane wisdom, his gentle unyielding tone, the grace of his dance with the poetics of W. H. Auden. When I read Paula Meehan I engage with her personal story as she chooses to dramatize it, with her profound compassion for the poor and powerless, her self-inscription in those ranks that tails back into her own childhood — but I also engage with her thoughtful and honest dance with the ghost of Akhmatova, her affinity for the poetry of Gary Snyder. When I read Michael Coady I am heartened by his profound love of music, just as I love the dignified wit in the face of despair that marks the poems of Tony Curtis, that and his unremarked but affecting affinity with Beckett. I hear the voices in Peter Sirr of long conversations with the poetic traditions of Holland and Italy, I discern the syntax of traditional music in Moya Cannon's deceptively quiet poems, I find the universal exuberance of a young woman discovering her body and the world in Leanne O'Sullivan, that and her recuperation of the storyscape of her native west Cork …

I want a scholarship that discloses these depths in a rigorous, respectful, even affectionate unveiling. I want a scholarship that flies free of the market, however defined or understood. I want a scholarship that understands poems are made in humility with a sense of wonder and privilege, a scholarship founded not on the poem as commodity but on the poem as instance of human process, on poems as small boats set afloat on the stream. I want a scholarship of contagious excitement and rigor, a scholarship that discloses the endlessness of poems, a scholarship in which I can feel at home and welcome.

I want a scholarship that understands we make poems in order to provoke, offer, and share instructed pleasure.

I want a scholarship in which no poet is left behind.

I want a scholarship brave enough to refuse the denatured, denaturing discourse of these terrible present times.

I beg the forgiveness of Michael Hartnett's ghost when I say I want a scholarship of refusal, a discourse where scholarship begins and continues as a rebel act.

It is true enough in its way, that with cherry-picked exceptions, the poetry that was written in the Republic during and since the prolonged agony of the war in the North has been neglected in academic discourse — with, I should not need to add, some few honorable exceptions. Inasmuch as this means that this poetry has not been subjected to the attentions of Procustes, that may well be a good thing, but it is not a good thing that this poetry has lacked the support of good, generous, and insightful critical dialogue.

My immediate purpose here has been to sketch in the lineaments of destructive, ultimately negative, critical practice. In drawing attention to some neglected Irish poets and poetry, in both languages, I make no special case for Irish poetry as such — I could make a similar plea for informed attention to Welsh, Scottish, Caribbean, and other poetries, but I have, unsurprisingly, a particular knowledge of what is being written in my own country, in my own time.

For a long time now, and I am not alone in this among my contemporaries, it feels as if a cold north wind has been blowing down from the heights of theory-driven criticism.

I thought I might let a southern wind blow through and out into the free lands of a wider possibility. I hope these words may be taken in good part.

NOTES

1. Sean Sayers, "The Concept of Alienation in Existentialism and Marxism: Hegelian Themes in Modern Social Thought" (paper presented at the Hegel Society of Great Britain Annual Conference, Oxford, UK, Sept. 2003), accessed online Aug. 24, 2016, http://www.academia.edu/3035430/The_Concept_of_Alienation_in_Existentialism_ and_Marxism_Hegelian_Themes_in_Modern_Social_Thought.

2. Nuala Ní Dhomhnaill, "Ceist na Teangan," *Pharaoh's Daughter* (Winston-Salem, NC: Wake Forest UP, 1993), 154. The translation is my own.

3. Michael Hartnett, from "A Farewell to English," *Selected and New Poems* (Winston-Salem, NC: Wake Forest UP, 1994), 50.

4. I remember a particularly absurd demonstration of this in the 90s: BBC Radio 4 had invited two well-known Irish women poets and a distinguished professor of literature

to take part in a discussion program, in the course of which the presenter asked the professor why it was that so many women poets were emerging in the Republic and so few in the North. Her response was startling. "Well," she said, and I am paraphrasing here, "you see the South is so backward, particularly in its treatment of women, that it threw up a woman's movement, and that in turn threw up a generation of young women poets." The (young, male) presenter, to his credit, managed not to burst out laughing, not least at the sectarian and inadvertently comic implication that Northern Ireland was an advanced liberal society which *therefore* had no need of women poets, and the poets, equally to their credit, generously forbore to respond to the good professor's explanation. Myself, listening to the program, I thought it an ingenious departure in literary studies, to explain the emergence of a cohort of writers in terms of projectile vomiting.

14

Three Contemporary Irish-American Poets: Michael Donaghy, Campbell McGrath, and Maureen McLane

James Chandler

How do we identify an Irish poet "post-Ireland"? My approach to this question will be to consider three American poets of Irish descent, each with a discernible relationship to Ireland and its poetic traditions. Very different as they are, both in their writing and in their responses to Irish culture, they are nonetheless alike in rewarding careful critical attention. All are poets who have emerged over the last quarter century or so, and in each case I have followed their work closely from the start, for all were once students at the University of Chicago. That is an institution known for its zealous academicism, and all three of these poets managed to secure gainful employment in a university setting. Each, moreover, has elaborated a complicated and interesting posture toward scholarship and academic life more broadly. I mean to attend to that posture in each case, even as I consider what it means to think about them as Irish poets post-Ireland.

They attended the University of Chicago in very different capacities. Michael Donaghy matriculated as an MA student in 1976. Campbell McGrath was an undergraduate there in the early 1980s. Maureen McLane successfully pursued her PhD in English in the early 1990s. All have written noteworthy criticism. In Donaghy's case, soon after his death nearly a decade ago at the age of fifty, there appeared a collection of essays and reviews titled *The Shape of the Dance* (2009).[1] McGrath has published a couple of dozen insightful critical essays and published interviews and, in the process, has turned himself into a very fine prose stylist. McLane, the youngest of the three, has already established herself as one of the finest scholars of Romantic literature and British poetry more broadly in her generation. This body of work would have earned her tenure at NYU, where she now teaches, had she written nothing else. And her public criticism is likewise voluminous and distinguished. As early as 2006 she was awarded the New York Book Critics Circle Award for her critical reviews of the previous year. The overall body of critical work produced by this trio is very rich indeed, and of course sheds some light on the poetry, but it is the poetry itself that I mean to address in what follows.

1. Michael Donaghy

When Donaghy came to graduate school at Chicago in the mid-1970s, he was certainly a bright student — probably the brightest I encountered in my first few years there — but he was also struggling with issues of social and personal dislocation. He was raised in the Bronx by Irish immigrant parents. His father was superintendent in an apartment building on Fifth Avenue — the family lived in the basement behind the boiler. He was now studying English literature in an elite graduate program. In spite of, or because of, what proved to be a kind of obsession with the writings of the sixteenth-century Italian maverick, Giordano Bruno, Donaghy did well enough in the MA program to win admission to Chicago's competitive PhD program. In spite of some brilliant writing about Coleridge, graduate school was not, for him, a good fit. He became disaffected with academic work. There was an unfortunate confrontation with Paul de Man in a seminar on Shelley (Donaghy later wrote amusingly about this). Eventually, Donaghy learned to play whistle and bodhrán, and joined a band that played some of the better folk clubs in Chicago. He started writing poetry. Like many such talents in our program he also turned to our excellent student-run literary magazine, *The Chicago Review*, where he served briefly as editor-in-chief. In 1985 he moved to London where he first earned a living by playing in pub bands, busking in tube stations, and teaching. He also began to gain recognition as a poet in the UK, republishing a chapbook, *Slivers*, as *Shibboleth* (1988), which won both the Faber and the Whitbread awards in quick succession.[2] Over the next two decades, he published three well-reviewed books of poems and had a one-third share of volume 11 in the Penguin Modern Poets series (with Andrew Motion and Hugo Williams). With the help of Paxman, Picador brought out a posthumous *Collected Poems* in 2009, introduced astutely by Sean O'Brien. It included a "fragment" on Irish folk music.[3]

I mention these details because, of the three poets under discussion here, Donaghy has the biggest reputation on the Irish side of the Atlantic, and the most developed ties to Ireland and Irish culture. Moreover, questions of Irish identity in particular are in play for Donaghy as they are not for the other two poets. When he moved to London he became a habitué of the Irish Cultural Center in Kilburn, and even more Irish-identified than in his trad-music years in Chicago. At the same time, he was gaining recognition within the British poetry establishment, and this was patently confusing. He had already lost much of his Bronx accent in Chicago, but after years in London he spoke, in certain circumstances, in a kind of Mid-Atlantic North London brogue, which can still be heard in his recorded readings.

In the poetry, to be sure, questions of identity are raised to a level beyond the Irish context, and tend rather to be framed as questions of identification. Consider the modest but telling title poem of the first volume, *Shibboleth*:

One didn't know the name of Tarzan's monkey.
Another couldn't strip the cellophane
From a GI's pack of cigarettes.
By such minutiae were the infiltrators detected.

By the second week of battle
We'd become obsessed with trivia.
At a sentry point, at midnight, in the rain,
An ignorance of baseball could be lethal.

The first morning of the first snowfall, I was shaving,
Staring into a mirror nailed to a tree,
Intoning the Christian names of the Andrews Sisters.
'Maxine, Laverne, Patty.'[4]

"Shibboleth" is a poem about passwords and passing, and about what kind of knowledge counts as and for identification. The speaker's dilemma is paradoxically about how to produce the identifying language that establishes precisely who he already takes himself to be. In order to get by the sentry point, that is, he must perform himself, call up whatever it is that allows him to be called by the generic name he bears. Nor is he alone in facing such a predicament. The first-personal plural is indeed crucial to the poem for two reasons. It locates the speaker's dilemma as collective, not personal — not "psychological," as one might imagine from looking only at the concluding lines about his work of memorization. "We'd become obsessed with trivia" (emphasis added). Who is this "we"? It is those who must perform who they already are, who must remember what they are supposed to be incapable of forgetting, but who fear that they are capable of such forgetfulness.

Are they wrong about this? That question leads us back to the first stanza, with its opening double-take — "One didn't know the name of Tarzan's monkey" — as if the "one" were the universalized, impersonal, and slightly snobbish English version of the French "on" or the German "Man." It turns out that the "one" in question is quite particular. It is a person who failed to pass the test at the sentry point, as did "another," who couldn't manage the cellophane on the cigarette pack. Did they fail because the test succeeded in detecting their true identities, or because they panicked and failed to perform what they knew? Or did they not know for other reasons: were there no non-smokers among the GI's? And what *is* the name of Tarzan's monkey? The speaker suggests that these were "infiltrators" caught out by the test. But then why the anxiety among the speaker's group, working away at their trivia? Why the fear of an exposed impersonation?

The poem never quite answers those last questions but it does raise them to another level. This is the level of Donaghy's own impersonation of the battle-tested soldier, the understated hardiness of shaving in the snow, the ritual skill of using a mirror nailed to a tree, the casual adoption of the soldier's temporality ("By the second week of battle," "The first morning of the first snowfall"). *That* act of passing, one might say, gets the poem past our own readerly checkpoint, and it does so by deploying the oldest trick in the book: a distracting maneuver. This passing is abetted, furthermore, by the poem's knowing way with an iambic pentameter norm, talky, like Frost's, but claiming license to greater variation.

We can already sense in this poem that questions of identity are closely tied, for Donaghy, with those of authentication. This connection becomes more explicit in "Smith," a longer and more ambitious poem, and one where this sort of issue is given an Irish inflection:

> What is this fear before the unctuous teller?
> Why does it seem to take a forger's nerve
> To make my signature come naturally?
> Naturally? But every signature's
> A trick we learn to do, consistently,
> Like Queequeg's cross, or Whistler's butterfly.
> Perhaps some childhood spectre grips my hand
> Every time I'm asked to sign my name.
>
> Maybe it's Sister Bridget Agatha
> Who drilled her class in Christ and penmanship
> And sneered 'affected' at my seven-year-old scrawl.

The signature embodies a certain contradiction as at once a quasi-natural authentication of identity and a result of lifelong practice, not all of it innocent, some of it caught up in affectation, as we see in the ensuing lines about some pretentious comments aimed to impress on a first trip to a Rodin exhibition, where the narrator recalls his comments as reflecting "the feelings I wanted to have." But such an anecdote, he explains, no more accounts for his uneasiness before the "unctuous teller" than does his penmanship classes with Sister Bridget Agatha:

> No, I'm sure it all began years later.
> I was twenty, and the girl was even younger.
> We chose the hottest August night on record
> And a hotel with no air-conditioning.
> We tried to look adult. She wore her heels
> And leant against the cigarette machine as,
> Arching an eyebrow, I added to the register
> The name I'd practised into spontaneity —
> Surely it wasn't — *Mr and Mrs Smith?*

This, the poem's titular vignette, offers its primary site of parodic self-inquiry. And as the vignette unfolds, the fraught tension between affectation and authenticity, both in relation to oneself and in relation to another, is worked through to what seems to be a kind of epiphany.

> It's all so long ago and lost to me,
> And yet, how odd, I remember a moment so pure,
> In every infinite detail indelible,
> When I gripped her small shoulders in my hands,
> Steadying her in her slippery ride,
> And I looked up into her half-closed eyes …
> Dear friend, whatever is most true in me
> Lives now and forever in that instant,
> The night I forged a hand, not mine, not anyone's,
> And in that tiny furnace of a room,
> Forged a thing unalterable as iron.[5]

Here we seem to have been delivered the recollection on the basis of which the speaker can claim to have discovered something genuine, authentic, "true" in himself, a "pure" moment in every detail "indelible," to use the poem's own term, like the effect of a holy sacrament, or a mortal sin.

The stylistic modulation in that last stanza, furthermore, seems to confirm this familiar lyric turn of events, the moment of self-discovery. It is a rhetoric one associates with the tradition of the Romantic conversation poem, from Coleridge and Wordsworth through Robert Hass. Think of that moment in Hass's celebrated poem of the 1970s, one of the most anthologized American lyrics of the period in which Donaghy matured as a poet. After a similarly-themed series of skeptical reflections about the capacity of language to offer authentic representation, real purchase, on the world, Hass turns to an act of lovemaking:

> There was a woman
> I made love to and I remembered how, holding
> her small shoulders in my hands sometimes,
> I felt a violent wonder at her presence
> like a thirst for salt, for my childhood river
> with its island willows, silly music from the pleasure boat,
> muddy places where we caught the little orange-silver fish
> called *pumpkinseed*. It hardly had to do with her.
> Longing, we say, because desire is full
> of endless distances. I must have been the same to her.
> But I remember so much, the way her hands dismantled bread ...[6]

These lines lead to a conclusion that falls squarely in the tradition of the kind of poem that M. H. Abrams once called "the greater Romantic lyric," in which a view of a landscape leads to a troubled meditation, which in turn resolves in a spontaneous epiphany made possible by the poem itself.[7] Think of "Frost at Midnight" or "Tintern Abbey." Shall we take the final epiphanic turn of Donaghy's poem in this same spirit?

It is true that Donaghy's poem displays the stylistic markers of this kind of authentic self-discovery: the concession of loss, qualified, perforce, by the seemingly involuntary assertion of true feeling: "And yet, how odd,

I remember a moment so pure." We seem meant to notice the register of intimacy, the simplicity of diction, the ease of rhythm, the self-interruption (in this case with an ellipsis). Donaghy even invokes the device of the late-poem apostrophe (the "Dear Friend") so characteristic of this Romantic sub-genre. But perhaps that very act of address is the sign of something slightly off about this stylistic signature, something "forged" about it in more ways than one. Who, after all, is this "Dear Friend"? Conventionally, this addressee would figure as a kind of stand-in for "us." In this case, however, I suggest the dear friend is no more "us" than the speaker is actually in the business of authentication, despite the anxiety expressed about questions of signature — or more expansively, about a characteristic style of writing.

In poems like "Shibboleth" or "Smith," or again in perhaps his best-known lyric, "Machines," a persona is developed, a space of performance is defined, and we are invited to join the poet in the working out of a trans-actional identity in a sort of dance. That's what Donaghy himself tends to call it, especially in "Wallflowers," the lead critical essay in *The Shape of the Dance*. In the first section of that essay, "Telling the Dancer from the Dance," he recalls a night in 1977 in a church on the south side of Chicago:

> … I'd been playing jigs and reels for a ceilidh, watching the set dancers spinning and stamping out with wild precision the rhythms of a dance which can be described (accurately) as a feral minuet…. Only after the dancers had left the floor did I notice the circular patterns of black scuffs and streaks their heels had made on the polished wood.
>
> This pattern, I recognized, was an enormous encoded page of poetry, a kind of manuscript, or, more properly, *pediscript*.[8]

Donaghy goes on to link this concept to poetry's roots in oral performance: "Like all literary poetry in our culture, the pediscript is the record of — or formula for — a social transaction, all that remains of that give and take between artist and participating audience in an oral tradition."[9] Donaghy's pediscript gives you, so to speak, the authenticated shape of the dance, the answer to Yeats's famous question, in case you thought it called for one.

For all that, there is lots of room for trouble in that little moment of apposition in the definition of the pediscript as "the record of — or formula for — a social transaction." And the comic diagrams of the pediscript further trouble the relation posited between a mark and the act that it indexes or anticipates.[10] We are back to the problem of the signature, in a way, but we should also be reminded of the St. Valentine's Day context of "Liverpool," and the tracings of a sentimental tattoo. It is a poem whose opening question perhaps shows something of the young Donaghy's interest in the young Paul Muldoon.

> Ever been tattooed? It takes a whim of iron,
> takes sweating in the antiseptic-stinking parlour,
> nothing to read but motorcycle magazines
> before the blood-sopped cotton, and, of course, the needle,
> all for — at best — some Chinese dragon.
> But mostly they do hearts....

"Liverpool's" witty meditation takes up the case of one "Tracy,"

> who confessed she'd had hers done
> one legless weekend with her ex.
> Heart. Arrow. Even the bastard's initials, R. J. L.
> somewhere where it hurt, she said,
> and when I asked her where, snapped 'Liverpool'.

The issue with this indexical mark is its indelibility. For Tracy "had it sliced away / leaving a scar, she said, pink and glassy / but small, and better than having his mark on her."[11] Like "Smith," "Liverpool" addresses the labile relation of the mark to the character, the signatory inscription to the authentic identity.

Many of Donaghy's character portraits, like the one about Tim, an Irish-American childhood friend who hoped to become a nun, are about Irish or Catholic subjects. Here are the first three stanzas of "City of God," which is certainly among Donaghy's most accomplished poems and may be his best:

When he failed the seminary he came back home
to the Bronx and sat in a back pew
of St Mary's every night reciting the Mass
from memory — quietly, continually —
into his deranged overcoat.
He knew the local phone book off by heart.
He had a system, he'd explain,
perfected by Dominicans in the Renaissance.

To every notion they assigned a saint,
to every saint an altar in the transept of the church.
Glancing up, column by column, altar by altar,
they could remember any prayer they chose.
He'd used it for exams, but the room went wrong —
a strip-lit box exploding slowly as he fainted.
They found his closet papered floor to ceiling
with razored passages from St Augustine.

He needed a perfect cathedral in his head,
he'd whisper, so that by careful scrutiny
the mind inside the cathedral inside the mind
could find the secret order of the world
and remember every drop on every face
in every summer thunderstorm.
And that, he'd insist, looking beyond you,
is why he came home.[12]

This is a character portrait in the mode of personal reminiscence, a combination that owes something perhaps to Heaney's "Casualty."[13] The sketch of the quirky Irish outsider is rendered in unmarked pronouns and telling details. Like "Casualty," too, this is a poem about a man denied community, including by the poet himself, who nonetheless in closing, produces a rapprochement, a reminiscence cum reverie of a certain connection. In Heaney's poem it is the dreamlike account "that morning" on the boat with the fisherman; in Donaghy's the anecdote heralded by the phrase "one evening."

I walked him back one evening as the snow
hushed the precincts of his vast invisible temple.
Here was Bruno Street where Bernadette
collapsed, bleeding through her skirt
and died, he had heard, in a state of mortal sin;
here, the site of the bakery fire where Peter stood
screaming on the red hot fire escape,
his bare feet blistering before he jumped;
and here the storefront voodoo church beneath the el
where the Cuban *bruja* bought black candles,
its window strange with plaster saints and seashells.[14]

Both "Casualty" and "City of God" seem to capture something about how community is denied to the outsider. Heaney's fisherman in Derry is out of the loop, no part of the band of brothers at the funeral for the fallen in Bloody Sunday, and his addictions lead him to ignore the warnings that were meant to keep safe the included ones. Heaney, too, denies him communion over the question of poetry, evading his queries, changing the subject. In the case of his neighbor in the Bronx, Donaghy, characteristically, sees the question of identity and belonging in terms of a coded performance of knowledge, rendered surreal by the mobilization of the Brunian system of *memoria technica*. Donaghy's outsider seems deranged, where Heaney's is a sane man on the dole on account of a drinking problem. (Nor do we find in Heaney loose bits of Bob Dylan floating in the poetic amber: "And I remember every face / Of every man who put me here.")[15]

In none of this work does Donaghy show much interest in the location of culture. Insofar as Donaghy's poems mark him as *Irish*-American, therefore, they tend to do so more by way of an interest in Irishness as an inheritance than in Ireland as a specific geography. Place reference typically turns into a kind of inside joke for Donaghy, as in the lines from "Liverpool," where the question of where the tattoo was done on the body is answered by way of where it was done in the world. In "City of God," questions of urban geography seem no more relevant to Donaghy's Bronx than to Augustine's heavenly metropolis. Unsurprisingly, Google Maps discloses no street or lane or avenue named "Bruno" anywhere in New York City, surely an inside reference to the very same system of placing memory that had so fascinated Donaghy himself during his studies at Chicago. By contrast, as we will see, the question of place looms much more prominently in the work of Campbell McGrath.

2. Campbell McGrath

Raised in Washington D.C. in a second generation Irish immigrant family, McGrath is a poet who also learned about systems during his studies at the University of Chicago, and he writes about them wittily in his early books, especially in the section of *"The Bob Hope Poem"* he entitled "The Triumph of Rationalism." This poem is from his third book, *Spring Comes to Chicago* (1996), one that swept several major US poetry prizes. It is an irreverent tribute to Hyde Park and to the University of Chicago's curious place in it, for McGrath a place of mismatched yet overlapping systems: from the readings in the University's famous (or notorious) common core classes, to the displays at the nearby Museum of Science and Industry, to the menu at Ho Wa Gardens, a Chinese restaurant just across the Midway on 63rd Street.[16]

McGrath has an anthropologist's keen idea for located culture and ethnographic detail, worked out in the cadences of a long line that can even assimilate anthropological prose, especially if the anthropologist is a good enough prose writer, like Marshall Sahlins, who taught a celebrated course on Systems at the University for years. In *"The Bob Hope Poem,"* McGrath actually manages to incorporate a paragraph from Sahlins's *Islands of History* (1985) in such a way as to submerge its rhythms, syntax, and semantics into the flow of the poem's catalogues of various rival systems. The Big System, for McGrath and Sahlins alike, is capitalism, and while still a student at the University, McGrath produced a broken series of poems in which the serial form itself produces a witty commentary on commodification. Thus, "Capitalist Poem #7," for example, is a childhood recollection of collecting money in a UNICEF box but then spending it all at the 7-Eleven convenience store.[17] The poem consists of two catalogues: one is the list of things for which the money was intended by UNICEF, the other the things on which the child McGrath squandered it all. It is an early instance of a

Whitmanesque instinct for the catalogue that would serve McGrath well over time.

Like his sensitivity to place, McGrath's exuberant instinct to catalogue diverse items creates certain tensions with systems understood abstractly. Wordsworth, another poet of place, said he wrote his *Lyrical Ballads* to demonstrate the manner in which we associate ideas in a state of excitement. Specificity of place and exuberance of associated response are, for both poets, an answer to the debilitating abstractions of system. And, perhaps not coincidentally, it is also true that McGrath seems to accept Wordsworth's contention that there is no essential difference between the language of poetry and the language of prose. McGrath himself has written prose poems alongside both formal poems and free verse poems from his earliest days. *Road Atlas* (1999), moreover, the book that appeared after *Spring Comes to Chicago*, consists almost entirely of prose poetry.[18] Indeed, it opens with a little manifesto, a prose poem titled "The Prose Poem." It follows this with "Plums," an appropriation *for* the prose poem of what might seem like the very antithesis *of* the prose poem — the imagist mode of W. C. Williams's poetic miniatures such as "This Is Just to Say" and "The Red Wheel Barrow."

"Plums," which belongs in the long tradition of prospect poems, begins: "I'm sitting on a hill in Nebraska, in morning sunlight, looking out across the valley of the Platte River."[19] It invokes, more broadly, the conventions of what used to be called the loco-descriptive poem. Sometimes this mode ends up being framed as an associationist form of memory, as in Wordsworth, and sometimes self-consciously so, as in "Plums": "Why do I still carry it, that moment in Nebraska?" This mode is everywhere present in McGrath's work. Just a partial list of international places described there would include Berlin, Jamaica, Vanuatu, Brazil, Manitoba, Amsterdam, Oaxaca, Nagasaki, and Spain. And the list of American places might seem to go on forever: Rosarito Beach (Baja California), Miami, Memphis, Los Angeles, North Dakota, Colorado, New Mexico, Las Vegas, Texas, Iowa, West Virginia, Chicago, Baltimore, Minneapolis, Rock Falls (Illinois), Biloxi (Mississippi), Caineville (Utah), the Mojave Desert, the Snake River Valley, the Gulf Coast. In many instances these places are investigated with an attention both to physical landscape and local customs, often with a sense of the fit between the two, but seldom without a light sense of irony. If this work were to be best compared to a body of contemporary filmmaking it would be the locally-inflected work of the Coen Brothers.

What about Ireland, and the Irish sense of place? Late in *Road Atlas* comes "Four Clouds Like the Irish in Memory," McGrath's first real effort to produce a poem that connects with his Irish heritage, and, perhaps tellingly, it is framed as a memory of origins (it opens, "First memory of school:") and a lesson about how to write poetry. In the second longish prose paragraph, about the elementary poetry lesson, one can provisionally distinguish three modes of representation. There are the teacher's words: the questions ("What do the clouds look like?") and the encouragements ("Good, good"). There are the child's responses: "Butterfly, banana split, polar bear, clown." And then there are the poet's own mature efforts at scene-setting: "Boisterous sun, orbital crab apples." One sees this third modality more starkly at work in the poem with the teacher's second question and its gloss: "What does the dogwood look like, its bracts and tiers and white cascades of flowers?" "Bracts," like "orbital," is diction that delaminates the gloss from the question, an early indication of the adult poet's interest in setting his own imagination free in the poem about liberating that faculty in the child.

When the poem takes off in mid-paragraph, the poet seizes on the license afforded by an appositive "Like," now in its third iteration, to pursue an associational logic in a way that the child in him could not, or anyhow to articulate pursuit in terms unavailable to the child.

> Like going to New York for the holidays, like heaven or the George Washington Bridge at night, its titanium spans and whirligigs, garlands of popcorn, garlands of cranberries, baked ham and my grandfather's accordion, my mother and her sisters trying out their old Shirley Temple routines amidst an Irish stew of relatives and well-wishers immersed for the day in the nostalgic mist and manners of the old sod.

The pivotal image in this catalogue, the one that redirects its paratactic series, is "garlands of popcorn," which figures the undulating amber lights on the suspension bridge into Manhattan and in turn becomes the ornamental strand on the Irish grandparents' Christmas tree. Once ushered, by this means, into the house of the grandparents, the poem can dwell there long enough to substitute for the child's list of associations with the four clouds from an adult list, offered as it were in behalf of the child: "Shamrock, whiskey bottle, subway train, diaspora." The shift in diction also marks the shift in modality, since "diaspora" clearly belongs to a semantic register that includes "orbital" and "bracts," thus inflecting the list as an expression of the mature poet's consciousness.

Ultimately, the poem carries us to the Upper West Side of the early 1970s for the sake of a memory about the drive home to Washington with the poet's grandfather, one Francis Daniel Campbell, and what seems to have been his first trip out of the metropolis since his coming to America. The associative reminiscence conveys the sense of something peculiar that the child must have caught in the manner of this accordion-playing Irish immigrant, something filled out with later knowledge and experience:

> ... this was my mother's father, a countryman from Donegal, famous for long strolls in Riverside Park collecting weeds for home remedies, for walking the bridge to save a penny on a pack of cigarettes. He worked forty years as a ticket taker in the subway, pent too long 'mid cloisters dim, and somewhere in southern New Jersey, in the backseat of the station wagon looking out past the turnpike traffic, he said, in his thick brogue, to no one in particular, *goodness, I had no idea there were such great forests left.*[20]

The closing reminiscence elaborates the logic of association inherent in the four terms that get substituted for the initial four terms that the child associates with the clouds. It dramatizes on more than one level the difference between the associations of the child's fancy and those of the adult's imagination — the latter deepened by a sense of location, and of dislocation, loss, and sympathy. What the child can register, evidently, is the oddity of his grandfather's remark, perhaps the thought that the scrubby pines of South Jersey could strike anybody as a great forest. No doubt the child wrote off the experience to his grandfather's faintly mysterious manners and means, though we are meant to understand that the old man's comment strikes the child forcefully enough to impress it deeply in his memory.

We are also meant to see that the mature poet can see far more of its implications. He can see not only that the country man from Donegal was starved for nature, limited in his experience of America, and oriented toward gratitude. He can also see that only for an Irishman can even the pine barrens — what in another poem he calls New Jersey's "dwarf-pine coastal midlands" — count as a great forest.[21] "Pent 'mid cloisters dim," a phrase used by Coleridge in an early conversation poem ("This Lime-tree Bower, my Prison") to describe his citified sensibility, sounds a self-consciously literary note in the poem, with the aim of establishing the larger cultural context that the poet has acquired since his childhood to make sense of his grandfather's pain, and the means he took to deal with it.

As a character portrait of a New York Irishman, the poem can be productively contrasted with Donaghy's "City of God." The immigrant experience matters to this poem as it does not to Donaghy, and this may have to do with the different emphasis on questions of location in each poet. McGrath's Romantic anthropology looks at the relationship of culture and customs, places and persons, chiefly as registered in the lives of others. Donaghy's poetry tends to register the effects of his own relocation to the UK, which is to say that it tends not to address the problem of location directly or straightforwardly. Of course, the locations dealt with directly in "Four Clouds" are not themselves Irish. They are primarily the Upper West Side of New York City and the pine barrens of South Jersey. Ireland is the displaced location, represented here chiefly by the grandfather's longing for it.

A closer approach to the matter of Ireland, and perhaps to a more straightforward loco-descriptive way with its places, can be found in a poem from *In the Kingdom of the Sea Monkeys* (2012) entitled "An Irish Word," in which an association of ideas leads more directly than in "Four Clouds" to Ireland itself. Some of the cast of characters is the same as in "Four Clouds." Wordsworth spoke of the association of ideas. Williams said, "no ideas but in things."[22] In this poem, the trigger of the association is not in the sight of the cloud or dogwood but the fact of a word — "canny" — that it calls up.

Here the poem works through certain clichés that the poet seems to have acquired about the Irish as a people, but as in "Four Clouds" he works through to a recollection of his mother's Donegal family. Here we learn that the maternal grandfather, Francis Daniel Campbell, is from Drimnaherk, in Donegal, that he and his four brothers left Ireland together, bound for Australia, South Africa, Liverpool, and Los Angeles, "losing track of each other at once and forever." We learn that his wife, née Anna Monaghan, lost her father in New York at a young age and had to return to their home in Donegal, the three girls and their seamstress mother "taking in mending and needlework to eat":

> Market days they rode the train into Derry
> to sell embroidered linens and hand-tatted lace,
> kerchiefs monogrammed *z* to *a*.
> She was nearing thirty
>
> when she married and recrossed the Atlantic
> and from her my own mother
> had a recipe for soda bread, piles of drop-stitch
> tablecloths, and a small stoneware pitcher
>
> hand-painted in folksy script —
> *Be Canny Wi' the Cream.*

Canny is the putatively "Irish word" with which the poem begins, and now helps it circle to a close, as we shift to a scene of the young McGrath children and their customary response to this word and the object on which it was hand-painted:

> Nothing could move my brother and I to screams
> of laughter like that tiny pitcher,
>
> so serious of purpose, so quaintly archaic,
> as we slurped down bowls of Frosted Flakes
> before school in the breakfast nook.
> The scrupulous economy of the world it bespoke,
>
> the frugality toward which it gestured,

were as inscrutable to us then
as the great sea cliffs at *Slieve League* when
we drove to the top at Amharc Mór.[23]

This poem works a bit like "Four Clouds," but in reverse, with the child's limited but alert imagination, in its memory of the word canny, providing the poem's actual starting point, which only delivered to us in the final lines, where the kitsch and the sublime stand in unstable juxtaposition.

Lately, McGrath has been writing more directly about Ireland and its landscapes, and he told me recently that he plans a book, to be called *Atlantic Studies*, that will incorporate some of these poems. The idea for the volume is a series of landscape meditations (loco-descriptive poetry again) on ocean-facing sites all around the Atlantic rim. But it may not be a coincidence that early pilot poems for the project have been poems about Irish landscapes. This one, for example, about Mount Errigal, in northern County Donegal, is nicely sensitive to the multi-layered temporalities of a remote coastal site:

On the seldom-visited, west-looking, wave-etched headland,
the ancient fortress buried in high grass has softened
into barrow mounds grazed by sheep,

its tumbled stones claimed by farmers across generations
to enclose their pastures in drystone walls
stitched like rough sutures across a quilt of green fields,

and the government has built a new lighthouse
beside the old castle
from which the beacon signals

like a jewel refracting sunlight from the mind's tower
and the sea reflects back
its prismatic imagination of the future.

In this moment of mirroring, the poem too seems to fold on itself to reflect on the complex temporalities it begins by registering:

So time is not a god but a golden mirror,
an aspect of self-consciousness,
frenzy of wild swans settling to the water

and when they insinuate their snakelike necks
below the surface what
can they perceive of the afterlife?

And when a fish breaches suddenly, leaping free
of its element, crossing over
to the suffocating, planar emptiness of our world,

is this what visionaries see?
Is this heaven, then,
this voluptuous, sun-stricken, gravity-ridden realm?

It is not difficult to sense thematic elements imported into this poem from
the Yeats of, say, "The Wild Swans at Coole." This is not only McGrath's
first extended poetic appropriation of Yeats but also an unwonted meld of a
loco-descriptive poem about a place with a style or voice that itself has come
to be associated with that place. "That place" is not just Ireland, but also
the general neighborhood of Yeats's Sligo and Ben Bulben. Mount Errigal
is, after all, the next mountainous peak north from Ben Bulben, and the
only one on that line between Ben Bulben and the sea. Yet even as he poses
quasi-mystical questions of the Irish landscape by way of its greatest lyric poet,
there is a note that reminds us of a certain pedantic skepticism and light-
hearted wit, especially in the distances from the vision of the visionaries in
those final questions and slightly "off" terms in which the landscape is recast.

Thus, when we make our return to the swans in a Yeatsian reprise of
their image, their appearance in the new moment, the poem's new "now,"
brings new words in its wake:

The birds on the water resemble sleepwalkers now,
and our words clatter like stones
on a shore slipping from sunlight to dense shadow.[24]

These words, however, do no more than clatter, as a darkness descends that seems closer to the end of Stevens's "Sunday Morning" than to anything by Yeats. We might consider this yet another example of the poetic hybridity that characterizes the work of all three of these poets.

3. *Maureen McLane*

Like McGrath, Maureen McLane is a self-consciously American poet — American in her idiom and in most of her poetic interlocutors — but again, like him, one with an interest in writing about the wider world. Her literary scholarship has mostly run to British Romanticism, especially the British ballad, but in her recent, acclaimed volume of essays — *My Poets* (2012) — she also avows commitments to a long line of American poets, from Emily Dickinson and Walt Whitman to Louise Glück and C. K. Williams.[25] Like McGrath, too, she often writes about places. She is perhaps again as different from McGrath and Donaghy, however, as they are from each other. For one thing, she almost never produces character portraits, even when she gestures at the genre.

A partial exception to this rule is "Tenancy," a poem from the first book (*Same Life*, 2008). It helps to see how differently McLane handles the figure of the Irish in New York from what we saw in Donaghy and McGrath.

> The old Irish aunts are dead
>   and thank god!
>   — They were plagues
>   on their nephew
>   himself a plague
>   on me his upstairs neighbor
>   prey to his paranoiac riffs
>   on nuns and shadowy city officials
>   and his sister
>   the absentee landlord.

Kinship's not all
   it's cracked up etcetera!
     If he forgets
       his dose he might lose it
     as he once unloosed his fists upon the admittedly
        querulous aunts
      the neighbors report.

But thankful are we
   for those spinsters
     he allegedly pummeled not least
   for keeping one known malcontent
     home: they gardened and tended and now the dead

their roses and asters and bleeding hearts
   are blooming year after
     each crazy year.[26]

In spite of the presence of a sketchy narrative and the insider Irish-studies reference to "the absentee landlord," this poem turns not on broad-strokes dramatic irony and self-conscious pedantry, like Donaghy's, nor on exuberant association and eclectic learning, like McGrath's, but rather on a trait that, in describing other poets, she calls "paradoxically bold humility."

In this case, what that means is making the short line do its work in turning the poem, and returning it, in successive moves across the width of the page. Consider how the three lines beginning "on ..." in the first stanza effect successive pivots in our narrative understanding of the poem's somewhat sordid mini-plot of victimization. Or again, how surprising elements in this compact account of neighborhood, kinship, and tenancy are produced with the six words that comprise the last two lines of that stanza: "and his sister / the absentee landlord." The poem turns again with the shallow pun on "crack up" and the revelation of the nephew's (reported) violence when he goes off his medications. This in turn prepares for the speaker's expression of gratitude and the closing metaphor of the perennial blooming of the flowers of the dead aunts, along with the dead themselves, presumably in the tended ground plot of this poem.

One can often tell much about a poet's own commitments by seeing what she praises in others. The phrase "paradoxically bold humility" comes from a 2007 review of volumes by Michael O'Brien and Pam Rehm, which celebrates these two writers for making "poetry against noise ... an anti-monumental poetry," offering instead "'only a constant disappearing / into the day's allowance.'" O'Brien in particular is singled out for his interest in "how a day acquires a pattern; how fragile membranes like moths' wings, or the mind's energy, might play across harder materials: these poems offer their own singular tracery." This theme of the day is sounded in the opening line of the review, where McLane cites a line from the Irish-born painter:

> "You have had your day, and each day is a short life." So says the painter
> Sean Scully, quoted on the wall text accompanying his painting "Night"
> hanging now (Jan. 2007) in the glorious retrospective of his work at the
> Metropolitan Museum of Art, "Wall of Light." One imagines Michael
> O'Brien would agree.

McLane offers a hint as to what such an agreement amounts to in this case. "Like Scully," she explains, O'Brien "orients us [to] the sensible impact of a day's passing." And the review, as I've suggested, elaborates this thought, pointing especially to O'Brien's "singular tracery."[27]

But what about in her own case? Three years later, she published her second book, *World Enough* (2010), with Farrar, Straus and Giroux, and in it is a poem nominally set in New York City that returns to the Scullian theme:

> *After Sean Scully: "You have had your day ..."*
> a bar
> on 3rd
> a beer
> or two
> first down
> and ten

number
the number
of Sundays
unchurched
uneven
unmarked
"each day
a short life" [28]

The poem might be seen as an engagement with the natural supernaturalism of Wallace Stevens's "Sunday Morning" negotiated by way of
the minimalism of W. C. Williams (one of "her poets," and a poet often
engaged with in her poetry). It offers, however, a stripped-bare version
of that story — the stark dystopian vision of a secular world with neither
nature nor super-nature to sustain it. In just twelve syllables — a mere
thirty-five letters — McLane manages to capture the seriality of the world
of the modern sports bar, the "culture" of the NFL, which plays its games
on Sundays. In its spare verse form and pointed resort to numbers (both
ordinal and cardinal), the poem suggests that the flip side of Stevens's
displacement of Christian ritual into secular aestheticism — "the green
freedom of a cockatoo / Upon a rug" — might prove to be a chain of
Sundays squandered among senseless pursuits in featureless haunts and
nameless places.[29] You have had your day, and you missed your chance,
and it was the chance of a short lifetime.

How does McLane herself manage the short life-saving act of disappearing into the day's allowances while making its pattern visible in a
singular tracery? One way she does this is with her own experiments in the
form of the series. Conspicuously bridging *World Enough* and its predecessor *Same Life* is a numbered pair of series — "Songs of a Season" (eighteen
short pieces — several, including the first three and the last, haikus, several
others 3–5–3 quasi-haikus) and "Songs of a Season II" (twenty-three pieces of
eight lines each). What links the two series is that both involve askesis and
aesthesis, as McLane disciplines herself to the confinements of miniature
form in order to enhance the sensible apprehension of the revolving world,
turning that world round again herself with new turn of phrase:

and while I was not thinking
the lake rolled on

and while I was thinking
on a soft summer day sitting by the lake
I missed the lake[30]

Taken together, these two series — Songs of a Season I and II — raise vexing questions about exactly how we understand the constitutions of a series. In the one case, we find the haiku norm with variations. In the other, the eight-line stanza is strictly observed. How much regularity is needed to make a series? How much variation can a series tolerate and remain a series?

Questions like these about what counts as seriality enliven other sequences within these two volumes. *Same Life* itself includes a series of six separately numbered poems — separately listed in the index — titled "*After Sappho*" I, II, III, etc. The individualized numbering suggests that what we might call the autonomy quotient in each part of the series runs higher in the Sappho set than in others. Contrariwise, there is another series of untitled, unnumbered poems (or poem-sections) under the heading "*Core Samples*," including the compelling one that begins: "It was under the spell of Yeats I fell / in love with you."[31] Are these both, the numbered and the unnumbered sequences, series in the same sense? How do the numbers of syllables, lines, and feet matter to the series question, and to the questions of daily life — that is, to tracing the pattern of the day's disappearance, and indeed, of the "short life" that, pace Sean Scully, every day amounts to?

To complicate matters further, the second book, *World Enough*, itself features a series of three series poems, "Passage I" (nine poem-sections), "Passage II" (nine poem-sections), and "Passage III" (twenty poem-sections). Among these, the poems in "Passage II" display the most regularity of line and form, consisting chiefly of stanzas of two short lines in the manner of "After Sean Scully," typically unimeter or dimeter. "Passage III" offers the widest play with line and form, with poems ranging from eight words to nearly a page and a half. But even this does not capture the imaginative forms of seriality produced (or traced) in the Passage poems. For while "Passage II" observes great regularity of line and stanza form, it also aggregates its short two-line stanzas in a variety of ways, so that we focus attention on a stanza's relative autonomy within a poetic section. The recurring question that animates "Passage II" is that of what authorizes a two-line stanza to be part of a poetic section, or conversely, what enables it to stand, so to speak, in its own room?

Finally, there is the quasi-narrative series that constitutes the sequence of poems or sections that bears the wonderful title "From Mz N: the serial." (N is McLane's middle initial, for Noelle.) We are encouraged, I think, to take this as McLane's rendering of a growth of the poet's mind, especially inasmuch as it concludes with a long, irreverent meditation on Wordsworth and his spots of time. This is natural supernaturalism in spades, but it is worked through a poetics caught up in problems of serial form. The penultimate entry in this sequence, indeed, is a sonnet — probably Western poetry's most prominent form of poetic seriality.

The American version of natural supernaturalism goes by the name of Transcendentalism, which lends its name to a poem in *World Enough* that begins: "I have seen something brighter / than realism / would allow." Here again we have a poem in sections, and sometimes stanzas within sections, raising questions of serial form at every level, including systematic permutations on the diction of the other sections in the three columns of words that constitute the third (unnumbered) section:

Snow	Geese	Pines
Geese	Snow	Pines
Pines	Snow	Geese
Snow	Pines	Geese
Geese	Pines	Snow
Pines	Geese	Snow [32]

Abstracted markers of the New England landscape are here disposed into a kind of minimal system. It is as if Emerson's transparent eyeball, in which words are taken as signs for natural facts and natural facts signs for spiritual facts, were fitted with a lens that revealed a New England winter's day as a kind of algorithm — something brighter, perhaps, than realism would allow. McLane's concern with seriality, numbered form, at once spontaneous and self-conscious, appears with equal insistence at the level of the foot, the line, the stanza, the section, the poem, the book, the oeuvre. It is deeply constitutive of her verbal art. We thus circle back to "After Sean Scully," which increasingly seems to me a kind of mini-manifesto, an *ars poetica* laid out in what amounts to two fourteeners. But now the final question: Is there something to be said about the Irish connection in this poem — the links to O'Brien and Scully? One notes the emphasis on Sunday, and perhaps on desacralization as well, perhaps the faint whiff of Guinness in the New York Irish sports bar. Can one go further?

In her most recent book, there is a difficult poem titled "Belfast" and, taken whole, it makes a good occasion for exploring this question:

> Your velvet hills came to me
> last night in the pool
> how they hugged the fraught city
> the pubs filled and buzzing
> the Europa unbombed now for years.
> Your political murals are kitsch
> and history's a ditch
> for lying if we let
> the gravediggers
> name us. Let's bury
> our pseudonyms
> all undisclosed.
> Was Scarlett O'Hara's father
> a blustering Ulsterman
> or was he a peasant
> like granddad from Wicklow
> tender and fond amidst the riot
> and kind to his slaves
> but for the obvious?

The speaker's apostrophe to "Belfast" is inspired by a vision of its hills experienced in a pool, the location of which is initially unspecified. The vision gives way to an exhortation to bury the *noms de guerre* rather than victims of a conflict, and that exhortation in turn leads to what seems to be a query about a fictional Irish figure in another bloody Civil War who cannot be readily identified with either side of the Troubles in Northern Ireland. But then the poem takes a strange turn toward these lines, which lead to some context for "the pool":

> Your storefronts
> were boarded, your university
> Victorian, the linen quarter
> defunct. The solid brick
> that shelters us unmortared
> smashed a window.
> Your sky hung low your beer
> rode high your visiting Masons
> sober and punctual.
> A Days Inn here
> is a Days Inn anywhere
> but for the marchers gathering
> their ribbons' gaud at odds
> with their drawn gaunt faces
> shut like a purse
> around an old watch
> that still keeps time

The poem thus flirts with the continuity we might associate with a mono-logue, in this case the single extended apostrophe to the city of Belfast, spoken by a visitor who may be recollecting a vision or memory in swim-ming pool, possibly a Days Inn swimming pool. It might be the Days Inn in downtown Belfast, not far from Queens, the "Victorian" university, though we are pointedly reminded that a Days Inn there is indeed a Days Inn any-where. The play between the specific Days Inn of Belfast and the generic form of the Days Inn resonates in other parts of the poem. The speaker may be a descendent of a Leinster peasant, a native of the South, but "grand-dad" may be generic rather than personal. And Scarlett O'Hara's father is so generic an Irish character as to leave the question of Ulster and Leinster ambiguous. Seriality enters the poem subtly in the sense that the empty homogeneity of the Days Inn, one might say, corresponds to the empty homogeneity of "days in" one place or another.

Seriality enters in another way as well, in that certain passages stand out from the putatively situated enunciation, the flow of the monologue and its Belfast occasion, to float in the poem as separately sequenced units, embedded serial items in a quasi-narrative sequence. They take the form of outré generalizations. I refer specifically to the three sentences that stretch over the eleven lines that follow the poem's only question and constitute its middle section:

> White people are weird
> with their vitamin D
> and sunravaged skin.
> So far from an equator
> it's hard to walk the line
> in a cleaved world.
> Orange, green, navy blue
> the colors are weapons
> as were some horses
> in the 19th century.[33]

One could imagine each of these versified sentences as separate sections in one of the series that I have already discussed. This poem about an Irish place keeps us wondering to what degree it is and is not a place like any other. A measure of its difference from McGrath's almost perfectly contemporary poem about Mount Errigal, therefore, is that the latter poem seems to wish to find a local idiom to be spoken with its American accent. In McLane, the very question of what makes a place a place, rather than a placeholder in a series, seems to be what is paramount.

Though McLane is at least as steeped in the Romantic tradition of poetry as either Donaghy or McGrath, her taste runs less to the conversation poem than to the literary ballad, with its commitments, disjunctions, impersonality, and, one might even say, serial form. "Belfast" is about as close as McLane comes to writing a meditation in the line of Coleridge and Wordsworth's transformative meditative poems of 1797–98 — a line that Hass's "Meditation at Lagunitas" is patently invoking, and Donaghy and McGrath make use of in their different ways. But it is not really possible to imagine in the course of McLane's loco-descriptive meditation on Belfast a transition like the one in Hass's poem about Lagunitas: "After a while I understood that, / talking this way, everything dissolves ..."[34] Nor could one quite imagine in Hass or Donaghy or McGrath the kind of serial disruption of the verse paragraph effected by McLane's: "So far from an equator / it's hard to walk the line / in a cleaved world."

4. Conclusion

We have been considering three poets whose reputations are very much in the making. McGrath's new volume of Atlantic studies should be out before too long and promises new treasures. McLane, with three volumes from FSG in the last seven years, seems only just to be taking off in her poetic career. And Donaghy has lately had some renewed critical attention: a memoir by Maddy Paxman, and a critical study of the poetry by the fine Scottish poet Don Paterson.[35] Highly valued as these three poets are now, it is not difficult to imagine a time in the near future when they will have achieved a new level of critical recognition and attention.

Might we then come to think of them more readily as Irish-American poets? It seems possible that we might, especially if McGrath and McLane continue to engage with the matter of Ireland as they have lately done. Still, one would not want to elide the differences in the ways in which they can be said to be "post-Ireland." These differences appear, as I have tried to stress, in the three poets' varying relations to memory, to place, and to questions of form. Perhaps, too, they show in the way each of these poets allows the British Romantic tradition to mediate Irish materials: Donaghy in his ventriloquistic performance of poetic identity, McGrath in his reworking of the loco-descriptive tradition, and McLane in her interest in the formal qualities of Romantic song. It is nothing new for Irish poets to invoke, even to inhabit, British Romantic figures like Wordsworth, Coleridge, and Shelley, as some of the poetry I've mentioned by Yeats and Heaney reminds us. Our three Irish-Americans, however, seem more focused in their specific invocations, very much in line with their specific talents and interests. Perhaps the best rubric for them, in the end, would have been "post-Ireland, post-Romanticism."

NOTES

1.   Michael Donaghy, *The Shape of the Dance: Essays, Interviews and Digressions*, ed. Adam O'Riordan and Maddy Paxman (London: Picador, 2009). I'd like to thank Maddy Paxman, Campbell McGrath, and Maureen McLane for cooperating with the investigation, and Andrew Yale for help in preparing the final text.

2.   Donaghy, *Shibboleth* (Oxford: Oxford UP, 1988).

3.   Donaghy, "Fragment. *Irish Folk Music: A Fascinating Hobby, With Some Account of Related Subjects*, by Police Chief Francis O'Neill, Chicago, 1910," in *Collected Poems* (London: Picador, 2009), 197–98.

4.   Donaghy, "Shibboleth," in *Shibboleth*, 17.

5.   Donaghy, "Smith," in *Shibboleth*, 10–11.

6.   Robert Hass, "Meditation at Lagunitas," in *Praise* (New York: Ecco Press, 1979), 4–5.

7.   M. H. Abrams, "Structure and Style in the Greater Romantic Lyric," in *The Correspondent Breeze: Essays on English Romanticism* (New York: Norton, 1984), 76–108.

8.   Donaghy, "Wallflowers," *The Shape of the Dance*, 3–4.

9.   Ibid., 4.

10.   Ibid., 3, 2.

11.   Donaghy, "Liverpool," in *Errata* (Oxford: Oxford UP, 1993), 23.

12.   Donaghy, "City of God," in *Errata*, 21–22.

13.   Seamus Heaney, "Casualty," in *Field Work* (London: Faber and Faber, 1979), 21–24.

14.   Donaghy, "City of God," in *Errata*, 21–22.

15.   "I Shall be Released," written by Bob Dylan and first released on The Band, *Music from Big Pink* (Capitol SKAO-2955, 1968).

16.   Campbell McGrath, "The Bob Hope Poem," in *Spring Comes to Chicago* (New York: Ecco, 1996), 9–80.

17.   McGrath, "Capitalist Poem #7," in *Capitalism* (Hanover, NH: Wesleyan UP, 1990), 18.

18.   McGrath, *Road Atlas: Prose & Other Poems* (Hopewell, NJ: Ecco Press, 1999).

19.   McGrath, "Plums," in *Road Atlas*, 5.

20. McGrath, "Four Clouds Like the Irish in Memory," in *Road Atlas*, 65–66.

21. McGrath, "Tabernacle, New Jersey," in *Road Atlas*, 67–69.

22. William Carlos Williams, *Paterson* (New York: New Directions, 1995), 6.

23. McGrath, "An Irish Word," in *In the Kingdom of the Sea Monkeys* (New York: Ecco, 2012), 11–13.

24. McGrath, "Mt. Errigal" (unpublished manuscript).

25. Maureen N. McLane, *My Poets* (New York: Farrar, Straus and Giroux, 2012).

26. McLane, "Tenancy," in *Same Life* (New York: Farrar, Straus and Giroux, 2008), 60–61.

27. McLane, "*Sleeping and Waking / Small Works*," *Zoland Poetry* 1 (2007), http://www.zolandpoetry.com/reviews/2007/v1/ObrienRehm.html.

28. McLane, "After Sean Scully: 'You have had your day…',," in *World Enough* (New York: Farrar, Straus and Giroux, 2010), 93.

29. Wallace Stevens, "Sunday Morning," in *The Collected Poems of Wallace Stevens* (New York: Vintage, 1990), 66.

30. McLane, "Songs of a Season," in *Same Life*, 53.

31. McLane, "It was under the spell of Yeats," in *Same Life*, 103.

32. McLane, "Transcendentalism," in *World Enough*, 89–92.

33. McLane, "Belfast," in *This Blue* (New York: Farrar, Straus and Giroux, 2014), 72–74.

34. Hass, "Meditation at Lagunitas," in *Praise*, 4–5.

35. Maddy Paxman, *The Great Below* (Reading, UK: Garnet, 2014), and Don Paterson, "*Smith*": *A Reader's Guide to the Poetry of Michael Donaghy* (London: Picador, 2014).

15

Ireland's Afterlives in Global Anglophone Poetry

Omaar Hena

As this collection of essays attests, there is no disputing how Irish poetry is *in* and *of* the world, especially as outside pressures have shaped the formation of Irish poetry and as Irish writing has become an important influence in shaping other poetries far beyond the island's borders. In recent years, Irish studies has taken a global turn which is due to the established influence of postcolonial studies and may further stem from globalization discourses in the humanities. But the worlding of Irish literature has a long history. We can look back to the eighteenth and nineteenth centuries, given experiences of transatlantic migration due to the famine and Irish participation in British imperialism. This was followed by periods of exile, migration, and cosmopolitanism under "high" and "late" modernisms in the twentieth century. And now in the twenty-first century, Irish cultural production in film, theater, fiction, and poetry has begun to address the challenges facing "the new Irish," considering the increasingly multiethnic, polyglot constitution of the polity.[1] In the relatively smaller domain of poetry studies, scholars have mapped the significance of US, Eastern European, Greek, French, and Japanese literary and cultural influences upon contemporary Irish poetry as well as the institutional networks connecting Ireland with Caribbean, African, and South Asian spaces of poetic production in the post–World War II era.[2] Whether looking outward by projecting the nation through transnational literary circuits and cosmopolitan interrelations or turning inward by representing local spaces and cultural practices as already saturated with outside influences, Irish writers and artists have adopted a range of strategies to imagine Ireland both within and beyond the geographic boundaries of the island.

"Post-Ireland." At play, here, are at least two senses of "post" that, at first blush, seem antithetical to one another: one sense carries with it a desire to announce (as in "to post") the presence of Ireland and thereby drive "toward"; the other sense, conversely, describes an impulse to move "beyond." What might it mean to pose "Post-Ireland" not as a declarative statement but, rather, as a still unresolved question concerning the various ways writers — Irish and non-Irish alike — have displayed an irrepressible "desire for" and a concomitant imperative to "think beyond" the nation by repeatedly returning to questions of difference and cross-cultural comparison?

In light of the ways scholars have traced the global inflections informing contemporary Irish literature, this chapter switches focus by examining how contemporary global anglophone poets recurrently look to Ireland to contend with the contradictions of modernity as they are locally embedded and globally imagined. Overall, we can see several reasons for Ireland's seminal position in postcolonial English-language poetry. For one, and as has been widely acknowledged, Ireland was one of Britain's oldest colonies (after Wales) — stretching back, depending on one's historical perspective, to the twelfth century when Henry II was declared lord of Ireland. This was followed by the series of invasions and plantations in the sixteenth century and onward, leading up to the Act of Union (1801), which formally incorporated Ireland under British colonial rule. It is by now a commonplace to acknowledge how the historical foundation of British imperialism in Ireland became a template for other colonial locations that have contended with the legacy of empire post-Ireland (or concurrently with Ireland). In the process, postcolonial authors have modeled their own struggles for political and literary independence through Irish authors. Given what Mark Quigley calls "Ireland's much earlier entry into postcoloniality," we need to "consider anew how the Irish experience might both inflect and be inflected by anticolonial and postcolonial formations emanating from other former imperial spaces."[3] It makes sense, then, that postcolonial authors would adapt Irish literary models to grapple with their own social, political, and cultural dislocations, as I discuss below.

Another related reason stems from the centrality of Irish literature in the formation of world literature more broadly. In the field of postcolonial studies and world literature, for instance, there have been extensive studies of the significance of Shaw, Wilde, Synge, Yeats, Joyce, and Beckett (to name only the most recognizable) upon canonical postcolonial authors, including Claude McKay, Jean Rhys, Chinua Achebe, Samuel Selvon, Wole Soyinka, Mustapha Matura, J. M. Coetzee, Salman Rushdie, Jamaica Kincaid, Arundhati Roy, Junot Díaz, and many others. These lines of influence are due to a wide array of sociological, historical, and political contexts. In *The World Republic of Letters* (1999, 2004), Pascale Casanova looks to Ireland's relatively "peripheral" relation to metropolitan, imperial centers of world literature such as Paris and London in the early- and mid-twentieth century. Over a short period of time, Casanova claims, modern Irish authors developed a series of strategies for contesting colonial rule and for subverting imperial centers of literary production, thereby forging an Irish national heritage and staging "a revolt against the literary order."[4] By linking "national" and "international" perspectives, Yeats, Shaw, Joyce, and Beckett furthermore staked a claim for their writing's relative autonomy from the political world and, in the process, enabled the emergence of "Ireland" as a new center of literary production. "The Irish Paradigm," for Casanova, has become exemplary for other minor literatures from the so-called peripheries. We might even go so far to say that once Ireland has become an institutional center in world letters (not such "the Irish Paradigm" but *a* paradigm), later postcolonial authors look to Irish writing to gain recognition and visibility in the literary marketplace.

A third reason, though, is due to the sheer sophistication of Irish literature and the versatile strategies Irish writers deploy in handling the flexibility of the English language, especially through a repeated emphasis on alterity and estrangement. As we will see, global anglophone poets repeatedly cite "the language issue" as a crucial means through which to reflect upon questions over identity and difference, national belonging and cosmopolitan attachment, and an overwhelming preoccupation over aesthetics and politics. Like their Irish predecessors, the poets studied here similarly question how experimentations with the English language can both express a "desire for" and a wish to "move beyond" local, geographic boundaries with an eye to the global energies animating poetic production and reception.

The generative possibilities encapsulated in "Post-Ireland," I hope, will provide a broad analytic concerning the numerous ways global anglophone poets turn to "Ireland" — here understood as a densely layered, multifaceted site, comprising its historical, political, cultural, aesthetic, and imaginative dimensions — as a relay through which to mediate a host of social-political preoccupations and across a range of contexts, from postwar periods of decolonization through twenty-first century globalization. "Literary texts," Amanda Tucker and Moira E. Casey argue in reference to the transnational energies of Irish literature, "not only serve as representations of transnational subjects and themes related to cross-border movements, networks, and affiliations; they become transnational connectivities themselves."[5] I begin with a comparison between W. B. Yeats and Derek Walcott (b. 1930, St. Lucia) before turning to Christopher Okigbo (1932–1967, Nigeria), E. A. Markham (1939–2008, Montserrat/UK/France), Sujata Bhatt (b. 1956, India/US/Germany), and Daljit Nagra (b. 1966, UK). Had I world enough and time, I would have also discussed A. K. Ramanujan (1929–1993, India/ US), Louise Ho (b. 1945, Hong Kong), Lorna Goodison (b. 1947, Jamaica/ US), Grace Nichols (b. 1950, Guyana/UK), Ingrid de Kok (b. 1951, South Africa), and Fred D'Aguiar (b. 1960, Guyana/UK/US). Though this chapter is by no means exhaustive, we can nonetheless see how English-language poets from around the world have contributed to a vibrant conversation over the many ways in which Irish cultural resources both survive (*sur-vivre*, "live on") and flourish as they become uprooted, appropriated, recycled, and renewed in the global era.

I would like to begin my exploration of Ireland's afterlives through a close reading of a now familiar pairing: W. B. Yeats and Derek Walcott. In 1936, Yeats composed his late poem "Lapis Lazuli," which in many ways crystallizes, and even pre-figures, many of the critical debates over the cross-cultural energies animating the production and reception of Irish literature over the past two decades. Before World War II, Yeats was already looking globally in "Lapis Lazuli" to question the role of art in responding to human suffering. "For everybody knows or else should know," Yeats memorably writes:

> That if nothing drastic is done
> Aeroplane and Zeppelin will come out,
> Pitch like King Billy bomb-balls in
> Until the town lie beaten flat.[6]

In order to represent the pressing immediacy of political crisis, Yeats notably overlays earlier historical moments of European conquest so as to show, at one and the same time, the "provinciality" of Europe's internal conflicts as well as the "globality" of the poet's imaginative reach — first to summon and then to yoke together discrepant temporalities and geographic spaces that otherwise would appear to be worlds apart. Indeed, the remainder of the poem proceeds, in its cross-rhymed strophes of varying length, to travel back in time and place to Shakespeare's Renaissance England, even further back to Callimachus's Greece in the fifth century BCE, and then forward in time and across a continent to Emperor Ch'ien Lung's Manchu Qing Dynasty in eighteenth-century China, where the poem ostensibly concludes.

In the final stanza, Yeats peers into the precious stone of lapis lazuli, given to him as a birthday gift by the poet Henry Talbot de Vere Clifton, and metaphorically transfigures "Every discolouration of the stone, / Every accidental crack or dent" into the semblance of natural tranquility, "a water-course or an avalanche, / or lofty slope."[7] All this happens before Yeats inserts *himself* into the exotic art object, where he shares company with the three distant Chinese figures who listen to "mournful melodies." Together, they stare from almost planetary heights upon "all the tragic scene" of catastrophe below:

and I
Delight to imagine them seated there;
There, on the mountain and the sky,
On all the tragic scene they stare.
One asks for mournful melodies;
Accomplished fingers begin to play.
Their eyes mid many wrinkles, their eyes,
Their ancient, glittering eyes, are gay.[8]

So what does it mean for the Western Yeats "to delight to imagine" the ancient, Eastern figures that he sees in the stone of lapis lazuli, and that he holds in his mind's eye? Yeats's "Lapis Lazuli," even beyond reflecting an ambivalent instance of orientalism, constitutes an incipiently globalized aesthetic whereby the Irish modernist, who is neither fully inside nor outside his Anglo-Irish identity, responds to the crises of modernity by imagining cross-cultural affiliations formed away from the imperial center and circulated transnationally, all the while remaining attuned to the spaces between cultures. Yeats goes to great lengths to preserve the gap between his speaker's location and the subjects he imagines, especially through the repetition of "them," "there," "their." Together, these words signify a self-conscious awareness of the singularity of cultural difference: that the Irish and Chinese experiences are neither identical with nor collapsible into one another. At the same time, Yeats's distancing mechanisms also invite a correspondence between "there" and "here," as when the arresting enjambment ("and I / Delight") suspends the poem's lyric "I," who straddles in-between the Western, modern "here" of the site of composition and the Eastern, ancient "there" of the "tragic scene." The poem compresses time and space so as to call into question the separation of spatial and temporal borders that usually cordon off cultures, geographies, and histories, all of which are, in truth, already entangled within one another, however unevenly.

Here and across this work, Yeats routes Irishness beyond the Irish-English binary, outward to India, China, and Japan, and it thus is not reducible to orientalism, primitivism, or cultural imperialism, though these are admittedly part of the story. Surely Yeats appropriates Chinese cultural artifacts. "Lapis Lazuli" manifests an instance of "Irish orientalism," in

Joseph Lennon's phrasing: that is, the semiotic presence of the East in Irish texts which constitutes a distinct and separate discourse from orientalism proper.[9] Irish orientalism simultaneously operates both within and at a distance from European orientalism because of what Lennon calls Ireland's "liminal" or in-between position as both colonized and colonizer, a position often enabling Irish writers to make productive cross-colonial identifications.[10] "Celtic-Oriental comparisons," he writes, "allowed Irish writers to rhetorically assert both their proximity to the metropole, or center of the Empire, and their proximity to the periphery, depending on the context, audience, and purpose of their argument or representation."[11] As we can see in this instance, Yeats "rhetorically takes advantage of both the orientalist perspective of the colonizer and the nationalist convictions of the colonized."[12] But as much as Yeats exemplifies Irish orientalism the poem also Hibernicizes China, overlaying the Eastern signifier with Yeats's own preoccupations within a "semicolonial" Irish context, in the words of Derek Attridge and Marjorie Howes.[13] In this sense, "China" becomes less a referent to real histories and subjects and more an imagined geography which Yeats channels along with "England" and "Greece": even as Yeats strives toward the incorporation of foreign artifacts into a coherent worldview, the poem equally demonstrates how its world-making project is necessarily incomplete and provisional. This maneuver on Yeats's part compels us to sustain a double vision: at once acknowledging the incommensurable differences *between* and the overlapping contiguity *across* discrete cultures and languages as they enter into conversation with one another.

In poetry studies, readers are now well aware of Derek Walcott's Irish affiliations and solidarities. He memorably describes the Irish as "the niggers of Britain" in a 1977 interview with Edward Hirsch. In his monumental epic *Omeros* (1990), the poet travels to Ireland, which he describes as "a nation split by a glottal scream."[14] Across his career, he repurposes Irish modernists to fashion what several scholars have described as a "discrepant cosmopolitanism," a term borrowed from cultural anthropologist James Clifford.[15] As Michael Malouf observes, Walcott looks to the migrant, exilic qualities of "Irish writing" to articulate the Caribbean as "a cosmopolitan culture of bricolage, where every individual part is only a figure for a larger whole located elsewhere."[16] But Walcott also looks to Irish authors to self-consciously meditate upon the powers and limitations of poetic language to name "a world" still caught between the demise of imperialism on the one hand and the acceleration of globalization on the other. In the process, Walcott also questions the fate of locality in the midst of tourism and poverty in the Caribbean and elsewhere.

Consider, for instance, his poem "The Lost Empire" from *White Egrets* (2010). In this later poem, the first strophe recounts with bitter sarcasm how the British empire's world-wide reach, previously encircling "Burma, Canada, Egypt, India, the Sudan," became "all of a sudden" nothing more than "air," "dirt," and "silence."[17] The poem then proceeds to recount the pageantry of decolonization — "the whited eyes and robes of surrendering hordes" — and the lure of western metropoles for postcolonial migrants in the "glittering cities, / Genoa, Milan, London, Madrid, Paris." The final strophe shifts perspective, however. Reminiscent of the pastoral tradition extending back to Virgil's *Eclogues*, the poem extols how:

> This small place produces
> nothing but beauty: the wind-warped trees, the breakers
> on the Dennery cliffs, and the wild light that loosens
> a galloping mare on the plane of Vieuxfort makes us
> merely receiving vessels of each day's grace,
> light simplifies us whatever our race or gifts.
> I'm as content as Kavanagh with his few acres;
> for my heart to be torn to shreds like the sea's lace,
> to see how its wings catch colour when a gull lifts.[18]

In these lines, Walcott's hexameters enlist local topography, place-names inherited from British and French colonialism, and the sights and sounds of natural ecology to articulate the ways "light simplifies" — or, the ways poetic illumination suspends — the racial antinomies and political hierarchies that the poem had previously indicted and, significantly, capitalized upon. Indeed, the deixis signaled by "this small place" refers to the small place of the stanza that itself "produces" the quotidian "beauty" that the text construes as "each day's grace." After having dilated the time of globalization to include the history of imperialism, decolonization, and post-War global economic exchange, the final lines turn to the local, ecological splendor of St. Lucia. It is as if the ceaseless flux of nature might gesture to a counter-discursive domain of globalism that would resist, or at least momentarily disrupt, the hegemonic effects of globalization. Put another way, his poem seeks to refresh the reader's perception of globalism so as to call into question who and what populates a world, whether they be empires, nations, and cities, or wind-warped trees, the sea's lace, and a lifting gull.

Walcott does so, however, by positioning his writing in relationship with another exemplar of self-fashioned locality, Patrick Kavanagh. Interestingly, however, the speaker's "content" in localism is betrayed by a quivering restlessness, which occurs on the levels of rhetoric and intertextuality. The simile comparing the speaker's heart "torn to shreds" *as if* it were "the sea's lace" might well signify the shreds of world literature that flow through Walcott's verse, producing redoubled localities that are threatened by erasure. Walcott's title, "The Lost Empire," signifies, along one interpretive line, the "lost empire of signs": the lost power of language to name a world anew as a social-political necessity set against what is often perceived as the homogenizing logic of globalization, which flattens the differences between discrete times and places. Along another line, however, the poem also enacts "signs at liberty" signaling his writing's participation in globalization through the wayward movement of literatures, thereby rejuvenating English-language poetry and expanding the domain of world literature.

Yeats and Walcott unite in casting *poiesis* as a performative enactment that can draw linkages between disparate geographies, histories, and languages. What's more, their trans-historical conception of poetic influence — as when Yeats compares himself to "the Tibetan monk who dreams at his initiation he himself is eater and eaten," thereby capturing the cyclical processes of consumption and production subtending the circulation of global culture;[19] or when Walcott conceives of Homer, Dante, Shakespeare, and Joyce not as European precursors that need to be shucked off but, on the contrary, as simultaneous contemporaries driven by a "filial impulse" through which literary language becomes a "living element" begetting new cultural attachments — seeks to advance polycentric models of poetic production and reception.[20]

Before Walcott articulated the vacillations of postcolonial subjectivity through Yeatsian ambivalence in "A Far Cry from Africa" (1962), other world poets turned to the Anglo-Irish modernist during the era of decolonization and subsequent struggles for national independence in the middle of the twentieth century. We can think, especially, of Nigerian authors such as Wole Soyinka and Christopher Okigbo. Born in 1932, Okigbo lived in Northern Nigeria before studying classics at University of Ibadan (his early poetic practice involved his own translations from Greek and Latin into English). After graduating in 1956, he became a school teacher, a librarian at the University of Nigeria (Nsukka), and a representative for Cambridge University Press before his untimely and tragic death fighting for the Biafran side during the bloody civil war (1967–70). While T. S. Eliot and Ezra Pound are typically named as the most dominant influences (among the many *Western* influences) upon his particular brand of postcolonial modernism, Yeats was also a seminal figure to Okigbo, at least in his "later" career.

As Okigbo's readers are well aware, he composed "Lament of the Masks" in honor of Yeats. The poem is featured in the opening pages of the collection *W. B. Yeats: 1865–1965: Centenary Essays*, published in Nigeria by the University of Ibadan Press and jointly edited by D. E. S. Maxwell and S. Bushrui. The table of contents lists essays placing Yeats in conversation with Shakespeare, Synge, Irish nationalism, and "the Oriental and Celtic elements" of his writing. But the collection also includes poems by South African writer L. D. Lerner and Northern Irish author James Simmons. These bibliographic details are well worth mentioning. As Nathan Suhr-Sytsma has shown, they form part of a broader pattern in which mid-century poets operate within transnational networks and institutions of print and, in doing so, address multiple and often overlapping publics at local, national, and international scales. Seeing Okigbo's poem in this framework, Suhr-Sytsma argues that " 'Lament of the Masks' looks less like evidence of a postcolonial African writer's debt to European innovation than part of a lively conversation about Yeats's legacy among anglophone poets from various non-metropolitan locations."[21] It makes sense that Yeats would have such a powerful effect upon Okigbo, particularly given Nigeria's tumultuous political climate during the late 1950s and 1960s. Okigbo likely saw in

Yeats the cosmopolitan modern poet-figure *par excellence*, one who also sought to forge a uniquely national consciousness against colonial rule by elevating local mythology and folklore into high art while, at one and the same time, maintaining a position of poetic autonomy by using masked personae to take on a public voice, or even many public voices, a feature which has become a hallmark of Yeats's oeuvre.

"Lament of the Masks" is written in the conventions of the Yoruba praise poem, or *oríkì*. The oral praise poem typically describes the features of the deceased hero or ancestor by listing his names and epithets, lauding his accomplishments and victories, and comparing him to animal symbolism and the natural world.[22] As other scholars have established, Okigbo adopts all of these features but transforms the *oríkì* into a thoroughly hybrid and fundamentally print form.[23] Okigbo's speaker enunciates in "Warped voices" and "from throats of iron," as if to signify the *oríkì*'s estrangement from itself.[24] The poem casts Yeats as "WAGGONER of the Great Dawn" (alluding to his immersion in the occult) who pursues and subdues "the white elephant," violently transforming its tusks into "ivory trumpets."[25] Throughout, Yeats takes on a sublime magnitude who evades containment, even at the level of lineation and enjambment: "They poured you into an iron mould / You burst the mould."[26] The poem concludes:

> But will a flutist never stop to wipe his nose?
> Two arms can never alone encircle a giant iroko.
> Night breezes drum on the plantain leaf:
> Let the plantain leaf take over the dance.[27]

Yeats's monumental stature compels Okigbo to figure him as the "giant iroko." In Yoruba myth, the iroko tree stands at the center of a forest and contains within it an ancestral spirit, often figured as an old man, a symbol of virility and strength. Any who dare to cut down the hallowed tree will release the man's spirit, potentially bringing ruin to the community. In these lines, Okigbo encases the spirit of the Irish poet within the iroko. Now housed within the iroko, Yeats suddenly becomes an authentic origin of Yoruba culture, whose power inspires something akin to terrible beauty for those who might encircle him.

Having paid homage to Yeats, the final lines, however, seem to displace him to clear a space for a new mode of praise poems that might blend Irish and Yoruba sources. It is as if the plantain leaf (a Yoruba figure of health and sustenance) might supplant ("take over") the Yeatsian dance, despite the continuing reverberations which we hear from "Among School Children." That is, the poem aspires for the local "breeze" and the native "leaf" to become its own lament for Yeats, thereby replacing the paltry artifice of song, dance, or poetry itself. In the end, the ambiguity of these final lines makes it difficult, if not impossible, to know "Yeatsian" symbology from "Yoruba" mythology: masks, horns, drums, trees, and the dance are now "native" to both traditions through their mutual imbrication. Here, Okigbo taps into and extends the global reach of Yeats's cultural storehouse, which now takes on new life when transplanted on Nigerian soil. In his later work, Okigbo seems to take on the role of the poet-prophet by fusing Igbo traditions with anglo-modernism (especially the T. S. Eliot of *The Waste Land*). It was after writing "Lament of the Masks" that Okigbo composed his apocalyptic sequence "Path of Thunder: Poems Prophesying War" (1965–66). Arguably, Okigbo's engagement with the apocalyptic Yeats may have furnished him with a powerful model to intertwine indigenous Yoruba idioms and high anglo-modernist poetics in the context of the struggle for national independence and civil war and, in the process, made possible a thoroughly postcolonial Nigerian *oríkì*.

Whereas Okigbo relates to Yeatsian sources from a distance, other poets have engaged Ireland — and its ambivalent relation to the British Empire — in more direct ways. E. A. Markham, for instance, was born in Montserrat, which he claims "is more organically Irish than any other [island] in the Caribbean" due to Ireland's colonial presence on the island stretching back to the seventeenth century.[28] Having grown up surrounded by Irish influences in the Lesser Antilles, Markham moved to Britain in the 1950s and held a Senior Lectureship in creative writing at Sheffield Hallam University. At different points in his life, he lived in France and Papua New Guinea but also spent time in Northern Ireland while writer-in-residence at the University of Ulster, Coleraine (1988–1991). During these years, he edited the literary magazine *Writing Ulster* and delivered a lecture (subsequently published as an essay) titled "Ireland's Islands in the

Caribbean: Poetry from Montserrat and St. Caesare" (1994). In his essay, Markham recalls how his home island was settled by a group of Irish dissidents fleeing British and French rule of St. Kitts in 1632. "This was not," Markham is clear to say, "a voyage of discovery."[29] Irish occupation of the island increased all the more in the aftermath of Cromwell's vicious campaign later in the seventeenth century, transforming Montserrat into "an outpost of Ireland in the Caribbean."[30] While not arriving as colonists and subsequently subject to British legal restrictions and anti-Catholic discrimination, the Irish also participated in land ownership and plantation slavery.[31] Markham bears a personal awareness of Ireland's imprint on the "Emerald Isle of the Caribbean," an imprint which quite literally appears through a number of national symbols. For instance, the ensign on Montserrat's flag features the figure of Erin holding a harp; and the Government House in the capital of Plymouth is engraved with a shamrock. Echoing Walcott, Markham likewise maintains that "Ireland's proximity to England and complex relationship to English makes it easier for us, from outlying areas of Englishness, or Britishness, or English-languageness, to adopt and adapt its literary models without the political self-consciousness that would arise if those models were English — or perhaps, even American."[32] Unlike other postcolonial writers who receive Irish resources from afar, such as Okigbo or Linton Kwesi Johnson whose Jamaican dub rhythms were informed by Irish accents broadcast over the BBC, Markham goes so far as to claim that Irishness and Irish consciousness is already native to the Caribbean's history of creolization.

During his residency at Coleraine, Markham wrote and later published his fifth collection of poems, *Letter from Ulster & The Hugo Poems* (1993). As the title suggests, the book is divided into two parts: those poems written from an "Irish perspective" in Ulster looking out to the world (spanning the Caribbean, North America, the UK, Eastern Europe, the Middle East, and South Africa) and, conversely, other poems situated in Montserrat concerning Hurricane Hugo, which devastated the island while Markham was living in Northern Ireland in 1989. His poem "Island" belongs to the first group and indirectly comments on Ireland's waves of invasions, from the Viking raids in the Middle Ages through the Early Modern and Modern era. "Island" places particular emphasis on the experiences of those who remain broken and fragmented due to historical violence, perhaps up to and including the Troubles. The poem concludes:

> Those for whom cracks were never mended
> are here, bits of them trying to assemble
> bits of you they care to claim. They attack —
> guns, bombs, badverbs — evacuated arguments.
> On the horizon, another island afloat. Ah,
> in a sea of salt, a line,
> a rope, a plan of rescue:
> how best to invade?[33]

In these lines, "Island" contains the "cracks" and "bits" which refuse mending only to expose how these same linguistic elements ("badverbs") risk perpetuating colonization. By underscoring the reversibility of "they" and "you," Markham highlights the tenuous, arbitrary relation between colonizer and colonized. In many ways, "Island" questions how and whether the poem might offer a way out of this cycle through "a line" or "plan of rescue": if anything, Markham seems to signal his own writing's immersion in colonial legacies, whether situated in Ulster or in the Caribbean. If spoken from a Northern Irish perspective, the poem casts "Ulster" as thoroughly divided within itself due to its long history of conquest, stretching back to Cromwell, the Act of Union, and through the Troubles, the aftermath of which were still reverberating when Markham was writing in the early 1990s. If spoken, though, from a Montserratian perspective, Markham would seem to cast himself as a Caribbean invader of Northern Ireland, as if to return Ulster's colonial legacy back to its British origins before it was transported across the Atlantic. And yet, it would seem as though Markham requires the reader to sustain both of these perspectives simultaneously. In doing so, the poem leaves open the possibility for a reciprocal intertwining of "Ulster" and "Montserrat" into one another, each "Island" now the uncanny double of the other, both in friction and harmony. Here and elsewhere in the collection, such as in the poems "Hinterland," "Letter from Ulster," "Maurice V.'s Dido," and "Kevin's Message to Montserrat," Markham brings to the surface what he calls "the floating images, the buried memories" of Irish-Caribbean "alliances."[34] In doing so, he points to provisional and shifting models of intercultural subjectivity circulating across the Atlantic.

Given the legacy of colonial education and mass migration in the post-war era, several poets from the Asian subcontinent have similarly grafted their own hybrid experiences of multilingualism and living-between-worlds through Irish sources. We can think, for instance, of the Yeatsian inflections informing the work of Indian-born poet A. K. Ramanujan (1929–93) and Kashmiri-born Agha Shahid Ali (1949–2001), both of whom made their careers while living in the US. Yeats's sustained engagement with poetry and politics — combined with his global expansiveness and immersion in Eastern cultures — has been profoundly significant for these poets to mediate the divisions of diaspora and to fashion cosmopolitan subjectivities.

South Asian diaspora women poets however face added difficulties given their triple condition of exclusion as female, ethnic minorities, and outside a male-centered lyric tradition. The Indian-born, US-educated, and now Germany-based poet Sujata Bhatt (b. 1956) takes up these and other concerns in her writing. In contrast to Ramanujan and Ali, Bhatt grew up primarily in the US (she learned English after moving to New Orleans at the age of five due to her father's profession as a virologist). Though less recognized than her elder male predecessors, Bhatt has published several collections with Carcanet Press: *Brunizem* (1988), which won the Commonwealth Poetry Prize (Asia); *Monkey Shadows* (1991); *Point No Point* (1997); *Augatora* (2000); and *Pure Lizard* (2008). Her writing has also earned recognition from the prestigious Poetry Book Society. Bhatt draws upon a wide range of references to write the conjunctures and disjunctures of gender, sexuality, and diaspora. For instance, she frequently switches back and forth between English and her mother tongue, Gujarati, to pattern the "foreignness" and "in-betweenness" of splitting periods of her life between the US, UK, Europe, and India.[35] What's more, she infuses her poems with allusions to classical Indian epic cycles such as the *Ramayana* and the *Mahabharata*, as well as poets in the American grain such as William Carlos Williams, Wallace Stevens, and Elizabeth Bishop, and British modernists including Thomas Hardy and Virginia Woolf. But she also cites "the importance of the Irish tradition," including "Yeats, Joyce, and Kavanagh," during her years pursuing an MFA at the University of Iowa.[36]

The sheer multiplicity of geographies, cultural references, and languages suffusing Bhatt's writing also carry a political edge. For her, they serve as her way of "'writing back' to history" and "break[ing] certain silences," given the gender restrictions and sexual prohibitions she perceives as imposed upon South Asian diaspora women.[37] Her poetry relishes in image, color, and sound, often imitating the visual and musical arts. Bhatt's sensualism and eroticism moreover flaunt boundaries of decorum and aesthetic taste as much as boundaries of ethnic belonging. Consider, for instance, "The Kama Sutra Retold" from *Brunizem*, which begins:

> You laugh,
> but I want to know
> how would we break the long silence
> if we had the same rules?
> It's not enough to say
> > she kissed his balls,
> > licked his cock long
> > how her tongue could not stop.[38]

Bhatt refuses a mere description of the sexual act ("it's not enough") through phallocentric discourse focusing on fellatio. In the subsequent verse paragraphs, the speaker proceeds to move back in time and recalls her seventeen-year-old self swimming out to an island with her male lover. Interestingly, Bhatt overlays the adolescent erotic encounter through Yeats, as the male figure in the poem "wishes they were swans / Yeats's swans" who "glide across other worlds; magical yet rustling with real reeds."[39] In recounting a moment of mutual seduction, the final verse paragraphs build toward "her" ecstasy, but now by way of "Leda and the Swan" (1924):

> She must have swallowed the sky
> > the lake, and all the woods
> > > veined with amber brown pathways;
>
> for now great white wings
> are swooping through

her thighs, beating stronger
>   up her chest,
the beak stroking her spine
feathers tingling her skin,

the blood inside
>   her groin swells

while wings are rushing to get out,
>   rushing.[40]

In what has become one of the most controversial poems in his oeuvre, Yeats deploys the figure of Leda to meditate on the relation between violence, sexuality, and women's mythic "knowledge" of — and relative agency in — history. In his broken sonnet, Yeats looks voyeuristically upon Leda's violation, questioning its horror all the while becoming "so caught up" in the moment of sexual conquest. We'll recall how the poem's onslaught of spondees ("A sudden blow: the great wings beating still"; "white rush"; "strange heart beating"; "brute blood of the air") mimic the traumatic "suddenness" of Leda's rape before the utter "strangeness" of the swan. Yeats leaves the speaker (and the reader) to question — in a moment of radical uncertainty as we are left vexed over the extent to which Leda is left utterly bereft — whether she took on "his knowledge with his power / before the indifferent beak could let her drop?"[41] One strength of Yeats's poem is, arguably, how it foregrounds the layers of mediation through which the speaker confronts, and finally fails to apprehend, sexual violence in its mythic proportions.

Bhatt takes a different tack. In the lines above, she repurposes Yeats's language by stripping "Leda" of her prior associations with masculine violence and now giving sublime expression to feminine sexuality in ways that are far more down-to-earth but nonetheless all-consuming. The swan, here, is for her pleasure. Consider, for instance, how Bhatt figures the multiple erotic zones of "her" body ("thighs," "chest," "spine," "skin," "groin") and through her breathless *jouissance*, which we can see and hear through ongoing present participles ("beating," "stroking," "tingling," "rushing").

Her open-ended syntactical patterning enacts the spreading and diffusion of female pleasure unleashed in *écriture feminine*. The conclusion swells to climax, as line spills over line, until it seems as though the poem will endure beyond itself through the "rushing," "rushing" flow of orgasm. In these ways, Bhatt performs a double transgression. For one, her eroticism shatters taboos concerning the proper subject matter befitting South Asian women's writing. But she does so, secondly, by interweaving *The Kama Sutra* and Yeats, appropriating masculinist mythic texts which now take on new kinds of significance in the context of postcolonial feminist concerns. Bhatt remakes "Leda" in her own diasporic image, rewriting the fecundity of feminine sexuality in the unruliness of everyday desire.

As readers will have noticed, Yeats has figured prominently thus far in my discussion of Ireland's afterlives in global anglophone poetry. This probably does not come as much of a surprise given the abiding influence of anglo-modernism generally in shaping postcolonial poetics in English. But what about contemporary Irish and Northern Irish poetry? In the past two decades, especially, post-war authors such as Seamus Heaney and Paul Muldoon have gained prominent recognition through publications with elite presses such as Faber, international awards such as the Nobel Prize and the Pulitzer Prize, appointments as the Oxford Professor of Poetry, university residencies at Harvard and Princeton respectively, and regular placement in university syllabi. Though both of these authors, in different ways, began at the margins of the poetry world in the US and UK, their writing's inventive engagement with a range of problems — concerning poetry and violence, the poet's divided relation to divided communities, the abiding question of the language issue, the problem of mediating between local and global perspectives, and self-reflexive meditations on how their writing is produced through, circulated by, and received within literary institutions and late capitalist mechanisms of commodification (to name a few) — has significantly contributed to their standing in the poetry establishment.

For London-born, British-Punjabi poet Daljit Nagra (b. 1966), the preoccupations of his Northern Irish precursors have taken on urgent significance in the context of Black and Minority Ethnic (BME) cultural production in twenty-first century Britain. After the publication of his award-winning first collection, *Look We Have Coming to Dover!* (2007),

Nagra was lionized as *the* voice of British-Asian poetry. In the pages of *The Guardian* and *The Independent,* he was lauded as rejuvenating English poetry through his buoyant humor, vibrant "Punglish," and use of multiple voices and masked personae to pattern the contradictions of belonging and alienation. Nagra, though, faces a particular set of challenges. In light of New Labour imperatives promoting diversity in the late 1990s and early 2000s, he writes with an awareness of how his writing will be perceived as "representative" of his South Asian community and used to advance multiculturalist agendas branded under "Cool Britannia." (As a former secondary teacher and now based at Brunel University London, he is especially sensitive to the ways minority writing is put to the service of educating young adults about "other cultures," such as in the General Certificate of Secondary Education.) Nagra, like other BME poets such as Bernardine Evaristo, Patience Agbabi, and Lemn Sissay, emphasizes how many of the social disparities and racial exclusions stemming from the Thatcher era have remained intact. One problem Nagra confronts is how to draw upon now elite, canonical Irish precursors to question nagging inequalities confronting minority communities when, by adopting these same sources, he accrues significant cultural capital and may risk confirming multicultural ideologies of diversity and assimilation.

Irish writers, overall, seem to serve a double function in Nagra's writing. Citing the importance of Heaney, Muldoon, and Ciaran Carson, he returns repeatedly to Irish authors "because of their energized attitude towards Englishness" and the ways in which "the Irish tradition challenges Englishness and [...] the English lineage."[42] From one perspective, then, Nagra repurposes Irish poetic sources to challenge and thereby insert himself into the English poetic tradition. And yet, from another perspective, Englishness is far from monolithic in his eyes, but figures instead through its inner alterity and ineluctable entanglement with myriad others due to the British Empire and the waves of migration in the post-war era. In poems such as "Yobbos!" and "Digging" from his first collection, Nagra directly alludes to Muldoon and Heaney, respectively, to draw cross-cultural comparisons between "Indians' and Irish people's shared oppression."[43] To be sure, he is also careful to distinguish Irish from British-Asian experiences, particularly given the absence of a distinct literary-cultural lineage for a newly arrived author such as Nagra. Still, Nagra forges Irish-Indian connections across his writing to invent flexible, capacious models of cross-cultural subjectivity for contemporary Britain.[44]

His second collection, *Tippoo Sultan's Incredible White Man Eating Tiger Toy Machine!!!* (2011), extends his exploration of the ways in which imperial conceptions of race and difference continue to frame and frustrate claims to "global Britishness." While he does not allude directly to Irish sources in his latter collection, we can nonetheless detect the continuing significance of Muldoon to Nagra's project. Consider, for instance, his poem "Octoroon":

> Ah sweet thing
> with yellow curls & aqua eyes
> the soapy bubbles that you blow
> gasp at your cocoa skin.
>
> I wonder do your True Blue parents
> still force a
> *pompompomp*
> for The Last Night of the Proms?[45]

Nagra's playful title (referring to a racially derogatory term for a mixed race person of one-eighth African ancestry) likely invokes the nineteenth-century stock character popularized by Irish playwright, Dion Boucicault, in the antebellum melodrama *The Octoroon* (1859). But he also adopts a number of Muldoonian strategies. Indeed, the lines above may echo Muldoon's dark meditation on miscegenation and hybridity in "Promises, Promises," whose speaker imagines Sir Walter Raleigh returning to the lost colony of Roanoke "Only to glimpse us here and there / As one fair strand in her braid, / The blue in an Indian girl's eye."[46]

The first stanza's abrupt apostrophic beginning ("Ah sweet thing") sets in tension the mixed race subject's "yellow curls & aqua eyes" with his or her "cocoa skin." However casual these lines may appear, they are densely layered through a chain of allusions and metonymies. For one, Nagra seems to allude to John Everett Millais's painting *A Child's View of the World* (1886), which became world famous as an advertisement for Pears' Soap, newly retitled as *Bubbles*:

Pears' Soap, *Bubbles*, 1900–05, Digital Image. Reprinted with permission from The Advertising Archives (London), http://www.advertisingarchives.co.uk, accessed June 2, 2016.

In 1887, Millais sold his painting and its copyright to Sir William Ingram (the owner of *Illustrated London News*) who, in turn, sold it to A&F Pears of Pears' Soap. As Anne McClintock has established, soap "flourished" in the nineteenth century "because, as a cheap and portable domestic commodity, it could persuasively mediate the Victorian poetics of racial hygiene and imperial progress."[47] Pears marketed soap as a racial commodity of imperialism, mobilizing discourses of whiteness to instruct precepts of cleanliness and to police the boundaries between the purity of white Englishness and the contamination of colonial alterity. We can see this quite literally through the caption in the advertisement above: "Pears' soap beautifies the complexion, keeps the hands white and imparts a constant bloom of freshness to the skin." In "Octoroon," it is as if the soapy bubbles acquire a racialized subjectivity of whiteness, which stands in contrast to and yet seductively "gasp[s] at / your cocoa skin." This last line insinuates yet another reference to empire's racialized commodities, the "sweet thing" of cocoa. Like soap, Britain's cocoa trade in West Africa and advertising campaign would gain ascendency in the early twentieth century, at the very moment when the British Empire was about to collapse.[48] In these ways, Nagra indirectly cues his readers into the ways imperial models of Englishness have reinforced racial hierarchies through the simultaneous disavowal of, fetishistic fascination with, and capitalist consumption of colonial otherness. "Octoroon" deliberately replays racial stereotype to uncover the fragile, insubstantial basis of Englishness itself, one whose soapy bubble might burst at any moment.

The second stanza, in turn, questions how nineteenth-century imperial histories impinge upon contemporary celebrations of postimperial Britishness. The speaker, we read, wonders whether the mixed race child's "True Blue," Tory parents feel compelled to participate in the pageantry of patriotism, such as the Last Night of the Proms and performances of Sir Edward Elgar's "Pomp and Circumstance" (whose title alludes to Othello's speech praising the glory of war). These lines bear the most visible and audible mark of Muldoon's poetics, especially through the repetition of the seemingly nonsense sounds of "*pompompomp*." In *To Ireland, I* (2000), Muldoon names this feature as the "contagyious" impulse in Irish writing, which revels in "the slip and slop of language, [showing] a disregard for the line between sense and nonsense."[49] As Muldoon's readers are well aware, his propensity for "contagyious" writing often works to mask a violent, traumatic reality as it is encoded through childlike sounds. In this instance, the "*pompompomp*" might invoke the sounds of the "pom pom" machine gun, deployed by the British in the Second Boer War in South Africa and World War I. It may further refer to a "pommy," a derogatory term for a British citizen who migrated to Australia or New Zealand. Or, it may register how the perpetuation of Englishness (as symbolized by Elgar and the Last Night of the Proms) "still" requires a "forced" repetition of its perceived imperial greatness, as orchestral sounds both conceal and reveal the violent conquest of other peoples and spaces through "the pride, pomp, and circumstance of glorious war."[50]

For all of the celebration of a post-racial British society through diversity campaigns such as Cool Britannia, Nagra slyly registers how imperial obsessions with racial classification and the consumption of difference have not gone away. At first blush, we may be tempted to perceive Nagra's writing as the bastard offspring of "True Blue" literary parentage which we can see on the poem's formal surface, its allusions to conventionally "English" literary lineages, and its shameless performance of stereotype. By titling his poem "Octoroon," Nagra indirectly critiques the radical insufficiency and tragic inevitability of racial stereotype to approach the multiplicity of cross-racial subjectivity. At the same time, though, Nagra strategically rein-scribes stereotype to alert his readers to the poem's messy layers of alterity which refuse easy containment: "Octoroon" comprises a composite mixture of various cultural sources drawn from high and low, from an array of time periods, and spanning diverse geographies (Boucicault, Millais, Pears adver-tising, the cocoa trade, Elgar, Shakespeare, Muldoon). In doing so, Nagra implicitly "wonders" about the many ways his own writing might be put to the work of advancing the "*pompompomp*" of postimperial Britishness by necessarily disguising its "dark," imperial underpinnings which reside just under the surface of the poem's cocoa skin.

We can take this one step further. If the title, "Octoroon," marks the failure of labels to account for irrepressible differences as they are shaped and molded into coherent conceptions of "identity," it equally registers how racialized labels — octoroon, British-Asian, BME, postcolonial, or global British — are also branding mechanisms for newly visible minority artists such as himself. In this way, Nagra performs his own self-branding to self-re-flect upon the ways his poetry is enmeshed within and cannot overcome the commodification of difference through the commercialization of poetry in the contemporary British scene. This awareness on his part serves as his way of patterning global Englishness by carrying forward its imperial legacy, imagining it within and beyond strictly national frameworks, all the while underscoring how BME cultural production participates in the inequalities of the literary marketplace. The institutional centrality of Irish writing — what Casanova calls "the Irish paradigm" — has partly enabled a peripheral British-Punjabi poet to gain visibility and recognition within the contested domain of the contemporary English poetry scene. As I have shown across this essay, though, global anglophone poets repeatedly turn to Ireland due to its long colonial legacy, which has resonated in other spaces of imperial and postcolonial cultural production. Nagra clearly taps into and extends these histories, recalling how the Irish have been othered. Like the other poets in this chapter, Nagra further recognizes how Irish writers estrange the English language, uncovering the differences, alterities, and mixtures which exist under the surface of "standard English." In the end, the slip and slop of Nagra's language octoroons — that is, sardonically stereotypes *and* others — the wily Muldoon, recalling to us the unruly cross-contaminations of poetic influence as they spill across racial, national, and historical boundaries.

To bring my discussion full circle, I would like to return to the phrase with which I began this essay. In my eyes, "Post-Ireland" functions less as a descriptive reality (political borders have decidedly *not* gone away, no matter how transnational our critical lens), than as an open-ended question, a horizon of possibility, even an ongoing problem for mediating difference and alterity. Earlier, I mentioned the worldly constitution of Irish literature, especially as Irish authors repeatedly display a double-movement, in their dual "desire for" and wish to "move beyond" the nation. At the center of this doubleness, however, is an insurmountable alterity that is not separate from but constitutive of Irish literature, revealing Irishness as non-identical-to-itself and criss-crossed through other times, other places, other influences and confluences. In some instances, forms of otherness appear as foreign, non-Irish elements in the moment of cross-cultural encounter while, in others, they figure as modes of difference native to the local. In both cases, we can see how poets and poems mediate past and present, local and global, familiar and strange, self and other, so as to lay bare forms of difference already internal to "Irish" literature, given its long and varied histories of conquest and cross-cultural encounter at home and abroad. In these ways, "Irishness" has become a translatable identity, readily repurposed by other non-Irish writers and poets. If Irish literature has historically questioned diverse ways of signifying difference when the act of comparison is no longer a choice but a necessity, then it makes perfect sense why so many global anglophone poets have looked through the dark glass of Irish literature to see their own fractured reflection in a wide array of social-political contexts.

Across this chapter, I have charted a few pathways, both real and imagined, that English-language poets have pursued in turning to "Ireland" as a relay for making partial sense of their own personal experiences, historical circumstances, and social preoccupations. As has become clear by now, figures such as Yeats, Kavanagh, Heaney, and Muldoon loom large in this body of poetry. It seems likely that relatively peripheral poets need to draw upon now established, canonical Irish authors in order to gain literary recognition within the highly competitive domain of English-language poetry. Still, I have sought to emphasize how "Ireland's afterlives" take on fresh significance as they are molded and adapted on both sides of the Atlantic and under disparate contexts of decolonization (Okigbo), migration (Markham), diaspora (Bhatt), resettlement (Nagra), the rapid acceleration of globalization (Walcott), and shared experiences of cultural in-betweenness and estrangement connecting all of these authors to one another.

It remains uncertain, of course, what role Ireland will play in the writing of future world poets. What does seem likely, though, is that twenty-first-century Irish poetry will be written from increasingly cross-cultural perspectives. One such example is Nigerian-born, Irish poet Lind Grant-Oyeye, whose writing tends to focus on questions of globalization, social equality, and political justice. In January 2016, Grant-Oyeye won the Universal Human Rights Student Network award for "M-Moments," a poem initially published in *The New Verse News*, an online magazine featuring "politically progressive poetry on current events and topical issues."[51] "M-Moments" takes its inspiration from May 2015 news reports concerning the conditions of 1,600 refugees who fled religious and ethnic persecution in Myanmar and Bangladesh and were found (and subsequently detained) in Malaysia. The poem concludes:

> On strange lands were some feet planted. They kissed strangers
> and slept with enemies — red juices pressed against their lips,
> with the firm force of a heavy weight boxer's strength, kissing Judas' doppelgänger
> to the sweet sound of the language from Babel, spoken with a lover's passion.
>
> Faint memories show M in the alphabet song, is for Migration, for marriage.

Grant-Oyeye writes with an ethical awareness of the necessity of giving a textual face and a voice to the conditions of the dispossessed, especially for those who would otherwise seem invisible and insignificant. At the same time, she also signals how her poetry self-reflexively transforms distant experiences of suffering and displacement into aesthetic forms, which we can see through the "some feet" of the poem's meter and "the sweet sound" of her writing. In the process, "M-Moments" compels readers to question the discursive mechanisms which mediate social realities of migration — and how certain people's lives are heard while others are silenced in the alphabet song of language. Given Ireland's increasingly cross-cultural constitution in the present century, I delight to imagine how future Irish poetry will become transformed yet again to take on new voices, new idioms, and new ways of writing the complexities of being in the world.

NOTES

1. The scholarship on transnational approaches to Irish literature is extensive. See Richard Kearney, *Postnationalist Ireland: Politics, Culture, Philosophy* (London: Routledge, 1997); Declan Kiberd, *The Irish Writer and the World* (Cambridge: Cambridge UP, 2005); Mícheál Mac Craith, "Literature in Irish, c. 1550–1690: from the Elizabethan Settlement to the Battle of the Boyne," in *The Cambridge History of Irish Literature, Vol. 1,* eds. Margaret Kelleher and Philip O'Leary (Cambridge: Cambridge UP, 2006), 191–231; Pilar Villar-Argáiz, ed., *Literary Visions of a Multicultural Ireland: The Immigrant in Contemporary Irish Literature* (Manchester: Manchester UP, 2014); Aisling Byrne, "The Circulation of Romances from England in Late-Medieval Ireland," in *Medieval Romance and Material Culture,* ed. Nicholas Perkins (Suffolk: Boydell & Brewer, D. S. Brewer, 2015), 183–98; Nels Pearson, *Irish Cosmopolitanism: Location and Dislocation in James Joyce, Elizabeth Bowen, and Samuel Beckett* (Gainesville: University of Florida Press, 2015).

2. See Jahan Ramazani, *The Hybrid Muse: Postcolonial Poetry in English* (Chicago: The University of Chicago Press, 2001); Steven Matthews, "Translations: Difference and Identity in Recent Poetry from Ireland and the West Indies," in *Irish and Postcolonial Writing: History, Theory, Practice,* ed. Glenn Hooper and Colin Graham (New York: Palgrave, 2002), 109–26; Robert Faggen, "Irish Poets and the World," in *The Cambridge Companion to Contemporary Irish Poetry,* ed. Matthew Campbell (Cambridge: Cambridge UP, 2003), 229–49; Charles Pollard, *New World Modernisms: T. S. Eliot, Derek Walcott, and Kamau Brathwaite* (Charlottesville: University of Virginia Press, 2004); Maria McGarrity, *Washed by the Gulf Stream:*

The Historic and Geographic Relation of Irish and Caribbean Literature (Newark: University of Delaware Press, 2008); Michael Malouf, *Transatlantic Solidarities: Irish Nationalism and Caribbean Poetics* (Charlottesville: University of Virginia Press, 2009); Nathan Suhr-Sytsma, "Haiku Aesthetics and Grassroots Internationalization: Japan in Irish Poetry," *Éire-Ireland* 45, nos. 3–4 (Fall–Winter 2010): 245–77; Irene De Angelis, *The Japanese Effect in Contemporary Irish Poetry* (New York: Palgrave, 2012); and Suhr-Sytsma, *Poetry, Print, and the Making of Postcolonial Literature* (Cambridge: Cambridge UP, forthcoming 2017).

3. Mark Quigley, *Empire's Wake: Postcolonial Irish Writing and the Politics of Modern Literary Form* (New York: Fordham UP, 2013), 14, 24.

4. Pascale Casanova, *The World Republic of Letters*, trans. M. B. DeBevoise (Cambridge, MA: Harvard UP, 2004), 304–5.

5. Amanda Tucker and Moira E. Casey, eds., *Where Motley is Worn: Transnational Irish Literatures* (Cork: Cork UP, 2014), 9.

6. W. B. Yeats, "Lapis Lazuli," *The Collected Poems of W. B. Yeats* (New York: Scribner, 1996), 294.

7. Ibid., 295.

8. Ibid.

9. Joseph Lennon, *Irish Orientalism: A Literary and Intellectual History* (Syracuse: Syracuse UP, 2008), xvi.

10. Ibid., xvii.

11. Ibid., xvi.

12. Ibid., xxviii.

13. Derek Attridge and Marjorie Howes, eds., *Semicolonial Joyce* (Cambridge: Cambridge UP, 2000), 1.

14. Derek Walcott, *Omeros* (New York: Farrar, Straus and Giroux), 199.

15. On Clifford's notion of "discrepant cosmopolitanism" see *Routes: Travel and Translation in the Late Twentieth Century* (Cambridge, MA: Harvard UP, 1997), 36; on Walcott's particular version of "discrepant cosmopolitanism" see Pollard, *New World Modernisms*, 16–19; and Malouf, *Transatlantic Solidarities*, 132.

16. Malouf, *Transatlantic Solidarities*, 171.

17. Derek Walcott, *White Egrets* (New York: Farrar, Straus and Giroux, 2010), 36–37.

18. Ibid., 37.

19. W. B. Yeats, "A General Introduction to My Work," in *Essays and Introductions* (New York: Macmillan, 1968), 519.

20. Derek Walcott, *What the Twilight Says: Essays* (New York: Farrar, Straus and Giroux, 1999), 36, 62.

21. Suhr-Sytsma, *Poetry, Print, and the Making of Postcolonial Literature* (Cambridge: Cambridge UP, forthcoming 2017).

22. Molara Ogundipe-Leslie, "The Poetry of Christopher Okigbo: Its Evolution and Significance," in *Critical Essays on Christopher Okigbo*, ed. Uzoma Esonwanne (Washington DC: Three Continents Press, 1984), 185.

23. Jahan Ramazani, *A Transnational Poetics* (Chicago: The University of Chicago Press, 2009), 102–3; Suhr-Sytsma, *Poetry, Print, and the Making of Postcolonial Literature*.

24. Christopher Okigbo, "Lament of the Masks," in *W. B. Yeats: 1865–1965: Centenary Essays*, eds. D. E. S. Maxwell and S. Bushrui (Ibadan: University of Ibadan Press, 1965), xii.

25. Ibid., xiv.

26. Ibid.

27. Ibid., xv.

28. E. A. Markham, "Ireland's Islands in the Caribbean," in *The Cultures of Europe: The Irish Contribution*, ed. James P. Mackey (Belfast: The Institute of Irish Studies, The Queen's University of Belfast, 1994), 142–43.

29. Ibid., 140.

30. Ibid., 136.

31. Ibid., 143.

32. Ibid., 139.

33. E. A. Markham, *Letter from Ulster & The Hugo Poems* (Lancaster, UK: Littlewood Arc, 1993), 13–14.

34. Markham, "Ireland's Islands," 143.

35. Sujata Bhatt, "In Conversation with Sujata Bhatt," interview with Helen Tookey, *PN Review* 40, no. 1 (2013): 30.

36. Sujata Bhatt, "Interview with Sujata Bhatt," interview with Vicki Betram, *PN Review* 138 (2001), accessed online Apr. 8, 2016, http://www.carcanet.co.uk/cgi-bin/scribe?showdoc=4;doctype=interview.

37. Sujata Bhatt, "In Conversation with Sujata Bhatt," 32.

38. Sujata Bhatt, "The Kama Sutra Retold," *Brunizem* (Manchester: Carcanet, 1998), 39.

39. Ibid., 40.

40. Ibid., 40–41.

41. Yeats, "Leda and the Swan," *The Collected Poems*, 214.

42. Daljit Nagra, "'Meddl[ing] with my type': An Interview with Daljit Nagra," interview with Claire Chambers, *Crossings: Journal of Migration and Culture* 1 (2010): 94.

43. Ibid.

44. On Nagra's rewritings of Muldoon and Heaney, see Dave Gunning, "Daljit Nagra, Faber Poet: Burdens of Representation and Anxieties of Influence," *Journal of Commonwealth Literature* 43 (2008): 95–108; and Omaar Hena, *Global Anglophone Poetry: Literary Form and Social Critique in Walcott, Muldoon, de Kok, and Nagra* (New York: Palgrave, 2015), 133–36, 147–52.

45. Daljit Nagra, "Octoroon," *Tippoo Sultan's Incredible White Man Eating Tiger Toy Machine!!!* (London: Faber and Faber, 2011), 33.

46. Paul Muldoon, "Promises, Promises," *Poems 1968–1998* (New York: Farrar, Straus and Giroux, 2001), 85.

47. Anne McClintock, *Imperial Leather: Race, Gender, and Sexuality in the Colonial Contest* (London: Routledge, 1995), 130.

48. On empire and the cocoa trade, see Emma Robertson, "Bittersweet Temptations: Race and the Advertising of Cocoa," in *Colonial Advertising and Commodity Racism*, eds. Wulf D. Hund et al. (Berlin: Lit Verlag, 2013), 171–96.

49. Paul Muldoon, *To Ireland, I* (Oxford: Oxford UP, 2000), 107.

50. William Shakespeare, *Othello (Folger Shakespeare Library)* (New York: Washington Square Press, 1993), 143.

51. Lind Grant-Oyeye, "M-Moments," *The New Verse News*, May 16, 2015, accessed online May 3, 2016, http://newversenews.blogspot.com/2015/05/m-moments.html.

Acknowledgments

The editors warmly acknowledge the assistance of the following people, all of whom contributed greatly to the compilation and creation of this book: Denise Ayo, Matthew Campbell, Eimear Clowry, Omaar Hena, Emily Hershman, Tara MacLeod, Rachel McEvoy, Thomas Merluzzi, and Ryan Shirey. Thanks are also due to Amanda Keith and the many committed interns at Wake Forest University Press: Christina Berry, Nicole Cahill, Lena Hooker, Katie Huggins, Sophie Leveque, Melissa Libutti, Shannon Magee, Ashley Mellon, Alana Mills, Alex Muller, Fahad Rahmat, Emily Smith, Rachel Stewart, and Blair Wessels.

We gratefully acknowledge permission to reprint copyrighted material in this book as follows:

SARAH ANNES BROWN: Excerpts from *The Metamorphis of Ovid: from Chaucer to Ted Hughes* are used by permission of Bristol Classical Press, an imprint of Bloomsbury Publishing Plc. COLETTE BRYCE: Excerpts from "Hide-and-Seek," "A Clan Gathering," "The Search," "Derry," "The Analyst's Couch," "North to the South," and "Re-entering the Egg" from *The Whole and Rain-domed Universe*; "Car Wash" from *Self Portrait in the Dark*; "Stones," "Last Night's Fires," "1981," "Device," and "The Full Indian Rope Trick" from *The Full Indian Rope Trick*; and "Line" and "Form" from *The Heel of Bernadette* reprinted by permission of Picador. PASCALE CASANOVA: Excerpts from *La République Mondiale des Lettres* are reprinted by permission of Editions du Seuil. VONA GROARKE: Excerpts from "Furrow" from X are reprinted by permission

CONOR O'CALLAGHAN: Excerpts from "Kingdom Come," "Lordship," "Among Other Things," "Wild Strawberries," "Woodsmoke," "A Nest of Tables," "The Server Room," and "Sospeso" from *The Sun King* are reprinted by permission of Wake Forest University Press and The Gallery Press. CAITRÍONA O'REILLY: Excerpts from "Ariadne," "Amanita Virosa," "Everything Flowers," and "Geis" from *Geis* are reprinted by permission of Bloodaxe Books and Wake Forest University Press. JUSTIN QUINN: Excerpts from translations of "Scéal Syrinx" ("Syrinx Story") by Aifric Mac Aodha are reprinted with permission of the translator. DAVID WHEATLEY: Excerpts from translations of "File" ("Poet"), "La Tricoteuse," "Focal Faoisimh" ("The Soothing Word"), and "Sop Préacháin" ("A Crow's Wisp") by Aifric Mac Aodha are reprinted with permission of the translator.

Every effort has been made to trace and contact copyright holders before publication. If notified, the publisher will rectify any errors or omissions at the earliest opportunity.

Bibliography

Abrams, M. H. "Structure and Style in the Greater Romantic Lyric." In *The Correspondent Breeze: Essays on English Romanticism*, 76–108. New York: W. W. Norton & Company, 1984.

Acquisto, Joseph. "The Place of Poetry; Nature, Nostalgia, and Modernity in Jaccottet's Poetics." *Modern Language Review* 105, no. 3 (July 2010): 679–94.

Agamben, Giorgio. "The End of the Poem." In *The End of the Poem: Studies in Poetics*. Stanford: Stanford University Press, 1999.

Agee, Chris, ed. *The New North: Contemporary Poetry from Northern Ireland*. Winston-Salem, NC: Wake Forest University Press, 2008; London: Salt Publishing, 2011.

Alighieri, Dante. *The Divine Comedy 3: Paradise*. Translated by Dorothy Sayers and Barbara Reynolds. Middlesex: Penguin, 1962.

Allen, Michael. "Rhythm and Revision in Mahon's Poetic Development." In *Close Readings: Essays on Irish Poetry*, edited by Fran Brearton, 98–122. Sallins, Kildare: Irish Academic Press, 2015.

Almqvist, Bo and Roibeard Ó Cathasaigh, eds. *Ó Bhéal an Bhab: Cnuas-Scéalta Bhab Feiritéar*. Indreabhán: Cló Iar-Chonnacht, 2002.

Alofsin, Anthony. *Frank Lloyd Wright — the Lost Years 1910–1922: A Study of Influence*. Chicago: The University of Chicago Press, 1993.

Andrews, Elmer. *The Poetry of Seamus Heaney: All the Realms of Whisper*. London: Macmillan, 1988.

Archambeau, Robert. "Postnational Ireland." *Contemporary Literature* 50, no. 3 (2009): 610–18.

Arkins, Brian and Patrick F. Sheeran. "Coloniser and Colonised: The Myth of Hercules and Antaeus in Seamus Heaney's *North*." *Classical and Modern Literature* 10, no. 2 (1990): 127–34.

Attridge, Derek and Marjorie Howes, eds. *Semicolonial Joyce*. Cambridge: Cambridge University Press, 2000.

Auden, W. H. *The Complete Works of W. H. Auden*, Volume 1 and 2. Edited by Edward Mendelson. Princeton: Princeton University Press, 1997/2002.

——— and Louis MacNeice. *Letters from Iceland*. London: Faber and Faber, 1937.

Batten, Guinn. "'He Could Barely Tell One from the Other': The Borderline Disorders of Paul Muldoon's Poetry." *South Atlantic Quarterly* 95, no. 1 (Winter 1996): 171–204.

———. "'Where All the Ladders Start': Identity, Ideology, and the Ghosts of the Romantic Subject in the Poetry of Yeats and Muldoon." In *Romantic Generations: Essays in Honor of Robert F. Gleckner*, edited by Ghislaine McDayter, Guinn Batten, Barry Milligan, and Peter Manning, 245–80. Lewisburg, PA: Bucknell University Press, 2001.

Beckett, Samuel. *Molloy*. In *The Trilogy*. London: Picador, 1979.

Benjamin, Walter. *One-Way Street and Other Writings*. Translated by J. A. Underwood. London: Harcourt Brace, 1979.

———. "The Translator's Task." Translated by Steven Rendall. *TTR: Traduction, Terminologie, Rédaction* 10, no. 2 (1997): 151–65.

Bhatt, Sujata. *Brunizem*. Manchester: Carcanet, 1988.

———. "In Conversation with Sujata Bhatt." Interview with Helen Tookey. *PN Review* 40, no. 1 (2013): 30–32.

———. "Interview with Sujata Bhatt." Interview with Vicki Betram. *PN Review* 138 (2001). Accessed online, April 8, 2016, http://www.carcanet.co.uk/cgi-bin/scribe?showdoc=4;doctype=interview.

Blake, Séamus. "Seán Ó Tuama and Irish Gaelic in the Twentieth Century." *American Journal of Irish Studies* 8 (2011): 117–36.

Boland, Rosita. "What Daffodils Were to Wordsworth, Drains and Backstreet Pubs Are to Me." *The Irish Times*, March 12, 2011.

Brearton, Fran. "'The Nothing-could-be-simpler-line': Form in Contemporary Irish Poetry." In *The Oxford Handbook to Modern Irish Poetry*, edited by Fran Brearton and Alan Gillis, 629–50. Oxford: Oxford University Press, 2012.

Brennan, Livia. "Ailbhe Ní Ghearbhuigh." *Poetry International* Rotterdam. Accessed online, http://www.poetryinternationalweb.net/pi/site/poet/item/18333/30/Ailbhe-Ni-Ghearbhuigh.

Brodsky, Joseph. *Watermark*. New York: Farrar, Straus and Giroux, 1992.

Brody, Saul. *The Disease of the Soul: Leprosy in Medieval Literature*. Ithaca and London: Cornell University Press, 1974.

Brogan, T. V. F. "Rhyme." In *The Princeton Encyclopedia of Poetry and Poetics*, 4th edition, edited by Roland Greene et al. Princeton: Princeton University Press, 2012.

Brown, Sarah Annes. *The Metamorphosis of Ovid: from Chaucer to Ted Hughes*. London: Gerald Duckworth, 1999.

Brown, Marshall. "Periods and Resistances." *Modern Language Quarterly* 62, no. 4 (2001): 309–16.

Bryce, Colette. *The Full Indian Rope Trick*. London: Picador, 2005.

———. *The Heel of Bernadette*. London: Picador, 2000.

———. "Omphalos." *The Poetry Review* 103, no. 3 (Autumn 2013). Accessed online, August 15, 2016. http://poetrysociety.org.uk.gridhosted.co.uk/wp-content/uploads/2014/12/1033-Bryce.pdf.

———. *Self-Portrait in the Dark*. London: Picador, 2008.

———. *The Whole and Rain-domed Universe*. London: Picador, 2014.

Campbell, Matthew. *Irish Poetry Under the Union, 1801–1924*. Cambridge: Cambridge University Press, 2013.

———. "Muldoon's Remains." In *Paul Muldoon: Critical Essays*, edited by Tim Kendall and Peter McDonald, 170–88. Liverpool: Liverpool University Press, 2004.

Caplan, David. *Rhyme's Challenge: Hip Hop, Poetry, and Contemporary Rhyming Culture*. New York: Oxford University Press, 2014.

Carpenter, Dorothy M. "The Pilgrim from Catalonia / Aragon: Ramon de Perellós, 1397." In *The Medieval Pilgrimage to St. Patrick's Purgatory: Lough Derg and the European Tradition*, edited by Michael Haren and Yolande de Pontfarcy, 99–119. Enniskillen: Clogher Historical Society, 1988.

Carragher, Alvy. "Meet the Poet." *HeadStuff* website, April 17, 2015. http://www.headstuff.org/2015/04/doireann_ni_ghriofa/.

Carson, Ciaran. Review of *North* by Seamus Heaney. *The Honest Ulsterman* 50 (Winter 1975): 184.

Carson, Liam. "Taking literature in Irish out of the Gaelic ghetto." *The Irish Times*, October 6, 2014.

Casanova, Pascale. *La République Mondiale des Lettres*. Paris: Seuil, 1999.

———. *The World Republic of Letters*. Translated by M. B. DeBevoise. Cambridge, MA: Harvard University Press, 2004.

A Catalogue of the Manuscripts, Typescripts, and Correspondences of Nuala Ní Dhomhnaill. Dublin: Kenny's Bookshop & Art Gallery, 1994.

Chesterton, G. K. *The Autobiography of G. K. Chesterton*. New York: Sheed and Ward, Inc., 1936.

Clifford, James. *The Predicament of Culture: Twentieth-Century Ethnography, Literature, and Art*. Cambridge, MA: Harvard University Press, 1988.

———. *Routes: Travel and Translation in the Late Twentieth Century*. Cambridge, MA: Harvard University Press, 1997.

Clifton, Harry. *The Holding Centre: Selected Poems 1974–2004*. Northumberland, UK: Bloodaxe; Winston-Salem, NC: Wake Forest University Press, 2014.

Coleman, Philip. "'At ease with elsewhere': Pearse Hutchinson's Transnational Poetics," Review of *Collected Poems* and *At Least for a While* by Pearse Hutchinson. *Dublin Review of Books* 1, no. 5 (2009). http://www.drb.ie/essays/at-ease-with-elsewhere.

Conboy, Sheila. "What You Have Seen is Beyond Speech: Female Journeys in the Poetry of Eavan Boland and Eiléan Ní Chuilleanáin." *The Canadian Journal of Irish Studies* 16, no. 1 (1990): 65–72.

Corcoran, Neil. *Poets of Modern Ireland: Text, Context, Intertext*. Carbondale: Southern Illinois University Press, 1999.

Coupe, Laurence. *Myth*. London and New York: Routledge, 1997.

Cronin, Michael. *An Ghaeilge san Aois Nua / Irish in the New Century*. Dún Laoghaire: Cois Life, 2005.

Culin, Stewart. *Games of the North American Indians: Games of Skill*, Volume 2. Lincoln: University of Nebraska Press, 1992.

Cummings, Philip. "Who can now be considered Ireland's leading poets in the aftermath of Seamus Heaney's passing? Five contemporary Irish poets everyone should read." *The Irish Post*, September 28, 2013.

Cussen, Clíodhna and Micheál Ó Ruairc. *Síoda ar Shíoda*. Dublin: Coiscéim, 2008.

Darcy, Ailbhe. "Dorothy Molloy's Gurlesque Poetics." *Contemporary Women's Writing* 8, no. 3 (2014): 319–38.

Davie, Donald. *Articulate Energy*. London: Routledge, 1955.

Davis, Alex. *A Broken Line: Denis Devlin and Irish Poetic Modernism*. Dublin: University College Dublin Press, 2000.

De Angelis, Irene. *The Japanese Effect in Contemporary Irish Poetry*. New York: Palgrave, 2012.

Denman, Peter. "Know the one? Insolent Ontology in Derek Mahon's Revisions." *Irish University Review* 24, no. 1 (Spring-Summer 1994): 27–37.

———. "Rude Gestures? Contemporary Women's Poetry in Irish." *Colby Quarterly* 28, no. 4 (1992): 251–59.

de Paor, Louis. *Leabhar Na hAthghabhála: Poems of Repossession*. Northumberland, UK: Bloodaxe Books, 2016.

Dickinson, Emily. *The Complete Poems of Emily Dickinson*. Edited by Thomas H. Johnson. Boston: Little, Brown and Company, 1960.

Dillon, John. Interview with Nuala Ní Dhomhnaill. August 7, 2014.

Donaghy, Michael. *Collected Poems*. London: Picador, 2009.

———. *Errata*. Oxford: Oxford University Press, 1993.

———. *The Shape of the Dance: Essays, Interviews and Digressions*. Edited by Adam O'Riordan and Maddy Paxman. London: Picador, 2009.

———. *Shibboleth*. Oxford: Oxford University Press, 1988.

Dorgan, Theo. "Twentieth Century Irish-Language Poetry." *Archipelago* 7, no. 3. Accessed online, http://www.archipelago.org/vol7-3/dorgan.htm.

Eagleton, Terry. *The Event of Literature*. New Haven and London: Yale University Press, 2012.

Eco, Umberto. *Foucault's Pendulum*. San Diego: Harcourt Brace Jovanovich, 1989.

Eliot, T. S. "The Social Function of Poetry." In *On Poetry and Poets*, 4th edition, 15–25. London: Faber and Faber, 1965.

———. "*Ulysses*, Order and Myth." *The Dial* 75 (November 1923): 480–84.

Ellmann, Richard. "Joyce and Yeats." *Kenyon Review* 12, no. 4 (Autumn 1950): 636.

Enniss, Stephen. *After the Titanic: A Life of Derek Mahon*. Dublin: Gill & MacMillan, 2014.

Faggen, Robert. "Irish Poets and the World." In *The Cambridge Companion to Contemporary Irish Poetry*, edited by Matthew Campbell, 229–49. Cambridge: Cambridge University Press, 2003.

Falci, Eric. *Continuity and Change in Irish Poetry, 1966–2010*. Cambridge: Cambridge University Press, 2012.

Fitt, Gerry. Lecture to College Historical Society. Trinity College, Dublin, February 12, 1973.

Flannery, Eóin. "Listening to the Leaves: Derek Mahon's Evolving Ecologies." In *Ireland and Ecocriticism: Literature, History and Environmental Justice*, 22–55. New York: Routledge, 2016.

Foer, Jonathan Safran. "Jonathan Safran Foer on Paul Muldoon." *Poetry Society of America*. https://www.poetrysociety.org/psa/poetry/crossroads/tributes/jonathan_safran_foer_on_paul_mul/.

Foster, R. F. *Vivid Faces: The Making of a Revolutionary Generation*. London: Allen Lane, 2015.

Foucault, Michel. "Of Other Spaces: Utopias and Heterotopias." *Architecture/Mouvement/Continuité* (October 1984): 46–49.

French, Percy. *Prose, Poems and Parodies*. Edited by De Burgh Daly. Dublin: Talbot Press, 1929.

Freud, Sigmund. *Standard Edition of the Complete Psychological Works of Sigmund Freud*, Volume 15. Translated and edited by James Strachey. London: Hogarth Press, 1953–1974.

Frost, Robert. *The Poetry of Robert Frost*. Edited by Edward Connery Lathem. New York: St. Martin's Press, 2002.

Frye, Northrop. *The Educated Imagination*. Bloomington: Indiana University Press, 1971.

Gillis, Alan. "Heaney's Legacy." *Irish Review* 49–50 (2015): 144–46.

Gonzáles-Ariaz, Luz Mar. "'A Pedigree Bitch, Like Myself': (Non)Human Illness and Death in Dorothy Molloy's Poetry." In *Animals in Irish Literature and Culture*, edited by Kathryn Kirkpatrick and Borbála Faragó, 119–35. London: Palgrave Macmillan, 2015.

Grant-Oyeye, Lind. "M-Moments." In *The New Verse News*, May 16, 2015. Accessed online, May 3, 2016, http://newversenews.blogspot.com/2015/05/m-moments.html.

Grigsby, Byron Lee. *Pestilence in Medieval and Early Modern English Literature*. New York: Routledge, 2003.

Groarke, Vona. *X*. Loughcrew, County Meath: The Gallery Press, 2014.

Gunning, Dave. "Daljit Nagra, Faber Poet: Burdens of Representation and Anxieties of Influence." *Journal of Commonwealth Literature* 43 (2008): 95–108.

Haffenden, John, ed. *Viewpoints: Poets in Conversation with John Haffenden*. London: Faber and Faber, 1981.

Hammer, Langdon. "Useless Concentration: Life and Work in Elizabeth Bishop's Letters and Poems." *American Literary History* 9, no. 1 (Spring 1997): 162–80.

Hart, Henry. *Seamus Heaney: Poet of Contrary Progressions*. Syracuse, NY: Syracuse University Press, 1992.

Hartnett, Michael. *Selected and New Poems*. Loughcrew, County Meath: The Gallery Press; Winston-Salem, NC: Wake Forest University Press, 1994.

Hass, Robert. *Praise*. New York: Ecco Press, 1979.

Haughton, Hugh. *The Poetry of Derek Mahon*. Oxford: Oxford University Press, 2007.

Heaney, Seamus. *Articulations: Poetry, Philosophy and the Shaping of Culture*. Dublin: Royal Irish Academy, 2008.

———. *Death of a Naturalist*. London: Faber and Faber, 1966.

———. *Door into the Dark*. London: Faber and Faber, 1969.

———. *Electric Light*. London: Faber and Faber, 2001.

———. *Field Work*. London: Faber and Faber, 1979.

———. *Finders Keepers, Selected Prose 1971–2001*. London: Faber and Faber, 2002.

———. *Government of the Tongue*. London: Faber and Faber, 1989.

———. Interview by Gerald Dawe. *The Poetry Programme*. Dublin: RTÉ Radio 1, January 31. 2009.

———. Interview by Seán Rocks. *Arts Show Special*, radio broadcast. Dublin: RTÉ Radio 1, April 13, 2009. Last accessed October 19, 2015, http://www.rte.ie/heaneyat70/radio.html.

———. *North*. London: Faber and Faber, 1975.

———. *Opened Ground: Poems 1966–1996*. London: Faber and Faber, 1998.

———, trans. "Pangur Bán." *Poetry* 188, no. 1 (April 2006): 4.

———. *Place and Displacement*. Cumbria, UK: Frank Peters, 1984.

———. "The Poet as a Christian." *The Furrow* 20, no. 10 (1978): 603–6.

———. *Preoccupations: Selected Prose, 1968–1978*. London: Faber and Faber, 1984.

———. *The Redress of Poetry: Oxford Lectures*. London: Faber and Faber, 1995.

———. *The Riverbank Field*. Loughcrew, County Meath: The Gallery Press, 2007.

———. *Seeing Things*. London: Faber and Faber, 1991.

———. *Station Island*. London: Faber and Faber, 1984.

———. "A Tale of Two Islands: Reflections on the Irish Literary Revival." In *Irish Studies 1*, edited by P. J. Drudy, 1–20. Cambridge: Cambridge University Press, 1980.

———. "Translator's Note." *Poetry* 188, no. 1 (April 2006): 4–5.

———. "View." *The Listener*, December 31, 1970, 102.

Hegel, George Wilhelm Friedrich. *Aesthetics: Lectures on Fine Art.* Translated by T. M. Knox, 2 vols. Oxford: Clarendon Press, 1975.

Hena, Omaar. *Global Anglophone Poetry: Literary Form and Social Critique in Walcott, Muldoon, de Kok, and Nagra.* New York: Palgrave, 2015.

Hill, Geoffrey. " 'The Conscious Mind's Intelligible Structure': A Debate." *Agenda* 9, no. 4–10, no. 1 (Autumn-Winter 1971–72): 14–23.

———. "Poetry as Menace and Atonement." In *Collected Critical Writings*, edited by Kenneth Haynes. Oxford: Oxford University Press, 2008.

Hoggard, Liz. "The revolutionary artists of the 60s' colourful counterculture," *The Observer*, September 4, 2016.

Holdridge, Jefferson. *The Poetry of Paul Muldoon.* Dublin: The Liffey Press, 2008.

Hughes, Eamonn. " 'Weird/Haecceity': Place in Derek Mahon's Poetry." In *The Poetry of Derek Mahon*, edited by Elmer Kennedy-Andrews, 97–110. Buckinghamshire: Colin Smythe, 2002.

Jarvis, Simon. "Musical Thinking: Hegel and the Phenomenology of Prosody." *Paragraph* 75 (July 2005): 57–71.

———. "Why rhyme pleases." *Thinking Verse* I (2011): 17–43.

Jenkinson, Biddy. "A Letter to an Editor." *Irish University Review* 21, no. 1 (Spring/ Summer 1991): 27–34.

———. "Máire Mhac an tSaoi: The Clerisy and the Folk (P.I.R. 24): A Reply." *The Poetry Ireland Review* 25 (Spring 1989): 80.

Johnson, Maria. "Reading Irish poetry in the New Century: *Poetry Ireland Review* 2000–2009." *Poetry Ireland Review* 100 (March 2010): 35–46.

Kant, Immanuel. *Critique of Pure Reason.* Translated by Norman Kemp Smith. London: Macmillan, 1929.

Kavanagh, Patrick. *Collected Poems.* Edited by Antoinette Quinn. London: Penguin Classics, 2005.

Kearney, Richard. "The IRA's Strategy of Failure." In *The Crane Bag Book of Irish Studies*, edited by Mark Patrick Hederman and Richard Kearney, 699–707. Dublin: Blackwater Press, 1982.

———. *Myth and Motherland.* Derry: Field Day Publications, 1984.

———. *Postnationalist Ireland: Politics, Culture, Philosophy.* London: Routledge, 1997.

Kendall, Tim. *Paul Muldoon.* Chester Springs: Dufour, 1996.

Kennedy-Andrews, Elmer, ed. Introduction to *The Poetry of Derek Mahon*. Buckinghamshire: Colin Smythe, 2002.

———. *Writing Home: Poetry and Place in Northern Ireland, 1968–2008*. Cambridge: D. S. Brewer, 2008.

Kerrigan, John. "Ulster Ovids." In *The Chosen Ground: Essays on the Contemporary Poetry of Northern Ireland*, edited by Neil Corcoran, 237–69. Chester Springs, PA: Dufour Editions, 1992.

Kiberd, Declan. "After Ireland?" *The Irish Times*, August 29, 2009. http://www. irishtimes.com/news/after-ireland-1.728344.

———. *Inventing Ireland: The Literature of a Modern Nation*. London: Jonathan Cape, 1995.

———. *The Irish Writer and the World*. Cambridge: Cambridge University Press, 2005.

Kilroy, Ian. "Transatlantic Poet" (interview with Paul Muldoon). *The Irish Times*, April 19, 2003, B7.

Kinsella, Thomas. *The Táin*. Oxford: Oxford University Press, 2002.

Kinsey, Tara Christie. "Rave on, John Donne: Paul Muldoon and Warren Zevon." *The Yellow Nib* 8 (Spring 2013): 33–51.

Kirsch, Adam. *The Wounded Surgeon: Confession and Transformation in Six American Poets*. New York: W. W. Norton & Company, 2005.

Kristeva, Julia. *Revolution in Poetic Language*. New York: Columbia University Press, 1984.

Lakoff, George and Mark Johnson. *Metaphors We Live By*. Chicago: The University of Chicago Press, 1980/2003.

Larkin, Philip. *The Whitsun Weddings*. New York: Random House, 1964.

Lennon, Joseph. *Irish Orientalism: A Literary and Intellectual History*. Syracuse: Syracuse University Press, 2008.

Lloyd, David. *Anomalous States: Irish Writing and the Post-colonial Moment*. Durham, NC: Duke University Press, 1993.

Longenbach, James. "Paul Muldoon: The Poet of Giddiness." *Slate* (November 28, 2006). http://www.slate.com/articles/arts/books/2006/11/paul_muldoon.html.

Longley, Edna. *The Living Stream: Literature and Revisionism in Modern Ireland*. Newcastle-upon-Tyne: Bloodaxe Books, 1994.

———. "*North*: 'Inner Émigré' or 'Artful Voyeur'?" In *The Art of Seamus Heaney*, edited by Tony Curtis, 63–96. Dublin: Wolfhound, 1994.

Lyotard, Jean-François. *The Inhuman, Reflections on Time*. Translated by Geoffrey Bennington and Rachel Bowlby. Cambridge: Polity Press, 1991.

Lysaght, Seán. "What is Eco-Poetry?" *Poetry Ireland Review* 103 (April 2011): 74–82.

Mac Aodha, Aifric. *Gabháil Syrinx*. Maynooth: An Sagart, 2010.

———. "Sop Préacháin." *Poetry*, September 2015. http://www.poetryfoundation.org/poetrymagazine/poem/250798.

———. "'A Talkative Corpse': The Joys of Writing Poetry in Irish." *Columbia: A Journal of Literature and Art*, October 25, 2011. http://columbiajournal.org/902.

Mac Lochlainn, Gearóid. *Sruth Teangacha / Stream of Tongues*. Indreabhán: Cló Iar-Chonnacht, 2002.

MacNeice, Louis. *Collected Poems*. London: Faber and Faber, 2007; Winston-Salem, NC: Wake Forest University Press, 2013.

———. *Modern Poetry*. Oxford: Oxford University Press, 1938.

Madden, Ed. "Queering the Irish Diaspora: David Rees and Padraig Rooney." *Éire-Ireland* 47, nos. 1 & 2 (Earrach/Samhradh [Spring/Summer] 2012): 173–201.

Mahon, Derek. *An Autumn Wind*. Loughcrew, County Meath: The Gallery Press, 2010.

———. *Collected Poems*. Loughcrew, County Meath: The Gallery Press, 1999.

———. *The Hudson Letter*. Loughcrew, County Meath: The Gallery Press, 1995; Winston-Salem, NC: Wake Forest University Press, 1996.

———. *Life on Earth*. Loughcrew, County Meath: The Gallery Press, 2008.

———. *New Collected Poems*. Loughcrew, County Meath: The Gallery Press, 2011.

Malešević, Siniša. "Irishness and nationalisms." In *Are the Irish different?* edited by Tom Inglis. Manchester: Manchester University Press, 2014.

Malouf, Michael. *Transatlantic Solidarities: Irish Nationalism and Caribbean Poetics*. Charlottesville: University of Virginia Press, 2009.

Markham, E. A. "Ireland's Islands in the Caribbean." In *The Cultures of Europe: The Irish Contribution*, edited by James P. Mackey, 136–54. Belfast: The Institute of Irish Studies, The Queen's University of Belfast, 1994.

———. *Letter from Ulster & The Hugo Poems*. Lancaster, UK: Littlewood Arc, 1993.

Matthews, Steven. "Translations: Difference and Identity in Recent Poetry from Ireland and the West Indies." In *Irish and Postcolonial Writing: History, Theory, Practice*, edited by Glenn Hooper and Colin Graham, 109–26. New York: Palgrave, 2002.

McAuliffe, John. "Contemporary Irish poetry impresses in inventive mode." *The Irish Times*, January 2, 2016.

———. "Sound, rhythm, a soft-top and a disco ball's bright distortions." Review of *The Sun King* by Conor O'Callaghan. *The Irish Times*, June 15, 2013.

McClintock, Anne. *Imperial Leather: Race, Gender, and Sexuality in the Colonial Contest*. London: Routledge, 1995.

McDonald, Peter. *Collected Poems*. Manchester, UK: Carcanet Press, 2013.

———. *Mistaken Identities: Poetry and Northern Ireland*. Oxford: Clarendon Press, 1997.

———. *Sound Intentions: The Workings of Rhyme in Nineteenth-Century Poetry*. Oxford: Oxford University Press, 2012.

McGarrity, Maria. *Washed by the Gulf Stream: The Historic and Geographic Relation of Irish and Caribbean Literature*. Newark: University of Delaware Press, 2008.

McGrath, Campbell. *Capitalism*. Hanover, NH: Wesleyan University Press, 1990.

———. *In the Kingdom of the Sea Monkeys*. New York: Ecco, 2012.

———. "Mt. Errigal." Unpublished manuscript.

———. *Road Atlas: Prose & Other Poems*. Hopewell, NJ: Ecco Press, 1999.

———. *Spring Comes to Chicago*. New York: Ecco, 1996.

McKibben, Bill. *The End of Nature* (1989). Revised with a new introduction. New York: Anchor, 1999.

McLane, Maureen N. *My Poets*. New York: Farrar, Straus and Giroux, 2012.

———. *Same Life*. New York: Farrar, Straus and Giroux, 2008.

———. "Sleeping and Waking / Small Works." *Zoland Poetry* 1 (2007). http://www.zolandpoetry.com/reviews/2007/v1/ObrienRehm.html.

———. *This Blue*. New York: Farrar, Straus and Giroux, 2014.

———. *World Enough*. New York: Farrar, Straus and Giroux, 2010.

McMillen, Robert. "Agallamh: Véarsaí ón mbreacGhalltacht le Séamus Barra Ó Súilleabháin." *Tuairisic.ie*, Deireadh Fómhair 11, 2016. http://tuairisc.ie/agallamh-vearsai-on-mbreacghalltacht-le-seamus-barra-o-suilleabhain/.

Miller, Timothy S. and John W. Nesbitt. *Walking Corpses: Leprosy in Byzantium and the Medieval West*. Ithaca, NY: Cornell University Press, 2014.

Mills, Lia. "Hidden Irelands." *Dublin Review of Books* (March 2014). Accessed online, http://www.drb.ie/essays/hidden-irelands#.

Molloy, Dorothy. *Gethsemane Day*. London: Faber and Faber, 2006.

———. *Hare Soup*. London: Faber and Faber, 2004.

———. *Long-Distance Swimmer*. County Clare: Salmon Poetry, 2009.

Moore, Geoffrey, ed. *The Penguin Book of American Verse*. London: Penguin Books, 1977.

Morrissey, Sinéad. *Between Here and There*. Manchester, UK: Carcanet Press, 2002.

———. *The State of the Prisons*. Manchester, UK: Carcanet, 2005.

———. *Through the Square Window*. Manchester, UK: Carcanet, 2009.

Morrison, Blake. "Speech and Reticence: Seamus Heaney's *North*." In *British Poetry Since 1970: A Critical Survey*, edited by Peter Jones and Michael Schmidt, 103–11. Manchester, UK: Carcanet Press, 1980.

Muldoon, Paul. *Collected Poems*. London: Faber and Faber, 2001.

———. *The End of the Poem: Oxford Lectures in Poetry*. London: Faber and Faber, 2006.

———. "Getting Round: Notes Towards an *Ars Poetica*." *Essays in Criticism* XLVIII, no. 2 (April 1998): 107–28.

———. *Hay*. London: Faber and Faber, 1998.

———. *Horse Latitudes*. New York: Farrar, Straus, and Giroux, 2006.

———. "An Interview with Paul Muldoon." By Lynn Keller. *Contemporary Literature* 35, no. 1 (Spring 1994): 1–29.

———. *Madoc*. London: Faber and Faber, 1990.

———. *Moy Sand and Gravel*. New York: Farrar, Straus and Giroux, 2002.

———. *Poems 1968–1998*. New York: Farrar, Straus and Giroux, 2001.

———. *The Prince of the Quotidian*. Loughcrew, County Meath: Gallery Press; Winston-Salem, NC: Wake Forest University Press, 1994.

———. *Shining Brow*. London: Faber and Faber, 1993.

———. *A Thousand Things Worth Knowing*. London: Faber and Faber, 2015.

———. *To Ireland, I*. Oxford: Oxford University Press, 2000.

Murphy, Gerard, ed. and trans. *Early Irish Lyrics*. Oxford: Oxford University Press, 1956.

Nagra, Daljit. "'Meddl[ing] with my type': An Interview with Daljit Nagra." Interview with Claire Chambers. *Crossings: Journal of Migration and Culture* 1 (2010): 87–96.

———. *Tippoo Sultan's Incredible White Man Eating Tiger Toy Machine!!!* London: Faber and Faber, 2011.

Nic Congáil, Ríona et al. "An Lucht Fileata." *Comhar* 70, no. 9 (September 2010): 13–15.

Ní Chatháin, Proinseas. "Themes in Early Irish Lyric Poetry." *Irish University Review* 22, no. 1 (1992): 3–12.

Ní Chléirchín, Caitríona. "Abjection and Disorderly Elements of Corporeal
    Existence in the Irish-Language Poetry of Nuala Ní Dhomhnaill and Biddy
    Jenkinson." *Proceedings of the Harvard Celtic Colloquium* 30 (2010): 157–74.

———. "Todhchaí na Scríbhneoireachta Gaeilge: bláthú, péacadh agus dóchas."
    Comhar 70, no. 6 (June 2010): 6–9.

Ní Chuilleanáin, Eiléan. *The Magdalene Sermon and Earlier Poems.* Winston-Salem,
    NC: Wake Forest University Press, 1991.

Nic Íomhair, Caitlín. "In praise of Biddy Jenkinson," *The Irish Times,* August 4, 2015.

Ní Dhomhnaill, Nuala. *An Dealg Droighin.* Dublin: Cló Mercier, 1981.

———. *The Astrakhan Cloak.* Loughcrew, County Meath: The Gallery Press, 1992;
    Winston-Salem, NC: Wake Forest University Press, 1993.

———. *Féar Suaithinseach.* Maynooth: An Sagart, 1984.

———. *The Fifty Minute Mermaid.* Translated by Paul Muldoon. Loughcrew,
    County Meath: The Gallery Press, 2007.

———. "Filíocht a cumadh: Ceardlann Filíochta." *Leachtaí Chomh Cille XVII*
    (1986): 147–70.

———. Nuala Ní Dhomhnaill Papers, 1974–2000. (MS1997-12) John J. Burns Library,
    Boston College.

———. *Pharaoh's Daughter.* Loughcrew, County Meath: The Gallery Press, 1990;
    Winston-Salem, NC: Wake Forest University Press, 1993.

———. *Selected Essays.* Edited by Oona Frawley. Dublin: New Island, 2005.

———. *The Water Horse.* Loughcrew, County Meath: The Gallery Press, 1999;
    Winston-Salem, NC: Wake Forest University Press, 2000.

Ní Ríordáin, Clíona. "Liam Ó Muirthile, *An Fuíoll Feá—Rogha Dánta/Wood
    Cuttings—New and Selected Poems." Études Irlandaises* 39, no. 1 (2014): 223–27.

O'Brien, Peggy, ed. *The Wake Forest Book of Irish Women's Poetry.* Winston-Salem,
    NC: Wake Forest University Press, 2011.

O'Callaghan, Conor. *The Sun King.* Loughcrew, County Meath: The Gallery Press;
    Winston-Salem, NC: Wake Forest University Press, 2013.

———, ed. *The Wake Forest Series of Irish Poetry,* Volume 3. Winston-Salem, NC:
    Wake Forest University Press, 2013.

O'Casey, Sean. *Drums Under the Windows.* Volume 3 of *Autobiography.* London:
    Macmillan, 1972.

Ó Coigligh, Ciarán. *An Fhilíocht Chomhaimseartha 1975–1985.* Dublin: Coiscéim, 1987.

Ó Conchubhair, Brian. "The Right of Cows and the Rite of Copy; an Overview of Translation from Irish to English." *Éire-Ireland* 35, nos. 1/2 (2000): 92–111.

Ó Dónaill, Niall. *Foclóir Gaeilge-Béarla*. Baile Átha Cliath: An Gúm, 1977.

O'Driscoll, Dennis. *Stepping Stones: Interviews with Seamus Heaney*. London: Faber and Faber, 2008.

Ó Dúill, Greagóir. *Fearann Pinn: Filíocht ó 1900–1999*. Dublin: Coiscéim, 2000.

———. "Infinite Grounds for Hope?: Poetry in Irish Today." *Poetry Ireland Review* 39 (Autumn 1993): 10–27.

———. "Simon Ó Faoláin." *Poetry International Rotterdam*. Accessed online, http://www.poetryinternationalweb.net/pi/site/poet/item/22528/30/Simon-O-Faolain.

Ó Dúshláine, Tadhg. "The Magnanimous Poetry of Eithne Strong." *SouthWord* 2, no. 1 (Winter 1999): n.p.

Ó Faoláin, Simon. "Ailbhe faoi Agallamh: Márta 31ú, 2016." *NÓS*. Accessed online, http://nos.ie/cultur/leabhair/ailbhe-faoi-agallamh/.

Ó Floinn, Tomás. "Art Ó Maolfabhail." In *Cion Fir: Aistí Thomáis Uí Fhoinn in Comhar*, edited by Liam Prút, 411–16. Dublin: LeabharComhar, 1997.

Ogundipe-Leslie, Molara. "The Poetry of Christopher Okigbo: Its Evolution and Significance." In *Critical Essays on Christopher Okigbo*, edited by Uzoma Esonwanne, 185–94. Washington DC: Three Continents Press, 1984.

O'Kane Mara, Miriam. "Reproductive Cancer: Female Autonomy and Border Crossing in Medical Discourse and Fiction." *Irish Studies Review* 17, no. 4 (2009): 467–83.

Okigbo, Christopher. "Lament of the Masks." In *W. B. Yeats: 1865–1965: Centenary Essays*, edited by D. E. S. Maxwell and S. Bushrui, xiii–xv. Ibadan: University of Ibadan Press, 1965.

Olson, Charles. "Projective Verse" [1950]. In *The Norton Anthology of Modern and Contemporary Poetry*, edited by Jahan Ramazani, Richard Ellmann, and Robert O'Clair, Volume 2, 1053–61. New York: W. W. Norton & Company, 2003.

O'Mahony, Niamh, ed. *Essays on the Poetry of Trevor Joyce*. Bristol: Shearsman Books, 2015.

Ó Muirthile, Liam. "Offshore on Land—Poetry in Irish Now." In *A New View of the Irish Language*, edited by Caoilfhionn Nic Pháidín and Seán Ó Cearnaigh, 140–51. Dublin: Cois Life, 2008.

O'Reilly, Caitríona. *Geis*. Northumberland, UK: Bloodaxe Books; Winston-Salem, NC: Wake Forest University Press, 2015.

———. "'It felt like a breaking of some taboo I'd placed myself under': Caitríona O'Reilly on writing *Geis*." By Shannon Magee and Alexander Muller. Wake Forest University Press website, October 7, 2015. http://blog.wfupress.wfu.edu/2015/10/07/it-felt-like-a-breaking-of-some-taboo-id-placed-myself-under-caitriona-oreilly-on-writing-geis/.

———. *The Nowhere Birds*. Northumberland, UK: Bloodaxe Books, 2001.

———. *The Sea Cabinet*. Northumberland, UK: Bloodaxe, 2006.

Ó Ríordáin, Seán. *Eireaball Spideoige*. Dublin: Sáirséal/Ó Marcaigh, 1952.

———. *Selected Poems*. Edited by Frank Sewell. New Haven & London: Yale University Press and Cló Iar-Chonnacht, 2014.

O'Toole, Tina. "*Cé Leis Tú?* Queering Irish Migrant Literature." *Irish University Review* 43, no. 1 (2013): 131–45.

Ó Tuama, Seán. "Coiscéim na hAoise seo – agus duanairí eile." *Comhar* 51, no. 5 (May 1992): 68–74.

———. "Pádraig Ó Mileadha agus Traidisiún Filíochta an Gaeilge." *Aguisíní*. Dublin: Coiscéim, 2008.

Parini, Jay. *Robert Frost: A Life*. New York: Holt, 1999.

Parker, Michael. "Back to the Heartland: Seamus Heaney's 'Route 110' sequence in *Human Chain*." *Irish Studies Review* 21, no. 4 (2013): 374–86.

Paterson, Don. "*Smith*": *A Reader's Guide to the Poetry of Michael Donaghy*. London: Picador, 2014.

Paulin, Tom. "*Letters from Iceland*: Going North." In *The 1930s: A Challenge to Orthodoxy*, edited by John Lucas, 59–77. Sussex: Harvester Press, 1978.

Paxman, Maddy. *The Great Below*. Reading, UK: Garnet, 2014.

Pearson, Nels. *Irish Cosmopolitanism: Location and Dislocation in James Joyce, Elizabeth Bowen, and Samuel Beckett*. Gainesville: University of Florida Press, 2015.

Perloff, Marjorie. *The Poetics of Indeterminacy*. Princeton: Princeton University Press, 1981.

Póirtéir, Cathal. *Éigse an Aeir*. Dublin: Coiscéim, 1998.

Pollard, Charles. *New World Modernisms: T. S. Eliot, Derek Walcott, and Kamau Brathwaite*. Charlottesville: University of Virginia Press, 2004.

de Pontfarcy, Yolande. "The Historical Background to the Pilgrimage to Lough Derg." In *The Medieval Pilgrimage to St. Patrick's Purgatory: Lough Derg and the European Tradition*, edited by Michael Haren and Yolande de Pontfarcy, 7–34. Enniskillen: Clogher Historical Society, 1988.

Potts, Robert. "Daddy's Growling Girl." *The Guardian*, May 27, 2006. http://www.
theguardian.com/books/2006/may/27/featuresreviews.guardianreview17.

———. "The Poet at Play." *The Guardian*, May 11, 2001. http://www.theguardian.com/
books/2001/may/12/poetry.artsandhumanities.

Quigley, Mark. *Empire's Wake: Postcolonial Irish Writing and the Politics of Modern
Literary Form*. New York: Fordham University Press, 2013.

Quinn, Justin. *The Cambridge Introduction to Modern Irish Poetry, 1800–
2000*. Cambridge: Cambridge University Press, 2008.

———. "The Disappearance of Ireland." In *The Cambridge Introduction to Modern
Irish Poetry, 1800–2000*, 194–210. Cambridge: Cambridge University Press, 2008.

———. "The Irish Effloresence." *Poetry Review* 91, no. 3 (Autumn 2001): 46.

Ramazani, Jahan. *The Hybrid Muse: Postcolonial Poetry in English*. Chicago: The
University of Chicago Press, 2001.

———. *Poetry of Mourning: The Modern Elegy from Hardy to Heaney*. Chicago: The
University of Chicago Press, 1994.

———. *A Transnational Poetics*. Chicago: The University of Chicago Press, 2009.

Randall, James. "An Interview with Seamus Heaney." *Ploughshares* 5, no. 3 (1979): 7–22.

Randolph, Jody Allen. "Cathal Ó Searcaigh, January 2010." In *Close to the Next
Moment: Interviews from a Changing Ireland*. Manchester, UK: Carcanet, 2010.

Redmond, John. "Willful Inconsistency: Derek Mahon's Verse Letters." *Irish
University Review* 24, no. 1 (Spring-Summer 1994): 94–116.

Redshaw, Thomas Dillon. "The Living Voice." *Poetry Ireland Review* 104 (September
2011): 129–33.

Regan, Stephen. "Irish Elegy after Yeats." In *The Oxford Handbook to Modern Irish
Poetry*, edited by Fran Brearton and Alan Gillis. Oxford: Oxford University Press,
2012.

Reisfield, Gary M. and George R. Wilson. "Use of Metaphor in the Discourse on
Cancer." *Journal of Clinical Oncology* 22, no. 9 (2004): 4024–27.

Rich, Adrienne. "When We Dead Awaken: Writing as Re-Vision." *College English* 34,
no. 1 (1972): 18–30.

Robertson, Emma. "Bittersweet Temptations: Race and the Advertising of Cocoa."
In *Colonial Advertising and Commodity Racism*, edited by Wulf D. Hund et al.,
171–96. Berlin: Lit Verlag, 2013.

Rosenstock, Gabriel and Ciaran Carson. "Aspects of Irish-language Poetry and Its
Miraculous Survival." *Poetry Ireland Review* 105 (December 2011): 21–34.

Rose, Richard. *Governing Without Consensus: An Irish Perspective*. London: Faber and Faber, 1971.

Roth, Philip. *Nemesis*. Boston: Houghton Mifflin Harcourt, 2010.

Sayers, Sean. "The Concept of Alienation in Existentialism and Marxism: Hegelian Themes in Modern Social Thought." Paper presented at the Hegel Society of Great Britain Annual Conference, Oxford, UK, September 2003.

Schmidt, Michael. "A Jester in the Earnest World." *PN Review* 173 33, no. 3 (January/February 2007). http://www.pnreview.co.uk/cgi-bin/scribe?item_id=2914.

Schrage-Früh, Michaela. *Emerging Identities: Myth, Nation and Gender in the Poetry of Eavan Boland, Nuala Ní Dhomhnaill and Medbh McGuckian*. Trier: WVT, 2004.

Sexton, Anne. *The Complete Poems*. Boston: Houghton Mifflin, 1981.

Shakespeare, William. *Othello (Folger Shakespeare Library)*. New York: Washington Square Press, 1993.

Shay, Cary A. *Of Mermaids and Others: An Introduction to the Poetry of Nuala Ní Dhomhnaill*. Bern: Peter Lang, 2014.

Sheils, Barry. *W. B. Yeats and World Literature: The Subject of Poetry*. New York: Ashgate, 2015.

Sirr, Peter. "How Things Begin to Happen: Notes on Eiléan Ní Chuilleanáin and Medbh McGuckian." *Southern Review* 31, no. 3 (1995): 450–68.

Snyder, Gary. *No Nature: New and Selected Poems*. New York: Random House, 1992.

Sontag, Susan. *Illness as Metaphor and AIDS and its Metaphors*. New York: Picador, 1990.

Spender, Stephen. *New Collected Poems*. London: Faber and Faber, 2004.

Steiner, George. *After Babel: Aspects of Language and Translation*, 3rd edition. Oxford: Oxford University Press, 1998.

Stevens, Wallace. *The Collected Poems of Wallace Stevens*. New York: Vintage, 1990.

Stewart, Susan. *Poetry and the Fate of the Senses*. Chicago: The University of Chicago Press, 2002.

Storr, Anthony. *Freud*. Oxford: Oxford University Press, 2001.

——. *Jung*. London: Fontana, 1973/1995.

Suhr-Sytsma, Nathan. "Haiku Aesthetics and Grassroots Internationalization: Japan in Irish Poetry." *Éire-Ireland* 45, nos. 3–4 (Fall-Winter 2010): 245–77.

——. *Poetry, Print, and the Making of Postcolonial Literature*. Cambridge: Cambridge University Press, forthcoming 2017.

Synge, John Millington. *In the Shadow of the Glen.* In *The Playboy of the Western World and Other Plays.* New York: Signet Classics, 2006. 82–94.

———. *Letters to Molly: John Millington Synge to Maire O'Neill, 1906–1909.* Edited by Ann Saddlemyer. Cambridge, MA: Harvard University Press, 1971.

———. *Poems.* Volume 1 of *Collected Works.* Edited by Robin Skelton. London: Oxford University Press, 1962.

Tennyson, Alfred. *Poems.* Edited by Christopher Ricks, 2nd edition, 3 vols. London: Longmans, 1987.

The Band. *Music from Big Pink.* Capitol SKAO-2955, 1968.

Thurneysen, Rudolf, ed. *Old Irish Reader.* Dublin: Institute for Advanced Studies, 1981.

Tillinghast, Richard. "The Future of Irish Poetry?" In *Finding Ireland,* 193–217. Notre Dame: Notre Dame University Press, 2008.

Titley, Alan. *Nailing Theses: Selected Essays.* Belfast: Lagan Press, 2011.

Tomlinson, Charles. *Collected Poems.* Oxford: Oxford University Press, 1985.

Tucker, Amanda and Moira E. Casey, eds. *Where Motley is Worn: Transnational Irish Literatures.* Cork: Cork University Press, 2014.

Twiddy, Iain. "Cancer and the Ethics of Representation in Paul Muldoon's *Horse Latitudes.*" *New Hibernia Review* 16, no. 4 (Winter 2012): 18–36.

———. *Pastoral Elegy in Contemporary British and Irish Elegy.* London and New York: Bloomsbury Academic, 2012.

Vendler, Helen. "Anglo-Celtic Attitudes." *New York Review of Books* (November 6, 1997).

———. "Fanciness and Fatality." Review of *Horse Latitudes* by Paul Muldoon. *The New Republic* 235 (November 9, 2006): 26–33.

———. *Seamus Heaney.* Cambridge, MA: Harvard University Press, 1998.

Villar-Argáiz, Pilar. "The Female Body in Pain: Feminist Re-Enactments of Sexual and Physical Violence in Dorothy Molloy's Poetry." *Contemporary Women's Writing* 4, no. 2 (2010): 134–52.

———, ed. *Literary Visions of a Multicultural Ireland: The Immigrant in Contemporary Irish Literature.* Manchester: Manchester University Press, 2014.

Walcott, Derek. *The Arkansas Testament.* London: Faber and Faber, 1987.

———. "The Muse of History." Lecture, South Bank, London, March 3, 1995.

———. *Omeros.* New York: Farrar, Straus and Giroux, 1990.

———. *What the Twilight Says: Essays.* New York: Farrar, Straus and Giroux, 1999.

————. *White Egrets.* New York: Farrar, Straus and Giroux, 2010.

Wheatley, David, trans. "A Crow's Wisp." *Poetry* (September 2015). http://www.poetryfoundation.org/poetrymagazine/poem/250798.

————, trans. "Poet." *The Stinging Fly* 20, no. 2 (Winter 2011/2012): 80.

————, trans. "The Soothing Word." *Poetry International*, October 2, 2015. http://www.poetryinternationalweb.net/pi/site/poem/item/24202/auto/0/The-Soothing-Word.

————, ed. *The Wake Forest Series of Irish Poetry*, Volume 4. Winston-Salem, NC: Wake Forest University Press, 2017.

Wheatley, David and Ailbhe Ní Ghearbhuigh. "Ní hAnsa." *Comhar* 72, no. 8 (September 2012): 24–25.

White, Jerry. "Place, Dialect, and Broadcasting in Irish: Plus ça change …" *Éire-Ireland* 50, nos. 1 & 2 (Spring/Summer 2015): 113–36.

Whitman, Walt. *November Boughs.* In *Complete Poetry and Collected Prose*, 1163–64. New York: Library of America, 1982.

Williams, William Carlos. *Paterson.* New York: New Directions, 1995.

Wills, Clair. *Improprieties: Politics and Sexuality in Northern Irish Poetry.* Oxford: Clarendon Press, 1993.

————. *Reading Paul Muldoon.* Newcastle-upon-Tyne: Bloodaxe Books, 1998.

Wilson, James S. F. "Paul Muldoon: The Art of Poetry, No. 87." *The Paris Review* 169 (Spring 2004). http://www.theparisreview.org/interviews/30/the-art-of-poetry-no-87-paul-muldoon.

Wittgenstein, Ludwig. *Culture and Value.* Chicago: The University of Chicago Press, 1980.

————. *Philosophical Investigations.* Chichester, West Sussex, UK: Wiley-Blackwell, 2009.

————. *Remarks on Frazer's Golden Bough.* Newark: Brynmill, 1991.

Wordsworth, William. *Poetical Works.* Edited by Ernest de Selincourt. Oxford: Oxford University Press, 1904–1969.

————. *Prose Works of William Wordsworth.* Edited by W. J. B. Owen and J. W. Smyser, 3 vols. Oxford: Clarendon, 1974.

Yeats, W. B. *Collected Poems.* London: Macmillan, 1952.

————. *The Collected Poems of W. B. Yeats.* New York: Scribner, 1996.

————. *The Complete Poems.* Edited by Daniel Albright. London: Dent, 1992.

————. *Essays and Introductions.* New York: Macmillan, 1968.

———. *Explorations*. New York: Macmillan, 1962.

———. *Letters on Poetry from W. B. Yeats to Dorothy Wellesley*. Oxford: Oxford University Press, 1964.

———. *The Major Works*. Edited by Edward Larrissy. Oxford: Oxford University Press, 1997.

———. *Memoirs*. Edited by Denis Donoghue. London: Macmillan, 1972.

———. *The Poems*. Edited by Daniel Albright. London: J. M. Dent, 1994.

———. *The Variorum Edition of the Poems of W. B. Yeats*. Edited by Peter Allt and Russell K. Alspach. New York: Macmillan, 1957.

Zapf, Hubert. "Literary Ecology and the Ethics of Texts." *New Literary History* 39, no. 4 (Autumn 2008): 847–68.

Notes on Contributors

MATTHEW CAMPBELL writes mainly about poetry from the beginning of the nineteenth century to the present day. He taught Victorian, Modern, and Irish literature at Sheffield University before going to York as Professor of Modern Literature in 2011. His first book was on Victorian poetry, and he was the editor of *The Cambridge Companion to Contemporary Irish Poetry*. In 2013 Cambridge University Press published his *Irish Poetry under the Union, 1801–1924*, a book about the invention of Irish poetry in English by figures like Moore, Ferguson, Mangan, and Yeats across the period in which Ireland was part of the United Kingdom. Current projects include a history of the last two centuries of Irish poetry.

JAMES CHANDLER is Barbara E. and Richard J. Franke Distinguished Service Professor in the Department of English, Director of the Franke Institute for the Humanities, Founder and Director of the Center for Disciplinary Innovation, and Chair of the Department of Cinema and Media Studies at the University of Chicago. His research interests include British and Irish literature since the early Enlightenment, American cinema, the politics of interpretation, and the relationship of literary criticism to film criticism. *England in 1819* (University of Chicago Press, 1998), his study of literary historicism and its limits, won the Press's Laing Prize in 2000. Recent publications include *The Cambridge History* of *English Romantic Literature* (2009) and *An Archaeology of Sympathy: The Sentimental Mode in Literature and Cinema* (University of Chicago Press, 2013), which traces the formal foundations of modern narrative cinema to the early sentimentalist moment of literature and moral philosophy. He is currently at work on a book about practical criticism in literature and cinema. He is a Fellow of the American Academy.

AILBHE DARCY is Lecturer in Creative Writing at Cardiff University. A collection of her poetry, *Imaginary Menagerie*, is available from Bloodaxe Books and a second volume is forthcoming. In 2017 a selection of her work will appear in *The Wake Forest Series of Irish Poetry*, Volume 4, edited by David Wheatley. *Subcritical Tests*, written in collaboration with the English avant-gardist S. J. Fowler, will be published by Gorse in the same year. Darcy is the co-editor of a special forum on religious faith and innovative poetic forms with Romana Huk for *Religion & Literature*, and her article "Dorothy Molloy's Gurlesque Poetics" appears in *Contemporary Women's Writing*. New poems appear in *Poetry*, *Éire-Ireland*, *Poetry Ireland Review*, and *The Stinging Fly*.

JOHN DILLON is a postdoctoral research fellow of the University Writing Program and the Kaneb Center for Teaching and Learning at the University of Notre Dame. His dissertation, "The Servants of Modernism: Aesthetics and Tradition in Yeats, Lorca, and Woolf," constellates hard-won archival research with Digital Humanities methods to argue that domestic servants played a critical role in the advent and burgeoning of European modernism. His primary fields of research are European modernism, digital humanities, text analysis, and learning analytics. His current project, which draws on computational text analysis and archival materials, focuses on modeling the relationship between dreaming and lyric creativity. A launch-pad article for this project is forthcoming with Cambridge University Press. He has also published an edited translation of Seán Ó Ríordáin's preface to *Eireaball Spideoige* with Yale University Press. He is the co-founder and director of *Breac: A Digital Journal of Irish Studies*. In addition to his literary critical work, he recently won an IBM/USAID Research fellowship to work with IBM Research, India, on a project using Natural Language Processing and Machine Learning to better understand student emotion and its significance in online learning environments.

THEO DORGAN is a poet who is also a novelist, non-fiction prose writer, editor, translator, broadcaster, librettist, and documentary scriptwriter. He has published five books of poetry. His most recent collections are *Greek* and *Nine Bright Shiners*, both published by Dedalus Press. His two prose accounts of crossing the Atlantic under sail — *Sailing For Home* and *Time On The Ocean: A Voyage from Cape Horn to Cape Town* — won wide acclaim, as has his recently published first novel, *Making Way* (New Island Books, 2013). His work has been widely translated: two full collections have been published in Italian as well as a selected poems in French. *La Hija De Safo* was published by Ediciones Hiperion, Madrid, in 2001. He has been editor of, among other titles, *Foundation Stone, Notes Towards a Constitution for a 21st Century Republic* (New Island Books, 2013), *Irish Poetry Since Kavanagh, Revising The Rising* (with Máirín Ní Dhonnchadha), *A Book of Uncommon Prayer, What We Found There, Watching The River Flow*, and, with Gene Lambert, *Leabhar Mór na hÉireann/The Great Book of Ireland*, a unique manuscript volume on vellum. Awarded the O'Shaughnessy Prize for Poetry in 2010, he is the 2015 winner of the *Irish Times* Poetry Now Award for the best book of poetry published in 2014. He is a member of Aosdána.

ERIC FALCI is Associate Professor of English at the University of California, Berkeley. He is the author of *Continuity and Change in Irish Poetry, 1966–2010* and the *Cambridge Introduction to British Poetry, 1945–2010*, both published by Cambridge University Press, as well as various essays on modern and contemporary Irish and British poetry. He is currently working on a book about the relationship between poetry and music in the nineteenth and twentieth centuries.

OMAAR HENA is an Associate Professor of English at Wake Forest University, where he teaches courses in modern and contemporary poetry in English, postcolonial literature, and global literary studies. His publications have appeared in *Contemporary Literature, Minnesota Review, The Princeton Encyclopedia of Poetry and Poetics, The Oxford Handbook of Contemporary British and Irish Poetry, A Companion to*

Modernist Poetry, and *The Cambridge Companion to Postcolonial Poetry.* In 2015, his book *Global Anglophone Poetry: Literary Form and Social Critique in Walcott, Muldoon, de Kok and Nagra* was published with Palgrave's series in *Modern and Contemporary Poetry and Poetics.*

JEFFERSON HOLDRIDGE is Director of Wake Forest University Press and Professor of English at Wake Forest University in North Carolina. His main research interests are modern and contemporary Irish poetry, though he has written on such earlier writers as Swift, Goldsmith, Lady Morgan, and William Carleton. He has written two critical books, entitled *Those Mingled Seas: The Poetry of W. B. Yeats, the Beautiful and the Sublime* (2000), and *The Poetry of Paul Muldoon* (2008). He has also edited and introduced *The Wake Forest Series of Irish Poetry,* Volume 1 (2005) and Volume 2 (2010).

FLORENCE IMPENS is a Leverhulme Early Career Fellow at the John Rylands Research Institute at the University of Manchester. She previously worked as a National Endowment for the Humanities Fellow at the Keough-Naughton Institute for Irish Studies at the University of Notre Dame. She was educated in France before moving to Ireland, where she received a PhD in English from Trinity College, Dublin in 2013. Her research focuses on twentieth- and twenty-first-century British and Irish poetry, with a particular interest in translation and classical reception studies, and in comparative literature. She is currently working on a project on poetry in translation in the UK and Ireland after 1962, supported by the Leverhulme Trust. She has published essays and reviews in several academic and literary journals, including *Irish Studies Review, The Dublin Review of Books,* and *Poetry Ireland's Trumpet.* Articles relating to classical presences in contemporary Irish poetry are forthcoming in *Irish Unversity Review,* in Volume V of *The Oxford History of Classical Reception in English Literature,* and in *Seamus Heaney in Context,* published by Cambridge University Press.

DECLAN KIBERD is Keough Professor of Irish Studies at the University of Notre Dame. He has published many books on Irish writing: *Synge and the Irish Language, Idir Dhá Chultúr, Inventing Ireland, Irish Classics, The Irish Writer and the World,* and *Ulysses and Us.* His most recent work is *Handbook of the Irish Revival 1891–1922,* coedited with P. J. Mathews.

He has been Director of the Yeats International Summer School and a member of the Irish Manuscripts Commission. He has served on the Board of Directors of the Abbey Theatre. He writes regularly in newspapers on Irish themes and for the *Times Literary Supplement*. He taught Anglo-Irish Literature and Drama for thirty-two years at University College Dublin.

AILBHE MCDAID has published on contemporary poetry, migration, and popular culture. She holds degrees from University College Cork and Trinity College Dublin, and completed her PhD in 2015 at the Centre for Irish and Scottish Studies at the University of Otago, New Zealand. Her doctoral research was entitled "'Neither here nor there, and therefore home': A Poetics of Migration in Contemporary Irish Poetry" and is under preparation for publication as a monograph by Palgrave Macmillan in 2017. She is currently working on a research project entitled "Homeward Bound — A Liverpool–West Africa Maritime Heritage" at Liverpool John Moores University. Her articles and reviews have been published in *Irish Studies Review, Nordic Journal of Irish Studies, Australasian Journal of Irish Studies,* and *Journal of Franco-Irish Studies.*

NATHANIEL MYERS is a postdoctoral fellow at the University of Notre Dame. His research interests include post-1900 Irish and British poetry and poetics, lyric and lyric studies, affect theory, and the posthuman in contemporary literature and film. Currently, he is at work on a monograph examining affect and ethics in Irish and British elegy from Seamus Heaney to Denise Riley. He has been a frequent contributor of reviews for *New Hibernia Review,* and he is the Associate Director and co-editor of *Breac: A Digital Journal of Irish Studies* (breac.nd.edu).

BRIAN Ó CONCHUBHAIR is Associate Professor of Irish Language and Literature at the University of Notre Dame where he serves as Director of the Center for the Study of Languages & Cultures since 2013. He published *Fin de Siècle na Gaeilge: Darwin, An Athbheochan agus Smaointeoireacht na hEorpa* in 2009. Other edited publications include *Éire-Ireland: Ireland and Sport* 48, no. 1 & 2 (Spring/Summer 2013); *The Language of Gender, Power and Agency in Celtic Studies* (2013); *Darkness: Liam O'Flaherty's Tragedy* (2013); and *Lost in Connemara: Stories from the Irish/Caillte i gConamara: Scéalta Aniar* (2014). He currently serves as President of the American Conference for Irish Studies.

KELLY SULLIVAN is Assistant Professor/Faculty Fellow in Irish Studies at New York University's Glucksman Ireland House. She has a PhD in British and Irish literature from Boston College. Her recent publications include "Harry Clarke's Modernist Gaze," *Éire-Ireland* 47, nos. 3–4 (2012); "Not Knowing as Aesthetic Imperative: Tim Robinson's Stones of Aran" in *Unfolding Irish Landscapes: Tim Robinson, Culture, and Environment* (Manchester University Press, 2015); and "A Portfolio of New Irish Poets" (selection editor and introduction) in *Éire-Ireland* 48, nos. 3–4 (2013). Her current book project, *Epistolary Modernism*, looks at fictional letters and verse epistles in literature from the 1920s through the Second World War, and argues that late modernist writers felt a renewed commitment to the purpose and principle of literature as public speech even as they saw privacy curtailed and surveillance increased. She co-founded the NYU Global Modernisms Group, grant-funded through NYU's Center for the Humanities, and she is the Arts Representative for the American Conference for Irish Studies. She published a novel, *Winter Bayou* (Lilliput Press, Dublin) in 2005, and has poetry and short fiction published or forthcoming in *Poetry Ireland Review, Salmagundi, Many Mountains Moving,* and elsewhere.

DANIELA THEINOVÁ has taught Irish literature at Charles University, Prague since spring 2014. Her research focuses on contemporary Irish and British poetry, modernist poetry, Irish-language writing, and feminist theory. Her PhD project examined the role of language and marginality in Irish women's poetry of the last forty-five years. Theinová's articles have appeared in *Litteraria Pragensia, Revue Souvislosti,* A2, and a number of other periodicals, and she has contributed to *The Politics of Irish Writing* (2010) and *Boundary Crossings* (2012). She has translated extensively from English and Irish into Czech, including novels by Colm Tóibín, Kate Atkinson, and Marilynne Robinson, short stories by Pádraic Ó Conaire, Lorrie Moore, Tessa Hadley, and Seán Mac Mathúna, plays by J. M. Synge, and poetry by Vona Groarke, Louis MacNeice, Medbh McGuckian, Máirtín Ó Direáin, Michael Davitt, Aifric Mac Aodha, and Nuala Ní Dhomhnaill. Her translation of *Deoraíocht* by Pádraic Ó Conaire (2004) was historically the first translation of a novel from Irish into Czech.

Index

environment, 59, 63, 69, 79–81, 85, 88, 96, 180, 301, 303, 398

epistolary, 80, 82, 89–92, 398

ethics, 79, 80, 90, 262, 285, 397

Europe/European, 10, 12, 13, 15, 21, 33, 77–81, 83, 85, 89, 92, 98–99, 105, 112, 122, 134, 180, 255, 257, 340, 343, 345, 347–48, 351, 353, 394

European Union, 10, 13

Evans, Martina, 169

Evaristo, Bernardine, 357

exile, 78, 82, 138, 190, 339

Expressionism, 180–81

Falci, Eric, 225, 241

Fanning, Gerard, 97, 285

Feiritéar, Bab, 155–56

feminine/femininity, 38, 102, 121, 128, 355, 356

feminist/feminism, 59, 104, 181, 182, 356, 398

Fiacc, Padraic, 300

Fitt, Gerry, 132

Fleuron, Svend, 79

Foer, Jonathan Safran, 25–27, 34, 36

folklore, 12, 146, 155, 156, 189, 206, 216, 251, 257, 267, 349

formalism, 28–30, 108, 176

Foster, Roy, 31

Foucault, Michel, 170

France/French, 21, 22, 38, 99, 146, 180, 183, 189, 190, 193, 278, 310, 340, 342, 346, 350, 351, 395, 396

Paris, 188–89, 255, 341, 346

Versailles, 77, 278

Frazer, James George, 158, 286

free verse, 28–29, 31, 200, 319

See also blank verse

French, Percy, 39

"Shlathery's Mounted Fut," 39

Freud, Sigmund, 151, 158, 187

Friel, Brian, 134

Frost, Robert, 278, 280, 282, 287, 311

"Directive," 280

Frye, Northrop, 284–85

The Educated Imagination, 284

Gaelic, 30, 123, 125, 129, 138, 189, 212, 295

gender, 16, 57, 99, 102–4, 111, 165, 171, 179, 182, 295, 298, 301–3, 353, 354, 397

See also feminine

See also masculine

Germany/German, 22, 77, 79, 176, 198, 218, 231, 310, 342, 353

Gillis, Alan, 42

Ginsberg, Allen, 41

globalization, 10, 22, 180, 286, 295, 339, 342, 344, 346–47, 363

Gluaiseacht Cearta Sibhialta na Gaeltachta, 180

Gonzáles-Ariaz, Luz Mar, 108

Goodison, Lorna, 342

Gorman, Michael, 303

Gould, Glenn, 87, 92

Goya, Francisco, 126

Graham, Jorie, 41

Grant-Oyeye, Lind, 363

"M-Moments," 363–64

Greece/Greek, 21, 37, 146, 190, 209, 245–48, 250–53, 271, 292–93, 340, 343, 345, 348

Gregory, Lady Augusta, 251, 254